Light points

OR HACHASSIDUS PUBLICATIONS

LIGHTPOINTS ON THE TORAH

Copyright © 2020 by
OR HACHASSIDUS PUBLICATIONS
Brooklyn, NY 11213
oh@chasidus.net

Original Hebrew/Yiddish text
© Copyright Kehot Publication Society

First printing, March 2020

Published by
KEHOT PUBLICATION SOCIETY
770 Eastern Parkway Brooklyn, NY 11213
718-774-4000 / Fax 718-774-2718
editor@kehot.com
www.kehot.org

ORDER DEPARTMENT:
291 Kingston Avenue Brooklyn, NY 11213
718-778-0226 / Fax 718-778-4148
www.kehot.com

All rights reserved, including the right to reproduce this book
or portions thereof, in any form, without permission,
in writing, from Or Hachassidus Publications.

The Kehot logo is a registered trademark
of Merkos L'Inyonei Chinuch.

ISBN: 978-0-8266-0105-6

Editorial and production team (partial list):
Rabbi Baruch S. Davidson
Rabbi Leibel Schapiro
Rabbi Shmuly Avtzon
Rabbi Mendy Drookman
Rabbi Avraham Mann
Ms. Miriam Szokovski
Ms. Chaya Sarah Cantor

Design & Layout
Shimon Gorkin
Spotlight Design
Mendy Angyalfi

THE WEISS EDITION

Light points

FROM THE TEACHINGS OF
THE LUBAVITCHER REBBE ON THE
WEEKLY TORAH PORTION

ADAPTED BY
BARUCH SHALOM DAVIDSON

*This "Lightpoints" Sefer is
generously sponsored by*

הרה"ת

ר' **משה אהרן צבי**

בן מרים

וזוגתו

מרת **העניא רבקה רות**

בת צפורה

וייס

שיחיו

Rabbi Moshe Aharon Tzvi
ben Miriam

And his wife,
Mrs. Henya Rivkah Rus
bas Tziporah
Weiss
שיחיו

Sherman Oaks, California

*May God fulfill all their wishes for good; with health,
long life, and much success in all of their endeavours,
physical and spiritual, and with true abundance.*

And for their children

שלום אליעזר, מנחם מענדל,
יונה מרדכי, חנה פערל
שיחיו

Sholom Eliezer, Menachem Mendel,
Yonah Mordechai, Chanah Pearl
שיחיו

*May they grow up to be Chassidim,
God-fearing Jews and Torah scholars,
with good health and long life.*

About this Publication

ב"ה

טַעֲמוּ וּרְאוּ כִּי טוֹב ה' (תהלים לה, ט)

"Taste and you will see that Hashem is good."
(Tehillim 34:9)

We give thanks to Hashem for granting us the *zechus* to present this collection of Torah insights gleaned from the teachings of the Lubavitcher Rebbe, Rabbi Menachem Mendel Schneerson, זצוקללה"ה נבג"מ זי"ע.

This work attempts to provide the English-speaking reader with a taste of the Rebbe's profound, complex and extensive contributions to Talmudic, Halachic, Kabbalistic and Chassidic teachings.

In the interest of providing material that is both accessible to the layperson and short enough for a quick burst of inspiration, these particular insights were selected for their relative simplicity. Moreover, many of the ideas have been stripped of the artful build-up which the Rebbe uses to develop and support his interpretations. Every effort has been made, however, to remain true to the content of the original, and to give the reader an authentic representation of the Rebbe's ideas.

The insights vary in style and content. Some focus more on the literal interpretation of the Torah and its commentaries; others highlight the relevance of the Torah's lessons in our day and age. As their name indicates, the *Light-points* are intended to be short and easy to read, but more importantly, they are points of light to illuminate our perspective on the Torah, and to direct us along the path of truth and holiness that guides our lives. They were originally published as a daily e-mail and print publication, and were enthusiastically received by thousands of subscribers.

Some of these insights originally appear as mere parenthetical and marginal notes within the Rebbe's lengthy expositions of the Torah portion. Others are the writer's attempt to condense some of the Rebbe's brilliant explanations into a few short lines, with the hope that the reader will go back to the source and study the Rebbe's treatment of the topic in depth. Understandably, a reader may find that he or she disagrees with the writer's interpretation or presentation of the Rebbe's ideas, and we welcome all feedback, and will correct any mistakes in future editions.

This collection was compiled and written by **Rabbi Baruch Shalom Davidson**, a member of the Machon Or Hachassidus editorial team, and the content was reviewed for publication by **Rabbi Yehuda Leib Schapiro**, Rosh Yeshiva of the Yeshiva Gedola Rabbinical College of Greater Miami and rabbi of Congregation Beis Menachem in Miami Beach, Florida.

This volume has been published through the generosity of **Rabbi Moshe Aharon Tzvi** and **Ruty Weiss**, Shluchim of the Rebbe in Sherman Oaks, California, in tribute to their parents, **R' Berel** and **Miriam Weiss** and **R' Sholom** and **Tzipora Lapidus**, of blessed memory, whose love and admiration of the Rebbe knew no bounds.

We also extend our sincerest thanks to **Rabbi Zushe Wilhelm**, dean of Mesivta Oholei Torah, who initiated this project, and whose vision and unwavering support have been a driving force in seeing it through from dream to reality.

Machon Or Hachassidus
11 Nissan 5780

Contents

  v About this Publication

BEREISHIS | בראשית

  3 Seeking Aleph
  5 The First Question
  7 You Will, but When Already?
  9 The New Perfect
11 Born to Work
13 A Mountain, a Molehill, or Your Most Important Next Step?

NOACH | נח

15 Staying Afloat
17 Don't Get the Wrong Impression
19 The Only Self to Sacrifice is Your Own
21 Living the Dream
23 The Maturing of Humankind
25 You See what You Need to See

LECH-LECHA | לך לך

27 Where Our Story Really Begins
29 It's About the Departure
31 Food of Fanatics
33 The Reasonable Bad Guy
35 Old Enough for What?
37 Lasting Effect

VAYEIRA | וירא

39 Do You Feel an Urge to Be Kind?
41 The Basics of Hospitality
43 Judging by the Weather
45 A Legacy of Dust and Ashes
47 Sacrificing Your Faith for Your G-d
49 A Seat for G-d, a Stage for Mankind

CHAYEI SARAH | חיי שרה

51 Life is What You Make of It
53 127 Varieties
55 Aging Well
57 Parenting is Forever
59 Mitzvos for Misses and Mrs.
61 Your Candles, Your Home

TOLDOS | תולדות

63 The Fighter
65 Be Practical, but Spiritual
67 Better Off Blind
69 Beneath Eisav's Surface
71 Gifts from a Minimalist
73 Earning the Unearnable

VAYEITZEI | ויצא

- 75 Don't Let It Go to Your Head
- 77 Good Night, Yaakov
- 79 There is No Place like Home
- 81 Make the Time to Build a Home
- 83 How Yaakov Made His Fortune
- 85 The Rest of the Story

VAYISHLACH | וישלח

- 87 Don't Make Yourself at Home
- 89 It's Not Petty When it's Your Child
- 91 You Should Really Get Out a Bit
- 93 The Jewish Way in Responsible Adulthood
- 95 Eisav's Yom Kippur
- 97 The Unsettled Jew

VAYEISHEV | וישב

- 99 Between Pebbles and Pearls
- 101 A Jew and His Dreams
- 103 Dreaming to Toil
- 105 Filled with Emptiness
- 107 What Does Not Go Up
- 109 A Picture Worth More than a Thousand Words

MIKEITZ | מִקֵּץ

- 111 Living the Dream
- 113 How Low Can You Bow?
- 115 Localized Humility
- 117 Got Faith, Won't Travel
- 119 Independence from Foreign Aid
- 121 Teshuvah: Accepting Personal Responsibility

VAYIGASH | וַיִּגַּשׁ

- 123 The Urgent Need for Change
- 125 A Time to Weep
- 127 Surviving or Thriving?
- 129 No Pain, No Gain
- 131 One-Track Education
- 133 Judge My Actions, Not My Plans

VAYECHI | וַיְחִי

- 135 Made in Egypt
- 137 A Mother's Sacrifice
- 139 Insider Information
- 141 If You Can Beat Them
- 143 Bearers of the Aron
- 145 A Local Source of Energy

SHEMOS | שמות

151 Save Your Children from Pharaoh's Decree
153 Hands Down
155 The Scary Truth about Lashon Hara
157 The Power of Positive Thinking
159 A Donkey with a History
161 Don't Mind Your Own Business

VA'EIRA | וארא

163 The Fathers
165 Discovering the Real Motive
167 Escaping the Cold
169 Blood Before Frogs
171 When the Bare Minimum is Optimal
173 Fire and Ice

BO | בא

175 When the Gates of Teshuvah Close
177 Not the Time and Place for Miracles
179 Sacred Time
181 The Deprogramming
183 Egypt Syndrome
185 The Miracle of Freedom

BESHALACH | בשלח

187 Praying for a Living
189 Stop, Drop and Care
191 From Sea to See
193 The Women's Dance
195 A Time for War
197 Think Outside the Cloud

YISRO | יתרו

199 United: Verb or Adjective?
201 Shock and Awe
203 Who Wouldn't Want the Torah?
205 Ten for Ten
207 The Correct Response
209 The Egyptian Me

MISHPATIM | משפטים

211 Same Law, Different Court
213 Free to Steal
215 Are You All Ears?
217 Far Be It from Me
219 Speaking of Nature
221 It's Not All About You

TERUMAH | תרומה

- 223 Man's Highest Calling
- 225 Plant a Tree from Israel
- 227 Have Poles, Will Travel
- 229 The People's Mishkan
- 231 Baby Face
- 232 Brazen as Brass, Soft as Soil

TETZAVEH | תצוה

- 233 Nameless
- 235 Sounds from a Distance
- 237 To Wear or to Serve?
- 239 Fasten Your *Avnet*
- 241 The Altar of Anonymity
- 243 Don't Sacrifice Your Heart

KI SISA | כי תשא

- 245 Rinse Well Before Serving
- 247 Positively Fulfilling the Negative Prohibitions
- 249 A Conflict of Interest
- 251 Learned from the Pro
- 253 A Role Model
- 255 When Broken Comes Before Whole

VAYAKHEL | ויקהל

257 Preoccupied
259 Taking Donationsfrom Children
261 The Shabbos Spell
263 The Mishkan Again?
265 The Gifts of the Gifted
267 The Rearview Mirror

PEKUDEI | פקודי

269 The Collateral
271 The Testimony
273 Mass-Energy Equivalence
275 It's How You Wear It
277 Self-Construction
279 The Closing Pitch

VAYIKRA | ויקרא

285 It's All in the Aleph
287 Why Korbanos? That's Why
289 The Pure
291 The Selfless Fuel of Sacrifice
293 The Best and Finest
295 What Do You Crave?

TZAV | צו

- 297 Limits and Permits
- 299 Kohanim Without Borders
- 301 Dare to Prepare
- 303 Cynical is Criminal
- 305 Burning Fats, Fueling Flames
- 307 What does Joyful Judaism Mean?

SHEMINI | שמיני

- 309 Drawing Down vs. Drawing Up
- 311 Expectations
- 313 No Instructions Necessary
- 315 Act Now, Perfect Later
- 317 Fins and Scales
- 319 A Fish's Tale

TAZRIA | תזריע

- 321 Seeds of Rebirth
- 323 The Hardest Thing to Change is Yourself
- 325 The Costly Effects of Cheap Talk
- 327 The Qualified Judge
- 329 The Mitzvos of a Sinful Jew
- 331 Preventive Medicine

METZORA | מצורע

- 333 Skin Deep
- 335 Ready or Not
- 337 Words of Worth
- 339 Treasure Land
- 341 Precious Possessions
- 343 Keeping Your Head Underwater

ACHAREI | אחרי

- 345 The Afterdeath
- 347 Business before Pleasure
- 349 Homeward Bound
- 351 The Insincere Vidui
- 353 Total Makeover
- 355 Bloodless

KEDOSHIM | קדושים

- 357 The Motivation Behind It All
- 359 You Can Be Holy
- 361 The Power of Judging Favorably
- 363 Knowing Means Doing
- 365 Love on Demand
- 367 Love in Two Dimensions

EMOR | אמור

369 Warn and Shine
371 Slave Rights
373 Self-Sacrifice with a Capital "S"
375 The Ultimate Kiddush Hashem
377 Animals First
379 Sheepish Bread

BEHAR | בהר

381 A Little Big
383 Goal-Oriented
385 Give Me Your Tired
387 A Jew's Red Line
389 Out of Control
391 Well Paid

BECHUKOSAI | בחוקותי

393 When the Going Gets Tough
395 The Art of Carving
397 Timing
398 The Messianic Age: Out of This World?
400 Chores or Passions?
402 Exchange Rate

BAMIDBAR | במדבר

407 Numbers that Matter
409 Just a Number?
411 The Differences We Have in Common
413 You Must Be a Levi Too
415 Choose Your Neighbors Carefully
417 Hide and Go

NASO | נשא

419 By a Raise of Heads
421 Holistic Healing
423 How to Give
425 Returning Shortly
427 I am Holy, Therefore I Am Different
429 Where More is Less

BEHA'ALOSCHA | בהעלתך

431 Step Up
433 Lamps and Flames
435 Searching for Connection
437 Fight for Your Rights
439 Not Just a Stopover
441 Your Honor

SHELACH | שלח

- 443 Telling Priorities
- 445 Manufacturer's Instructions
- 447 Where the Angels Failed
- 449 The Theory of Dough
- 451 Intentions Alone Won't Do
- 453 Committed Clothing

KORACH | קרח

- 455 In Memoriam: Korach
- 457 Protecting Your Information
- 459 Separate is Better than Equal
- 461 Same but Different
- 463 A Morning Person's Teshuvah
- 465 To Save Those You Love

CHUKAS | חקת

- 467 Irrational Judaism
- 469 Is Death Final? Depends Whom You Ask
- 471 The Cow and the Calf
- 473 Living on Edge
- 475 How I Really Feel about You
- 477 When Moshe Forgives

BALAK | בלק

- 479 Outnumbering
- 481 Uncountable Mitzvos
- 483 Live Prey
- 485 Beauty is in Detail
- 487 Radical Blessings
- 489 Moshiach and You

PINCHAS | פנחס

- 491 Grassroots Initiative
- 493 A Legacy of Love
- 495 An Eternal Reward
- 497 A Breach of Nature
- 499 Just a Thought
- 501 Don't Forget Your Father

MATOS | מטות

- 503 Tough Staff
- 505 No Ordinary Matter
- 506 To Abstain or Not to Abstain
- 508 Tapping into the Sanctity Line
- 510 Greater Israel
- 512 The Villager

MASEI | מסעי

- 514 What Goes Down
- 516 Journeys with the King
- 518 Reciprocating the Gift of the Land of Israel
- 520 24-Hour Security
- 522 One Nation, One Soul
- 524 Local Judge, Distant Sentence

DEVARIM | דברים

- 529 Filtered, Not Altered
- 531 War of Words
- 533 Being Productive isn't Enough
- 535 Jewish Nationality
- 537 Incontestably Yours
- 539 War? What For?

VA'ESCHANAN | ואתחנן

- 541 The Unstoppable Sound
- 543 The One and Only Word Echad
- 545 The Martyr's Shema
- 547 The Tefillin Line of Attack
- 549 Controlling Your Mind and Heart
- 551 Mezuzah: Protecting the Citizens of Israel

EIKEV | עֵקֶב

553 The Greatest Reward of All

556 The Faith Diet

558 To the Exclusion of All Others

560 First Words

562 What's On Your Mind?

564 Speak as G-d Speaks

RE'EH | רְאֵה

566 Under Renovation

569 Let Them Eat Meat

571 What Spring Teaches Us about Winter

573 Appreciating the Joy of Yom Tov

575 The Holiday that was Left Out

577 Expectations

SHOFTIM | שֹׁפְטִים

579 Counseling Law

581 The Real King

583 A Little Remorse, A Lot of Merit

585 Planting Smart

587 Love what You Learn

589 Equipped for Life

KI SEITZEI | כי תצא

- 591 Just Go Out
- 593 Beware of Heights
- 594 Don't Put Others at Risk
- 596 Collecting Dues
- 598 Holy Matrimony
- 600 Being Kind by Accident

KI SAVO | כי תבוא

- 602 Your Happiness is My Happiness
- 604 Earn your Keep
- 606 Don't Make Yourself Too Comfortable
- 608 Raising Children: The Hardest Job of All
- 610 The King's Hidden Treasures
- 612 Graduation

NITZAVIM | נצבים

- 614 Solid Backing
- 616 The Pact
- 618 What Makes You Jewish Today?
- 620 Can Teshuvah Be an Obligation?
- 622 To Cure the Heart
- 624 A Hint of Love

VAYEILECH | וילך

626 The Perfectly Timed Yahrzeit
628 Hakhel: Bracing for Change
630 Welcome to the Faith. Hakhel!
632 Two Last Instructions
634 When G-d Hides
636 Moshe's Retirement

HA'AZINU | האזינו

638 Close to the Heavens
640 When Distance is a Virtue
642 Finding Faith
644 Angels At Risk
646 Humble As Ever
648 Some Things Can't Wait

VEZOS HABRACHA | וזאת הברכה

650 The Choicest Choice
653 The Inheritance
655 The Joy of Achievement
656 Keep Your Enemies at a Distance
658 The Greatest Praise of All
660 The Peak

בראשית
BOOK OF BEREISHIS

חומש בראשית מוקדש לעילוי נשמת
Chumash Bereishis is dedicated in loving memory of

ר' יעקב
בן ר' דובער
Yaakov ben Dov Ber

מרת אלישבע בתי'
בת ר' מאיר זלמן
Elisheva Batya bas Meir Zalman

ר' יואל דוב
בן ר' ארי' לייב
Yoel Dovid ben Aryeh Leib

מרת רבקה
בת ר' זאב
Rivka bas Zev

❖ ❖

מרת גיטל רייזל
בת ר' דוד הירש
Gittel Raizel bas Dovid Hirsh

ר' יהושע משה
בן ר' יעקב
Yehoshua Moshe ben Yaakov

❖ ❖

ר' חיים מתתיהו
בן ר' אהרן מאיר הלוי
Chaim Matisyahu ben Aharon Meir Halevi

מרת יהודית
בת ר' יצחק
Yehudis bas Yitzchak

❖ ❖

נדבת נכדיהם
צבי וזוגתו געלמאן ומשפחתו
שיחיו

Dedicated by their grandchildren
Mr. and Mrs. Tzvi Gellman and family
שיחיו

בראשית
Bereishis

1:1 | א:א

בְּרֵאשִׁית בָּרָא אֱלֹקִים אֵת הַשָּׁמַיִם וְאֵת הָאָרֶץ

In the beginning, G-d created the heaven and the earth.

Seeking Aleph

The first letter in the Torah is ב—the second letter of the Hebrew alphabet. Everything in the Torah is precise, so by beginning with the second letter rather than the first, the Torah indicates that the studied word of the Torah is "Part 2," and we must preface our study with "Part 1."

What is the Torah's "Part 1"?

The prophet Yirmiyahu lamented the exile of the Jewish people from the Land of Israel and identified its cause, saying, "Why is the land ruined, withered like a wilderness, with no one passing through? Said G-d, 'Because they have forsaken My Torah.'"[1] The Talmud asserts that the abandonment of G-d's Torah that the prophet refers to was "that they did

---

1. Yirmiyahu 9:11–12.

not first utter the blessing over the Torah [before studying it]."[2] The Jews in Yirmiyahu's era did not forsake the study of the Torah, yet their neglect of the *berachah* indicated that although they appreciated the Torah's wisdom, they did not focus on its holiness and Divine origin.[3]

This passage in the Talmud illustrates that studying and understanding its teachings is only one aspect of our relationship with the Torah. Before approaching the Torah with our tools of intellect, we must establish and affirm the other aspect of our relationship—our primary objective in Torah study: to attach ourselves to the Divinity of the Torah that transcends human comprehension. As the Talmud emphasizes, we must "*first* utter the blessing over the Torah," in which we bless and acknowledge G-d, "the Giver of the Torah." Thereafter, when we study the Torah, we attach ourselves not only to the Torah's wisdom and ideas, but to the G-dliness of the Torah as well.

The Torah therefore starts with a ב, to remind us that first we must recognize that our primary goal is to unify ourselves, through our Torah study, with the Giver of the Torah. Then we can proceed to part 2—the letter ב of בראשית, with which we begin the process of reading and understanding the Torah.

—*Likkutei Sichos, vol. 15, pp. 1–3*

---

2. Bava Metzia 85b.
3. See Bach, Orach Chaim 47.

1:1 | א:א

בְּרֵאשִׁית בָּרָא אֱלֹקִים אֵת הַשָּׁמַיִם וְאֵת הָאָרֶץ

In the beginning, G-d created the heaven and the earth.

The First Question

Rashi's very first comment on the Torah begins with a question: "Said Rabbi Yitzchak: The Torah should not have begun from anywhere other than 'This month shall be for you...,'[4] the first mitzvah given to the Jewish people. Why then does it begin with 'In the beginning...'?" Only after answering this question does Rashi begin his interpretation of the first verse in the Torah.

The order of Rashi's comments is puzzling. The objective of Rashi's commentary is, in his own words, "[to teach] the simple meaning of the Scripture."[5] If so, why does he begin with a theoretical question about the Torah's structure before addressing the difficulties in the literal meaning of the verse?

This unusual opening serves as an introduction to Rashi's commentary throughout the Torah, and in fact to Torah study in general. With this opening discussion, Rashi addresses the first question that a child, or anyone, should ask as they begin to study Torah, even before they begin to analyze its words.

A child begins his study of the Torah expecting that in the Torah he will find G-d's message to the world and the laws that He gave to the Jewish people (some of which the child has already begun to observe). When the first thing he reads is the story of Creation, he instinctively asks, "What does this

---

4. Shemos 12:2.
5. Rashi, Bereishis 3:8.

story have to do with G-d's expectations from me? Why am I reading about Creation, or any other story, instead of reading about the mitzvos that G-d commanded the Jewish people?" As such, the first thing that Rashi must explain is that this story, too, contains a message for the Jewish people. Only then can he continue with his interpretation of the Torah's words.

This explains another peculiarity in Rashi's words. Normally, Rashi answers the difficulties in the verse without spelling out the questions. Here, however, Rashi elaborates on the question, thereby emphasizing the validity of this question, and teaching us the attitude with which we must approach every aspect of the Torah. Like the child who begins to read the story of Creation, we must constantly ask, "What does this teaching in the Torah tell me about G-d's expectations of me today?"

—*Likkutei Sichos, vol. 5, p. 2, fn. 6;*
Toras Menachem 5744, vol. 1, pp. 349–353

| 1:31 | א:לא

וַיְהִי עֶרֶב וַיְהִי בֹקֶר יוֹם הַשִּׁשִּׁי

...And it was evening and it was morning, the sixth day.

You Will, but When Already?

At the conclusion of its account of the first day of Creation, the Torah sums up the day by saying, "It was evening and it was morning, one day." On the second day it concludes, "It was evening and it was morning, a second day." On the third day, "...a third day," and so on. On the sixth day of Creation, however, the Torah concludes with, "It was evening and it was morning, *the* sixth day." Based on the Talmud,[6] Rashi explains that the Torah thereby hints to another well-known and important "sixth day"—the sixth day of the month of Sivan, the day the Jewish people accepted the Torah 2448 years after Creation. Meaning, says the Talmud, that "G-d stipulated with all of creation" that its existence was contingent on the Jewish people accepting the Torah, which would eventually take place on the 6th of Sivan.

Why does the Torah allude to this important "stipulation" by highlighting the date the Jewish people accepted the Torah, the 6th of Sivan, and not with a more general allusion to the giving of the Torah?

In doing so, the Torah seeks to demonstrate the unparalleled greatness before G-d of the actual deeds of a Jew in this world.

---

6. Shabbos 88a.

Unlike the creation that waited in abeyance, "uncertain" if the Jewish people would accept the Torah, before G-d there were no doubts. G-d knows the future just as He knows the present and the past, and the Jewish people's future acceptance of the Torah was already an established fact. Yet despite His advance knowledge, G-d still "marked" the significance of "the sixth" day of Sivan (hinted in "the sixth day" of creation), demonstrating the importance of this future date. Because despite G-d's knowledge that the Jewish people would accept the Torah (and the significance of their future acceptance of the Torah before Him even before the fact), nothing can compare to the moment in earthly time when the Jewish people actually accepted the Torah.

Though the future is as real to G-d as the present and the past, He still awaits the moment that a Jew in this world will act and realize his potential.

—Toras Menachem, Sefer Hamaamarim
Melukat, vol. 2, pp. 145–146

2:3 | ב:ג

וַיְבָרֶךְ אֱלֹקִים אֶת יוֹם הַשְּׁבִיעִי וַיְקַדֵּשׁ אֹתוֹ כִּי בוֹ
שָׁבַת מִכָּל מְלַאכְתּוֹ אֲשֶׁר בָּרָא אֱלֹקִים לַעֲשׂוֹת

G-d blessed the seventh day and sanctified it, for on it He abstained from all His work that G-d created to do.

The New Perfect

On the seventh day from the start of Creation, G-d rested from His creation of the world—"His work that G-d created to do."

What is the meaning of this phrase? Would it not have been more accurate to refer to Creation as the work "that G-d created and did"?

The Midrash explains that indeed G-d created the world "to do"—i.e., to be perfected by humankind. In the words of the Midrash, "Anything created in the six days of Creation requires enhancement."[7]

This perspective seems to contradict the oft-repeated teaching of our Sages that the world was entirely perfect and complete upon creation.[8] Which one is it? Was the world perfect upon creation, or does it require further improvement—"to do"?

These two views are not contradictory, however, when we consider the context of the verse that refers to creation as the work "that G-d created to do"—a verse which speaks about the seventh day, Shabbos.

In the first six days of Creation, the creation met all "expectations": it was perfect and complete. When the seventh

---

7. See Bereishis Rabbah 11:6 and commentaries ad loc.
8. See Bereishis Rabbah 12:6, 13:3 and 14:7.

day arrived, however, and G-d sanctified that day as Shabbos, the additional holiness drawn into the world made it suddenly possible for the world to attain greater heights than it had been capable of before, rendering its initial state of perfection deficient. Thus began the requirement for humankind "to do"—to bring creation to its newly endowed potential, for greater potential obligates greater responsibility and accomplishment.

—*Likkutei Sichos, vol. 25, pp. 14–17*

3:1 | ג:א

וְהַנָּחָשׁ הָיָה עָרוּם
The serpent was cunning...

Born to Work

"Man is born for toil."[9] Already from the very beginning of man's existence, G-d placed him in the Garden of Eden and gave him a task: "To work it [the Garden] and to guard it."

Why is toil so central to man's existence? Why is happiness contingent on hard work, unattainable without effort? After all, G-d is the ultimate source of goodness; why does He require us to endure the pain and difficulty of toil?

Granted, it is man's nature to enjoy the work of his own hands more than he enjoys what is given to him without any effort on his part. ("A man prefers one *kav* [a measurement] of his own to nine *kav* of his neighbor's."[10]) But this nature itself was created by G-d! Why did G-d create man to have a natural preference for the fruits of his own labor, instead of allowing him to enjoy that which comes without any effort or challenge?

In truth, however, the necessity for toil exemplifies the ultimate gift that G-d grants humankind. By requiring us to toil, G-d gives us the ability to experience what is truly in the realm of the Creator. By creating us in a state where our needs are not provided for automatically, requiring us to "make things happen" and contribute toward our own destiny, G-d

---

9. Iyov 5:7.
10. Bava Metzia 38a.

gives us the opportunity to emulate Him—our Creator Who causes everything to exist.

And because of that ability to emulate G-d, to "contribute" and to be a creator, we are inherently uncomfortable with being "takers"—beneficiaries of the labor of others. In the words of our Sages, "One who eats from the food of another is ashamed to look at his benefactor's face,"[11] for man naturally senses that his purpose is to be like G-d, to make a difference through his own efforts, and not to be dependent on others.

—Haggadah Shel Pesach im Likkutei Taamim Uminhagim, vol. 2, pp. 641-643; Likkutei Sichos, vol. 15, pp. 94-95

---

11. Talmud Yerushalmi, Orlah 1:3.

3:1 | ג:א

וְהַנָּחָשׁ הָיָה עָרוּם
The serpent was cunning...

A Mountain, a Molehill, or Your Most Important Next Step?

According to the Midrash, G-d's decree not to eat from the Tree of Knowledge applied only on the sixth day of Creation, the day that Adam and Chava were created. With the onset of Shabbos that evening, the prohibition would have been removed.[12] Moreover, per Talmudic account of the day's events, when G-d gave the command, only three hours remained until Shabbos.[13] But an hour later, Adam had already sinned.[14]

The fact that Adam—who heard the command directly from G-d—could not wait a mere three hours and disobeyed G-d's simple instructions so quickly is nothing short of astonishing. We see from here, however, that a man's temptation to sin is not an indication of how truly difficult that particular law is for him to abide by, but of how critical it is that he keep it. The greater the mitzvah's urgency, the greater the efforts of the *yetzer hara*, the "evil inclination" tasked with inciting man to sin. Because the command not to eat from the Tree of Knowledge was of such colossal importance (as is evident from the dire consequences of Adam's transgres-

---

12. See Bereishis Rabbah 21:7.
13. Sanhedrin 38b.
14. Ibid.

sion), the *yetzer hara*, embodied here in the serpent,[15] made even this easy, short-term prohibition too tempting for Adam to withstand.

The lesson this teaches us is obvious. When we find ourselves struggling with a particular observance or prohibition, regardless if its origins are biblical, rabbinic, or merely Jewish custom, we must recognize that the difficulty is simply a mirage created by the *yetzer hara*. In fact, our temptation to transgress is the greatest indicator that at that moment, in that place, for us as individuals, it is the fulfillment of this mitzvah in particular that is absolutely crucial.

—*Likkutei Sichos, vol. 3, pp. 747–749*

---

15. See Zohar 1:35b.

נח
Noach

6:9 | ו:ט

נֹחַ אִישׁ צַדִּיק תָּמִים הָיָה בְּדֹרֹתָיו

Noach was a righteous man, perfect in his generations.

Staying Afloat

Parshas Noach begins by describing Noach as "a righteous man, perfect in his generations." Why does the Torah limit Noach's righteousness to "in his generations"?

Rashi offers two explanations:

> Some of our Sages interpret this in praise of Noach: How much more so that if he had lived in a generation of righteous people, he would have been even more righteous. Others interpret it disparagingly: Relative to his generation he was righteous, but if he had been in Avraham's generation, he would not have been regarded as significant at all.

We know that the Torah goes to great lengths to avoid shaming even non-kosher animals.[1] Certainly, the Torah

---

1. See Bava Basra 123a.

would not add words just to shame Noach! So why are we told that Noach was not objectively righteous, and was regarded as such only in comparison to the people of his time?

Evidently, Noach's imperfection teaches us an important lesson that we could not have learned without knowing this detail.

Chassidus explains that the Hebrew word for "ark," *teivah*, also means "word." The same way the physical *teivah* provided Noach and his family with safety from the fierce waters of the Flood, the spiritual *teivah* saves a person from drowning in the flood of material concerns that occupy his mind. In order to save yourself from the flood, says the Torah, you must "enter the *teivah*"—immerse yourself in the words of *tefillah* (prayer) and Torah.[2] One might argue, however, that perhaps this is effective only for the righteous, like Noach. Maybe those who are spiritually deficient cannot save themselves from the "raging floods of worry" by merely "entering the *teivah*" of Torah and *tefillah*?

To dispel this misconception, the Torah emphasizes that the refuge provided by the *teivah* is not only for the perfect and righteous—for if Noach had lived in the generation of Avraham, "he wouldn't have been regarded as significant at all." This teaches that whether you are actually righteous or not, you too can be saved by "entering the *teivah*"—immersing yourself energetically in the words of *tefillah* and Torah. And like Noach, whose family was saved along with him (and even the animals), your entry to the *teivah* will also impact everyone around you, and in fact all of existence.

—*Likkutei Sichos, vol. 5, pp. 281-283*

---

[2]. See Keser Shem Tov, Hosafos 11; Torah Ohr, Noach 8c–9a.

6:9 | ו:ט

נֹחַ אִישׁ צַדִּיק תָּמִים הָיָה בְּדֹרֹתָיו

*Noach was a righteous man,
perfect in his generations.*

Don't Get the Wrong Impression

Rashi brings two opinions as to why the Torah emphasizes that Noach was righteous "in his generations":

> Some of our Sages interpret this in praise of Noach: How much more so that if he had lived in a generation of righteous people, he would have been even more righteous. Others interpret it disparagingly: Relative to his generation he was righteous, but if he had been in Avraham's generation, he would not have been regarded as significant at all.

The two views Rashi outlines are not necessarily arguing about Noach's level of righteousness. It is possible that everyone agrees that in comparison to Avraham, Noach's conduct was impressive but not ideal. Nevertheless, Noach was not entirely to blame. For all can agree that had he lived in a more righteous generation, the positive environment would have helped him become even greater!

The Sages were debating only what the Torah seeks to communicate by saying that Noach was "perfect in his generation." Some Sages interpret these words in praise of Noach: despite the negative influences around him, Noach remained righteous, and had he lived in another era, he surely would have been even greater. According to the second opinion, however, the Torah's emphasis on Noach's righteousness "in his generation" warns us that although Noach's inner strength was certainly praiseworthy, not all aspects of his behavior should be emulated (such as his failure to pray for the people of his generation to be saved).[3] Noach's perfection was only relative to his environment; in some areas we must strive to be even greater than Noach was, just as he would have been had he lived in better times.

—*Likkutei Sichos, vol. 25, pp. 19–21*

---

3. See Zohar 1:67b.

7:23 | ז:כג

וַיִּשָּׁאֶר אַךְ נֹחַ וַאֲשֶׁר אִתּוֹ בַּתֵּבָה

And only Noach and those with him in the ark survived.

The Only Self to Sacrifice is Your Own

Noach's dedication to the animals' needs aboard the ark teaches us the extent to which we must go when we are charged with a Divine mission. Particularly, Noach's devotion to providing his passengers with their sustenance serves as a metaphor for those who have been tasked with providing others with spiritual sustenance.

Rashi describes the physical toll that tending the animals took on Noach:

> He was groaning and spitting blood because of the burden of tending to the cattle and the beasts. And some say that he delayed feeding the lion, and it struck him; concerning him it is said:[4] 'Behold, a righteous man is requited [for his sins] in this world.'[5]

Noach was a spiritual person, the most righteous in his time, yet he fully dedicated himself to the exhausting job of feeding the animals, unabated even by the detriment this caused to his physical health. Emulating Noach, we too must commit ourselves to carrying out our mission to bring the Torah's message of G-dliness and holiness to the world under any circumstances, even if it comes at the expense of our

---

4. Mishlei 11:31.
5. Bereishis 7:23.

physical comfort. We must not be discouraged, even if we find ourselves "groaning and spitting blood" from the challenges that present themselves.

At the same time, however, we must learn from Noach not to impose this "readiness for discomfort" on others. As Rashi concludes, "Some say that he delayed feeding the lion, and it struck him." Noach was punished for delaying the lion's food to teach us that while we must readily sacrifice our own comfort for the success of our vital and lofty mission, the next person's needs, or even their conveniences, are not ours to sacrifice or delay.

—*Likkutei Sichos, vol. 5, pp. 53-56*

8:16-17 | ח:טז-יז

צֵא מִן הַתֵּבָה אַתָּה וְאִשְׁתְּךָ וּבָנֶיךָ וּנְשֵׁי בָנֶיךָ אִתָּךְ: כָּל הַחַיָּה אֲשֶׁר אִתְּךָ מִכָּל בָּשָׂר בָּעוֹף וּבַבְּהֵמָה וּבְכָל הָרֶמֶשׂ הָרֹמֵשׂ עַל הָאָרֶץ הוצא אִתָּךְ

Go out of the ark, you and your wife, and your sons, and your sons' wives with you. Every living thing that is with you of all flesh, of fowl, and of animals and of all the creeping things that creep on the earth, bring out with you.

Living the Dream

In his prophecies of the messianic era, Yeshayahu foretells that "the wolf shall dwell with the lamb, the leopard shall lie down with the young goat… and a small child shall lead them."[6]

A similar atmosphere prevailed in Noach's ark, where even the most fierce and predatory animals coexisted peacefully, despite their confinement to tiny quarters for an entire year. Moreover, the animals were so peaceful that Noach and his family alone successfully maintained them all and tended to their needs—an operation that would normally require a much larger team of caretakers. Chassidus explains that the peace between all the ark's occupants was brought about by the extraordinary Divine revelation that was felt in the ark, comparable in nature to the revelations of the era of Moshiach. This remarkable feeling of G-d's presence overwhelmed the animals and changed their nature, causing even ferocious animals of prey to become peaceful and approachable.

---

6. Yeshayahu 11:6.

This explains Rashi's commentary on the word הוצא—"bring out": "It is written הוֹצֵא, but it is read הַיְצֵא. הַיְצֵא means: tell them that they should come out. הוֹצֵא means: if they do not wish to come out, you take them out."

According to Rashi, when the land was finally dry and livable again, and the time came to leave the confines of the ark, G-d alerted Noach that he might have to forcibly remove the animals. One would imagine that after spending a year cooped up in an ark, the animals would be more than happy to leave! But the opposite was true. In the ark's cramped conditions, the animals were given a taste of the utopian era of Moshiach, and who would want to walk away from that?

—*Likkutei Sichos, vol. 25, pp. 28–31*

8:21-22 | ח:כא-כב

וַיָּרַח ה' אֶת רֵיחַ הַנִּיחֹחַ וַיֹּאמֶר ה' אֶל לִבּוֹ...
וְלֹא אֹסִף עוֹד לְהַכּוֹת אֶת כָּל חַי כַּאֲשֶׁר עָשִׂיתִי:
עֹד כָּל יְמֵי הָאָרֶץ זֶרַע וְקָצִיר וְקֹר וָחֹם
וְקַיִץ וָחֹרֶף וְיוֹם וָלַיְלָה לֹא יִשְׁבֹּתוּ

G-d smelled the appeasing fragrance, and G-d said to Himself, "...Never again will I strike down all life as I have done. As long as the earth lasts, seedtime and harvest, cold and heat, summer and winter, and day and night will never cease."

The Maturing of Humankind

In the aftermath of the Flood, two seemingly opposite extremes were introduced into the world. On the one hand, the earth achieved stability and permanence: after the Flood, G-d swore to never again destroy the world. On the other hand, the human lifespan was drastically shortened: whereas prior to the Flood people lived for almost 1000 years, after the Flood people began to die at a much younger age.

These changes are not unrelated. Together they reflect the change in human potential that was brought about through the Flood—a change that is likewise expressed in the rainbow, the sign of G-d's promise to never again destroy the entire world.[7]

A rainbow is caused when moisture that rises from the earth catches and refracts the light of the sun. The moisture rising from the earth represents mortal man's contribution to creation—"from below," as it were. Now, the generations

---

7. See Bereishis 9:15.

prior to the Flood were sustained by G-d's benevolence alone. After the Flood, however, G-d gave humanity the ability to refine the world and make it receptive to G-dliness, whereby the world became capable of "earning its own keep." Therefore, after the Flood, G-d created the rainbow. He caused the rising moisture to be less dense and more receptive of the light of the sun, reflecting the world's new reality—its potential to be elevated and to become receptive to G-dliness.

Accordingly, the extremes described above are really two sides of the same coin. On the one hand, the world now has the ability to earn and, if necessary, restore G-d's desire in its existence—for eternity, just as He is eternal. By the same token, however, the world's existence is now contingent on mortal man's efforts to deserve life—efforts that are inherently limited and finite. Consequently, the average human lifespan is much shorter now than it was before the Flood, when life was granted by G-d's limitless kindness alone.

—*Likkutei Sichos, vol. 15, pp. 51–54*

9:23 | ט:כג

וַיִּקַּח שֵׁם וָיֶפֶת אֶת הַשִּׂמְלָה
וַיָּשִׂימוּ עַל שְׁכֶם שְׁנֵיהֶם וַיֵּלְכוּ אֲחֹרַנִּית
וַיְכַסּוּ אֵת עֶרְוַת אֲבִיהֶם
וּפְנֵיהֶם אֲחֹרַנִּית וְעֶרְוַת אֲבִיהֶם לֹא רָאוּ

And Shem and Yefes took the garment, and placed it on both of their shoulders. They walked backwards, and they covered their father's nakedness; their faces were turned backwards, and they did not see their father's nakedness.

You See what You Need to See

The Baal Shem Tov taught: Flaws that you see in someone else are a reflection of your own imperfections. From heaven you were led to notice these shortcomings in someone else, for your own deficiencies in that particular area would have otherwise gone unnoticed.

Now, you might argue that perhaps you were made aware of your friend's weaknesses in order for you to assist him in dealing with them. This might be true, but in that case your detection of your friend's weaknesses would have been primarily of a practical nature: in his flaws you would "see" and sense your responsibility to help him—not the fact that he is less than perfect. But instead you were "shown" a critical view of your friend, meaning that what you see is that your friend is imperfect, even more than you sense your responsibility to help him. This "chance discovery," says the Baal Shem Tov, is not only about helping your friend; there's something in it for you too—it brings attention to the areas in which you too could use critique and improvement.

The incident of Shem and Yefes protecting their father's honor alludes to this idea. The Torah relates that when Noach was drunk and lying naked in his tent, Shem and Yefes entered backward—so as not to see their father's nakedness—and they covered him. Now, the Torah states that Shem and Yefes faced backward, in which case they obviously couldn't see their father, who lay naked in front of them. Nevertheless, the verse emphasizes that Shem and Yefes "did not see their father's nakedness." In other words, not only did they not see their father naked since they faced the opposite direction, they also did not "see" his nakedness and shame; all they saw was a situation that demanded their assistance.

—*Likkutei Sichos, vol. 10, pp. 24-28*

לֶךְ לְךָ
Lech-Lecha

12:1 | יב:א

וַיֹּאמֶר ה' אֶל אַבְרָם לֶךְ לְךָ מֵאַרְצְךָ
וּמִמּוֹלַדְתְּךָ וּמִבֵּית אָבִיךָ אֶל הָאָרֶץ אֲשֶׁר אַרְאֶךָּ

G-d said to Avram, "Go forth from your land and from your birthplace and from your father's house, to the land that I will show you."

Where Our Story Really Begins

Avram's accomplishments in the first several decades of his life are not recorded in the Written Torah. We are not offered even a brief description (as we were with Noach) of the righteous Avram who discovered the Creator on his own and risked his life to teach the world about monotheism—many years before G-d began to communicate with him.[1]

Instead, the Torah introduces Avram by telling us that G-d commanded him to leave his home, his country, his family and

---

1. See Talmud, Nedarim 32a; Mishneh Torah, Hil. Avodah Zarah 1:3.

all that was familiar, and travel to the land that G-d would show him.

In doing so, the Torah defines the unique nature of Avram's—the first Jew's—relationship with G-d, distinguishing him and the Jewish nation from the rest of civilization.

All of humankind is capable of discovering G-d and committing to Him. What makes us unique, however, is that our primary relationship with Him lies not in our recognition of G-d and our decision to attach ourselves to Him, but in His choice of us as His people. Likewise, the primary significance of the mitzvos that G-d gave the Jewish people lies not in their impact on the individual or the world, but in G-d's desire that we fulfill these observances and adhere to His will.

The Torah therefore leaves out any background information about Avram's piety and the good deeds he did before G-d spoke to him. Instead, it begins with G-d's first command to him, "Go forth from your land," to emphasize that man's finite efforts to develop a meaningful relationship with G-d are utterly insignificant in comparison to the connection that is forged by G-d singling out the Jew and commanding him, and the Jew in turn observing G-d's commands.

—*Likkutei Sichos, vol. 25, pp. 47–50*

12:1 | א:יב

וַיֹּאמֶר ה' אֶל אַבְרָם לֶךְ לְךָ מֵאַרְצְךָ
וּמִמּוֹלַדְתְּךָ וּמִבֵּית אָבִיךָ אֶל הָאָרֶץ אֲשֶׁר אַרְאֶךָּ

G-d said to Avram, "Go forth from your land and from your birthplace and from your father's house, to the land that I will show you."

It's About the Departure

Lech-Lecha begins with G-d's instruction to Avram, "Go forth from your land and from your birthplace and from your father's house, to the land that I will show you."

Aren't the details about the place that Avram will be leaving superfluous? A journey to any new land automatically requires leaving your current location, and obviously your home and place of birth, so why mention them? Moreover, some details about where he would be relocating would surely have helped Avram plan and prepare for the journey, yet Avram was told only about his point of departure, but given no details at all about his destination!

With this command, however, G-d mapped out the steps a Jew must take to reach his ultimate destination in his Divine service. It is a journey of many steps, requiring that one transcend all his personal constraints and motives, in order to make the fulfillment of G-d's will the defining feature of his life.

These steps are hinted at in G-d's command to Avram.

"Go forth from your land": Land represents nature. This first command means: abandon your natural preferences.

"Your birthplace": Your environment shapes your habits and lifestyle. This second step demands that you transcend the trends and influences of your surroundings.

"Your father's house": This alludes to your education, provided by the parents who raised you. This command tells you that in order to reach the "Promised Land," your devotion to G-d must supersede your academic sophistication and intellectual achievement.

"To the land that I will show you": To a person who devotes himself unconditionally to G-d, surrendering any personal preferences, calculations, or biases—the specific destination is irrelevant. His readiness to fulfill whatever G-d wills is always the same, regardless of the particulars.

—*Sefer Hasichos 5750, pp. 96–100*

14:13 | יד:יג

וַיָּבֹא הַפָּלִיט וַיַּגֵּד לְאַבְרָם הָעִבְרִי

The fugitive came and told Avram the Hebrew...

Food of Fanatics

In Parshas Lech-Lecha, a "fugitive" comes to Avram's home and informs him that his nephew Lot has been taken as a prisoner of war.

The Midrash[2] elucidates this encounter:

> The fugitive was Og. Why was he called Og? Because when he came, he found Avram busy with the mitzvah of *ugos* [spelled עוגות in Hebrew, similar to the name עוג, Og].

Literally translated as "cakes," matzah is called עוגות in Shemos 12:39. According to the Midrash, Avraham was preparing matzah when Og arrived.

The Midrash continues:

> Og's intentions were not for the sake of heaven. Rather, he thought, "This Avram is a zealot. I'll tell him, 'Your nephew has been taken captive,' and he will go out to war and be killed. Then I will take Sarai, his wife."

These seemingly unrelated facts about Og's name and his motives are written in immediate succession because, evidently, seeing Avram's preoccupation with the mitzvah of matzah upon his arrival played a critical role in molding Og's plans.

Matzah is "food of faith."[3] Avram's intense preoccupation

---

2. Bereishis Rabbah 42:8.
3. See Zohar 2:183b.

with this faith-building activity reflected his suprarational commitment to G-d—a relationship that focused more on faith than on reason.

Such a person, reasoned Og, is a fanatic, and prone to acting irrationally. He was therefore certain that despite the obvious risks and questionable outcome, Avram would unreasonably jeopardize his own life to try to save his nephew—likely, never to return.

Thus, the matzah that Og found Avram preparing when he arrived led him to conclude that if he told Avram that Lot had been taken captive, it would create the perfect opportunity for him to swoop in and take this "fanatic's" wife as his own.

—*Reshimos, no. 17*

14:13 | יד:יג

וַיָּבֹא הַפָּלִיט וַיַּגֵּד לְאַבְרָם הָעִבְרִי

*The fugitive came
and told Avram the Hebrew...*

The Reasonable Bad Guy

Og was a cynic,[4] but he could respect humanitarian causes. So it's not surprising that when Avram's nephew Lot was taken as a prisoner of war, Og came to break the news to Avram and encouraged him to save his relative.

Yet the Midrash tells us that Og's motives were actually immoral:

Og's intentions were not for the sake of heaven. Rather, he thought, "This Avram is a zealot. I'll tell him, 'Your nephew has been taken captive,' and he will go out to war and be killed. Then I will take Sarai, his wife."[5]

Though the cause was justified and logical, Og didn't actually believe that Avram could be victorious over the mighty kings who had taken Lot captive. Rather, Og played on Avram's zealous nature, encouraging him to take on a suicidal mission, trusting that Avram would never return and Sarai would then be Og's for the taking.

This demonstrates the moral danger inherent in following a system of principles based on human understanding alone. A person who, like Og, is guided and motivated only by logic,

---

4. See Bereishis Rabbah 53.
5. Ibid, 42:8.

and not by a G-dly ideal that transcends reason, can justify having someone killed in order to take that person's wife, and all the while believe that he is doing the right, reasonable and humanitarian thing.

—*Reshimos, no. 17*

17:12 | יז:יב

וּבֶן שְׁמֹנַת יָמִים יִמּוֹל לָכֶם כָּל זָכָר לְדֹרֹתֵיכֶם

And at the age of eight days, every male among you shall be circumcised, throughout your generations.

Old Enough for What?

When making a covenant, the parties commit to remain devoted to each other even if eventual discoveries or circumstances might cause them to lose favor in each other's eyes. Nevertheless, human beings are inherently limited, and are therefore constantly changing. As a result, their treaties are not guaranteed to last eternally.

The covenant of *bris milah* (circumcision), however, is different. Regarding *bris milah*, G-d says, "My covenant shall be in your flesh as an everlasting covenant"—meaning that through circumcision the Jew enters a truly eternal covenant with G-d. A finite and ever-changing human can indeed not effect something so timeless, but the eternal One can.

Hence, circumcision is not an act through which man attaches himself to G-d, but one through which G-d binds Himself to the individual circumcised—forever, as only G-d can.

This explains why we perform *bris milah* on an eight-day-old infant, even though the baby is too young to actively participate and contribute toward entering the covenant. For although the act of *bris milah* is performed by man, the "entering of the covenant" is effectuated by G-d Himself. Since the eternal covenant of *bris milah* does not require (nor can it be achieved through) human input, the age and readiness of the one being circumcised is irrelevant. As such, when the first opportunity arrives, and the baby is eight days old and strong enough to endure the circumcision, we immediately grant him the great fortune of entering the *bris milah*—our eternal covenant with G-d.

—*Likkutei Sichos, vol. 25, pp. 86–88*

17:13 | יז:יג

וְהָיְתָה בְרִיתִי בִּבְשַׂרְכֶם לִבְרִית עוֹלָם

*My covenant shall be in your flesh
as an everlasting covenant.*

Lasting Effect

"Our father Avraham observed the entire Torah before it was given," says the Talmud.[6] Chassidus explains, however, that the mitzvos our forefathers observed of their own initiative did not have the ability to impact and transform the physical world in a lasting way. After their observance of any particular "future mitzvah," the objects with which they fulfilled the mitzvah remained as mundane as before.[7]

In contrast, when a mitzvah is performed upon G-d's command, the holiness drawn into the world through the fulfillment of that mitzvah becomes part of the reality of the physical object with which the mitzvah was performed. For example, the physical *tefillin* that a Jew wears become holy, maintaining their holiness even after they are removed from one's head or arm.

Still, our Sages tell us that the actions of our ancestors, and the events that transpired in their lives, pioneered what would become their descendants' destiny.[8] In a spiritual sense, this means that the mitzvos performed by our forefathers grant us the ability to fulfill mitzvos today. As such, it was crucial that G-d instruct our forefathers to observe at least one mitzvah,

---

6. Kiddushin 82a.
7. See also Shir Hashirim Rabbah 1:3.
8. See Ramban, Bereishis 12:6; Bereishis Rabbah 40:6.

granting it the ability to impact physical reality in the same manner as those later observed by the Jewish people. In this way, all the mitzvos of our forefathers would have an association with those performed after the giving of the Torah, and could serve as their precedent.

This unique mitzvah was *bris milah*, circumcision, which distinguishes itself because the mitzvah and holiness it imparts remain imprinted on the flesh of the physical body forever. As G-d told Avraham, "My covenant shall be in your flesh as an everlasting covenant."

That is why Avraham waited to circumcise himself until G-d instructed him to do so (when he was 99 years old), rather than doing so earlier on his own initiative. Through G-d's command, our forefathers' observance of this mitzvah was endowed with the ability to imbue lasting holiness in the physical and material, akin to the effect of *every* mitzvah that a Jew performs today.

—*Likkutei Sichos, vol. 3, pp. 757–759*

וירא
Vayeira

18:1 | יח:א

וַיֵּרָא אֵלָיו ה' בְּאֵלֹנֵי מַמְרֵא וְהוּא יֹשֵׁב פֶּתַח הָאֹהֶל כְּחֹם הַיּוֹם

G-d appeared to him in the plains of Mamre, and he was sitting at the entrance of the tent when the day was hot.

Do You Feel an Urge to Be Kind?

The Torah tells us that on the third day after Avraham's circumcision, "G-d appeared to him… and he was sitting at the entrance of his tent when the day was hot."

The Torah makes a point of telling us about the extreme weather conditions at the time of this episode because, as Rashi explains, "G-d took the sun out of its sheath so as not to trouble Avraham with visitors." Nevertheless, Rashi continues, "When G-d saw that he was troubled that no guests were coming, He brought angels to him in the likeness of men."

According to Rashi's explanation, G-d caused that day to be unnaturally hot in order to spare Avraham the burden of entertaining visitors, but this unnatural absence of guests ultimately anguished Avraham. Did G-d's plan go awry? Was His interference with the normal weather a waste? Of course not. Clearly, although the plan was successful, as Divine plans always are, something changed that turned the absence of guests from a convenience into a source of distress.

What caused that change for Avraham? The answer lies in the words of the verse: "G-d appeared to him."

Avraham was instinctively generous. Being kind and hospitable to people in need came naturally to him. Yet even Avraham's generous spirit was stimulated only when he knew or saw someone in need. Therefore, in the absence of a situation requiring his attention, such as when the unbearable heat kept all travelers from passing through his area, Avraham was able to rest and recuperate from the circumcision he had undergone a few days earlier. G-d's plan worked out to a T.

But things changed for Avraham when G-d appeared to him. G-d's immeasurable kindness, revealed to Avraham on that day, evoked within Avraham an even greater spirit of generosity than before. Mirroring G-d's benevolence, Avraham became filled with such drive and motivation to be kind and giving that the lack of passerby suddenly became a terrible source of anxiety, and he desperately wished he could find someone with whom to share.

Sensing his anguish, G-d granted Avraham's new desire: "He lifted his eyes and saw, and behold, three men were standing beside him..."

—*Likkutei Sichos, vol. 5, pp. 329–330, fn. 99*

18:2 | יח:ב

וַיִּשָּׂא עֵינָיו וַיַּרְא וְהִנֵּה שְׁלֹשָׁה אֲנָשִׁים
נִצָּבִים עָלָיו וַיַּרְא וַיָּרָץ לִקְרָאתָם

He lifted his eyes and he saw,
and behold, there were three men standing beside him,
and he saw and he ran toward them.

The Basics of Hospitality

In Parshas Vayeira, Avraham interrupts a visit from G-d Himself in order to host three passersby (angels disguised as travelers). This teaches us the tremendous value of the mitzvah of *hachnosas orchim*, hosting guests. Per the Rambam:

> This is the tenet that our patriarch Avraham established, and the path of kindness that he followed. He would feed wayfarers, provide them with drink and accompany them. Showing hospitality for guests surpasses receiving the Shechinah, the Divine Presence, as is written: 'He saw, and behold, there were three men.'[1]

Yet considering that Avraham's guests were actually angels, who had no need for the food and drink he offered, did Avraham actually fulfill the mitzvah of *hachnosas orchim* with this act of hospitality? In hindsight, it seems that Avraham disturbed his meeting with G-d for guests who do not even qualify for *hachnosas orchim*!

From here we see that *hachnosas orchim* is defined primarily by the heartfelt concern that the host shows for his guests' wellbeing, and not by the accommodations he provides

---

1. Mishneh Torah, Hil. Avel 14:2.

(in which case the extent of the beneficiary's need would be relevant). Although other acts of kindness too are certainly better with a smile than without, yet the ideal way of giving charity is actually when the donor and recipient never even meet face to face.[2] Not so the mitzvah of *hachnosas orchim*, where the fulfillment of this mitzvah is first and foremost through showing your guests your *personal* and sincere concern for their comfort and wellbeing.

Thus, regardless of whether the angels visiting Avraham needed or ate the food that he prepared for them, Avraham fulfilled the mitzvah of *hachnosas orchim* to the fullest with the care *he exhibited* toward them. Moreover, knowing (better than anyone) just how much Avraham was cherished by G-d, the guests too could appreciate the sincere interest this great man took in them, putting his meeting with G-d on hold in order to provide them with food and to escort them on their way.

—*Likkutei Sichos, vol. 25, pp. 76-78*

---

2. Mishneh Torah, Hil. Matnos Aniyim 10:8.

18:1 | יח:א

וַיֵּרָא אֵלָיו ה' בְּאֵלֹנֵי מַמְרֵא
וְהוּא יֹשֵׁב פֶּתַח הָאֹהֶל כְּחֹם הַיּוֹם

G-d appeared to him in the plains of Mamre, and he was sitting at the entrance of the tent when the day was hot.

Judging by the Weather

In the midst of conversing with G-d, Avraham sees three men approaching and runs to welcome them to his home. From Avraham's behavior we learn that welcoming guests is greater than receiving the Shechinah, the Divine Presence.[3]

But, having no precedent from which to learn, how did *Avraham* know that it was permissible to welcome human company during his reception of the Divine Presence? Was he not concerned that such behavior was inappropriate and disrespectful to his esteemed Guest?

Avraham's conclusion that it was permissible to welcome guests in the midst of meeting with G-d was based simply on the weather. Rashi notes that it was unusually hot that day, as G-d sought to spare Avraham the trouble of welcoming guests: "G-d took the sun out of its sheath so as not to trouble him with visitors."

Noticing G-d's interference with the weather patterns, Avraham realized what was going on. He wondered: if a meeting with G-d may not be interrupted to welcome people into your home, then what need is there for Divine intervention

---

3. Talmud, Shabbos 127a.

to keep the passersby away right now? From the fact that G-d "took the sun out of its sheath" even *while* appearing to Avraham, in order to prevent guests from disturbing him, Avraham deduced that if guests *would* pass by, it was obviously still a mitzvah to welcome them even if it would disturb his meeting with G-d. Hence, concluded Avraham, welcoming guests must be greater than receiving the Shechinah! So when three men approached during G-d's visit, "He [Avraham] saw, and he ran toward them..."

—*Likkutei Sichos, vol. 25, p. 82, fn. 45*

18:27 | יח:כז

וַיַּעַן אַבְרָהָם וַיֹּאמַר הִנֵּה נָא הוֹאַלְתִּי לְדַבֵּר אֶל ה' וְאָנֹכִי עָפָר וָאֵפֶר

Avraham answered and said,
"Behold, now I have begun to speak to G-d,
although I am but dust and ashes."

A Legacy of Dust and Ashes

As a reward for our patriarch Avraham having said, 'I am but dust and ashes,' his descendants merited to receive two commandments: the ashes of the red heifer, and the dust that is mixed with water for a *sotah*.[4]

These two mitzvos correspond to more than just the metaphor of "dust and ashes" that Avraham used to describe his humble existence. The red heifer and the *sotah* water reflect the essence of Avraham's conduct, which he expressed with the words "I am but dust and ashes."

With these words Avraham effectively described the motivation behind his life of selflessness: his utter humility. Avraham was so insignificant in his own eyes that he felt certain that everyone else was surely entitled, equally or more, to the goodness with which he had been blessed. In fact, Avraham did not hesitate to help another person even when it might have caused him personal harm or loss. Thus, saving his nephew from captivity warranted risking his own life in battle;[5] tending to the physical needs of travelers whom he

---

4. Sotah 17a.
5. See Bereishis 14:1–24.

imagined to be pagan nomads justified forfeiting his time with the Divine Presence.[6]

As a reward, Avraham's descendants, the Jewish people, were given two mitzvos that exemplify this attribute of selflessness—the ashes of the *parah adumah*, the red heifer, used to purify those who contract impurity from a corpse; and the *sotah* water, used to prove the innocence of a suspected adulteress.

By Divine decree, all who were involved in preparing the ashes of the *parah adumah* contracted a degree of impurity themselves. Similarly, the preparation of the *sotah* water required erasing (into water) the ink of several verses from the Torah, including G-d's holy name. A Jew's ability to allow himself to become impure in order to spare someone else the inconvenience of impurity, or to actively desecrate G-d's holy name in order to save someone else's marriage, is truly the legacy of Avraham, who put all others before himself, viewing himself as nothing "but dust and ashes."

—*Likkutei Sichos, vol. 25, pp. 79–83*

---

[6]. See Bereishis 18:1–4 and Rashi ad loc.

22:2 | כב:ב

קַח נָא אֶת בִּנְךָ אֶת יְחִידְךָ אֲשֶׁר אָהַבְתָּ אֶת יִצְחָק
וְלֶךְ לְךָ אֶל אֶרֶץ הַמֹּרִיָּה וְהַעֲלֵהוּ שָׁם לְעֹלָה

Please take your son, your only one, whom you love, Yitzchak, and go away to the land of Moriah and bring him up there for a burnt offering.

Sacrificing Your Faith for Your G-d

To knowingly give up your life runs contrary to the basic human instinct for survival. Yet our history is filled with *kedoshim*—holy martyrs who chose to die rather than submit to a belief contrary to the Torah. Chassidus explains that they drew their strength from Avraham, who "opened the channels of self-sacrifice,"[7] enabling his descendants to access the soul's supernatural ability to part with life itself for the sake of sanctifying G-d's name.

But people of other faiths, too, have sacrificed their lives for their beliefs. What makes Avraham's sacrifice different?

Martyrdom on its own can be driven by a desire for rewards promised in the afterlife, or by a feeling that life without following your beliefs is not worth living, both of which are motivated by the desire to *improve* one's current state of existence. Avraham's spirit of self-sacrifice, however, was unique: not only was he ready to give up his *life* for G-d, he was ready to surrender his entire sense of identity and purpose of existence for G-d.

---

7. See Sefer Hamaamarim 5678, p. 283.

Avraham had dedicated his life to propagating his belief in One G-d, Creator of heaven and earth, contrary to all the pagan beliefs of his time. Avraham's willingness to sacrifice his *own* life to stand by his convictions, one could argue, was not in defiance of his identity—it was his very purpose in life! To sacrifice Yitzchak, on the other hand, especially with no one around to witness it, would not further this belief but defeat it. It would extinguish any hope that the belief system that had been Avraham's *raison d'être* would be passed along to future generations. This was truly a sacrifice of everything that Avraham lived for.

Therein lies the singularity of Avraham's self-sacrifice, and consequently his descendants', which was evident in the Akeidah, the Binding of Yitzchak. In the act of the Akeidah, Avraham demonstrated that his self-sacrifice was not driven by hopes of achievement or even spiritual gain; it was motivated solely by his unbreakable devotion to G-d's every command.

—*Likkutei Sichos, vol. 20, pp. 74-77;*
　ibid., vol. 18, p. 322

22:14 | כב:יד

וַיִּקְרָא אַבְרָהָם שֵׁם הַמָּקוֹם הַהוּא ה' יִרְאֶה
אֲשֶׁר יֵאָמֵר הַיּוֹם בְּהַר ה' יֵרָאֶה

Avraham named that place "G-d shall see," so it is said to this day: On the mountain, G-d will be seen.

A Seat for G-d, a Stage for Mankind

After the Akeidah, the Binding of Yitzchak, Avraham named the mountain upon which it took place "G-d shall see." As Rashi explains, this name reflected Avraham's wish that "G-d shall choose and 'see' [i.e., identify] this place to be for Him, to cause His Divine Presence to rest therein and for sacrifices to be offered here."

Avraham's prayers were granted. G-d chose the location of the Akeidah for the *mizbeiach*, the altar in the Beis Hamikdash, the Holy Temple. The Beis Hamikdash would be both the epicenter of Divine worship, "a house for G-d, prepared for sacrifices to be offered within it,"[8] as well as the place where G-d would "be seen," perceived by all the pilgrims on the holidays.[9]

These two themes in the Beis Hamikdash reflect the two principles of Jewish belief and worship that the episode of the Akeidah established. Firstly, "From this action [the Akeidah]... all people shall learn how far we must go in the fear of G-d."[10]

---

8. Mishneh Torah, Hil. Beis Habechirah 1:1.
9. See Shemos 23:17 and Talmud, Chagigah 2a.
10. Moreh Nevuchim 3:24.

Secondly, the Akeidah "informs us of the degree to which the prophets are certain about their revelations from G-d in prophecy... Avraham agreed to offer his only and beloved son as he was commanded, even though this command came in a dream or a vision... He would not have done so if he had even the slightest doubt about the vision's veracity."[11]

The designation of the place of the Akeidah as the stage for Divine *worship*—the sacrifices that were offered on the *mizbeiach*—corresponds to first theme of the Akeidah: the *devotion* to G-d's will that Avraham inspired in the world through his readiness to sacrifice his son at G-d's request.

The establishment of the site of the Akeidah as the primary seat of G-d's future *revelation* to humankind corresponds to the second aspect of the Akeidah: the faith in G-dly *revelation* through prophecy that was confirmed by Avraham's confidence that the command to sacrifice his son, which he heard prophetically, was indeed the word of G-d.

—*Likkutei Sichos, vol. 30, pp. 73–74*

---

11. Ibid.

חיי שרה
Chayei Sarah

23:1 | א:כג

וַיִּהְיוּ חַיֵּי שָׂרָה מֵאָה שָׁנָה וְעֶשְׂרִים שָׁנָה
וְשֶׁבַע שָׁנִים שְׁנֵי חַיֵּי שָׂרָה׃

The life of Sarah was one hundred years and twenty years and seven years, the years of the life of Sarah.

Life is What You Make of It

Sarah's life was far from uneventful: she was born and raised in one part of the world, but moved a number of times, spending the last half of her life in the Land of Israel. She was also taken captive *twice* by powerful kings who desired to marry her against her will.

Yet when the verse says "The life of Sarah was one hundred years and twenty years and seven years, the years of the life of Sarah," Rashi explains that the phrase "the years of the life of Sarah" summarizes all 127 years of Sarah's life, saying, "They all were equally good." Considering everything that Sarah endured, how can Rashi suggest that all 127 years of her life were equally good?

The answer lies in the Torah's unusual phrasing. Usually, when stating how long a person lived, the Torah says, "All the *days* of so-and-so were...,"[1] or "These are the *days of the years* of so-and-so's life."[2] Here, however, the Torah refers to the number of Sarah's years as "the *life* of Sarah," not "the years of Sarah."

The Torah's wording indicates that this verse is not only telling us how many years Sarah lived, but also that all 127 years were "Sarah's life," i.e., perfectly and equally filled with the meaning and purpose by which she defined her life.

To Sarah, living meant being in a vibrant relationship with G-d, first and foremost through the mitzvos entrusted to the Jewish woman. As our Sages tell us, a cloud (representing the Divine Presence) hovered constantly over Sarah's tent because she carefully maintained the purity of her married life; the dough she prepared was particularly blessed in the merit of her separation of *challah*; and the Shabbos candles that she lit burned miraculously throughout the following week.[3]

The physical and emotional distresses that Sarah experienced certainly pained her, but the pursuits by which she defined her life were never diminished or changed. Thus, the "life of Sarah"—her spiritual passions and endeavors—were perfect and good throughout all her 127 years.

—*Likkutei Sichos, vol. 35, pp. 92-93*

---

1. See Bereishis 9:29.
2. See Bereishis 25:7.
3. See Rashi, Chizkuni and Gur Aryeh, Bereishis 24:67.

23:1 | א:כג

וַיִּהְיוּ חַיֵּי שָׂרָה מֵאָה שָׁנָה וְעֶשְׂרִים שָׁנָה וְשֶׁבַע שָׁנִים שְׁנֵי חַיֵּי שָׂרָה׃

The life of Sarah was one hundred years and twenty years and seven years, the years of the life of Sarah.

127 Varieties

In the story of Purim, the miraculous salvation of the Jewish people came about through Queen Esther, who ruled over 127 provinces. The Midrash comments: "Why would Esther merit to rule over 127 provinces? As Esther was the granddaughter of Sarah, who lived 127 years, let her come and rule over 127 provinces."[4]

The correlation between Sarah and Esther is certainly not only a numerical parallel; the matching numbers indicate that Sarah's life and the miracle of Purim have something in common.

Rashi's interpretation of the words "the years of the life of Sarah" at the beginning of Parshas Chayei Sarah hints to the common feature between Sarah and the miracle of Purim. Rashi wonders: after we read that Sarah lived for 127 years, why is it necessary to recap that "these were the years of the life of Sarah"? He concludes that this phrase comes to summarize all 127 years, saying, "They all were equally good."

Now, no person's life is unmarked by change; yet remarkably, the Torah attests to Sarah having experienced all 127 years of her life as equally good.

---

4. Bereishis Rabbah 58:3.

When we encounter the same number, 127, in the book of Esther, the Midrash understands that this serves to draw our attention to Sarah's life, based on which we can understand why the Jews merited that miracle of Purim. During the Persian exile, the Jewish people lived scattered across 127 different lands. Each place was unique in climate, culture, language and character. Inevitably, outside of their Torah observance, the lifestyles of the Jews in these diverse locations varied tremendously. Yet when the decree to annihilate the Jews reached each province, not even one Jew considered the option to renounce his Judaism and be spared![5] Like the 127 years of Sarah that were astonishingly "all equally good," the Jews of 127 different "varieties" were identical in their steadfast belief and devotion to G-d. They therefore merited, says the Midrash, "that the granddaughter of Sarah" would "come and rule over 127 provinces."

—*Sichos Kodesh 5730, vol. 1, pp. 638–639*

---

5. See Torah Ohr 91b.

24:1 | כד:א

וְאַבְרָהָם זָקֵן בָּא בַּיָּמִים

Avraham was old, advanced in days.

Aging Well

The Torah describes Avraham as "old, advanced in days." Whereas the term "old" refers to Avraham's chronological age, the term "advanced in days" refers to the extent to which Avraham "lived" his life and the effect each day had on him.

A person might be old but not advanced in days, if life merely passed him by without deeply affecting him. Avraham, however, was "advanced in days"—he had advanced, entered and immersed himself in the happenings and changes of every day of his life, such that inevitably, experiencing life's ups and downs so deeply and personally took a physical toll on him as well.

This idea is reflected in the Zohar's understanding of the words "advanced in days" to mean that Avraham "lacked none of his days" in this world—i.e., he had utilized every single day of his life in the service of G-d. In the words of the Zohar, "When Avraham passed from this world, he rose and vested himself in his days, for he was not lacking even one of these precious garments..."[6] Just as Avraham was "advanced in days" in the literal sense, having profoundly experienced all the events of his life physically, so had he experienced and fully lived the spiritual significance of every day; there had

---

6. Zohar 1:224a.

not been even one day in Avraham's life during which he had not immersed himself in the spiritual calling of the moment.

—*Likkutei Sichos, vol. 35, pp. 90–92*

24:10 | כד:י

וַיִּקַּח הָעֶבֶד עֲשָׂרָה גְמַלִּים מִגְּמַלֵּי אֲדֹנָיו וַיֵּלֶךְ וְכָל טוּב אֲדֹנָיו בְּיָדוֹ

The servant took ten of his master's camels and he went; and his master's entire fortune was in his hand...

Parenting is Forever

Yitzchak was a grown man when Eliezer set off to find him a wife. The strong education that he had received from his parents had clearly had the desired impact, and Yitzchak lived by the same values of devotion to G-d as his parents had. (Thus, for example, when G-d commanded Avraham to offer Yitzchak as a sacrifice, Yitzchak was equally as willing to go ahead with it as was Avraham.[7]) Now that Yitzchak was 40 years old, one would assume that he could be left to his own devices to find a wife, without needing parental assistance to ensure that he'd continue on the right path.

But good wasn't good enough for Avraham. Avraham wanted to make certain that Yitzchak would encounter no hindrance whatsoever in marrying the right person and building a life on the path that G-d desired. Therefore, though Avraham still had many years to live, he parted with all his worldly possessions and gifted everything to Yitzchak in order to make him a more attractive suitor. As Rashi says, "Avraham wrote a deed gifting all he owned to Yitzchak, so that they

---

7. See Rashi, Bereishis 22:8.

[family of the prospective bride] would be eager to send him their daughter."[8]

Avraham demonstrated that even once our children and students are grown and mature, ready to build independent lives of their own, we mustn't cease in guiding them in the right direction. We must continue to guide them toward the proper path even at the cost of tremendous personal sacrifice, thereby ensuring that they build their lives in accordance with the Torah's eternal ways.

—*Sichos Kodesh 5730, vol. 1, pp. 209–210*

---

8. Rashi ad loc.

24:67 | כד:סז

וַיְבִאֶהָ יִצְחָק הָאֹהֱלָה שָׂרָה אִמּוֹ וַיִּקַּח אֶת רִבְקָה
וַתְּהִי לוֹ לְאִשָּׁה וַיֶּאֱהָבֶהָ וַיִּנָּחֵם יִצְחָק אַחֲרֵי אִמּוֹ

Yitzchak brought her to the tent of his mother Sarah, and he wedded Rivkah and she became his wife, and he loved her; and Yitzchak was comforted after losing his mother.

Mitzvos for Misses and Mrs.

Miraculous things happened in Yitzchak's home when his new bride Rivkah arrived. Rashi tells us:

> He [Yitzchak] brought her to the tent, and beheld that she was like his mother Sarah... As long as Sarah was alive, the candle burned from one Shabbos eve to the next, blessing was found in the dough, and a cloud hovered on the tent. These things ceased when Sarah died, but when Rivkah arrived they resumed.

Strangely, Rashi lists these miracles in exactly the opposite sequence than the order in which Yitzchak noticed them. The cloud began hovering over the tent immediately upon Rivkah's arrival. Later, when she settled in and began going about her daily activities, the blessing in the food she prepared became evident. And finally, Yitzchak saw the full extent of the miracles associated with Rivkah when the candles she lit before Shabbos were still burning a full week later.

Why does Rashi list the miracles in the opposite order? In doing so, Rashi alludes to the mitzvos that are associated with these miracles, and the order in which every Jewish woman begins to observe them.[9]

The cloud hovering on the tent represented the Shechinah, the Divine Presence, which dwells in homes where the laws maintaining the purity of married life are observed. Because the observance of this mitzvah begins only with marriage, Rashi mentions it last. Before that, Rashi tells us of the blessing found in Rivkah's dough, which was due to her observance of the mitzvah to separate *challah* from the dough she prepared—a mitzvah that a girl can fulfill as soon as she is old enough to help with the household chores, even before she starts a family of her own. But long before she is capable of helping in the home, a girl can already observe the mitzvah of lighting candles for Shabbos.

Rashi therefore mentions the miracle associated with the Shabbos candles first, to teach us that, like Rivkah (who lit Shabbos candles at the age of three), even young girls should begin lighting the Shabbos candles as soon as they can understand the significance of this mitzvah (even before they become *bas mitzvah*, actually obligated in the mitzvos).

—*Likkutei Sichos, vol. 15, pp. 167–173*

---

9. See Chizkuni and Gur Aryeh, Bereishis 24:67.

BOOK OF BEREISHIS — CHAYEI SARAH

24:67 | כד:סז

וַיְבִאֶהָ יִצְחָק הָאֹהֱלָה שָׂרָה אִמּוֹ וַיִּקַּח אֶת רִבְקָה וַתְּהִי לוֹ לְאִשָּׁה וַיֶּאֱהָבֶהָ וַיִּנָּחֵם יִצְחָק אַחֲרֵי אִמּוֹ

Yitzchak brought her to the tent of his mother Sarah, and he wedded Rivkah and she became his wife, and he loved her; and Yitzchak was comforted after losing his mother.

Your Candles, Your Home

After Sarah's passing, Avraham and Yitzchak assumed the duty of lighting the Shabbos candles in their tent each Friday (as is required by Jewish law in circumstances where the woman of the house cannot light them). But whereas Sarah's Shabbos candles (and later those lit by Rivkah) miraculously burned for the entire week, the candles lit by Avraham and Yitzchak did not. As Rashi tells us, miraculous things occurred in Yitzchak's home when his new bride Rivkah arrived:

> He brought her to the tent, and beheld that she was like his mother Sarah… As long as Sarah was alive, the candles burned from one Shabbos eve to the next, blessing was found in the dough, and a cloud hovered on the tent. These things ceased when Sarah died, but when Rivkah arrived they resumed.

This demonstrates the woman's unique ability to nurture her home and her family. As the Talmud rhetorically asks, "If a man brings home wheat, does he then chew raw wheat?"[10] A man's strength lies in what he brings home from the outside,

---

[10]. Yevamos 63a.

but a woman's strength lies in developing the home from within. Mirroring the distinct impact that a woman has on her home, the Shabbos candles lit by the Matriarchs miraculously brightened their homes throughout the entire week, whereas the candles lit by Avraham and Yitzchak did not.

Even though this miracle was physically visible only in the candles lit by the Matriarchs, in a spiritual sense the same is true of the Shabbos candles kindled by every Jewish woman and girl. Like the candles lit by Sarah and Rivkah, the Jewish woman's Shabbos candles illuminate her home for an entire week with the light of mitzvah observance. In this respect, the candles lit by a girl before even she becomes *bas mitzvah*, obligated in the mitzvos (like Rivkah, who was lighting candles at the age of three) have a power that even the candles lit by the holy Avraham did not have!

—*Likkutei Sichos, vol. 15, pp. 168–172*

תולדות
Toldos

25:22 | כה:כב

וַיִּתְרֹצֲצוּ הַבָּנִים בְּקִרְבָּהּ

The children struggled within her.

The Fighter

Our patriarchs and matriarchs were perfectly righteous. In the words of the Tanya, "Throughout their lives they sanctified their every limb to serve exclusively as a 'chariot' for the implementation of G-d's will."[1]

Yet, when our matriarch Rivkah was pregnant with twins, "the children struggled within her."[2] Rashi explains, "When she passed the Torah study hall of Shem and Eiver, Yaakov struggled to emerge, and when she passed places of idolatry, Eisav struggled to emerge." How was Eisav, the child of the saintly Yitzchak and Rivkah, already so innately attracted to

---

1. Tanya, chapter 23.
2. Bereishis 25:22.

idol worship when he was but a fetus in his mother's womb, causing him to stir each time she passed a house of idolatry?

Our Sages tell us that the deeds and lives of our patriarchs and matriarchs paved the way for their descendants, the Jewish people, to fulfill their destiny.[3] One aspect of this legacy is that through their unassailable commitment to G-d, our forefathers endowed every Jew with an inner strength of devotion to G-d. With this strength, a Jew can overcome any challenge to his Jewishness—be it adversity from the outside, or his personal struggles from within.

Yitzchak and Rivkah themselves were perfectly righteous, but because the path to G-dliness for some of their descendants would involve struggling with temptation, the legacy of Yitzchak and Rivkah also includes a natural inclination towards sin—in order to overcome it. They thus bore not only Yaakov, whose passions were entirely holy and pure, but also Eisav, who was born with an allure to sin and the inner strength to overcome it.

In fact, the Zohar states that as a child, Eisav, like Yaakov, excelled in the education he received from his grandfather Avraham—"Avraham's merit assisted and caused them to thrive, training them in the observance of mitzvos."[4] Undeniably, Eisav made the wrong choices as an adult. But until he went off on his own path, Eisav's attraction to idolatry was simply a natural part of being Yitzchak's child and Avraham's disciple: he exemplified the Jew who is born to struggle and is naturally endowed with the strength it takes to win.

—*Likkutei Sichos, vol. 20, pp. 109-113*

---

[3]. See Ramban, Bereishis 12:6; Bereishis Rabbah 40:6.
[4]. Zohar 1:138b.

26:5 | כו:ה

עֵקֶב אֲשֶׁר שָׁמַע אַבְרָהָם בְּקֹלִי וַיִּשְׁמֹר
מִשְׁמַרְתִּי מִצְוֹתַי חֻקּוֹתַי וְתוֹרֹתָי

*Because Avraham heeded My voice,
and kept My restrictions, My commandments,
My statutes and My instructions.*

Be Practical, but Spiritual

The Talmud states that long before the Torah was given on Mount Sinai, our forefathers observed all of its commandments. This is derived from a verse in Parshas Toldos:

> "We find that our father Avraham observed the entire Torah before it was given, as it is written,[5] 'Because Avraham heeded My voice, and kept My restrictions, My commandments, My statutes and My instructions.'"[6]

But could Avraham have observed all the mitzvos in their physical form? In order to observe the mitzvah of wearing *tefillin*, for example, the *tefillin* must contain certain portions of the Torah, some of which speak about the exodus from Egypt. As the Exodus took place more than three centuries after Avraham's passing, Avraham's fulfillment of the mitzvah of *tefillin* could not have been identical to ours. Rather, Chassidus explains that our forefathers observed the spiritual *equivalent* of the mitzvos, meaning that they affected in the

---

5. Bereishis 26:5.
6. Mishnah, Kiddushin 4:14.

spiritual realm what we affect through our physical observance of the mitzvos.[7]

The Torah's teachings are not a mere documentation of history; they serve as a guide for every Jew in his or her service of G-d. Accordingly, our forefathers' uniquely spiritual observance of the mitzvos must provide a lesson for us as well.

How can we observe the mitzvos spiritually (in addition to observing them practically)? By being the inspiration and encouragement behind another person's mitzvah observance.

When we encourage someone else to keep Shabbos or to increase their Torah study, they alone can actually fulfill their personal obligation to observe that mitzvah. *our* involvement is only spiritual; *their* observance is driven by the words we spoke and the motivation that we inspired, but we cannot physically do those mitzvos in their stead.

The spiritual observance of mitzvos by our forefathers thus teaches us that besides for observing mitzvos physically (i.e., performing mitzvos ourselves), we must also engage in mitzvos that we fulfill spiritually (the mitzvos fulfilled by others at our encouragement).

—*Toras Menachem 5745, vol. 1, p. 575*

---

7. See Torah Ohr, Lech-Lecha 11d.

27:1 | כז:א

וַיְהִי כִּי זָקֵן יִצְחָק וַתִּכְהֶיןָ עֵינָיו מֵרְאֹת
It came to pass when Yitzchak was old, and his eyes were too dim to see…

Better Off Blind

The Torah tells us that Yitzchak was blind in his old age. According to one explanation provided by Rashi, G-d caused this to happen "in order to enable Yaakov to take the blessings."

Now, to say that blindness is debilitating is an understatement, as Rashi comments, "Because Yitzchak's eyes had become dim and he was confined to his house… he was as though dead."[8] Nevertheless, because Yitzchak planned to bestow the greatest blessings upon Eisav, not knowing the full extent of his wickedness, G-d caused him to become blind in order for Yaakov to successfully disguise himself as Eisav and receive the blessings instead.

Consider this: Yitzchak was 123 years old at the time of the blessings, and he lived until the age of 180. So for 57 years Yitzchak suffered from blindness, confined to his house "as though dead," all because he was unaware of Eisav's wickedness and therefore desired to bless him. Was this really necessary? Why didn't G-d simply inform Yitzchak that Eisav wasn't worthy of the blessings, just as He communicated many other things to him?

(Moreover, Yitzchak already had suspicions about Eisav. He disapproved of Eisav's wives,[9] and he was aware that Eisav

---

8. Bereishis 28:13.
9. Bereishis 26:35.

did not have the praise of G-d on the tip of his tongue.[10] So why did G-d not reveal the whole truth about Eisav, instead of causing Yitzchak to be blind for the last 57 years of his life?)

From here we see the extent to which one must be willing to go in order to avoid speaking negatively about another Jew. G-d deemed it preferable to cause Yitzchak to be *blind for over five decades* rather than to tell him *lashon hara* about the wicked Eisav!

If this is true concerning Eisav, how much more careful must we be when speaking about our fellow Jews, the most sinful of whom are certainly not nearly as wicked as Eisav was!

—*Likkutei Sichos vol. 15, pp. 215–216*

---

10. See Rashi, Bereishis 27:21

27:1-4 | כז:א-ד

וַיִּקְרָא אֶת עֵשָׂו בְּנוֹ הַגָּדֹל וַיֹּאמֶר אֵלָיו...
בַּעֲבוּר תְּבָרֶכְךָ נַפְשִׁי בְּטֶרֶם אָמוּת

He summoned his elder son Eisav and said to him, "...so that I may grant you my soul's blessing before I die."

Beneath Eisav's Surface

Yitzchak was not entirely oblivious to Eisav's unrefined character and conduct, yet he intended to bestow upon him the most powerful blessings.[11] Surely, his desire to bless Eisav was not based only on what he did *not* know about him, but also on what he *did* see in him.

The Torah relates that Yitzchak devoted a great deal of energy to digging water wells, restoring old wells, and searching for and developing new sources of fresh water. Chassidus explains that this hobby was not a meaningless detail in Yitzchak's life, but a reflection of his distinctive nature and his unique path in the service of G-d. Where others saw dirt and gravel, Yitzchak dug deeply to reveal springs of lifegiving water that ran beneath the earth. This means, in spiritual terms, that Yitzchak devoted himself to refining the unrefined, unearthing and cultivating the potential within all creation to recognize its G-dly source.

Accordingly, we can understand why Yitzchak desired to bless Eisav. Despite Eisav's disreputable behavior, Yitzchak had the ability to see the great spiritual potential associated

---

11. See Bereishis 26:35; Rashi, Bereishis 27:21.

with Eisav's soul. Yitzchak therefore hoped that his powerful blessings would successfully excavate the spiritual treasures that lay hidden in his child.[12]

Today there are no Eisavs, but like Yitzchak, who labored to reveal the connection to G-d buried even within the wicked Eisav, we too must endeavor to draw near even those who seem distant from the lifegiving waters of the Torah. With toil and effort, we can reveal within them their innate connection to the Source of Life.

— *Likkutei Sichos, vol. 15, pp. 195-198*

---

12. Nevertheless, despite Eisav's immense potential, his actual lowly state was such that in reality the blessings would not have had the desired effect on him. Rivkah therefore deemed it necessary for Yaakov to receive the blessings instead of Eisav.

27:2 | כז:ב

וַיֹּאמֶר הִנֵּה נָא זָקַנְתִּי לֹא יָדַעְתִּי יוֹם מוֹתִי

He said, "Behold now, I have grown old;
I do not know the day of my death."

Gifts from a Minimalist

Yitzchak was 123 years old when he summoned his son Eisav and said, "Behold now, I have grown old; I do not know the day of my death." He instructed Eisav to prepare a meal for him, so that he could bless him before he died.

What was the occasion that inspired Yitzchak's words? Rashi explains:

> If a person is approaching the age at which his parents died, he should worry five years beforehand and five years afterwards. Yitzchak was 123 years old. He thought, "Perhaps I will live to my mother's age; she died at 127. I am thus within five years of her age." He therefore said, "I do not know the day of my death: I may reach my mother's age, or perhaps my father's."

At that point Yitzchak was five years younger than his mother had been at her passing, and there was still a good chance that he would live another 50 years or more, as his father had. (In fact, he ultimately lived to the age of 180, five years longer than his father did.) Moreover, his mother's passing at the age of 127 had been due to unnatural causes,[13] so it was safe to assume that he would live longer than she did. Yet Yitzchak began concerning himself with his end-of-life

---

13. See Rashi, Bereishis 23:2.

affairs at the age of 123, the youngest age—according to his calculations—when it was likely for him to die.

This degree of caution was not out of character for Yitzchak, whose dominant personality trait was *gevurah*—discipline and restraint.[14] He therefore viewed every aspect of life from a cautious and moderate perspective.

Nevertheless, despite Yitzchak's nature of discipline and moderation, the blessings that he bestowed (ultimately, upon Yaakov) were the most rich and extensive blessings given in the Torah, from the "dew of the heaven" to "the fat of the earth."

Yitzchak's paradoxical behavior teaches us—his descendants and spiritual heirs—that even if we are extremely disciplined and hard on ourselves, this cannot have any bearing on the way we relate to and give to others. Our relationship with our fellow Jew must always be one of affection and benevolence, generously sharing "from the dew of heaven and the fat of the earth."

—*Likkutei Sichos, vol. 15, p. 220*

---

14. See Zohar 3:4a (Raaya Meheimna).

27:13 | כז:יג

וַתֹּאמֶר לוֹ אִמּוֹ עָלַי קִלְלָתְךָ בְּנִי

And his mother said to him,
"Let your curse be upon me, my son."

Earning the Unearnable

When Rivkah heard about Yitzchak's plan to bestow his greatest blessings upon Eisav, their wicked son, she told Yaakov, the righteous son, to trick Yitzchak into giving him the blessings instead. But Yaakov was concerned that Yitzchak would catch on to his act, and that Yaakov would end up with curses instead of blessings. Rivkah therefore guaranteed him that she took full responsibility, saying, "Let your curse be upon me, my son," whereupon Yaakov agreed to go ahead with the plan.

Now, Yaakov was a devoted son, and was certainly as concerned for his mother's welfare as he was for his own. Clearly, then, his mother's guarantee that any curse would transfer to her could not have been very convincing!

Rather, what persuaded Yaakov was Rivkah's willingness to take such great risk in order for him to receive the blessings. Through her offer, Rivkah demonstrated that these blessings were worth any risk involved in receiving them. In fact, the risk-taking itself would made Yaakov worthy of receiving them.

Rivkah understood that these blessings were so extraordinary and unfathomable that they could not be earned through normal and rational means. She realized that to be the fertile soil in which these transcendent blessings could take root, one needed to be willing to transcend the security of his perfectly calculated and balanced lifestyle—he must be ready for *mesiras nefesh*, self-sacrifice.

Through her readiness to take such great risks for Yaakov to receive the blessings, Rivkah inspired within Yaakov an "uncalculated" readiness for *mesiras nefesh*, whereby he became worthy of blessings that surpass anything the mind could possibly grasp.

—*Likkutei Sichos, vol. 1, p. 56*

ויצא
Vayeitzei

28:11 | כח:יא

וַיִּקַּח מֵאַבְנֵי הַמָּקוֹם וַיָּשֶׂם מְרַאֲשֹׁתָיו

He took some of the stones of that place, and placed [them] at his head.

Don't Let It Go to Your Head

On his journey to Charan, Yaakov stopped for the night. Before going to sleep, he gathered some stones and arranged them around his head. Rashi explains: "He arranged them like a gutter pipe around his head, because he feared the wild beasts."[1]

If Yaakov wanted to protect himself through natural means rather than relying on a miracle, why did he erect the stone barrier only around his head? On the other hand, if the reason he did not build a blockade around the rest of his body was because he trusted that G-d would protect him, why did he take extra measures to guard his head?

---

1. Bereishis 28:11.

Clearly, Yaakov's placing the stones around his head to ward off intruders must hold deeper significance.

Yaakov was about to enter a new stage of life. Until now, the Torah tells us, Yaakov was "an innocent man who dwelled in tents"[2]—a reference to his extended studies in the "tents of Shem and Eiver,"[3] the centers of Torah study at that time. Now, on the cusp of marriage, Yaakov would be entering the workforce, living in Charan and working with the sly Lavan. He realized that the journey to Charan alone already exposed him to "wild animals," an allusion to the spiritual dangers that even the lead-up to his impending transition could pose. At this critical point, says the Torah, Yaakov protected his head.

In doing so, Yaakov demonstrated that to ensure our commitment to Torah values, even when we are engrossed in earning a living, our *heads* must be guarded. In the words of Tehillim, "If you eat the toil of *your hands*, you are praiseworthy, and it is good for you."[4] Invest and preoccupy only your hands—your physical energy—in your toil and labor; save your head and heart for the study of Torah and for passionate prayer.

As long you keep your head safe, taught Yaakov, and reserve your higher faculties for your relationship with G-d, then your integrity and sense of direction will stay secure even when your body goes to work.

—*Likkutei Sichos, vol. 1, pp. 61-62*

---

2. Bereishis 25:27.
3. Rashi ad loc.
4. Tehillim 128:2.

28:11 | כח:יא

וַיִּפְגַּע בַּמָּקוֹם וַיָּלֶן שָׁם כִּי בָא הַשֶּׁמֶשׁ...
וַיִּשְׁכַּב בַּמָּקוֹם הַהוּא

He arrived at the place and overnighted there because the sun had set... He lay down at that place.

Good Night, Yaakov

On his way to Charan, Yaakov stopped for the night and lay down to sleep at "the place"[5]—precisely the spot where the Beis Hamikdash, our Holy Temple, would be built.[6]

According to the Midrash, the Torah emphasizes that "at that place" he lay down, because "here he lay down to sleep, but during the 14 years when he studied under Eiver he did not lie down... Here he lay down, but during the 20 years he spent in Lavan's house he did not lie down."[7] Meaning that over a period of 34 years, the only place that Yaakov lay down for a good night's sleep was the site of the Beis Hamikdash! How could it be that Yaakov lay down for a relaxing and peaceful sleep specifically here, the holiest spot in the world?

The Torah's account of Yaakov's rest on the Temple Mount alludes to the great revelation of G-dliness that would one day take place there.

The structure of the human body reflects the superiority of a person's spiritual identity (represented by the spiritual faculties found in his brain) over the physical aspects of his life (represented by his feet). When we stand, our feet and

---

5. Bereishis 28:11.
6. See Rashi.
7. Bereishis Rabbah 68:11; see Rashi, Bereishis ad loc.

lower faculties are lower than—beneath and subject to—our minds, the seat of our spiritual awareness.

When we lie down, however, the head and feet are level. On the one hand, this represents a compromise of the "head's" superiority; on the other hand, it reflects the reality that before G-d, Who transcends all, physicality and spirituality are equal. This recognition reminds us that although our spiritual lives must obviously dominate our physical lives, ultimately both can and must be used to reveal G-d's transcendent essence.

It therefore came to be that Yaakov lay down to sleep specifically at the future site of the Beis Hamikdash, his feet level with his head. For in the presence of G-d, the height of spirituality is on equal footing with the lowly material world that it must guide and uplift.

—*Sefer Hasichos 5752, vol. 1, pp. 140–142*

30:20 | ל:כ

וַתֹּאמֶר לֵאָה... הַפַּעַם יִזְבְּלֵנִי אִישִׁי כִּי יָלַדְתִּי
לוֹ שִׁשָּׁה בָנִים וַתִּקְרָא אֶת שְׁמוֹ זְבֻלוּן

Leah said... "Now my husband will reside with me, for I have borne him six sons," so she named him Zevulun.

There is No Place like Home

When our matriarch Leah bore her sixth son, she named him Zevulun, a derivative of the word *zevul*—place of residence, saying, "Now my husband will reside with me." As Rashi explains, "His [Yaakov's] principal residence will be only with me, because I have as many sons as all his other wives combined."

According to the Kabbalah, your given name is not merely a product of your parents' personal preference. Rather, G-d endows parents with the wisdom to choose names that are uniquely associated with their child's soul.[8]

As such, the name Zevulun signifies not only the milestone that Leah reached with his birth, but also the nature of this specific child.[9]

Zevulun's association with "places of residence" can be explained in light of the well-known arrangement that the tribe of Zevulun had with the tribe of Yissachar. "Zevulun and

---

8. Shaar Hagilgulim, Chapter 23.

9. Moreover, the change that Zevulun's arrival precipitated—i.e., Leah's tent becoming Yaakov's primary home—was due not only to Zevulun's status as Leah's sixth son, but also to his distinct character. Since he was associated with the idea of *zevul*, a place of primary and permanent residence, his arrival brought a similar blessing to his mother's life.

Yissachar established a partnership: Zevulun will dwell at the seashore, and go out in ships to trade and make profit. They will thereby provide food for the tribe of Yissachar, who will sit and occupy themselves with the study of Torah."[10]

The tribe of Zevulun's immersion in commerce afforded them unique opportunities to infuse G-dly meaning into the material world and its ways. Their dealings "for the sake of Heaven"—in their case, to support Torah study—and their utilization of material means for the fulfillment of G-d's commands transformed this lowly physical world into a G-dly place to an even greater degree than was accomplished by the Torah study of their partners, the tribe of Yissachar, who hardly engaged in worldly affairs.

Hence the name Zevulun. For it is specifically the Zevulun, the businessperson, who has the greatest potential to develop this world into a *zevul*, a place that G-d can call home.

—*Likkutei Sichos, vol. 30, pp. 134–136*

---

10. Rashi, Devarim 33:18.

30:20 | ל:כ

וַתֹּאמֶר לֵאָה... הַפַּעַם יִזְבְּלֵנִי אִישִׁי כִּי יָלַדְתִּי
לוֹ שִׁשָּׁה בָנִים וַתִּקְרָא אֶת שְׁמוֹ זְבֻלוּן

Leah said... "Now my husband will reside with me, for I have borne him six sons," so she named him Zevulun.

Make the Time to Build a Home

Yaakov and his son Zevulun represent opposite ends of the Torah-study spectrum. Yaakov is called "an innocent man who dwelled in tents,"[11] a reference to his extended studies in the "tents of Shem and Eiver,"[12] the centers of Torah study of his time. Zevulun, on the other hand, arranged with his brother Yissachar that "Zevulun will dwell at the seashore, and go out in ships to trade and make profit. They will thereby provide food for the tribe of Yissachar, who will sit and occupy themselves with the study of Torah."[13]

We find, however, that upon the birth of Zevulun his mother said, "From now on, his [Yaakov's] principal residence (*zevul*) will be only with me."[14] Meaning, in spiritual terms, that Torah study—represented by Yaakov—finds its "permanent home" specifically in the company of Zevulun, the person preoccupied with business and worldly affairs.

Practically, this means that the strength and endurance of the Jewish people's dedication to G-d and His Torah is

---

11. Bereishis 25:27.
12. Rashi ad loc.
13. Rashi, Devarim 33:18.
14. Bereishis 30:20; see Rashi ad loc.

revealed when a Jew sets aside time for Torah study *despite* his engagement with the world—more so than in the diligent study of those who do not engage at all with the outside world.

It was therefore specifically upon the arrival of the worldly Zevulun that his mother's tent became the permanent and principal residence of Yaakov, who represents Torah study, because the (limited) Torah study of the worldly Zevulun is imbued with a tenacity and "permanence" that the Torah study of others does not have.

—*Likkutei Sichos, vol. 30, pp. 137–140*

31:6 | לא:ו

וְאַתֵּנָה יְדַעְתֶּן כִּי בְּכָל כֹּחִי עָבַדְתִּי אֶת אֲבִיכֶן

And you well know that I served your father with all my might.

How Yaakov Made His Fortune

The Rambam's Mishneh Torah is dedicated strictly to documenting the Torah's laws, and does not typically discuss the Divine reward promised to us for the observance of specific commandments.

The Rambam makes an exception when describing the extent to which an employee must invest himself in his job. In the Rambam's words:

> He [the employee] is obligated to put all his energy into his work, as the righteous Yaakov said: "I served your father with all my might." Therefore he received reward for this even in this world, as is written,[15] "The man became prodigiously wealthy."[16]

The Rambam's uncharacteristic elaboration of Yaakov's reward for his faultless work ethic indicates that this detail contributes to our understanding of the employee's obligations in Jewish law.

Prior to this law, the Rambam writes: "The employee is cautioned not to steal from the labor that is due his employer by neglecting his work slightly here and there, spending the

---

15. Bereishis 30:43.
16. Mishneh Torah, Hil. Sechirus 13:7.

entire day in deceit." This law is obviously a financial obligation from the employee to his employer.

In contrast, the Rambam's next statement, requiring a person to invest all his energy into the job (besides for fully utilizing his time and doing the job properly), would seem to be a matter of good faith, an ethical ideal "between you and G-d," more than a duty between employee and employer.

The Rambam dismisses this notion with his description of Yaakov's reward. His words emphasize that Yaakov was not only Divinely rewarded as one would be for any other mitzvah, but that the reward for his sincere effort was evident even in the compensation he received from his *employer*: though Lavan had hoped to deceive Yaakov, through Divine intervention the wages he was ultimately forced to pay accurately reflected Yaakov's hard work, making Yaakov an exceedingly wealthy man. The fact that Yaakov's *devotion* to his job was Divinely rewarded within the compensation he received from his *employer* underscores that putting your fullest effort into your job is not merely a matter of good faith; it is the *financial* duty of the employee to his employer, and therefore duly rewarded by G-d in the most direct and natural manner.

—*Likkutei Sichos, vol. 25, pp. 141–144*

לא:כב-כג | 31:22-23

וַיֻּגַּד לְלָבָן בַּיּוֹם הַשְּׁלִישִׁי כִּי בָרַח יַעֲקֹב: וַיִּקַּח אֶת אֶחָיו עִמּוֹ וַיִּרְדֹּף אַחֲרָיו דֶּרֶךְ שִׁבְעַת יָמִים

On the third day, Lavan was informed that Yaakov had fled. He took along his kinsmen and pursued him for the distance of a seven-day journey.

The Rest of the Story

The Baal Shem Tov taught that if a Jew is standing in prayer and someone tries to harass him and disturb him from praying, he should not be disheartened, for the disturbance itself must have a G-dly purpose. Namely, its purpose is to motivate him to delve even more fervently into the prayers he is reciting, to the point that he cannot even hear the disturbance.[17]

The underlying principle behind this idea is that, in truth, what prompted this disturbance is the harasser's spiritual source, which genuinely seeks to contribute to the realm of *kedushah*, holiness. The negative form that this drive assumes, i.e., a disturbance to a Jew's prayers, is only because the *medium* through which this energy is channeled into the physical world is unholy. At its core, however, this disturbance is purely a means of adding depth and passion to the Jew's communion with G-d.

In a similar vein, the Maggid of Mezeritch explained why Lavan chased after Yaakov and his family when they left Charan. The goal of Yaakov's stay with Lavan had been to extract the spiritual "sparks of holiness" that were hidden there, and

---

17. See Tanya, Iggeres Hakodesh 25.

to restore them to their rightful place—their G-dly purpose. When Yaakov left, however, there were still some holy sparks left behind. Lavan was therefore compelled to pursue Yaakov, in order to cause those sparks to be restored. Those restored sparks are the holy letters in the Torah that tell the story of Lavan's chase of Yaakov and their encounter.[18]

In light of this explanation, the story of Lavan chasing after Yaakov teaches us the perspective with which we must approach any difficulties we encounter in our efforts to do G-d's bidding. Instead of allowing an obstacle to weaken our resolve, we must recognize that even a disturbance can be a catalyst for bringing about greater *kedushah* in this world. By carrying on with our efforts unabated, we will reveal that, at its core, a challenge is only a means of generating greater motivation and resolve in our service of G-d.

—*Likkutei Sichos, vol. 1, pp. 80-81*

---

[18]. See Or Hatorah, Hosafos 5.

וישלח
Vayishlach

32:5-6 | לב:ה-ו

עִם לָבָן גַּרְתִּי... וַיְהִי לִי שׁוֹר וַחֲמוֹר צֹאן וְעֶבֶד וְשִׁפְחָה

I have sojourned with Lavan...
And I have acquired oxen and donkeys, flocks,
manservants, and maidservants.

Don't Make Yourself at Home

After living with Lavan for 20 years, Yaakov and his family finally left for the land of Canaan. To announce their arrival, Yaakov sent a message to his brother, Eisav: "I have sojourned (גַּרְתִּי) with Lavan and I have tarried until now."[1]

The literal meaning of the word גַּרְתִּי is "I stayed there as a foreigner." Yaakov used these words to emphasize that despite spending 20 years in Lavan's company, and amassing much material wealth there—"oxen and donkeys, flocks, manser-

---

1. Bereishis 32:5-6.

vants and maidservants—" he continued to view himself as a stranger in Charan. It never became his natural home.

Yaakov's view of himself as a stranger to Lavan and everything Lavan represented was the secret behind the other interpretation that Rashi suggests for the word גַּרְתִּי: "גַּרְתִּי has the numerical value of 613. That is to say: I lived with the wicked Lavan, but I kept the 613 commandments, and I did not learn from his evil deeds."[2] Yaakov's success at maintaining his observance of תרי"ג, the 613 mitzvos, was due to his firm resolve to keep his relationship with his material affairs in a state of גַּרְתִּי, foreignness. He therefore never allowed it to disturb his worship of G-d, and could proudly say, "Despite 20 years of Lavan's company, I kept the 613 commandments."

—*Likkutei Sichos, vol. 1, pp. 68–69*

---

2. Rashi ad loc.

32:33 | לב:לג

עַל כֵּן לֹא יֹאכְלוּ בְנֵי יִשְׂרָאֵל אֶת גִּיד הַנָּשֶׁה אֲשֶׁר עַל כַּף הַיָּרֵךְ עַד הַיּוֹם הַזֶּה׃

Therefore the Bnei Yisrael may not eat the gid hanasheh, *which is on the socket of the hip, until this day.*

It's Not Petty When it's Your Child

In the middle of the night Yaakov encounters an angel of G-d, wrestles with him and wins. But the angel, who is Eisav's spiritual source and advocate on high, wounds Yaakov's sciatic nerve. In commemoration, the Torah prohibits eating this nerve in any animal.

The significance of this mitzvah is explained in the Sefer Hachinuch:

> This mitzvah serves as a reminder to the Jewish people that though they will suffer many hardships in their exiles at the hands of the nations and at the hands of the children of Eisav, they should be confident that they will never be wiped out.[3]

The prohibition of eating the sciatic nerve seems to be a mere technicality in the laws of *kashrus*, applicable only to the specific nerve that the angel wounded, which is itself only a minor detail in the story of Yaakov's miraculous salvation. Why do we commemorate such a crucial aspect of Jewish faith—our eternal hope of survival—with a law so narrow in scope?

---

3. Mitzvah 3.

The emphasis that this mitzvah places on one detail is, in truth, extremely significant. It highlights that G-d's providence and concern for the Jewish people extends even to the most minor details in their lives!

Although the Baal Shem Tov taught that every aspect of creation is orchestrated by Divine Providence and serves a specific role in the Divine plan, the *significance* of every detail before G-d still varies, depending on how central a role it serves in the ultimate purpose of creation.

When it comes to details that affect the life of a Jew, however, there are no such distinctions; a nerve in a Jew's hip is as significant to G-d as the entire creation. Since every Jew is uniquely chosen and cherished by G-d, and imbued with a soul that is essentially one with G-d Himself, even the seemingly minor details in the life of a Jew are of infinite significance before G-d.

—*Likkutei Sichos, vol. 30, pp. 148–154*

34:1 | לד:א

וַתֵּצֵא דִינָה בַּת־לֵאָה אֲשֶׁר יָלְדָה לְיַעֲקֹב לִרְאוֹת בִּבְנוֹת הָאָרֶץ

Dinah, the daughter of Leah, whom she had borne to Yaakov, went out to see the daughters of the land.

You Should Really Get Out a Bit

The Torah's account of Dinah's abduction begins, "Dinah, the daughter of Leah… went out to see the daughters of the land." Rashi notes the Torah's emphasis on Dinah being Leah's daughter, and explains that Dinah inherited her social nature from her mother:

> She is identified as "the daughter of Leah" because she ventured out. For Leah too was an "out-goer," as it is written, "Leah went out to greet him [Yaakov]."[4] Regarding her it has been said, "Like mother, like daughter."

On the surface, it seems that the Torah views these two "out-goers" disapprovingly—their excursions are considered excessive by the Torah's standards of modesty. But would the Torah really go out of its way to disparage not only Dinah, but Leah too, when we know that "the Torah avoids disparaging even a non-kosher animal"?[5]

It must be that the Torah associates Dinah's conduct with Leah's as an indication of praise, rather than criticism. Just as Leah's motives were admirable when *she* "went out" ("she

---

4. Bereishis 30:16.
5. Bava Basra 123a.

desired and was seeking means to increase the number of tribes"),[6] Dinah's intentions were noble too.

What were Dinah's intentions?

When Yaakov prepared his family to meet Eisav, he hid Dinah in a crate so that Eisav would not see her and desire her. Yaakov was later punished for doing so, because had they married, Dinah might have positively influenced the wicked Eisav.[7] Certainly, if Dinah's chances of affecting Eisav were slim, Yaakov would not have been punished for hiding her! Evidently, Dinah's remarkable character meant that she was more than likely to succeed in transforming the wicked Eisav, had she only been given the opportunity.

As such, we can understand that Dinah's excursions were likewise motivated by her ability to affect people outside the pure environment of her family. She did not go out "to see the daughters of the land" in order to see and be seen among them, or to acquaint herself with their ways, but to attract them to hers—the righteous path of Yaakov.

Indeed, like her mother, Dinah went out with the purest of intentions.

—*Likkutei Sichos, vol. 35, pp. 150–151*

---

6. Rashi, Bereishis 30:17.
7. Rashi, Bereishis 32:33.

34:25 | לד:כה

וַיִּקְחוּ שְׁנֵי בְנֵי־יַעֲקֹב שִׁמְעוֹן וְלֵוִי אֲחֵי דִינָה אִישׁ חַרְבּוֹ וַיָּבֹאוּ עַל־הָעִיר בֶּטַח וַיַּהַרְגוּ כָּל־זָכָר

Two of Yaakov's sons—Shimon and Levi, Dinah's brothers—each man took his sword, and they came upon the city with confidence, and they slew every male.

The Jewish Way in Responsible Adulthood

Shimon and Levi are each referred to in this verse as איש, a man. The Midrash[8] calculates that this story took place just 13 years after the birth of Levi, the younger of the two brothers, and yet Levi is called a man, indicating that at the age of 13 he had the emotional maturity of an adult. This is one of the sources from which Jewish law establishes 13 years as the age of maturity, whereupon a boy becomes bar mitzvah—biblically responsible to observe the mitzvos.

Ironically, the context in which the 13-year-old Levi is called a man is not an instance in which he acted with the levelheadedness that comes with maturity: he and Shimon react heatedly to Shechem's exploitation of their sister, attacking the city, putting their own lives in grave danger.

This unusual source for the age of bar mitzvah highlights the true definition of mitzvah responsibility. Certainly, we can be held responsible for the mitzvos only when we have the capacity to understand and appreciate their importance. That is why the obligation to observe mitzvos begins only when

---

8. Bereishis Rabbah 80:10.

one becomes intellectually and emotionally mature— a "man." But understanding and discernment are only the tools—not the foundation—with which to serve G-d. The foundation of Divine service is *kabbolas ol*, "accepting the yoke of Heaven," submitting oneself to G-d's will with a commitment that transcends understanding and reason.

The Torah alludes to Levi and Shimon's adulthood in the episode of Shechem, for their actions demonstrated that their capacity for critical judgment stood firmly on foundations of *kabbolas ol*, submission to a higher cause. Thus, when defending their values necessitated personal risk and self-sacrifice, they readily put their own interests aside, and "each man took his sword…"

—*Likkutei Sichos, vol. 15, pp. 289-292*

36:2-3 | לו:ב-ג

עֵשָׂו לָקַח אֶת נָשָׁיו... וְאֶת בָּשְׂמַת בַּת יִשְׁמָעֵאל

Eisav chose his wives...
and Bosmas daughter of Yishmael.

Eisav's Yom Kippur

One of Eisav's wives was Bosmas, the daughter of Yishmael, who was previously[9] referred to as "Mochalas." The reason for this change, explain the Sages, is that the name Mochalas alludes to the remarkable spiritual transformation she experienced through marriage. According to Rashi:

> There are three whose sins are forgiven: a convert, someone promoted to a high position, and one who marries. The proof [for the last-named] is from here: she was called Mochalas (מָחֲלַת) because her sins were forgiven [נִמְחֲלוּ, *nimchalu*, in Hebrew, sharing a common root with Mochalas.]

The Torah alludes to this remarkable power of marriage specifically in reference to the *wicked* Eisav, to make evident that it is the marriage, in and of itself, that causes the bride and groom to be forgiven: their very decision to build a Jewish family, fulfilling the fundamental mitzvah to "be fruitful and multiply," brings about their extraordinary elevation and transformation.

The Talmud teaches, "He who teaches Torah to another person's child, the Torah considers it as if he fathered him."[10] Accordingly, just as a person who resolves to marry and build

---

9. Bereishis 28:9.
10. Sanhedrin 19b.

a family is forgiven for all his sins, so is one who resolves to fulfill the spiritual equivalent of this mitzvah by drawing others closer to the Torah.

Moreover, by using Eisav's marriage to Bosmas to teach us that marriage brings atonement for one's sins, the Torah is teaching us that even if you are not perfect, even if you view yourself as unworthy as "Eisav," G-d forbid, and have plenty to work on yourself, you should not hesitate to build your spiritual family—to devote yourself to drawing others closer to the Torah way of life. For through the marriage alone—i.e., through your very resolve to devote yourself to this vital mission—G-d will assist you and raise you to spiritual heights.

—*Likkutei Sichos, vol. 30, pp. 163–168*

36:6-8 | לו:ו-ח

וַיִּקַּח עֵשָׂו אֶת נָשָׁיו וְאֶת בָּנָיו וְאֶת בְּנֹתָיו
וְאֶת כָּל נַפְשׁוֹת בֵּיתוֹ וְאֶת מִקְנֵהוּ וְאֶת כָּל בְּהֶמְתּוֹ
וְאֵת כָּל קִנְיָנוֹ אֲשֶׁר רָכַשׁ בְּאֶרֶץ כְּנָעַן וַיֵּלֶךְ אֶל אֶרֶץ
מִפְּנֵי יַעֲקֹב אָחִיו... וַיֵּשֶׁב עֵשָׂו בְּהַר שֵׂעִיר

Eisav took his wives, his sons, and his daughters, and all the people of his household, and his cattle, and all his animals, and all his possessions that he had acquired in the land of Canaan; and he moved to another land, because of his brother Yaakov... And Eisav settled on Mount Se'ir.

The Unsettled Jew

Eisav's move from the land of Canaan to Mount Se'ir was motivated by practical considerations. He knew that the land of Canaan had been promised to the descendants of his grandfather Avraham, but it came with a price tag. Whoever would inherit the Promised Land would first pay off the "family debt"—G-d's decree that Avraham's descendants would be "strangers in a land that is not theirs."[11] Eisav reasoned, "Let me move away from here. I will share neither in the gift nor in the payment of the debt."[12]

But why was Eisav's move to Se'ir regarded as avoiding the debt? Couldn't his move be considered paying it off? After all, G-d decreed that Avraham's descendants would be "strangers in a land that is not theirs"—but not necessarily in Egypt. In what way was Eisav's moving his entire family and fortune to

---

11. Bereishis 15:13.
12. Rashi, Bereishis 36:7.

Se'ir less payment of the debt than Yaakov's relocating with his family to Egypt?

Careful analysis of the above mentioned decree shows, however, that the debt left for Yaakov to pay was not that his family would have to merely leave their homeland, as Eisav did, but that "גר יהי' זרעך—your children will be strangers": they will never assimilate with their host nation.

Eisav "*settled* on Mount Se'ir." He wanted his children to have the comfort of blending in with their new neighbors rather than remaining perpetual outsiders. Yaakov's children, however, never became citizens of their host country. The payment of the family debt meant they would remain foreigners throughout their stay in the land of Egypt.

The same is true of the Jewish people, the descendants of Yaakov, in the current exile—the debt of which we continue to pay until the coming of Moshiach. Unlike Eisav and his descendants in their new surroundings in Se'ir, we must constantly maintain our unease with the norms of exile, anxiously awaiting the Geulah, the Redemption, when we will be able to collect our long-awaited inheritance and finally settle peacefully in the Land of Israel.

—*Likkutei Sichos, vol. 10, p. 114*

וישב
Vayeishev

37:1-2 | ל״ז:א-ב

וַיֵּשֶׁב יַעֲקֹב... אֵלֶּה תֹּלְדוֹת יַעֲקֹב

Yaakov dwelled... These are the descendants of Yaakov.

Between Pebbles and Pearls

The Torah relates the events of Yaakov's life in detail, pauses briefly to mention Eisav's family and where they settled, and then resumes the story of Yaakov. Rashi explains:

> The Torah describes Eisav's settlements and his descendants only briefly... It describes Yaakov's settlements, the growth of his family, and all the events that brought these about in detail, since their importance before G-d warrants dwelling upon them at length... This can be compared to a pearl that falls into the sand: A person searches in the sand and sifts it with a sieve until he finds the pearl. Upon finding it, he casts the pebbles from his hand and keeps the pearl.[1]

---

1. Bereishis 37:1.

Rashi's analogy refers not only to the Torah's detailed account of Yaakov's life in contrast to its abbreviated history of Eisav; it also alludes to the Jewish people's primary mission throughout history—to sift through "the settlements of Eisav." The search for the pearl symbolizes our mission to find the holiness—the G-dly meaning and potential—hidden in the mundane world.

In view of that, we can understand why it was necessary for Rashi to note that upon finding the pearl one "*casts away the pebbles.*" Is it not obvious that once he has the pearl in his hands, he loses all interest in the pebbles and sand through which he was merely sifting to find?

By including this detail, however, Rashi teaches us that "casting away the pebbles" is indeed a crucial component of our mission. In order to extract and elevate—and indeed be elevated by—the sparks of G-dliness found in the mundane world, we must be certain that "the pebbles," the material setting in which those sparks lay hidden, are not what actually appeals to us. Otherwise we can easily be dragged down by materialism, instead of drawing out the positive elements that the material world contains. Only by casting away any personal interest in "the settlements of Eisav" can we successfully extract "the pearls"—the great spiritual wealth that is hidden therein.

—*Likkutei Sichos, vol. 15, pp. 305-307*

37:5 | לז:ה

וַיַּחֲלֹם יוֹסֵף חֲלוֹם

Yosef dreamed a dream.

A Jew and His Dreams

In Parshas Vayeishev we read about Yosef's dreams, both of which foretold that his family would one day bow to him. In the first dream, Yosef and his brothers were represented by sheaves of wheat. Eleven sheaves—the brothers—bowed to Yosef's single sheaf. In the second dream, his family—represented by the sun, moon and stars—again bowed to him.

In Parshas Mikeitz we read that, like Yosef, Pharaoh had two dreams, and his dreams also shared a theme, both foretelling seven years of plenty that would visit Egypt, followed by seven years of famine. And, like Yosef's, in Pharaoh's dreams the imagery changed from one dream to the next. In the first, the years of plenty and famine were represented by seven heavy, well-fed cows and seven sickly, emaciated cows. In the second, they were represented by seven healthy, plump ears of grain and seven limp, underdeveloped ears of grain.[2]

Interestingly, Yosef's dreams featured celestial beings—the sun, moon and stars—whereas Pharaoh's did not. Moreover, Pharaoh's dreams "deteriorated," as it were. His first dream involved animal life, but his second dream featured vegetation—a much lower lifeform. In contrast, Yosef's dreams progressed from the earthly to the heavenly.

---

2. Bereishis 41:1–32.

The contrast between these two sets of dreams highlights the differences between the dreamers. Pharaoh's dreams were devoid of anything heavenly, symbolizing a person whose mind is wholly engrossed in earthly pursuits. It comes as no surprise that such a person gradually becomes increasingly entrenched in his material obsessions, as is represented by the "degenerative" sequence of Pharaoh's dreams.

Yosef's dreams, however, were different. A Jew, even as he goes about the physical world, is always thinking about the heavenly aspects of his life—his spiritual development and G-dly purpose. Yosef therefore dreamed of the earthly as well as the heavenly, and in an order of "progression," because his life as a whole was in a constant state of growth.

—*Likkutei Sichos, vol. 3, pp. 805-806*

37:7 | לז:ז

וְהִנֵּה אֲנַחְנוּ מְאַלְּמִים אֲלֻמִּים בְּתוֹךְ הַשָּׂדֶה
*And behold, we were binding
sheaves in the midst of the field.*

Dreaming to Toil

Both Yosef's and Pharaoh's dreams involved grain, but a significant difference between them reflects the fundamental disparity between what they each represent.

Yosef's dream began with a scene of toil: he and his brothers were working the fields, binding sheaves of grain. Pharaoh's dream, on the other hand, involved no labor: ears of grain grew from the ground spontaneously.

The contrast between their dreams highlights the difference between those who draw sustenance from *kedushah*, holiness, and those who are sustained by *kelipah*, unholy sources.

Deriving nourishment from unholy sources involves little or no effort. As Bnei Yisrael told Moshe, "We remember the fish that we ate in Egypt free of charge,"[3] which, Rashi explains, means not that the Egyptians provided them with food at no cost, but that their lives in Egypt were free from mitzvah obligations.[4] They referred to their food as "free of charge," because nourishment from Egypt, an allusion to all things unholy, comes easily, without effort or toil.

Conversely, when one's life is nurtured exclusively by *kedushah*, everything is earned through hard work. This is, in

---

3. Bamidbar 11:5.
4. See Rashi ad loc.

fact, G-d's means of granting us the greatest degree of delight, for ultimately, things that come without effort are not truly enjoyable. In the words of the Talmud Yerushalmi, "One who eats from the food of another is ashamed to look at his benefactor's face."[5] The blessings we enjoy most are those we've earned, not those that are handed to us for free.

It is therefore only natural that the dreams of Yosef—representing the good and holy—began with toil and labor, while the dreams of Pharaoh—representing the unholy—were of growth that did not involve labor.

One who follows the demanding path of Yosef, however, can rest assured that his successes will follow the pattern of Yosef's dreams: though his beginnings may be humble, he will ultimately reach great heights, like Yosef's dreams, which progressed from the plant kingdom on earth to the celestial beings on high.

—*Likkutei Sichos, vol. 3, pp. 807–808, 820*

---

5. Orlah 1:3.

37:24 | לז:כד

וְהַבּוֹר רֵק אֵין בּוֹ מָיִם

*Now the pit was empty;
there was no water in it.*

Filled with Emptiness

The Torah describes the pit in which Yosef was held captive, saying, "Now the pit was empty; there was no water in it."

Rashi asks: "Do the words 'now the pit was empty' not imply that the pit contained no water? For what purpose did the Torah add that 'there was no water in it'? The added phrase saying that 'there was water in it' teaches us," replies Rashi, "that it was empty only of water, but it was in fact occupied by snakes and scorpions."

Water is often used as a metaphor for Torah study.[6] Accordingly, we can understand why the Torah alludes to the presence of snakes and scorpions in the pit by emphasizing that "there was no water in it," instead of stating explicitly that the pit was inhabited by harmful creatures.

The arrival of snakes and scorpions—symbolic of the spiritual ills that can plague a person's life—is not an "additional" risk faced by those who do not fill their lives with Torah study. Rather, the presence of these negative elements is *synonymous* with the absence of Torah study: they are its inevitable consequence. For the vacuum created when a person does not occupy his free time with Torah does not remain neutral.

---

6. See Bava Kamma 17a.

When "there is no water in it," the void automatically fills with "snakes and scorpions"—ideas that are incompatible with a holy lifestyle.

—*Likkutei Sichos, vol. 15, pp. 324–325*

38:13 | לח:יג

וַיֻּגַּד לְתָמָר לֵאמֹר הִנֵּה חָמִיךְ עֹלֶה תִמְנָתָה לָגֹז צֹאנוֹ

It was told to Tamar, saying, "Behold, your father-in-law is going up to Timnah to shear his sheep."

What Does Not Go Up

Rashi tells us that the city of Timnah was built on the slope of a mountain. We thus find that whereas Yehudah is said to have gone *up* to Timnah,[7] Shimshon went *down* to Timnah.[8] As Rashi explains, "You go up to Timnah when coming from one direction, but you go down to it when coming from the other."[9]

Rashi's words describe not only the topography of the region, but also a fundamental truth regarding the nature of Divine worship, which can be compared to ascending a mountain.[10]

While we read of people who *ascended* or *descended* to Timnah, the Torah never mentions anyone being *stationed* in this mountainside city or simply *going* there. For on a slope, you are either ascending or descending; if you do not climb upward, you will inevitably slide in the opposite direction.

The same is true with regard to our devotion to G-d and His service. We must constantly work toward greater heights

---

7. Bereishis 38:13.
8. Shoftim 14:1.
9. Bereishis 38:13.
10. Tehillim 24:3.

in our spiritual climb, if only to maintain the degree of devotion to G-d that we have already attained. For on a mountain, if you are not going up, you are almost certainly going down.

—*Likkutei Sichos, vol. 10, pp. 127–128*

39:12 | לט:יב

וַיַּעֲזֹב בִּגְדוֹ בְּיָדָהּ וַיָּנָס וַיֵּצֵא הַחוּצָה

But he left his garment in her hand,
and fled and went outside.

A Picture Worth More than a Thousand Words

When Potiphar's wife tried to seduce Yosef, "the image of his father's face appeared to him in the window," and stopped him from sinning, just moments before he would have succumbed to her advances.[11]

The Talmud's words imply that simply remembering the ethical standards with which he was raised would not have sufficed to stop Yosef from sinning; it was specifically the appearance of Yaakov's face that gave him the courage not to resist the immoral act. What did the appearance of Yaakov's face convey that so significantly influenced Yosef's decision?

Elsewhere, the Talmud tells us that "our forefather Yaakov's beautiful countenance was akin to that of Adam, the first man."[12] The Kabbalists attribute this physical resemblance to the spiritual bond that Adam and Yaakov shared. What was the spiritual bond? Through their spiritual endeavors, the forefathers, Yaakov in particular, undid the damage brought upon the world by Adam's sin of eating from the Tree of Knowledge.[13]

---

11. Sotah 36b.
12. Bava Metzia 84a.
13. See Keser Shem Tov, sec. 311; Zohar 3:111b.

Thus, seeing Yaakov's face reminded Yosef of his father's famous lookalike, Adam, an individual whose sin brought devastation upon the world. At the same time, he was reminded of Yaakov's efforts to bring healing (from the damage caused by Adam's sin) to the entire world. This caused Yosef to recognize that his decision whether or not to resist the advances of his master's wife would not be inconsequential or temporary. Like Yaakov and Adam, his actions would affect the entire world for all time!

To be sure, Yosef could have relied upon all sorts of rationalizations to justify sinning just this once, in order to avoid the inevitable life sentence for denying the wishes of his master's wife. But upon seeing his father's face, Yosef was reminded that the decisions of every individual at every moment have the ability to bring harm to the entire world, as did Adam's, or to repair the universe, as did Yaakov's. When he realized that his "personal" decision would affect the entire world for all eternity, Yosef raised himself above his rationalizations and fled.

—*Toras Menachem, vol. 29, pp. 262-265*

מקץ
Mikeitz

41:1 | מא:א

וַיְהִי מִקֵּץ שְׁנָתַיִם יָמִים וּפַרְעֹה חֹלֵם

At the end of two years, it came to pass that Pharaoh was dreaming...

Living the Dream

The Egyptian exile came about through a series of dreams. Yosef's brothers hated him because of his dreams, ultimately selling him as a slave. After changing hands several times, Yosef wound up in Egypt, where he was eventually jailed. In jail he earned fame as a dream interpreter, and his interpretation of Pharaoh's dreams landed him the second most powerful position in the country—viceroy. As a result, Yosef's family decided to temporarily settle near him in Egypt, a move that resulted in some 200 years of Egyptian subjugation and oppression.

The significant role dreams played in bringing about the Egyptian exile is explained in chassidic teaching[1] as an allusion to the spiritual reality of *galus*, exile.[2] And in light of the Arizal's teaching that every subsequent exile is rooted in the original Egyptian exile,[3] it follows that the dreamlike reality that characterized the Egyptian exile defines our current exile too.

In dreams, blatant contradictions seem plausible. The subject of a dream might reflect our conscious reality, but the context is often entirely unrealistic. Similarly, the conditions of *galus* cause our lives to abound with spiritual contradictions. We might experience selfless love of G-d while praying, yet simultaneously lust for things that are prohibited by the Torah.

But we must not be discouraged by the contradictions that plague our spiritual lives in *galus*, because the dreamlike nature of exile that allows us to increase our devotion to G-d despite our internal flaws also brings about another similarity between *galus* and dreams. Just as we are forced awake from our dreams when we are surrounded by bright light, by abundantly adding in the light of Torah and mitzvos we will ultimately force ourselves awake from the dream of *galus* to the bright world of Moshiach.

—*Likkutei Sichos, vol. 1, pp. 85–88*

---

1. Torah Ohr, Vayeishev 28c.
2. See Tehillim 126:1: "We have been like dreamers."
3. Likkutei Torah, Ki Seitzei.

41:43 | מא:מג

וַיַּרְכֵּב אֹתוֹ בְּמִרְכֶּבֶת הַמִּשְׁנֶה אֲשֶׁר לוֹ וַיִּקְרְאוּ לְפָנָיו אַבְרֵךְ וְנָתוֹן אֹתוֹ עַל כָּל אֶרֶץ מִצְרָיִם.

He had him ride in his chariot of second rank, and they called out before him "Avreich," appointing him over the entire land of Egypt.

How Low Can You Bow?

According to one interpretation cited by Rashi, the word *avreich* comes from the word *birkayim*, knees. Thus, the phrase "They called out before him '*Avreich*'" indicates that the Egyptians kneeled before Yosef.

In contrast, Yosef's brothers fully "prostrated themselves before him with their faces to the ground."[4]

The distinction between Yosef's brothers and the Egyptians can be understood in light of his position as "supplier for all the people of the land."[5] According to the Kabbalistic interpretation, he furnished his generation not only with food, but also with their spiritual needs—i.e., he inspired and nurtured their devotion and submission to G-d. Accordingly, the manner in which they bowed before him hints to the varying degrees of submission to G-d that he instilled in the people of his generation.

Kneeling connotes humility and obedience. The kneeler lowers his body and head in reverence of the person before whom he is kneeling. Nevertheless, a person who kneels maintains his upright posture, symbolizing a sense of self-worth.

---

4. Bereishis 42:6.
5. Ibid.

In contrast, prostration represents the complete nullification of any sense of self or ego. The person prostrating himself places his head—his mind and identity—on par with his feet, the organs representing total obedience.

Yosef's submission to G-d was one of prostration—one who surrenders every aspect of his identity (not only his actions, but also his inner thoughts and feelings) to G-d and His will. He likewise elevated his brothers, who were holy individuals in their own right, to a level of Divine worship equal to his own.

According to those who interpret *avreich* to mean that the Egyptians merely kneeled before Yosef, the Egyptians were not capable of assimilating the high level of Divine worship of Yosef and his brothers. Yosef's spiritual influence over them was therefore limited: he was able to lead them to acknowledge G-d and revere Him, but not to fully surrender themselves to His will. They therefore kneeled, but did not prostrate themselves.

—*Likkutei Sichos, vol. 5, p. 211*

41:48 | מא:מח

וַיִּתֶּן אֹכֶל בֶּעָרִים אֹכֶל שְׂדֵה הָעִיר
אֲשֶׁר סְבִיבֹתֶיהָ נָתַן בְּתוֹכָהּ

He placed food in the cities; the food of the field surrounding the city he put within it.

Localized Humility

According to Rashi, Yosef made sure to mix some local soil into the grain when placing it in storage, as a means of preservation.

Preserving grain by mixing it with soil reflects, in spiritual terms, the phrase we say at the conclusion of *Shmoneh Esrei*, וְנַפְשִׁי כֶּעָפָר לַכֹּל תִּהְיֶה, פְּתַח לִבִּי בְּתוֹרָתֶךָ—"Let my soul be like dust before all; open my heart to Your Torah." By regarding ourselves as lowly "soil," we ensure that our hearts will absorb and maintain the Torah that we study, which is compared to "produce" in the Talmud.[6]

Rashi emphasizes, however, that the grain is protected from decay only when it is stored with *local* soil, for even humility has its place. For example, to be meek and modest when you're needed to reach out to others and teach them Torah would be misplaced humility. The humility necessary to maintain our Torah study must be local—i.e., we must be humble within our actual study of the Torah, by prefacing and pervading our Torah study with an awareness of the Torah's sanctity and divinity that utterly transcends human

---

6. Sanhedrin 42a.

comprehension. Then we will approach Torah study not as a means of personal satisfaction and pride, but with the goal of awakening within ourselves even greater awe and love of G-d.

—*Likkutei Sichos, vol. 25, pp. 224–225*

42:1 | מב:א

וַיַּרְא יַעֲקֹב כִּי יֶשׁ־שֶׁבֶר בְּמִצְרָיִם
וַיֹּאמֶר יַעֲקֹב לְבָנָיו לָמָּה תִּתְרָאוּ

Yaakov saw that there was grain being sold in Egypt. Yaakov said to his sons, "Why should you purport [to be content]?"

Got Faith, Won't Travel

When hunger descended upon the land of Canaan, Yaakov encouraged his sons to travel to Egypt to buy grain. According to Rashi, they still had some food, but Yaakov said to his sons, "Why should you show yourselves before the sons of Yishmael and Eisav as though you are sated?"

Why was Yaakov concerned about the resentment of the sons of Yishmael and Eisav, who lived some distance away, and not the envy of his immediate neighbors?

Yaakov's concern was not simply about envy. (And rightfully so, as he and his family did not actually have a long-term supply of food, and their supplies did eventually become depleted.[7]) Rather, he was concerned about certain accusations and criticisms that would come specifically from the children of Yishmael and Eisav.

Despite their limited supply of food, Yaakov's sons were entirely content, as though they had all the grain that they would ever need. They were confident that G-d would provide for their needs without requiring them to relocate, or even to travel to Egypt to buy food.

---

7. See Bereishis 43:2.

But Yaakov was concerned that such behavior might draw unwanted attention from the sons of Yishmael and Eisav. There had been other famines in the land of Canaan that had forced Avraham and Yitzchak to move—Avraham to Egypt, and Yitzchak to Gerar. Yaakov worried that the sons of Yishmael and Eisav would ask, "Do the sons of Yaakov think that they are more worthy than our common grandparents, the saintly Avraham and Yitzchak, and that G-d will provide for them without requiring them to relocate?"

In truth, Avraham and Yitzchak had not moved solely because of the famine; other factors had also motivated them to migrate.[8] Yaakov, however, knew that the children of Yishmael and Eisav might not be aware of those reasons, so he instructed his sons to travel to Egypt to restock their provisions the natural way, so as not to draw attention from their "cousins" and put their earnestness in question.

If not for this concern, Yaakov would have agreed to remain in Canaan, confident that G-d would provide for them miraculously.

—*Likkutei Sichos, vol. 30, pp. 190–194*

---

8. See Rashi, Bereishis 12:10.

42:1 | מב:א

וַיַּרְא יַעֲקֹב כִּי יֶשׁ־שֶׁבֶר בְּמִצְרָיִם
וַיֹּאמֶר יַעֲקֹב לְבָנָיו לָמָּה תִּתְרָאוּ

Yaakov saw that there was grain being sold in Egypt, so Yaakov said to his sons, "Why should you purport [to be content]?"

Independence from Foreign Aid

When the land of Canaan was struck by famine, Yaakov encouraged his sons to travel to Egypt to buy grain. According to Rashi, he told them, "Why should you show yourselves before the sons of Yishmael and the sons of Eisav as though you are sated?" Rashi's words imply that if not for the resentment of the sons of Yishmael and Eisav, Yaakov's family could have subsisted without purchasing additional grain from Egypt.

Grain, the staple of the human diet, is analogous to wisdom and knowledge. Just as food is absorbed into the bloodstream and becomes one with the body, the wisdom one studies is absorbed by the brain and becomes one with the mind.

Egypt was once the world capital of science and wisdom.[9] (As an indication of this, the wisdom of King Shlomo, the wisest of all men, is lauded as being "even greater than the wisdom of Egypt."[10]) And, corresponding to its role of providing civilization with "intellectual sustenance," Egypt became the world's primary supplier of physical sustenance. As such, Rashi's implication that Yaakov and his family were not actually dependent on Egypt for their food alludes to the

---

9. See Zohar 1:125a.
10. I Melachim 5:10.

Jewish people's inherent independence from Egypt for their knowledge and wisdom.

Instead, the Jewish people were given the Torah from which to draw their wisdom. Even the knowledge of the sciences that is necessary for comprehension and observance of the Torah is essentially contained within the Torah itself. In addition, where necessary, the Jewish Sages themselves composed scientific works. In the era of the prophets, for example, sages from the tribe of Yissachar wrote texts explaining principles of astronomy and geometry relevant to the workings of the Jewish calendar.[11] This allowed a Jew's knowledge of the sciences to be entirely independent of secular influence.

Alas, due to the travails of exile we must now rely to some degree on secular scholarship for knowledge of the sciences relevant to the Torah. With the coming of Moshiach, however, the Jewish people's intellectual independence from "Egypt" will be restored, and we will once again draw all our wisdom from the Torah alone.

—*Likkutei Sichos, vol. 30, pp. 194–197*

---

11. See Mishneh Torah, Hil. Kiddush Hachodesh 17:24.

42:21-22 | מב:כא-כב

וַיֹּאמְרוּ אִישׁ אֶל אָחִיו אֲבָל אֲשֵׁמִים אֲנַחְנוּ עַל אָחִינוּ אֲשֶׁר רָאִינוּ צָרַת נַפְשׁוֹ בְּהִתְחַנְנוֹ אֵלֵינוּ וְלֹא שָׁמָעְנוּ עַל כֵּן בָּאָה אֵלֵינוּ הַצָּרָה הַזֹּאת: וַיַּעַן רְאוּבֵן אֹתָם לֵאמֹר הֲלוֹא אָמַרְתִּי אֲלֵיכֶם לֵאמֹר אַל תֶּחֶטְאוּ בַיֶּלֶד וְלֹא שְׁמַעְתֶּם

They said to one another, "Indeed, we are guilty for our brother, that we witnessed the distress of his soul when he begged us, and we did not listen. That is why this trouble has come upon us." Reuven answered them, saying, "Didn't I tell you, saying, 'Do not sin against the lad,' but you did not listen?"

Teshuvah: Accepting Personal Responsibility

In the troubles they encountered in Egypt, the sons of Yaakov perceived a form of Divine retribution for heartlessly selling their brother Yosef into slavery many years earlier. Upon hearing his brothers admit to their guilt, Reuven reminded them that they had been well aware of their actions at the time but had proceeded with Yosef's sale undeterred: "Didn't I tell you, saying, 'Do not sin against the lad,' but you did not listen?"

With his words of rebuke, Reuven was not merely rubbing salt on his brothers' wounds; he was guiding them towards true and complete *teshuvah*, repentance.

Complete *teshuvah* requires that the penitent make a genuine decision to change, to the extent that "[G-d], who knows the hidden, will testify concerning him that he will never return to this sin again."[12] The penitent must fully acknowledge the inherent wrongfulness of his actions and wholeheartedly commit to permanently avoid such behavior. Conversely, if one's *teshuvah* is motivated by external factors, such as the negative consequences that he is suffering because of his sin, his remorse does not reflect a genuine change of attitude.

In addition, in order to wholeheartedly and unequivocally abandon past behavior, one must take full responsibility for his willful decision to sin. Otherwise, one cannot sincerely commit to refrain from making those decisions again in the future.

Therefore, when the troubles that befell Yosef's brothers in Egypt led them to regret the cruelty they had shown towards him, Reuven told them that such remorse alone was not enough. "You must recognize the inherent evil in the act of selling of Yosef," said Reuven, "which I have stressed to you all along, even before our current situation. Moreover, you must acknowledge that at the time you were fully aware of the wrongfulness of your actions, yet you willfully chose to sell him."

Once the brothers heard and internalized Reuven's words, their *teshuvah* could be complete.

—*Likkutei Sichos, vol. 30, pp. 198-202*

---

12. Mishneh Torah, Hil. Teshuvah 2:2.

ויגש
Vayigash

45:9 | מה:ט

מַהֲרוּ וַעֲלוּ אֶל אָבִי וַאֲמַרְתֶּם אֵלָיו כֹּה אָמַר בִּנְךָ יוֹסֵף שָׂמַנִי אֱלֹקִים לְאָדוֹן לְכָל מִצְרָיִם רְדָה אֵלַי אַל תַּעֲמֹד

Hurry and go up to my father, and say to him, "So said your son Yosef: G-d has made me master over all of Egypt. Come down to me; do not tarry."

The Urgent Need for Change

Upon revealing his identity to his brothers, Yosef instructed them to return home immediately, and quickly bring Yaakov to Egypt. "Come down to me; do not tarry!" he insisted.

The urgency stressed in Yosef's plea was deliberate. Yaakov hadn't seen his son Yosef for a full 22 years, corresponding to the 22 years during which Yaakov did not fulfill the mitzvah of honoring his own father and mother—the 20 years he lived with Lavan, and the two he spent lingering on his journey home.[1] Now that Yaakov's punishment had run its course, Yosef wanted to be reunited immediately, without causing his father even one extra moment of suffering.

At times we encounter situations that demand a harsh or even punitive response on our part, what our Sages refer to as "distancing with the left hand."[2] We learn from the urgency of Yaakov's reunion with Yosef, however, that we must be extremely careful to take this approach only to the extent that it is absolutely necessary. The moment that such strict discipline is no longer required, we must *urgently* revert to being compassionate and accepting—"bringing close with the right hand."

—*Likkutei Sichos, vol. 15, p. 390*

---

1. Rashi, Bereishis 37:34.
2. Sotah 47a.

45:14 | מה:יד

וַיִּפֹּל עַל צַוְּארֵי בִנְיָמִן אָחִיו וַיֵּבְךְּ וּבִנְיָמִן בָּכָה עַל צַוָּארָיו

He fell on his brother Binyamin's neck and wept, and Binyamin wept on his neck.

A Time to Weep

When Yosef revealed his identity to Binyamin, they embraced one another and wept. According to Rashi, they cried because they each prophetically foresaw the destruction that would take place in the other's territory in the Land of Israel. Yosef wept for the two Batei Mikdash, the First and Second Holy Temples, which would be built and ultimately destroyed in Binyamin's territory, and Binyamin wept for the Mishkan that would be erected and later destroyed in Yosef's territory.

Interestingly, Rashi implies they each cried only in anticipation of what would befall the other, but not for the misfortune that would happen in their own territory. Why didn't they grieve their own misfortune?

Practically, crying is only a coping mechanism. It may alleviate some of your pain and sorrow, but it cannot change the source of your grief.[3]

Now, the knowledge that a peer is bringing spiritual ruin upon himself should certainly make you upset, but only he can stop that destruction from happening. If you have prayed for him and made every effort to lead him to the right path, but have been unsuccessful, his impending ruin should bring you

---

3. The exception is tears of *teshuvah*, repentance, which are constructive in their own right. See, for example, Tehillim 56:9.

to tears, for the pain of such devastation is great, and there is nothing you can do to stop it.

Conversely, when you become aware that you are bringing ruin upon *yourself*, the correct response is not to alleviate your pain through tears, but actually to do something about it! In fact, crying can distract you from addressing the issue, as you may console yourself that your pain and awareness is enough.

This is why Yosef and Binyamin did not cry for the Temples that would be destroyed on their own territories, but for the misfortune that would befall the other. To cry over their own issues would entirely miss the point.

—*Likkutei Sichos, vol. 10, pp. 148–149*

45:26-27 | מה:כו-כז

וַיַּרְא אֶת הָעֲגָלוֹת אֲשֶׁר שָׁלַח יוֹסֵף לָשֵׂאת אֹתוֹ וַתְּחִי רוּחַ יַעֲקֹב אֲבִיהֶם: וַיֹּאמֶר יִשְׂרָאֵל רַב עוֹד יוֹסֵף בְּנִי חָי אֵלְכָה וְאֶרְאֶנּוּ בְּטֶרֶם אָמוּת

He saw the wagons that Yosef had sent to carry him, and the spirit of Yaakov their father revived. Yisrael said: "It is much! Yosef my son is still alive! I will go and see him before I die."

Surviving or Thriving?

In case his father doubted that he was indeed still alive, Yosef sent a sign with his brothers to confirm his identity.[4] Since the Hebrew words for "wagon" and "calf" are spelled the same, עגלה, Yosef sent wagons to his father to allude to the last topic he and Yaakov had studied together—the laws of *eglah arufah*, the calf that is decapitated to atone for an unsolved murder.[5]

When Yaakov saw the wagons, the verse says, "his *spirit* was revived": he was now certain that Yosef was alive both physically and spiritually, still "living" with the Torah they had studied together 22 years earlier. Yaakov's words in the next verse, "It is much! Yosef my son is still alive," likewise express his admiration for Yosef's spiritual strength: "The power of my son is great, since he endured so much suffering and yet he still stands in his righteousness! He is greater than I."[6]

Despite the theme shared by these two verses, we traditionally separate them in the public Torah reading. The words

---

4. Bereishis Rabbah 94:3.
5. See Devarim 21:1-9.
6. Bereishis Rabbah 94:3.

"The spirit of Yaakov their father revived" conclude the third portion of the reading, and the next verse opens the fourth. This underscores the two distinct aspects of Yosef's spiritual endurance that impressed Yaakov.

The first verse describes Yaakov's "revival of spirit" upon recognizing that Yosef had withstood his challenges and maintained his attachment to the Torah. But that feat alone was something that Yaakov had also accomplished when he lived with Lavan for 20 years: "I lived with the wicked Lavan, but I observed the 613 commandments—I did not learn from his evil ways."[7]

More remarkable, however, was Yosef's second achievement: not only had his environment not affected him, *he* had affected his environment! As the ruler of Egypt, he used his power to influence the Egyptians spiritually as well.[8] Of this second aspect, Yaakov said—in what we read as a separate portion of the reading—"The power of my son is great... he is greater than I."

—*Likkutei Sichos, vol. 30, pp. 222-228*

---

7. Rashi, Bereishis 32:5.
8. See Rashi, Bereishis 41:55.

46:3 | מו:ג

אַל תִּירָא מֵרְדָה מִצְרַיְמָה כִּי לְגוֹי גָּדוֹל אֲשִׂימְךָ שָׁם

Do not be afraid of going down to Egypt, for there I will make you a great nation.

No Pain, No Gain

As Yaakov and his family journeyed to Egypt, G-d appeared to Yaakov and told him: "Do not be afraid of going down to Egypt, for there I will there make you a great nation." What was Yaakov's concern? Rashi explains, "Because he [Yaakov] was anguished that he was compelled to leave [the land of Canaan] and go abroad."

Rashi's wording indicates that Yaakov was not only *afraid* of what his future held in store, but also *anguished* about leaving the land of Canaan. Yet it appears that G-d does not address Yaakov's anguish, only his fear. G-d tells him not to be afraid, because his family will emerge from Egypt even stronger than when they arrived; but evidently, his distress over leaving Canaan was still justified. In fact, Rashi's words can be interpreted as a hint to the reason Yaakov need not be afraid: his anguish itself would guarantee that his family would thrive there.

Yaakov's resultant mix of emotions—confidence in G-d's promise, while simultaneously anguished over being exiled from the eternal Jewish homeland—symbolize the paradoxical feelings that the Jewish people must have toward *galus*, our state of exile and subjection to foreign rule until the coming of Moshiach.

On the one hand, we must not be daunted by the intensity of *galus*. Knowing that we were exiled solely by G-d's will, we can be certain that G-d has endowed us with the strength necessary to overcome any challenge to His service that *galus* presents. On the other hand, we must never become comfortable with our state of exile, for it is precisely our distress and discomfort that give us the strength to transcend the awful darkness and confront its challenges.

—*Likkutei Sichos, vol. 30, pp. 234–235*

46:28 | מו:כח

וְאֶת יְהוּדָה שָׁלַח לְפָנָיו אֶל יוֹסֵף לְהוֹרֹת לְפָנָיו גֹּשְׁנָה

He sent Yehudah ahead of him to Yosef, to prepare Goshen in advance.

One-Track Education

Yaakov sent Yehudah to Egypt to establish a place of Torah study and education in Goshen before the rest of the family arrived.[9] Why was it necessary for this institution of learning to be established by Yehudah, rather than by Yosef, who was already living in Egypt, and who certainly had both the means and the conviction to do so? Yosef had even proven himself to be on a higher spiritual level than Yaakov's other sons, considering that his preoccupation with the governance of Egypt diminished neither his spiritual sensitivity nor his devotion to G-d. So why did Yaakov insist on sending Yehudah to establish the school, instead of Yosef?

Despite Yosef's spiritual greatness, excellence in Torah study requires something that he simply did not have—time and freedom to devote himself exclusively to Torah study, with no other care in the world. Granted, this does not reflect negatively on Yosef, who flawlessly fulfilled his G-dly mission that demanded wholly engrossing himself in Egypt's national interests; but the quality of his Torah study, in and of itself, could not be on par with that of his brothers, who were shepherds by trade, and for the most part entirely removed from the pressures of the world.

---

9. Rashi ad loc.

Yaakov therefore appointed Yehudah to establish the center of Torah study in Goshen. This academy would be the foundation of Yaakov's family's residence in Egypt, and the spiritual power plant for the entire world, so it was crucial that the students devote their minds to Torah alone, without worrying about the outside world. It was Yehudah alone, not Yosef, who was capable of founding such a school.

—*Likkutei Sichos, vol. 3, pp. 827–830*

47:12 | מז:יב

וַיְכַלְכֵּל יוֹסֵף אֶת אָבִיו וְאֶת אֶחָיו וְאֵת כָּל בֵּית אָבִיו לֶחֶם לְפִי הַטָּף

Yosef sustained his father and his brothers and his father's entire household [with] bread according to the young children.

Judge My Actions, Not My Plans

In the book of Tehillim G-d is called "The Shepherd of Israel... He who leads Yosef like flocks of sheep."[10]

The Midrash interprets this verse (non-literally) as the Jewish people's supplication before G-d that He lead us like flocks of sheep "just as Yosef did." Specifically, "Just as Yosef sustained each person according to his deeds, as it is written, 'Yosef sustained his father...,' [we ask that] we too should be sustained according to our deeds."[11]

This teaching is puzzling. Is it necessary to draw an analogy from Yosef—or anyone else, for that matter—to request that G-d treat us in accordance with our deeds? Wouldn't that be the most fair and reasonable thing to expect from G-d? In fact, the greatness of Yosef was that he *did not* treat people only according to their deeds; he sustained his brothers and their families *despite* what they had done to him! Why then does the Midrash regard Yosef as the paragon of "sustaining each person according to his deeds," and why must we make a special request that G-d treat us in a similar manner?

---

10. Tehillim 80:2.
11. Midrash Tehillim 80.

With its spotlight on Yosef, the Midrash is highlighting that Yosef treated his brothers "according to their deeds"—*notwithstanding their intentions*. As he benevolently told his brothers, "Indeed, you intended evil against me, [but] G-d designed it for good, in order to bring about what is today, to keep a great populace alive."[12] Disregarding his brothers' terrible intentions in selling him, Yosef focused only on the wonderful outcome of their deeds (by Divine plan), and rewarded them accordingly.

This then is also the meaning of our prayer, according to the Midrash, that G-d sustain us "according to our deeds." We are requesting that in instances where our good deeds were without feeling, or were perhaps wrongly motivated, may G-d ignore our intent, as Yosef did. May He consider only our deeds, reward us for the good we have done, and disregard our less-than-perfect intentions.

—*Likkutei Sichos, vol. 5, pp. 242-247*

---

12. Bereishis 50:20.

ויחי
Vayechi

48:5 | מח:ה

וְעַתָּה שְׁנֵי בָנֶיךָ הַנּוֹלָדִים לְךָ בְּאֶרֶץ מִצְרַיִם עַד בֹּאִי אֵלֶיךָ מִצְרַיְמָה לִי הֵם אֶפְרַיִם וּמְנַשֶּׁה כִּרְאוּבֵן וְשִׁמְעוֹן יִהְיוּ לִי

Now, your two sons who were born to you in Egypt before I came to you, to the land of Egypt, shall be [considered] mine; Ephraim and Menasheh shall be to me like Reuven and Shimon.

Made in Egypt

Yaakov conferred upon two of his grandsons, Ephraim and Menasheh, the same status as his own sons—i.e., they would each father an independent tribe. When promising this to Yosef, however, instead of simply saying, "Your two sons Ephraim and Menasheh shall be to me like Reuven and Shimon," he described them as, "Ephraim and Menasheh, your two sons who were born to you in Egypt before I came to you."

This description not only excluded any future children that Yosef might have;[1] it also explained why, of all Yaakov's

---

1. See Ramban, Bereishis 48:15.

grandchildren, only Ephraim and Menasheh merited this elite status.

Ephraim and Menasheh were raised in Egypt, where Yaakov's values and lifestyle were foreign and unpopular. In addition, they were born a number of years before Yaakov's arrival in Egypt—"before I came to you"—so their early education was not under his direct tutelage. Still, they conducted themselves in a manner befitting grandchildren of Yaakov.

Therefore, among all his grandchildren, Yaakov could confidently say of Ephraim and Menasheh, "They shall be considered mine," for they embodied the tried and tested continuity of Yaakov's path.[2] Their exemplary tribute to Yaakov's enduring legacy earned them a place among Yaakov's own sons.

—*Likkutei Sichos, vol. 15, p. 435*

---

[2]. Moreover, in this regard Ephraim and Menasheh exemplified the quality that was unique to Yaakov among all the patriarchs—his ability to ensure that all his children would remain righteous (see Rashi, Bereishis 47:31).

48:7 | מח:ז

וָאֶקְבְּרֶהָ שָּׁם בְּדֶרֶךְ אֶפְרָת הִוא בֵּית לָחֶם

I buried her there along the road to Efras, which is Beis-Lechem.

A Mother's Sacrifice

Rachel's burial place should naturally have been in Me'aras Hamachpelah, alongside her husband. Instead, Yaakov buried her on the roadside near Beis-Lechem. Before his passing, Yaakov explained to Yosef that his mother's burial there would one day serve an important role in hastening her children's return from exile: When the Jewish people, hopeless and downtrodden, would pass her grave as they were led into exile, Rachel would emerge from her grave, weeping and begging G-d to show them mercy. And indeed, as the prophet Yirmiyahu later chronicled, "A voice is heard on high, lamentation, bitter weeping: Rachel is crying for her children." G-d replied, "There is reward for your work… and the children shall return to their own border."[3]

With this Yaakov consoled Yosef over his mother's seemingly second-rate burial place, for considering the comfort that her burial there would bring to her children, certainly Rachel would herself have chosen to be buried there.

The willingness to sacrifice for her children that Yaakov attributed to Rachel epitomizes the Jewish woman's unique role as the *akeres habayis*, the mainstay of the family.

---

3. Yirmiyahu 31:14–16.

Whereas both men and women must serve G-d with every aspect of their lives, only men are obligated in mitzvos that are time-sensitive and in the constant mitzvah to study Torah.[4] Women are exempt from time-specific and constant obligations because they are constantly tending to the needs of their families and homes. In this sense, the Jewish woman "sacrifices" the satisfaction and spiritual experience that comes with the observance of those mitzvos, serving G-d instead by nurturing her family.

This explains why among Yaakov's wives it was specifically Rachel who was buried on the roadside, for as Rashi states elsewhere, Rachel was the *akeres habayis* of Yaakov's household.[5] Therefore, just as she personified the "woman's sacrifice" in her lifetime, in her passing too, her "compromised" place of burial allowed her to implore G-d on her children's behalf and to guarantee their return home.

—*Likkutei Sichos, vol. 30, pp. 239-240*

---

4. See Talmud, Kiddushin 29a–b.
5. Bereishis 31:4.

49:1 | מט:א

וַיִּקְרָא יַעֲקֹב אֶל־בָּנָיו וַיֹּאמֶר הֵאָסְפוּ וְאַגִּידָה לָכֶם
אֵת אֲשֶׁר־יִקְרָא אֶתְכֶם בְּאַחֲרִית הַיָּמִים

*Yaakov called for his sons and said,
"Gather, and I will tell you what will happen
to you at the end of days."*

Insider Information

The Talmud[6] explains that Yaakov wanted to reveal the end of the days (i.e., the time of the ultimate redemption) to his sons, but the Shechinah, the Divine Presence, withdrew from him, rendering him unable to do so.

What did Yaakov want to achieve by revealing this information to his children, and why did G-d disapprove? According to one explanation, Yaakov foresaw that the redemption from Egyptian bondage could potentially be the complete and ultimate redemption, after which the Jewish people would never again be exiled.[7] He desired to reveal this to Bnei Yisrael (who knew that the Egyptian exile would not be longer than 400 years[8]), in the hope that it would motivate them to maintain their righteousness and indeed merit the complete redemption at that time. Moreover, he hoped that their knowledge that the final redemption was potentially imminent would cause them to increase their good deeds and bring about that complete redemption even sooner.

---

6. Pesachim 56a.
7. See Zohar 3:221a.
8. As stated in Bereishis 15:13–14.

G-d restrained Yaakov from revealing this information, however, for the highest form of Divine worship is to serve G-d of one's own initiative, when one's drive to be righteous comes from within. To some degree, this would be lost if Bnei Yisrael's motivation to increase their good deeds was based on prophetic information regarding the potential of their deeds to bring about the ultimate redemption by a given date. Their righteousness would not be regarded as "their own," as it had been motivated by outside sources of inspiration, and their merit would therefore not be complete.

Whereas Yaakov preferred to bring about the final redemption sooner, G-d preferred to give Bnei Yisrael the opportunity to merit the redemption of their own accord, making it the most perfect and complete redemption possible.

—Likkutei Sichos, vol. 20, pp. 228–232

49:6-7 | מט:ו-ז

בְּסֹדָם אַל תָּבֹא נַפְשִׁי בִּקְהָלָם אַל תֵּחַד כְּבֹדִי כִּי בְאַפָּם הָרְגוּ אִישׁ... אָרוּר אַפָּם כִּי עָז וְעֶבְרָתָם כִּי קָשָׁתָה

Let my soul not enter their conspiracy, let my honor have no part in their assembly; for in their wrath they killed a man... Cursed be their rage, for it is fierce, and their fury, for it is harsh.

If You Can Beat Them

Before his passing, Yaakov rebuked Shimon and Levi and cursed their rage, "for in their wrath they killed a man..." The Midrash[9] explains that the "man" that Shimon and Levi are said to have killed actually refers to quite a few men: the entire adult male population of Shechem! Yaakov refers to all of them as "a man," because to defeat all of Shechem was as simple for them as defeating one man.

Why, while rebuking them for their actions, did Yaakov pay tribute to the ease with which Shimon and Levi—endowed by G-d with extraordinary strength—decimated the population of Shechem?

Evidently, this unnatural strength was part of the reason Yaakov was so displeased with Shimon's and Levi's rage-driven actions.

In theory, Yaakov agreed with Shimon and Levi that punishment of the people of Shechem was justified.[10] He was critical only of their deceitful method. They promised the

---

9. Cited by Rashi ad loc.
10. See Ohr Hachaim, Bereishis 34:25; Ramban, Bereishis 34:13; Mishneh Torah, Hil. Melachim 9:14.

people of Shechem peace if the entire male population would circumcise themselves, but then they exploited their weakness and pain, and attacked them in violation of their agreement. Such deceitfulness disgraced Yaakov and the belief system for which he stood.

Yaakov therefore rebuked Shimon and Levi, pointing out that considering their ability to wipe out the entire city with the ease of killing one man, they had no need to resort to deception. They could have confronted the people of Shechem directly and made them suffer the consequences of their behavior. "Cursed be their rage!" said Yaakov, for it blinded them from recognizing their ability to carry out judgment without resorting to trickery.

—*Likkutei Sichos, vol. 5, pp. 151–152*

50:13 | נ״ג:

וַיִּשְׂאוּ אֹתוֹ בָנָיו

His sons carried him...

Bearers of the Aron

All of Yaakov's sons, with the exception of Yosef and Levi, who were represented by Ephraim and Menasheh, carried Yaakov's coffin from Egypt to Canaan. According to Rashi, Yaakov instructed them, "Levi shall not carry it, because he (i.e., his tribe) is destined to carry the *aron*. Yosef shall not carry it, because he is a king."

We find, however, that although the tribe of Levi was precluded from carrying Yaakov's coffin, Moshe himself, who was of the tribe of Levi, carried Yosef's coffin out of Egypt. Evidently, carrying these two coffins represented two very different ideas, only one of which conflicted with the tribe of Levi's future as bearer of the *aron*.

Our Sages tell us that as long as Yaakov lived, his presence in Egypt prevented his family's enslavement.[11] Thus, Yaakov's passing and the transfer of his body from Egypt marked the early beginnings of Bnei Yisrael's slavery.

Levi and his tribe, however, were never subjected to the slave labor.[12] When Pharaoh originally came to recruit Bnei Yisrael to "join him" in his work effort, the tribe of Levi refused, reasoning that it was not appropriate to participate in building Pharaoh's cities when one day they would be the ones carrying the holy *aron*. As a result, when Pharaoh later

---

11. See Rashi, Bereishis 47:28.
12. See Rashi, Shemos 5:4.

forced his original workers into slave labor, the tribe of Levi was not affected.[13] Accordingly, it was unsuitable for Levi, who "transcended" the Egyptian bondage, to take part in carrying Yaakov's coffin, which represented the beginning of their bondage.

Carrying Yosef's coffin from Egypt, however, was a symbol of Bnei Yisrael's redemption, for Yosef's remains had been their greatest source of hope and belief in their redemption. As Yosef had assured them, "G-d will surely remember you, and you shall bring up my bones from here with you."[14] The one most suitable to carry Yosef's coffin was therefore Moshe, from the tribe of Levi, who led Bnei Yisrael to their long-anticipated redemption.

—*Likkutei Sichos, vol. 20, pp. 237–238*

---

13. See Baalei Hatosafos, Shemos 1:13.
14. Shemos 13:19.

50:26 | נ:כו

וַיָּמָת יוֹסֵף בֶּן מֵאָה וָעֶשֶׂר שָׁנִים וַיַּחַנְטוּ אֹתוֹ וַיִּישֶׂם בָּאָרוֹן בְּמִצְרָיִם

Yosef died at the age of one hundred and ten years, and he was embalmed and placed in a coffin in Egypt.

A Local Source of Energy

When we conclude the public reading of any of the five books of the Torah, it is customary for the entire community to call out, "*Chazak chazak v'nischazek!*"—"Be strong, be strong, and may we be strengthened!" to encourage one another in the continued study of the Torah. In particular, the proclamation "*Chazak chazak v'nischazek*" highlights the strength we draw from these concluding verses of the book we have read, as well as the strength that the message of these final verses imbues into the ensuing book of Torah that we will soon begin.

Yet the book of Bereishis concludes with what seems to be an unfavorable event—Yosef's interment in Egypt. Whereas Yaakov's body had been brought to the land of Canaan for immediate burial, Yosef's body was embalmed and remained in Egypt, "the shame of the earth."[15] How is Yosef's burial in Egypt a source of strength and encouragement?

Upon careful consideration, however, Yosef's burial is the ultimate embodiment of the theme of the book of Bereishis and its lead-up into the book of Shemos.

---

15. Bereishis 42:9.

Throughout Bereishis we read about the deeds of our patriarchs and matriarchs, which served to inspire and guide their descendants, the Jewish people, particularly during the dark times of *galus*, exile. Likewise, we learn of G-d's promise that Bnei Yisrael would not remain exiled in Egypt forever, and that they would return to their homeland even greater and richer than they were before. These accounts, as well as Yaakov's blessings to his children near the end of the book, assisted and empowered Bnei Yisrael to endure their exile in Egypt.

Ultimately, however, in order for Bnei Yisrael to survive and even thrive in the lengthy exile, they needed not only promises, blessings and a legacy to aspire to, but also the presence of an actual source of strength to help them overcome the darkness of *galus*.[16]

Yosef's burial in Egypt thus constitutes the most invigorating conclusion to the book of Bereishis. For the physical presence of the holy remains of Yosef, the one without whose permission "no one may lift his hand or his foot in the entire land of Egypt,"[17] was what gave Bnei Yisrael the strength to overpower the difficult *galus* that lay ahead.

—*Likkutei Sichos, vol. 25, pp. 476-479*

---

16. See Zohar 1:222b.
17. Bereishis 41:44.

שמות
BOOK OF SHEMOS

לזכות
הרה"ת **דוד אוריאל**
וזוגתו מרת **סאסיא מלכה**
ובני ביתם
שיחיו לאורך ימים ושנים טובות
סמיטאנא

שמות
Shemos

1:22 | א:כב

כָּל הַבֵּן הַיִּלּוֹד הַיְאֹרָה תַּשְׁלִיכֻהוּ וְכָל הַבַּת תְּחַיּוּן

You shall cast into the Nile every boy who is born, but every daughter you shall make live.

Save Your Children from Pharaoh's Decree

At first glance, it would seem that Pharaoh's decree targeted only the infant boys born to Bnei Yisrael, but not the baby girls. If so, why was it necessary for Pharaoh to add and emphasize, "but every daughter you shall keep alive"? This implies that keeping the daughters alive was an active and integral part of his evil plan.

Pharaoh's objective was to stop the growth and continuity of the Jewish people. As such, he decreed that half the children born to Bnei Yisrael be annihilated physically—and the others spiritually. Pharaoh did not tell the Egyptians to *allow* the Jewish baby girls to live; he told them, "Every daughter [of Bnei Yisrael] *you shall make* live." You—the very same Egyptians who are murdering the Jewish boys—should instill your Egyptian values and lifestyle into all the surviving children, thereby spiritually annihilating whatever remains of Bnei Yisrael.

Indeed, the first part of Pharaoh's decree—to drown the baby boys in the Nile—conveys a similar message. Since it seldom rained in Egypt, the Egyptians relied on the waters of the Nile to irrigate their crops, and as they depended on it for their very sustenance, they considered the Nile a deity. Accordingly, drowning Jewish children in the Nile is a metaphor for immersing our children in the values, culture and lifestyle of our secular surroundings, thinking that this immersion will grant them a secure future.

It is crucial that we recognize that this approach stems from the likes of the evil Pharaoh—those who seek to destroy Jewish growth and continuity, if not physically then spiritually. In order to give our sons and daughters life, we must grant them an education that focuses on their true livelihood—the vitality that we Jews receive from "the Torah of Life."

—*Likkutei Sichos, vol. 1, pp. 111-112*

2:13 | ב:יג

וַיֵּצֵא בַּיּוֹם הַשֵּׁנִי וְהִנֵּה שְׁנֵי אֲנָשִׁים עִבְרִים נִצִּים וַיֹּאמֶר לָרָשָׁע לָמָּה תַכֶּה רֵעֶךָ

He went out on the second day, and behold, two Hebrew men were quarreling. He said to the wicked one, "Why will you strike your friend?"

Hands Down

The Torah describes Moshe's encounter with two quarreling men. "He said to the wicked one, 'Why will you strike your friend?'"

Notably, Moshe's plea is in the future tense, indicating that the man he rebuked stood poised to hit his friend, but had not yet done so. Yet the Torah refers to him as "the wicked one," notes the Talmud.[1] Thus the Rambam rules, "It is forbidden to raise one's hand against a colleague. Whoever raises a hand against a colleague, even though he does not hit him, is considered a wicked person."[2]

One understanding of the Rambam's ruling is that raising your hand against a colleague is prohibited not only to prevent you from striking him, but because the negative character traits inherent in the act make it contemptible in and of itself.

Every aspect of human life exists in order to enable man to serve G-d, each limb in the human body contributing in its own unique way.[3] The hand, specifically, is synonymous with *giving*—benefiting others. Therefore, raising your hand

---

1. Sanhedrin 58b.
2. Mishneh Torah, Hil. Chovel U'Mazik 5:2.
3. See Sefer Chareidim in detail.

in a manner associated with strife is forbidden and regarded as wicked, even if you do not actually hit anyone. For the very motion of raising your hand in strife defies the hand's G-dly ordained purpose: to perform acts of giving and lovingkindness.

—*Likkutei Sichos, vol. 31, pp. 1-6*

ב:יד | 2:14

וַיִּירָא מֹשֶׁה וַיֹּאמַר אָכֵן נוֹדַע הַדָּבָר

Moshe became frightened and said, "Indeed, the matter has become known!"

The Scary Truth about Lashon Hara

The redemption from Egypt marked the birth of the Jewish people—when Bnei Yisrael were chosen by G-d to be His nation.

This status was not earned through their virtues or merits. (In fact, due to the many years they spent in Egypt, many of Bnei Yisrael had fallen so low as to be drawn to idolatry.[4]) Rather, they attained their status as G-d's nation simply by His *choice*. In contrast with a *decision*, based on the qualities of the object or person selected, "pure choice" means to select between options that may be of equal merit; the selection of one over the other is unrelated to its qualities. That is why it was possible for Bnei Yisrael in Egypt to be chosen by G-d (and therefore redeemed) despite their lowly spiritual state at the time.

Yet, when Moshe discovered that there were talebearers among Bnei Yisrael, he became alarmed. "Since this is so," worried Moshe, "perhaps they do not deserve to be redeemed."[5] Why did Moshe fear that *lashon hara*, gossip, would render

---

4. See Mishneh Torah, Hil. Avodah Zarah 1:3.
5. Rashi, Shemos 2:14.

Bnei Yisrael undeserving of being chosen and redeemed, more so than any other sin?

Lashon hara is unique among all other sins in its divisiveness. In addition to causing tension between people, gossiping about another person's deficiencies demonstrates that you lack empathy toward that person, even if you have no intention of causing that person actual harm, G-d forbid.

Accordingly, we can understand the cause for Moshe's concern upon discovering talebearers among Bnei Yisrael. Although G-d's selection of Bnei Yisrael as His nation was not contingent on their virtues, in order to be the Chosen Nation it was necessary for them to be a unit, and not a group of isolated individuals. Moshe therefore feared that the divisiveness of *lashon hara* could ruin their cohesiveness and their identity as a unit, thereby preventing them from becoming the Chosen *Nation*. Though they might not have required any other virtue or merit to qualify as G-d's choice, only through unity could Bnei Yisrael constitute a "nation" that G-d could choose as His own.

—*Likkutei Sichos, vol. 31, pp. 8–12*

2:14-15 | ב:יד-טו

וַיִּירָא מֹשֶׁה וַיֹּאמַר אָכֵן נוֹדַע הַדָּבָר:
וַיִּשְׁמַע פַּרְעֹה אֶת הַדָּבָר הַזֶּה וַיְבַקֵּשׁ לַהֲרֹג
אֶת מֹשֶׁה וַיִּבְרַח מֹשֶׁה מִפְּנֵי פַרְעֹה

Moshe became frightened and said, "Indeed, the matter has become known." Pharaoh heard of this incident, and he sought to slay Moshe; and Moshe fled from before Pharaoh.

The Power of Positive Thinking

When Moshe discovered that people knew he had killed an Egyptian taskmaster, he became fearful for his future. Indeed, Pharaoh learned of the episode shortly thereafter, and sought to have him killed.

With this episode, the Torah hints at the extraordinary power of *bitachon*—complete trust in G-d's goodness and grace.

Having *bitachon* requires more than mere belief that since G-d orchestrates every detail of existence at every moment, whatever happens to you will certainly be for the very best. Rather, to have *bitachon* means to *be at ease* and trust that G d will grant you goodness in the most obvious sense of the word.

How can you be confident that G-d will indeed bless you with revealed good? Does the Torah not promise that G-d will reward those who are worthy and punish those who are not?

Based on the verse "He who trusts in G-d, kindness will encompass him,"[6] the Sefer HaIkkarim explains: "Even if one

---

6. Tehillim 32:10.

is not worthy on his own accord, *bitachon* draws down gratuitous kindness [from Above] upon he who trusts in G-d."[7] In other words, fervent *bitachon* alone makes a person worthy of G-d's blessings. Thus, if a person genuinely trusts that he is in G-d's good hands (and therefore not subject to any natural limitations), then he can be certain that G-d will guard him and provide for him in a revealed way—even if he is not necessarily worthy of this for any other reason. To paraphrase the Tzemach Tzedek's famous advice, "If you think positively, the future *will be* positive."

The Torah alludes to this principle of *bitachon* by telling us about Moshe's worries, which preceded the actual threat to his life. Considering the Torah's usual conciseness, the fact that it makes special note of Moshe's unease even before Pharaoh sought to execute him suggests that Moshe's fear actually contributed to the outcome. Had Moshe not been afraid, the threat to his life would never have materialized.

—*Likkutei Sichos, vol. 36, pp. 1-6*

---

7. Sefer HaIkkarim 4:46.

4:20 | ד:כ

וַיִּקַּח מֹשֶׁה אֶת אִשְׁתּוֹ וְאֶת בָּנָיו וַיַּרְכִּבֵם עַל הַחֲמֹר

Moshe took his wife and sons,
and mounted them on the donkey.

A Donkey with a History

The donkey that Moshe's family rode on to Egypt was not your average donkey; it was what the Torah calls "The Donkey." Rashi explains, "This was the donkey that Avraham saddled to travel to the Akeidah of Yitzchak, and it is the one upon which Moshiach is destined to appear."

In view of this donkey's uniqueness, we can understand why the Torah makes mention of Moshe's means of transportation at all. Evidently, this illustrious animal carried particular significance for the mission upon which Moshe was about to embark.

For seven days, G-d implored Moshe to accept the mission of redeeming Bnei Yisrael.[8] Moshe argued that his brother, Aharon, was older and more suitable for the task than he was, and Moshe did not want to offend him. Additionally, Moshe said, "I know that I am not destined to take them into the Land of Israel and to be their Future Redeemer. You have other messengers (i.e., the future Moshiach)—send them!"[9]

Ultimately, G-d insisted, and Moshe accepted the mission. To address Moshe's concerns, G-d arranged that the donkey upon which his family traveled to Egypt was "The Donkey."

The donkey served as a reminder that although our fore-

---

8. See Rashi, Shemos 4:10.
9. Rashi, Shemos 4:13.

father Avraham had good reason to hesitate when G-d instructed him to offer his son Yitzchak as a sacrifice, he "arose early in the morning, and he saddled his donkey."[10] As Rashi explains there, out of love for G-d and eagerness to obey His command, Avraham hastened to saddle the donkey himself, instead of commanding his servants to do so. Thus, the donkey represents the eagerness with which one must approach G-d's instructions. Accordingly, even if Moshe was legitimately concerned for his brother's honor, the donkey hinted that he should emulate Avraham and not hesitate to carry out G-d's command that *he* redeem Bnei Yisrael.

Moreover, with this donkey's distinction as the one upon which Moshiach is destined to appear, G-d responded to Moshe's second argument as well. The donkey's destiny hinted to Moshe that the redemption of Bnei Yisrael through Moshiach is not a separate, future redemption; it is contingent upon and will be a continuation of the redemption from Egypt that Moshe was about to lead.

—*Likkutei Sichos, vol. 31, pp. 15–18*

---

10. Bereishis 22:3.

5:4 | ה:ד

וַיֹּאמֶר אֲלֵהֶם מֶלֶךְ מִצְרַיִם לָמָּה מֹשֶׁה וְאַהֲרֹן
תַּפְרִיעוּ אֶת הָעָם מִמַּעֲשָׂיו לְכוּ לְסִבְלֹתֵיכֶם

The king of Egypt said to them, "Why, Moshe and Aharon, do you disturb the people from their work? Go to your own labors."

Don't Mind Your Own Business

When Moshe and Aharon asked Pharaoh to allow Bnei Yisrael to leave Egypt and worship G-d in the wilderness, Pharaoh dismissed them, saying, "Why do you disturb the people from their work? Go back to your own labor!" The commentaries note that Pharaoh told Moshe and Aharon to return to their *own* labor, indicating that their work was unlike the rest of the nation's.[11] For as the Ramban explains, Pharaoh recognized the need for a nation to have spiritual leaders. He therefore exempted the tribe of Levi from slave labor, and allowed them to be the scholars and teachers of Bnei Yisrael.[12]

Accordingly, Pharaoh told Moshe and Aharon to be thankful that they themselves were free to study and teach Torah, and not to interfere with the rest of the nation's enslavement. Moreover, said Pharaoh, practically speaking (as well as by the Divine decree that they be slaves for 400 years) Bnei Yisrael are unable to escape Egyptian servitude at this time, so why waste your time trying to change the reality?

Moshe and Aharon, however, ignored Pharaoh's warnings. They were not content with being free to study on their own,

---

11. See Rashi ad loc.
12. See Ramban ad loc.

or even to occasionally teach the rest of Bnei Yisrael. Instead, despite the odds against them, they campaigned for the entire nation to be set free, ultimately saving them just in the nick of time. As the Arizal taught, had Bnei Yisrael remained in Egypt for even one moment longer, they could never have been redeemed from the spiritual abyss to which they would have plunged.[13]

From Moshe and Aharon's debate with Pharaoh we learn that to concern ourselves exclusively with our own Torah study and observance is an attitude that stems from Pharaoh. In contrast, a Jew strives to ensure that his fellow Jews are also serving G-d, and studying and observing His Torah, no matter how unlikely it seems for him to succeed at this mission. When there are lives to save from Pharaoh, or from the spiritual Pharaohs of our time, every chance is worth taking, and no moment is too soon.

—*Likkutei Sichos, vol. 16, pp. 29–31*

---

13. See Siddur HaArizal, Haggadah Shel Pesach, s.v. Matzah Zo.

ואראVa'eira

6:3 | ו:ג

וָאֵרָא אֶל אַבְרָהָם אֶל יִצְחָק וְאֶל יַעֲקֹב

And I appeared to Avraham, to Yitzchak and to Yaakov.

The Fathers

In the first verses of Parshas Va'eira, G-d assures Moshe that He will soon redeem Bnei Yisrael from Egypt, thereby fulfilling the promises He made when He appeared to Avraham, Yitzchak and Yaakov. Rashi quotes the word *"Va'eira*—And I appeared," and summarizes to whom G-d appeared: "To the fathers." In doing so, Rashi is pointing out that although they each had distinctive qualities, their primary virtue was the one they had in common—they were "the fathers."

The prophet refers to Avraham as "Avraham, who loved Me"[1]—his worship of G-d was characterized by love for his Creator. Yitzchak's relationship with G-d is described as "the

---

1. Yeshayahu 41:8.

fear of Yitzchak"[2]—his life was primarily defined by fear and awe of Heaven. Yaakov represented a balance of both approaches, as he attested, "Had not the G-d of my father, the G-d of Avraham and the Fear of Yitzchak, been for me...,"[3] meaning that he incorporated both his father's and grandfather's spiritual traits in his worship of G-d.

Although love and fear of G-d are obviously unalike, they do share a commonality: both inspire action. As explained in Tanya,[4] love of G-d motivates observance of the positive mitzvos, and fear of G-d ensures that one distances himself from transgressing any of His prohibitions.

Rashi hints to this with his emphasis that Avraham, Yitzchak and Yaakov were "the fathers." Our Sages teach, "The principal offspring of the righteous are their good deeds."[5] Hence, by describing Avraham, Yitzchak and Yaakov as "the fathers," Rashi is emphasizing that their emotional attachment to G-d did not remain abstract; it translated into "offspring", i.e., practical good deeds.

In addition, by highlighting that our forefathers were, first and foremost, "the fathers," Rashi illustrates that more than the remarkable qualities they each exhibited in their personal service of G-d, our forefathers' main accomplishments in life were that they bred and inspired successive generations to follow in G-d's path.

—*Likkutei Sichos, vol. 3, p. 860*

---

2. Bereishis 31:42.
3. Ibid.
4. Chapter 4.
5. See Rashi, Bereishis 6:9.

7:3 | ז:ג

וַאֲנִי אַקְשֶׁה אֶת לֵב פַּרְעֹה וְהִרְבֵּיתִי אֶת אֹתֹתַי וְאֶת מוֹפְתַי בְּאֶרֶץ מִצְרָיִם

But I will harden Pharaoh's heart, and I will increase My signs and My wonders in the land of Egypt.

Discovering the Real Motive

G-d struck the Egyptians with ten plagues to punish them for their cruel enslavement of Bnei Yisrael. These supernatural plagues also forced Pharaoh to recognize G-d's existence and might, as we read, "I have allowed you to stand in order to show you My strength, and in order to declare My name all over the earth."[6]

These reasons alone seem to provide sufficient cause for the Ten Plagues, yet Rashi brings a third reason. Commenting on the words "I will harden [Pharaoh's heart],"[7] Rashi explains:

> [G-d was saying:] "Since Pharaoh behaved wickedly and defied Me... it is better for Me that his heart be hardened, so that I can increase My signs and My wonders in him; thereby you will recognize My mighty deeds." Such is the custom of the Holy One, blessed be He. He brings retribution on the nations so that Israel should hear and fear.

According to this explanation, the primary goal of the plagues was not their effect on the Egyptians, but to inspire awe and wonder within Bnei Yisrael.

---

6. Shemos 9:16.
7. Shemos 7:3.

A principle that Rashi teaches on the very first verse in the Torah supports this approach. Rashi writes there that G-d created all of existence "for the sake of the Jewish people and for the sake of Torah." This is true not only of the initial creation of the world, but of every event that transpires at any time thereafter. Therefore, even when seemingly Divine Providence caused a particular event to occur for other reasons, the true objective is the direct impact the event will have on the Jewish people.

Accordingly, Rashi emphasizes that G-d brought the Ten Plagues upon the Egyptians not only in retribution for their treatment of Bnei Yisrael or to make them recognize the Creator, but for the effect that the plagues would have on Bnei Yisrael themselves—they would inspire within them a more profound fear of G-d.

—*Likkutei Sichos, vol. 36, pp. 33–36*

7:20 | ז:כ

וַיֵּהָפְכוּ כָּל הַמַּיִם אֲשֶׁר בַּיְאֹר לְדָם

And all the water that was in the Nile turned to blood.

Escaping the Cold

Bnei Yisrael's exile in Egypt seemed interminable. Slavery was such a deep part of their identity that they refused to believe that their redemption was imminent. Egypt's oppression of Bnei Yisrael was so severe that even Moshe struggled to understand how it could be part of G-d's plan. It was only when G-d struck the Egyptians with the Ten Plagues that Egypt's grip on the Jewish people began to crumble.

"In every generation and every day, one must regard himself as though he has come out of Egypt on that very day."[8] The Torah's name for Egypt, *Mitzrayim*, shares a common root with the Hebrew word *meitzar*, constraint. Accordingly, Chassidus explains that "in every generation and every day," one must constantly strive to escape his personal "Egypt"—the internal constraints that hinder and restrain his devoted service of G-d. In this context, the Ten Plagues represent ten steps through which we can breach even the toughest internal barriers, freeing our souls to fully experience our attachment to G-d.

In the first plague, the waters of the Nile River—which the Egyptians worshipped as a god—turned into blood.

---

8. Mishnah, Pesachim 10:5, cf. Tanya, chapter 47.

Water is naturally cold; thus, the waters of the Nile represent coolness and indifference toward things that are G-dly and holy. This attitude of coolness is the root of all spiritual ills, for it is impossible for a person to remain perpetually unexcited about both holiness and that which challenges holiness. Consequently, even if a person observes all the mitzvos but does so coldly and apathetically, his detachment will invariably bring him to interest in and attraction to ideas that are incompatible with a life of holiness.

The first and most crucial step toward our escape from Egypt is therefore to rid ourselves of the cold waters of the Nile, and infuse our Judaism and Torah observance with passion.

—*Likkutei Sichos, vol. 1, pp. 119-124*

7:28 | ז:כח

וְשָׁרַץ הַיְאֹר צְפַרְדְּעִים וְעָלוּ וּבָאוּ בְּבֵיתֶךָ וּבַחֲדַר מִשְׁכָּבְךָ וְעַל מִטָּתֶךָ וּבְבֵית עֲבָדֶיךָ וּבְעַמֶּךָ וּבְתַנּוּרֶיךָ וּבְמִשְׁאֲרוֹתֶיךָ

The river will swarm with frogs, and they will emerge and come inside your home and into your bedroom and upon your bed, and inside the homes of your servants and among your people, and into your ovens and your kneading troughs.

Blood Before Frogs

G-d's battering of the Egyptians began with the waters of the Nile turning into blood. Next, G-d smote the land with a plague of frogs, which swarmed from the waters of the Nile into the Egyptians' homes, bedrooms and kitchens.

The Torah's name for Egypt, *Mitzrayim*, shares a common root with the Hebrew word *meitzar*, constraint. Accordingly, the ten plagues that brought down mighty Egypt represent the steps we must take to break out of our personal "Egypts"—the internal limitations that hinder and constrain our service of G-d.

The first two plagues both involved water. Water, which is cold by nature, symbolizes an attitude of coolness—detachment and indifference. The first plague, in which the waters of the Nile were transformed to warm and lifegiving blood, symbolizes that we must imbue our service of G-d with warmth and excitement. In contrast, the second plague, in which creatures of the water, frogs, swarmed, everything related to Pharaoh and Egypt—and particularly, their ovens—symbolizes that breaking through our internal "Egypts" requires developing a coolness towards material pleasures.

Now, under normal circumstances, ridding ourselves of competing loyalties—symbolized by the plague of frogs—would be the first step to take before attempting to live a life devoted to G-d and G-dliness. We see, however, that the plague of frogs was not the first plague but the second; the plague of blood preceded it. The order of these two plagues teaches that even before we have succeeded at cooling down our material pleasures, we must already infuse our Torah and mitzvos with fervor, for the light and warmth of our passion-filled mitzvos will assist in dispelling any dark and undesirable passions that remain.

—*Likkutei Sichos, vol. 1, pp. 123–125*

8:2 | ח:ב

וַיֵּט אַהֲרֹן אֶת יָדוֹ עַל מֵימֵי מִצְרָיִם וַתַּעַל
הַצְּפַרְדֵּעַ וַתְּכַס אֶת אֶרֶץ מִצְרָיִם׃

Aharon stretched forth his hand over the waters of Egypt, and the frog came up and covered the land of Egypt.

When the Bare Minimum is Optimal

Our Sages place great emphasis on executing a mitzvah from start to finish, rather than leaving it incomplete.[9] Nevertheless, when it is unclear what exactly constitutes completion of a particular mitzvah, we must examine the mitzvah in question before rushing to complete it to the fullest measure. If the mitzvah is charity-related or the like, we should obviously extend our involvement beyond any risk of leaving it incomplete. In other instances, however, we are best off fulfilling only the bare minimum, even at risk of not seeing the project through from beginning to end.

For example, when a *beis din* must inflict *malkos*, lashes, upon transgressors of certain sins, the Torah warns, "He shall flog him with forty lashes; he shall not exceed, lest he give him a more severe flogging than these."[10] Since the Torah prohibits exacting excessive punishment, if we are in doubt regarding the extent of our obligations in this mitzvah, we suffice by fulfilling our duty to the bare minimum.[11]

---

9. See Rashi, Devarim 8:1.
10. Devarim 25:3.
11. In fact, though the verse implies that the *beis din* must administer 40 lashes per transgression, the maximum amount of lashes ever

This explains the Midrash which discusses how the plague of frogs was set into motion. Aharon was instructed to afflict the Egyptians with frogs—plural—that would swarm through the entire land,[12] yet the verse states, "Aharon stretched forth his hand... and *the frog* came up and covered the land," implying that only one frog emerged through Aharon's efforts. The Midrash explains that Aharon brought one frog from the Nile, but when people hit that frog, swarms of frogs miraculously streamed from it and covered the land.

Since G-d's instruction to Aharon involved inflicting pain on other human beings, the Midrash opines that Aharon was as minimally involved as possible in its completion; he drew only one frog out from the Nile, and allowed the rest of the plague to come about at the hands of others.

—*Likkutei Sichos, vol. 16, pp. 84-85*

---

meted out for a single sin is actually 39. According to some opinions, this is to avoid coming too close to exceeding the limit. See Targum Yonasan, Devarim 25:3.

12. See Shemos 8:1.

9:24 | ט:כד

וַיְהִי בָרָד וְאֵשׁ מִתְלַקַּחַת בְּתוֹךְ הַבָּרָד
There was hail, and fire flaming within the hail.

Fire and Ice

In the seventh of the Ten Plagues, G-d caused a devastating hailstorm to rain down upon Egypt, striking all the people and livestock that were not indoors, and crushing all the remaining crops and trees. In addition, says the Torah, the balls of ice miraculously contained fire.

The purpose of this unusual and doubly miraculous plague was not only to destroy Egypt's crops, but also to crush the Egyptians' delusional arrogance.

Egypt did not depend on rain for the irrigation of its crops. Rather, from time to time the waters of the Nile would rise, and through a system of pools and canals the entire land would be irrigated. This independence from rain led the people of Egypt to believe that they were entirely self-sufficient and not at G-d's mercy for their survival. The prophet Yechezkel therefore describes Pharaoh as "the great crocodile that lies down in the midst of its rivers, who said, 'My river is my own, and I made myself.'"[13] As the commentaries explain, Pharaoh felt that "I do not need the heavens, for my river provides all my necessities."[14]

To strike down their arrogance and false sense of security, G-d caused a supernatural mix of fire and ice to rain from the heavens.

---

13. Yechezkel 29:3.
14. Rashi ad loc.

Ice represents the conceited person's coldness—his aloofness and indifference to others. At the same time, the arrogant person can be heatedly passionate—about himself. These two manifestations of arrogance are in fact two sides of the same coin: the conceited person's iciness toward others is due to his adoration of himself.

Accordingly, G-d crushed the Egyptians' arrogance with the plague of hail—a combination of fire and ice.

—*Reshimos, no. 27*

בא
Bo

10:1 | י:א

וַיֹּאמֶר ה׳ אֶל מֹשֶׁה בֹּא אֶל פַּרְעֹה כִּי אֲנִי הִכְבַּדְתִּי אֶת לִבּוֹ וְאֶת לֵב עֲבָדָיו לְמַעַן שִׁתִי אֹתֹתַי אֵלֶּה בְּקִרְבּוֹ

G-d said to Moshe: "Come to Pharaoh, for I have hardened his heart and the heart of his servants, in order that I may place these signs of Mine in his midst."

When the Gates of Teshuvah Close

The Torah attests that G-d hardened Pharaoh's heart, effectively causing him to keep Bnei Yisrael enslaved until G-d inflicted all Ten Plagues upon the Egyptians.

The hardening of Pharaoh's heart was a punishment for his prior sins. The Rambam explains, "It is possible for a person to commit a sin so egregious, or to commit so many sins, that the judgment rendered before the True Judge is that his retribution for these sins, which he committed freely and of his own accord, is that he is prevented from repenting and is no longer able to abandon his evil ways—so that he dies and perishes on account of those sins he committed."[1]

This explains why G-d did not give Pharaoh a chance to repent and avoid punishment for his *previous* wrongdoings. We find, however, that even after hardening Pharaoh's heart, G-d warned him, "*If* you refuse to let My nation go, behold, tomorrow I will bring locusts into your borders."[2] How could Pharaoh be held accountable for decisions he made *after* G-d took away his freedom of choice?

Evidently, even after his heart was hardened, he retained the ability to change his ways, and was therefore punished when he did not.

Support for this can be found in the Tanya, where the Alter Rebbe writes, regarding the Talmud's assertion that certain sinners are not granted a chance to repent, "This means only that he [the sinner] is not granted an opportunity. But if he presses forcefully and overpowers his evil impulse and repents, then his repentance is accepted."[3] Similarly, even after G-d manipulated Pharaoh's feelings toward Bnei Yisrael, the ultimate decision regarding their freedom was still Pharaoh's to make, and he was held liable for refusing to do so.

This teaches us that hope for a person to repent and change his ways is *never* lost. On the contrary, the obstacles a Jew encounters in his path to repentance are there to arouse in him an even greater determination, to "force" his return to G-d.

—*Likkutei Sichos, vol. 6, pp. 64–66*

---

1. Mishneh Torah, Hil. Teshuvah 6:3.
2. Shemos 10:4.
3. Iggeres Hateshuvah, chapter 11.

10:22 | י:כב

וַיְהִי חֹשֶׁךְ אֲפֵלָה בְּכָל אֶרֶץ מִצְרַיִם

There was thick darkness over the entire land of Egypt.

Not the Time and Place for Miracles

One of the purposes of the plague of darkness was to allow Bnei Yisrael to enter the Egyptian homes and take note of their possessions. This facilitated their fulfillment of G-d's command[4] that, upon their redemption, they should empty Egypt of its valuables. As Rashi explains, "When they were leaving Egypt and requested [certain items], if the Egyptians told them, 'We have nothing,' they would reply, 'We saw it in your house, and it is in such-and-such a place.'"[5]

A similar account is found in the Midrash. The Midrash adds, however, that Bnei Yisrael canvassed the Egyptians' homes in a supernatural manner: "Wherever Bnei Yisrael went, light accompanied them and illuminated all that was in the barrels, closets and hidden recesses of the Egyptian homes."[6] In contrast, Rashi implies that though the darkness *enabled* the search by blinding the Egyptians, Bnei Yisrael actually combed through the homes via natural means.

Rashi's opinion supports the principle that the natural processes involved in performing a mitzvah are a significant component of the mitzvah itself. This is because the purpose

---

4. See Shemos 3:22 and 11:2.
5. Rashi, Shemos 10:22.
6. Shemos Rabbah 14:3.

of all mitzvos is to bring G-dliness into the world by utilizing material means for a G-dly purpose. When a person does a mitzvah, he sanctifies not only the object with which the mitzvah is performed (e.g., the *shofar* or *lulav*), but also any other physical means that contributed toward the fulfillment of the mitzvah. As such, when there is hardship or financial cost involved in fulfilling a mitzvah, we are provided with the opportunity for even more of our lives to be included in and elevated by the holy act. If these costs were circumvented through supernatural means, part of the mundane natural world would remain unaffected.

Rashi therefore deduces that the fulfillment of G-d's command that Bnei Yisrael empty Egypt of its valuables involved the effort of conducting an ordinary, natural search. Had Bnei Yisrael been shown the "hidden recesses" of the Egyptian homes by means of a miraculous light instead of going through the effort of conducting an ordinary search, the opportunity for this mitzvah to elevate the natural processes of life would have been diminished.

—*Likkutei Sichos, vol. 31, pp. 48-49; vol. 5, pp. 80-81*

יב:ב | 12:2

הַחֹדֶשׁ הַזֶּה לָכֶם רֹאשׁ חֳדָשִׁים
This month shall be for you the head of the months.

Sacred Time

The first mitzvah given to the Jews after they became a nation was to determine and sanctify the first day of every month—Rosh Chodesh—thereby creating the Jewish calendar. This command is expressed in the verse cited above, הַחֹדֶשׁ הַזֶּה לָכֶם רֹאשׁ חֳדָשִׁים. The words החדש הזה can also be translated as "this renewal," meaning that G-d showed Moshe the crescent moon and said, "This renewal—when the moon renews itself—shall be [what determines] for you the heads of the months."[7]

The priority given to this mitzvah suggests that sanctifying Rosh Chodesh is a model mitzvah, representing the underlying theme of all the other mitzvos.

The primary objective of all mitzvos is to transform the physical world from mundane to holy. By using any physical object to perform a mitzvah, we reveal the G-dly purpose for which that object was created, thereby sanctifying said item.

The sanctification of Rosh Chodesh embodies this idea, for in this mitzvah *time itself* is elevated. Namely, this mitzvah involves taking a day that was previously like any other, and declaring it Rosh Chodesh—no longer a regular weekday, but a day replete with special offerings brought in the Beis Hamikdash. In addition, setting up the calendar requires the Beis Din to calculate the constant cycles and patterns of the sun

---

7. Rashi ad loc.

and moon. Thus, the mitzvah to establish a Jewish calendar not only elevates the days sanctified as Rosh Chodesh (and by extension, the holidays observed on specific dates within the months), it reveals the G-dly purpose within the *entire* passage of time.

Rosh Chodesh was therefore the first mitzvah commanded, since it is a visible act of sanctifying the mundane—the essential theme of all the mitzvos. Moreover, time, which marks and is defined by change, is the first and *most basic* characteristic of every created being: the change from non-existence to existence. As such, just as time is the very first creation, its sanctification is the very first mitzvah.

—*Likkutei Sichos, vol. 26, pp. 61-65*

12:6 | יב:ו

וְהָיָה לָכֶם לְמִשְׁמֶרֶת עַד אַרְבָּעָה עָשָׂר יוֹם לַחֹדֶשׁ הַזֶּה

You shall keep it for inspection
until the fourteenth day of this month.

The Deprogramming

Bnei Yisrael were commanded to designate a lamb on the 10th of Nissan to be slaughtered as the Pesach offering four days later.

Rashi comments that these four days of waiting were necessary because "the time for the Redemption had arrived... but Bnei Yisrael were steeped in idolatry."[8] To leave Egypt's borders but to bring its undesirable influences—"the shame of the earth"[9]—with them would mean that the redemption was incomplete. The slaughtering of sheep—an Egyptian deity—for the Pesach sacrifice was the Jewish people's means of rehabilitation. But the Jews in Egypt had not only dabbled in idolatry, they were steeped in it. Therefore, a one-time act that renounced their previous obsession with idolatry was not enough to deprogram them from Egyptian influence. A longer process was required: four days of introspection.

Why four days?

When Avraham was commanded to offer his son Yitzchak as a sacrifice, he headed out the very next morning to do G-d's bidding, but he was shown the place where Yitzchak would be sacrificed only three days into his journey—i.e., four days after the initial command. Rashi explains that G-d delayed showing

---

8. Rashi ad loc.
9. Bereishis 42:9.

it to him immediately, "so that people should not say that He confused him and confounded him suddenly, overwhelming his mind, and that if Avraham had had time to think it over, he would not have done it."[10] A person's greatest passion is his children. Giving Avraham four days to contemplate parting with his child meant that when he ultimately lifted the knife over Yitzchak, it was indisputable that he did so completely sound of mind.

Therefore, to remove the shame of the Egyptian influence, the Jewish people were commanded not only to slaughter a sheep, but to start the process four days in advance, fully aware of what they were about to do. By slaughtering a creature that they had once considered a deity, after four days of thought and awareness, they effectively and indisputably purged themselves of their idolatrous state of mind.

—*Likkutei Sichos, vol. 16, pp. 117–119*

---

10. Rashi, Bereishis 22:4.

12:13 | יב:יג

וְהָיָה הַדָּם לָכֶם לְאֹת עַל הַבָּתִּים אֲשֶׁר אַתֶּם שָׁם וְרָאִיתִי אֶת הַדָּם וּפָסַחְתִּי עֲלֵכֶם וְלֹא יִהְיֶה בָכֶם נֶגֶף לְמַשְׁחִית בְּהַכֹּתִי בְּאֶרֶץ מִצְרָיִם

The blood will be for you for a sign upon the houses where you will be, and I will see the blood and spare you, and there will be no destructive plague in you when I smite the land of Egypt.

Egypt Syndrome

After guaranteeing that G-d will spare the Jewish homes from the final plague—death of the firstborn—the Torah adds, "And there will be no destructive plague in you." Rashi explains that these additional words address the query: "What if one of Bnei Yisrael was in an Egyptian's house? I would think that he would be smitten like him. Therefore, the verse states: 'And there will be no destructive plague in you.'"

The Jews who lingered in Egyptian homes on the night of the Exodus were in an appalling spiritual state, one more akin to that of their Egyptian oppressors than to that of their fellow Jews. Consider this: Not only had Bnei Yisrael suffered miserably at the hands of the Egyptians for hundreds of years, they had just witnessed the miraculous plagues with which G-d punished their captors. Now they had offered the Pesach sacrifice to commemorate their imminent redemption, and were explicitly warned, "No man shall leave the entrance of his house until morning."[11] We could assume that at this point,

---

11. Shemos 12:22.

a Jew who still chose to spend the night in the home of an Egyptian "would be smitten like him," in Rashi's words.

Yet, out of His love for the Jewish people, G-d Himself descended into the homes of the Egyptians in order to single out the Jews who might be among them. "I will go out into the midst of Egypt,"[12] says G-d, to save a Jew so spiritually hollow that even on this fateful night he still clings to his Egyptian friends and neighbors.

In doing so, G-d demonstrated the lengths to which we must go to save a Jew, either physically or spiritually—i.e., to draw him nearer to the service of G-d. Emulating G-d's ways, we must seek to reach even the Jew who is so assimilated that engaging him can require "descending" and compromising (within the guidelines of *halachah*) our own high spiritual standards. We must search for the Jew who cannot be found in a holy environment and is still "in an Egyptian home," to rescue him and draw his heart closer to his Father in Heaven.

—*Likkutei Sichos, vol. 36, pp. 50-51*

---

12. Shemos 11:4.

13:8 | יג:ח

וְהִגַּדְתָּ לְבִנְךָ בַּיּוֹם הַהוּא לֵאמֹר בַּעֲבוּר
זֶה עָשָׂה ה' לִי בְּצֵאתִי מִמִּצְרָיִם

You shall tell your son on that day, saying, "It is for this sake that G-d acted on my behalf when I went out of Egypt."

The Miracle of Freedom

The Torah tells us that in all generations we must convey to our children "that G-d acted *on my behalf* when *I* went out of Egypt." Our Sages learn from this verse that "in every generation, one is obligated to regard himself as if he himself has just come out of Egypt."[13]

Chassidus explains that freedom from Egypt is a constant and recurring miracle, and not just the natural and automatic state ever since the Exodus 3000 years ago.

The Zohar explains that the exodus from Egypt involved not only redemption from our physical slavery; the spiritual source of Egypt was entirely vanquished as well.[14] This is hinted at in the verse "For the Egyptians whom you see today, *you will never see again*."[15] Practically, this means that (even though the bondage in Egypt is the spiritual root from which all our subsequent exiles derived,)[16] the Jewish people will never again be subjugated in a manner as extreme as the Egyptian bondage.

---

13. Mishnah, Pesachim 10:5.
14. See Zohar 2:52b.
15. Shemos 14:13.
16. See Bereishis Rabbah 16:4.

For this reason we continue to celebrate the holiday of Pesach despite having been subsequently exiled and forced into captivity in other lands multiple times, because the freedom achieved through the redemption from Egypt can never be undone.

Our eternal freedom from the *possibility* of another "Egypt-like" exile defies nature, for in the natural order of the world a comparable exile is entirely possible. Hence, the *guarantee* of freedom that came with the Exodus is not a one-time miracle, but a continuous, nonstop defiance of the natural possibility of enslavement. Therefore, in every generation, and indeed every single day,[17] we can truly regard ourselves as having just been redeemed from Egypt.

—*Likkutei Sichos, vol. 5, pp. 175–178*

---

17. See Tanya, chapter 47.

בשלח
Beshalach

14:10 | יד:י

וַיִּצְעֲקוּ בְנֵי יִשְׂרָאֵל אֶל ה'

And Bnei Yisrael cried out to G-d.

Praying for a Living

Upon seeing Pharaoh and his army rapidly approaching, Bnei Yisrael became frightened and cried out to G-d for salvation.

Now, Bnei Yisrael knew that G-d had promised to bring them to the Land of Israel, and they were well aware of His ability to deliver on His promises. Why, then, did they deem it necessary to pray that G-d save them from Pharaoh's armies?

Rashi answers this question with his commentary on the words "and they cried out." In Rashi's words, "They seized the craft of their ancestors."

For Avraham, Yitzchak and Yaakov, crying out to G-d was part of everyday life; they prayed regularly, not only in times of crisis. Rashi therefore refers to prayer as our forefathers' *craft*: prayer came so naturally to them, it was as though it was their full-time occupation. Similarly, Bnei Yisrael's prayer did not stem from doubt that G-d would save them from the Egyptians. Rather, they prayed instinctively—"because that's what Jews do"—despite their certainty that they would be saved.

The same is true for us in every generation and era. As descendants of Avraham, Yitzchak and Yaakov, our service of G-d through prayer, and likewise our Torah study and mitzvah observance, should not be limited to fulfilling a specific requirement. We must emulate our ancestors and "seize their craft," engrossing ourselves in these activities constantly and instinctively—simply because this is who we are and that is what we do.

Similarly, when we endeavor to draw others closer to Torah observance, we must recognize that prayer, Torah study and mitzvah observance are the natural craft of every descendant of Avraham, Yitzchak and Yaakov. No matter how far removed from Jewish practice a fellow Jew may seem, we must approach him with the conviction that Judaism is essentially his craft—his most natural way of life.

—*Likkutei Sichos, vol. 11, pp. 52-54*

14:15 | יד:טו

וַיֹּאמֶר ה' אֶל מֹשֶׁה מַה תִּצְעַק אֵלָי

G-d said to Moshe, "Why do you cry out to Me?"

Stop, Drop and Care

Bnei Yisrael were surrounded by danger on all sides. Moshe, their leader, cried out to G-d in prayer. G-d replied, "Why do you cry out to Me? Speak to Bnei Yisrael and have them journey forth. And you, raise your staff and stretch out your hand over the sea and split it, and the children of Israel shall come in the midst of the sea on dry land."

Rashi notes that before G-d instructed Moshe to split the sea, He reprimanded him, saying, "Why do you cry out to Me?" As Rashi explains, "Moshe was standing and praying. G-d said to him, 'Now is not a time to pray at length, when Israel is in distress.'"

We can only imagine the profound union with G-d that Moshe experienced during prayer. Nevertheless, G-d reprimanded Moshe for his lengthy prayers here. For notwithstanding the value of Moshe's Divine worship, the moment had come for him to lead Bnei Yisrael to salvation—it was not time to engage in anything else.

With the words "Why do you cry out to Me," G-d was teaching Moshe, and in turn each and every one of us, that our responsibilities toward our fellow Jews may not be treated as an afterthought. When a Jew is at risk of devastation, whether physical or spiritual, we must put everything else aside and devote ourselves to saving him, even if this means sacrificing opportunities for our personal growth.

—*Toras Menachem, vol. 25, pp. 42–45*

14:29 | יד:כט

וּבְנֵי יִשְׂרָאֵל הָלְכוּ בַיַּבָּשָׁה בְּתוֹךְ הַיָּם

But the children of Israel went on dry land in the midst of the sea.

From Sea to See

"Everything that exists on land also exists in the sea," says the Talmud.[1] The difference is only the extent to which their occupants are visible to the human eye: unlike their counterparts on dry land, the creatures of the sea are mostly out of sight. Accordingly, Chassidus interprets *kerias Yam Suf*, when the sea was transformed into dry land, as a spiritual experience in which spiritual realities that are normally unseen became clear and visible.[2]

Kerias Yam Suf is not only a past event, but something we should strive for in our personal service of G-d as well.

One such form of spiritual *kerias Yam Suf* in our personal lives is to bridge the gap between the spiritual heights we experience during prayer and the activities we engage in the rest of the day. The focus of prayer is to arouse in our hearts and minds *conscious* feelings of attachment and subordination to G-d. Though daily prayer automatically impacts our conduct throughout the rest of the day as well, nevertheless, the intensity of our feelings during prayer tends to fade and be "hidden" from our conscious thoughts when we are preoccupied by the mundane demands that each day brings. *Kerias Yam Suf,* however, in which the hidden world of the sea became

---

1. Chullin 127a.
2. Likkutei Torah, Tzav 14c, and elsewhere.

exposed, teaches and empowers us to expose what is naturally "hidden," and make it conscious and "visible." Meaning that even while going about our ordinary activities, we can and must strive to maintain a constant and *conscious* submission before G-d like that which we experience during prayer.

—*Likkutei Sichos, vol. 3, p. 1016e*

15:20 | טו:כ

וַתִּקַּח מִרְיָם הַנְּבִיאָה אֲחוֹת אַהֲרֹן אֶת הַתֹּף בְּיָדָהּ
וַתֵּצֶאןָ כָל הַנָּשִׁים אַחֲרֶיהָ בְּתֻפִּים וּבִמְחֹלֹת

Miriam the prophetess, Aharon's sister, took a tambourine in her hand, and all the women came out after her with tambourines and with dancing.

The Women's Dance

The drowning of the Egyptians in the sea (after Bnei Yisrael had safely passed through) brought a complete end to the Egyptian exile, whereupon the Jews burst into song to thank G-d for their redemption. The Torah tells us that the women, led by Miriam, surpassed the men in their celebration. The men only sang, but the women also danced and played musical instruments.

The women's rejoicing was greater than the men's because their suffering in Egypt had also been greater. Harsher than the backbreaking labor that the Egyptians inflicted upon Bnei Yisrael were Pharaoh's decrees regarding the Jewish children. Most notoriously, Pharaoh decreed that all Jewish baby boys should be drowned, and later he bathed in the blood of Jewish children, as related in the Midrash.[3] Though these decrees obviously caused *all* the Jews anguish, such pain is naturally experienced more severely by the child's mother than by the father. Since the women's suffering in Egypt had been more painful than the men's, their joy upon the redemption was commensurately greater, too.

---

3. Shemos Rabbah 1:34.

This idea is highlighted by the fact that the women's rejoicing was led by Miriam, whose very name reflected the bitterness of exile: the root of מרים—Miriam is the Hebrew word מר—*mar*, which means "bitter."[4] Our Sages tell us that as a young girl Miriam prophesied about the redemption,[5] a prophecy whose fulfillment she witnessed only more than 80 years later. Having lived her life in painful anticipation of the end of the bitter exile, Miriam's joy upon the redemption knew no bounds, and she now led the women in their abundantly joyous celebration.

—*Likkutei Sichos, vol. 1, pp. 139-140;*
Sefer Hasichos 5752, vol. 1, pp. 303-304

---

4. See Shemos Rabbah 26:1.
5. See Rashi, Shemos 15:20.

17:9 | יז:ט

וַיֹּאמֶר מֹשֶׁה אֶל יְהוֹשֻׁעַ בְּחַר לָנוּ אֲנָשִׁים וְצֵא הִלָּחֵם בַּעֲמָלֵק

Moshe said to Yehoshua, "Choose men for us, and go out and fight against Amalek."

A Time for War

When Bnei Yisrael were under imminent threat of attack by Pharaoh and his army, Moshe told them not to be concerned, for "G-d will fight for you."[6] In contrast, when Amalek attacked Bnei Yisrael, Moshe instructed Yehoshua to band together a group of fighters and to take immediate military action.

Moshe's very different responses to these two threats reflect the underlying difference between what each attack represented. Pharaoh pursued Bnei Yisrael from behind, whereas Amalek attacked Bnei Yisrael to prevent them from proceeding to Mt. Sinai. Pharaoh stood between Bnei Yisrael and Egypt; Amalek stood between Bnei Yisrael and the Torah.

In this sense, Pharaoh's attack represents Egypt's desire to infringe on Bnei Yisrael's physical freedoms: Pharaoh insisted that they may partake of "the best of the land of Egypt... the fat of the land"[7] only if they are his slaves. Conversely, Amalek's attack threatened Bnei Yisrael's relationship with G-d through the study and observance of Torah.

Under normal circumstances, physical combat is foreign to Bnei Yisrael—"The voice is the voice of Yaakov, and the hands are the hands of Eisav."[8] Combat and conflict are for

---

6. Shemos 14:14.
7. Bereishis 45:18.
8. Bereishis 27:22.

Eisav, not for Yaakov or his descendants, Bnei Yisrael. Thus, when Pharaoh threatened to attack, Moshe told Bnei Yisrael to leave the fight to G-d.

Everything changed, however, when Bnei Yisrael's ability to receive the Torah was challenged. Despite physical warfare being entirely unnatural to a Jew, when Amalek attempted to halt Bnei Yisrael on their way to Sinai, Moshe instructed Bnei Yisrael to wage war against them. For when a Jew's connection to the Torah is at risk, we must set aside all natural preferences, and utilize all means possible to bring him closer to receiving and internalizing the Torah.

—*Likkutei Sichos, vol. 1, pp. 144–145*

17:9 | ט:יז

וַיֹּאמֶר מֹשֶׁה אֶל יְהוֹשֻׁעַ בְּחַר לָנוּ אֲנָשִׁים וְצֵא הִלָּחֵם בַּעֲמָלֵק

Moshe said to Yehoshua, "Choose men for us, and go out and fight against Amalek."

Think Outside the Cloud

The Ananei Hakavod, the protective Clouds of Glory, sheltered Bnei Yisrael (who lived and traveled within them) from enemy attack. Thus, Amalek was capable of assaulting only "the stragglers behind you"—i.e., those who were expelled from the Cloud on account of their sins.[9] Moshe, in turn, instructed Yehoshua to form an army to *"go out* and fight against Amalek," since saving these outcasts from Amalek's attack involved leaving the protective Cloud.

This explains why the Midrash[10] gives Yehoshua's lineage back to his ancestor Yosef: the campaign to save wayward Jews and bring them back into the safe confines of the Ananei Hakavod exemplified the spiritual identity of Yosef.

Yosef's name expressed his mother Rachel's prayer for more children: "יֹסֵף ה' לִי בֵּן אַחֵר—May G-d add *[yosef]* another son for me."[11] Notably, her request was not only that G-d grant her an additional child, but that He grant בן אחר, which literally means "an *other* child." Chassidus explains this to mean that Yosef, the bearer of this name, represents the ability to transform even someone who is an אחר, an "other," into a בן, a son. Yosef was able to influence even those for whom G-d

---

9. See Rashi, Devarim 25:18.
10. Pesikta d'Rav Kahana, Piska 3.
11. Bereishis 30:24.

seemed foreign and who behaved in a manner that is "other"—foreign—to Jews, leading them to recognize that they are truly a "son," a child of G-d, and motivating them to live their lives as such.

Therefore, it was Yehoshua, a descendent of Yosef, who was chosen to lead the war against Amalek. For the willingness to leave our own sheltered environment in order to save those who are "outside the cloud," and the ability to bring them back into G-d's miraculous Ananei Hakavod, is inspired by and drawn from the spiritual identity of Yosef.

—*Likkutei Sichos, vol. 26, pp. 87–88*

יתרו
Yisro

19:2 | יט:ב

וַיִּחַן שָׁם יִשְׂרָאֵל נֶגֶד הָהָר

And there Yisrael encamped opposite the mountain.

United: Verb or Adjective?

Bnei Yisrael's encampment opposite Mount Sinai is described by the Torah using the singular verb וַיִּחַן, "and *he* encamped." Rashi explains that the singular form denotes that Bnei Yisrael camped at Sinai in perfect unison—"as one man, with one heart," harmoniously readying themselves to receive the Torah.

Rashi offers a similar explanation on the verse "And behold, Egypt was advancing behind them,"[1] where the Torah uses the singular verb נֹסֵעַ to describe the thousands of Egyptians who pursued Bnei Yisrael after they left Egypt. There, too, Rashi explains that the Egyptians were unified—"with one heart, as one man"—in their pursuit of Bnei Yisrael. There is,

---

1. Shemos 14:10.

however, a noticeable difference between Rashi's explanations in these two places. Regarding the Egyptians, Rashi says that they were "with one heart, as one man," whereas regarding Bnei Yisrael, Rashi reverses the order, saying, they were "as one man, with one heart."

This distinction highlights a significant difference between the two types of unity.

The people of Egypt were obviously a diverse group, as the Torah itself distinguishes between the average Egyptians and the sorcerers, and between "those who feared the word of G-d"[2] and those who did not. They were unified, however, in their hatred of Bnei Yisrael.[3] Their mutual *feeling* of animosity toward Bnei Yisrael, "with one heart," led to their unified *actions*, "as one man."

Bnei Yisrael's unity in their preparation for the giving of the Torah, on the other hand, was not merely a uniform reaction to a shared feeling. Rather, their mutual feelings were due to an even deeper unity, an inherent unity that is part of their very identity as Jews. This essential Jewish oneness—"as one man"—is what caused Bnei Yisrael to share equal feelings of anticipation and desire to receive the Torah—"with one heart," despite their individual differences.

—*Likkutei Sichos, vol. 21, pp. 102-104*

---

[2]. Shemos 9:20.
[3]. See Rashi, Shemos 14:7.

19:16 | יט:טז

וַיְהִי בַיּוֹם הַשְּׁלִישִׁי בִּהְיֹת הַבֹּקֶר וַיְהִי קֹלֹת
וּבְרָקִים... וַיֶּחֱרַד כָּל הָעָם אֲשֶׁר בַּמַּחֲנֶה

And it came to pass on the third day as morning dawned, that there was thunder and lightning... and the entire nation that was in the camp shuddered.

Shock and Awe

Why was the giving of the Torah accompanied by thunder and lightning? If it was to drive home the awesomeness of the moment, surely the fright caused by the thunder and lightning paled in comparison to the profound sense of awe that Bnei Yisrael experienced from the revelation of G-d Himself!

Rather, the dramatic physical storm that accompanied the giving of the Torah reflected the earthshattering *spiritual* discovery that Bnei Yisrael and the world at large experienced at that historic moment.

The Midrash describes G-d's revelation at Sinai as the "annulment of the decree" that separated "the higher realms and the lower realms."[4] Meaning that the divide separating the spiritual reality and the physical world that derives from it was breached.

Until the revelation at Sinai, the "truth" of the physical reality was unquestionable. At the giving of the Torah, that perception was shattered. We were shown—and given the eternal ability to recognize—that the truth of all existence is

---

4. Tanchuma, Va'eira 15.

not its tangible matter, but its derivation from G-d, the One and only true Being, who constantly generates its existence.

Imagine the shock and inner upheaval of a person who discovers that everything he thought he knew until now was a gross distortion of the truth, that reality is in fact the complete opposite of what he perceived it to be. Such was the blow that the G-dly revelation at Sinai dealt to the world's consciousness.

Accordingly, the thunder and lightning at the giving of the Torah were merely the physical reflection of the spiritual storm that swept over and shocked all of existence at that incredible juncture.

—*Likkutei Sichos, vol. 33, pp. 23-24*

19:17 | יט:יז

וַיִּתְיַצְּבוּ בְּתַחְתִּית הָהָר
And they stood at the bottom of the mountain.

Who Wouldn't Want the Torah?

The Talmud interprets the words "And they stood at the bottom of the mountain" to mean that at the giving of the Torah, G-d raised Mt. Sinai over the Jewish people and said: "If you accept the Torah, good; if not, you will be summarily buried beneath this mountain." "This," concludes the Talmud, "furnished a strong disclaimer against the acceptance of the Torah," until the Jews willingly reaccepted it after the Purim miracle, almost 1,000 years later.[5]

Why was this coercion necessary? When Moshe told them that they would be given the Torah, had Bnei Yisrael not willingly committed themselves to its complete observance, proclaiming, "We will fulfill and we will listen?"[6]

The Talmud's assertion must therefore be understood to mean not that Bnei Yisrael were coerced into accepting the Torah *against* their will, but that their *willing* acceptance *itself* was coerced.

A person who recognizes and understands that a life of Torah observance is the ultimate blessing, and that the opposite is true of a life devoid of Torah, would find it virtually impossible to refuse to accept the Torah. Bnei Yisrael, however, having left Egypt a mere 50 days earlier, could not have independently undergone such an extreme paradigm shift—

---
5. Shabbos 88a.
6. Shemos 24:7.

from the influence of Egypt, "the shame of the earth,"[7] to an appreciation of the Torah's holy ideals. Thus, their willful and unconditional affirmation to live by the Torah was the result of *being shown* from Above that a life without Torah is no life at all; it was not an ideal that they had come to appreciate on their own yet.

When the G-dly revelation at Sinai ended, Bnei Yisrael faced their prior commitment, but without the level of appreciation for the Torah that they had been exposed to when they made that commitment. Observing the Torah now, without that inspiration, was thus much more difficult than it had been at the moment of their original acceptance. "This," says the Talmud, "furnished a strong disclaimer against the acceptance of the Torah," until they reaccepted it later on their own initiative.

—*Likkutei Sichos, vol. 26, p. 424*

---

7. Bereishis 42:9.

20:1 | כ:א

וַיְדַבֵּר אֱלֹקִים אֵת כָּל הַדְּבָרִים הָאֵלֶּה לֵאמֹר

G-d spoke all these words, to say.

Ten for Ten

When the Torah uses the phrase וַיְדַבֵּר... לֵאמֹר—"He spoke… to say," it usually means that the person being addressed should repeat what he is being told to a third party. For example, when G-d instructs Moshe regarding a particular mitzvah, the Torah writes, "G-d spoke to Moshe, to say," meaning that Moshe should relay the command to Bnei Yisrael.

In light of that, the verse "G-d spoke all these words, to say," which precedes the Aseres Hadibros, the Ten Commandments, demands explanation. Wasn't the entire nation present when G-d spoke the Aseres Hadibros? In fact, according to the Midrash, the souls of *all* Jewish people—past, present and future—were present at Sinai![8] If everyone to whom the Ten Commandments were directed was present when G-d stated them, to whom must they be repeated?

The Maggid of Mezeritch explains, homiletically, that here the word לֵאמֹר—"to say"—alludes to the Asarah Ma'amaros, the "Ten Utterances"[9] with which G-d created the world (e.g., "G-d *said*, 'Let there be light,' and there was light,"[10] "G-d *said*, 'Let the earth sprout vegetation,'"[11] etc.). Accordingly, the verse וַיְדַבֵּר... לֵאמֹר that precedes the Aseres Hadibros is to be under-

---

8. Shemos Rabbah 28:6.
9. See Avos 5:1.
10. Bereishis 1:3.
11. Ibid. 1:11.

stood as a directive to draw וַיְדַבֵּר—the Torah contained in the Aseres Hadibros—into לֵאמֹר—the world that G-d created with the Asarah Ma'amaros.

Practically speaking, the Maggid's explanation teaches us that we should not compartmentalize our lives, separating the Torah and holy aspects from the mundane. Our interactions with the "Asarah Ma'amaros," i.e., the day-to-day of our physical lives, must be permeated with a Torah attitude and framed by a Torah lifestyle. Even our mundane activities must be guided not by the attitudes of the secular world, but by an outlook that reflects our attachment to the Aseres Hadibros, the eternal Torah.

—*Likkutei Sichos, vol. 1, pp. 148–149*

20:1 | כ:א

וַיְדַבֵּר אֱלֹקִים אֵת כָּל הַדְּבָרִים הָאֵלֶּה לֵאמֹר

G-d spoke all these words, to say.

The Correct Response

The Midrash explains that the word לֵאמֹר—"to say"—in the verse that introduces the Ten Commandments is not an instruction to repeat what is being said, as לֵאמֹר generally indicates. Rather, in this instance, לֵאמֹר means, "to respond," meaning that Bnei Yisrael responded to G-d after each of the Ten Commandments. The subject of their response, however, is a matter of debate. According to Rabbi Akiva, they responded "Yes!" to both the positive commandments and the prohibitions, indicating their willingness to comply with whatever G-d demanded. Rabbi Yishmael disagrees and says that they responded "Yes!" to the positive mitzvos, indicating their willingness to *fulfill* those commandments, and "No!" to the prohibitions, indicating that they would *refrain* from what is forbidden.[12]

This debate is, in essence, a commentary on the nature of the mitzvos and what our primary focus in their fulfillment must be. Should our emphasis in the observance of a mitzvah be on experiencing its unique message and effect on our lives and on the world, or on the common theme shared by all the mitzvos—simply, that their observance fulfills the will of G-d?

Rabbi Yishmael believes that the ultimate purpose of a mitzvah's observance is the refinement of the individual (and

---

12. Mechilta, Shemos 20:1.

the world) that each mitzvah causes. He therefore asserts that as the Jewish people heard each commandment, they sensed its unique purpose and effect. In line with their experience, their responses alternated between "Yes!", expressing their excitement to implement the positive mitzvos in their lives, and "No!", voicing their aversion to the wrongness of the prohibitions.

Rabbi Akiva, in contrast, maintains that the highest form of worship is the *transcendence* that can be experienced through mitzvos. This is found equally in refraining from transgression as it is in fulfilling the positive commands—they are all opportunities to *surrender* ourselves to G-d and His will. Rabbi Akiva therefore asserts that the Jewish people at Sinai experienced this transcendent nature of mitzvos, and appropriately responded a uniform, affirmative "Yes!" to all ten commandments.

—*Likkutei Sichos, vol. 6, pp. 124-125*

20:2 | כ:ב

אָנֹכִי ה' אֱלֹקֶיךָ אֲשֶׁר הוֹצֵאתִיךָ מֵאֶרֶץ מִצְרָיִם
I am Hashem, your G-d,
Who took you out of the land of Egypt.

The Egyptian Me

Our Sages teach that the Ten Commandments given at Mount Sinai represent the sum total of the entire Torah: all 613 mitzvos are incorporated within these ten.[13] In fact, the Tanya explains that all mitzvos are, in effect, a means of fulfilling the first two commandments.[14] Taking this a step further, the Zohar states that the entire Torah is contained within the very first word, אָנֹכִי—"I," with which G-d introduced Himself simply as "I," making known His unfathomable essence that transcends any name.

Astonishingly, according to the Midrash, the word אָנֹכִי is actually Egyptian![15] According to this Midrash, the *most important word* in G-d's communication to mankind was spoken in Egyptian—the parlance of the most debased society of its time, "the shame of the earth."[16]

By using an Egyptian word here, G-d communicated the purpose for which the entire Torah was given: not merely to give depth to our spiritual lives, but to draw G-dly purpose and holiness into the lowest and most mundane aspects of

---

13. See Azharos of Rav Saadiah Gaon.
14. See Tanya, beginning of chapter 20.
15. Tanchuma, Yisro. The more common Hebrew word for "I" in the Torah is אני.
16. Bereishis 42:9.

life as well. The opening word of the Ten Commandments is therefore not in Hebrew, the holy tongue, but in a language utterly removed from holiness, Egyptian.

Similarly, the Talmud relates that Moshe refuted the angels' claims to the Torah by asking them, "Did you descend into Egypt?"[17] Moshe emphasized this detail because the descent into lowly "Egypt," and the struggle to refine the mundane parts of our lives, is the entire purpose for which the Torah was given. It is this "descent into Egypt," our endeavors to reveal G-dliness even in places that are not yet environments of holiness, that connects us with אָנֹכִי—G-d's very essence that was revealed at the giving of the Torah.

—*Likkutei Sichos, vol. 3, pp. 892–895*

---

17. Shabbos 88b.

מִשְׁפָּטִים
Mishpatim

21:1 | כא:א

וְאֵלֶּה הַמִּשְׁפָּטִים אֲשֶׁר תָּשִׂים לִפְנֵיהֶם

And these are the ordinances that you shall place before them.

Same Law, Different Court

This verse, said to Moshe in the context of a discussion about the Jewish elders, is the source from which the Talmud deduces that we must bring civil disputes only "before *them*"— the Jewish courts.[1]

Even if the ruling would be identical in either court (Jewish or secular), we are instructed to seek judgment specifically in courts based on Torah law. Why? By seeking out and abiding by the rulings of Torah law, the individual is submitting himself to the will of G-d. In contrast, to abide by the rulings of a secular court, even if their conclusions are identical to those of the Torah, is merely to acknowledge the justness of human conventions and logic.

---

1. Talmud, Gittin 88b; see Rashi and Tosafos ad loc.

The importance of observing the laws simply because they are G-d's will is likewise conveyed in the Talmud's description of the tactics of the *yetzer hara*—the voice inside us that draws us to sin. The *yetzer hara* does not initially suggest that we transgress the most grievous of sins. Rather, "Today he tells him, 'Do this'; tomorrow he tells him, 'Do that'; until he bids him, 'Go and serve idols,' and he goes and serves."[2] Chassidus explains that the *yetzer hara*'s initial "suggestion" does not involve transgressing even a minor prohibition. He begins by lending credence to mitzvah observance from a rational perspective. He says, "Do *this*!" meaning, "This mitzvah is justified, even by *my* standards."

In this way, the *yetzer hara* slowly infiltrates a person's attitude toward Torah observance. Instead of being centered on obedience to G-d's will, one's observance of the mitzvos becomes defined by the degree to which he finds a particular mitzvah sensible, useful and personally beneficial. And after successfully diverting a person's focus from obeying G-d's will and G-d's will alone, the *yetzer hara* can eventually lure him to transgress even the most severe sins.

The Torah therefore instructs us not to adjudicate our disputes in secular courts, even if they will reach the same conclusions as the Torah. For in order not to fall prey to the *yetzer hara*'s vices, our observance of the Torah's laws must not be contingent on human rationalization alone. We must approach all the mitzvos with an attitude of *kabbolas ol*, obeying the mitzvos primarily because they are G-d's will and we are His subjects.

—*Likkutei Sichos, vol. 3, p. 900*

---

2. Shabbos 105b.

21:2 | כא:ב

כִּי תִקְנֶה עֶבֶד עִבְרִי שֵׁשׁ שָׁנִים יַעֲבֹד וּבַשְּׁבִעִת יֵצֵא לַחָפְשִׁי חִנָּם

If you buy a Jewish slave, he shall work for six years;
in the seventh, he shall go out to freedom without charge.

Free to Steal

Parshas Mishpatim immediately follows the account of the giving of the Torah at Sinai, and begins with the laws regarding a thief who was sold into slavery in order to repay the money he stole.[3]

With the law of the thief, the Torah sets the tone for the reality Bnei Yisrael faced after Sinai.

The bedrock of Torah observance is *kabbolas ol*—submitting ourselves to G-d's kingship and authority. Once we choose to be His subjects, we serve Him by obeying His commands.

At Sinai, however, Bnei Yisrael were *shown* that "G-d, He is the L-rd: there is none else beside Him,"[4] and as a result, a foundation of *free-willed* acceptance of G-d's sovereignty could not be cemented. Under the influence of that awesome G-dly revelation, devotion to G-d was only natural. Genuine, willing submission to His authority became possible only *after* the revelation was over, when G-d's presence was no longer apparent.

But with the freedom to submit to G-d's authority came the freedom to ignore or reject it. The portion immediately following the giving of the Torah therefore begins by warn-

---

3. See Rashi, Shemos 21:2.
4. Devarim 4:35.

ing us about the fate of a thief. The Talmud[5] teaches that a thief, who steals covertly, is worse than a robber, who steals openly. The robber is ashamed of neither man nor G-d. The thief, on the other hand, recognizes his wrongdoing and fears being caught. Nevertheless, he disregards the watchful eye of G-d, whose will he is knowingly transgressing. The thief thus epitomizes the inherent "risk" of the post-Sinai freedom of choice: a person can recognize G-d's existence, yet freely choose not to submit to His authority.

By warning us about the consequences of thievery immediately after the revelation at Sinai, the Torah seeks to make us aware of the post-Sinai reality: the truth is out in the open, but you don't automatically feel compelled to live by it. The downside of this freedom? You can end up as disturbingly low as a thief. The upside? You can truly and internally accept G-d's kingship over you, and commit yourself to His service by your own volition and desire.

—*Toras Menachem, vol. 39, pp. 109–112*

---

5. Bava Kamma 79b.

21:5-6 | כא:ה-ו

וְאִם אָמֹר יֹאמַר הָעֶבֶד אָהַבְתִּי אֶת אֲדֹנִי
אֶת אִשְׁתִּי וְאֶת בָּנָי לֹא אֵצֵא חָפְשִׁי...
וְרָצַע אֲדֹנָיו אֶת אָזְנוֹ בַּמַּרְצֵעַ וַעֲבָדוֹ לְעֹלָם

*But if the servant says, "I am fond of my master,
my wife, and my children. I will not go free"...
his master shall pierce his ear with an awl, and he shall
then serve him forever.*

Are You All Ears?

If a Jewish servant does not wish to go free after six years of servitude, his master brings him before the court and pierces his ear in the presence of the judges. The servant may then remain with his master until the Yovel, the Jubilee year.

Why does the Torah single out the servant's ear for piercing, out of all the other limbs of the body? The Talmud explains:

> For the Almighty says: This ear, which heard My voice on Mount Sinai when I proclaimed, 'For Bnei Yisrael are slaves to Me'[6]—they are My servants, and not servants of servants, and yet went and acquired a master for himself, let it be pierced![7]

But was the revelation at Sinai only heard, not seen? Doesn't the Torah say, "And the entire nation *saw* the sounds"?[8] If the servant's ears are guilty for not abiding by what they

---

6. Vayikra 25:55.
7. Kiddushin 22b.
8. Shemos 20:15.

heard, why aren't his eyes held accountable for not living up to what they witnessed?

In truth, however, the Torah's "disappointment" with the servant is not that he is less spiritually sensitive than he was at Sinai, when he *heard and saw* the voice of G-d. The disappointment is that he is not living up to his current potential, *based on* what he experienced at Sinai. And therein lies the difference between what he saw and what he heard.

After the sounding of the Ten Commandments, the awesome G-dly revelation at Sinai ceased. Hence, a Jew can no longer be expected to relate to G-d on the level of "seeing," with the clarity of purpose that Bnei Yisrael had during the revelation at Sinai.

The purpose of this post-Sinai concealment, however, was to allow Bnei Yisrael to arrive at accepting the yoke of G-d on their own accord. Meaning, that our ability to "hear," i.e., to choose to be G-d's subjects even when His presence is concealed, is still intact. Accordingly, we are held accountable, even post-Sinai, if we fail to *hear* and recognize that "Bnei Yisrael are slaves to Me," and not "servants to servants."

—*Toras Menachem, vol. 39, pp. 110–113*

MISHPATIM

21:13 | כא:יג

וַאֲשֶׁר לֹא צָדָה וְהָאֱלֹקִים אִנָּה לְיָדוֹ וְשַׂמְתִּי לְךָ מָקוֹם אֲשֶׁר יָנוּס שָׁמָּה

And for he who did not ambush, but G-d caused it to happen to him, I shall provide you a place to which he shall flee.

Far Be It from Me

Why does the Torah first refer to a person who murdered by accident in the third person, saying, "G-d caused it to happen to *him*," and immediately afterward address the person directly, saying, "I shall provide *you* a place"?

In doing so, the Torah hints that to transgress G-d's will *even inadvertently* is entirely foreign to a Jew. Therefore, even when the Torah addresses the transgressor directly, it does not refer to his sin as something that "*you* did," but as something that "G-d caused to happen to *him*"—to someone absent, not your natural self. As Chassidus explains, a Jew's true identity is his G-dly soul, to whom sin is utterly unthinkable. It is only due to our "other" identity, the animal soul, that it is possible for a Jew to be drawn to sin.

Nevertheless, a person's sins not only drag his animal soul even lower, they harm his G-dly soul's sensitivity and conscious relationship with G-d as well. The end of the verse therefore states, "I shall provide *you*—the G-dly soul—a place to which *he* can flee," i.e., I will provide you an opportunity for repentance and repair, through which you elevate and repair your animal soul, too.

—*Likkutei Sichos, vol. 9, p. 302*

21:28 | כא:כח

וְכִי יִגַּח שׁוֹר

If an ox gores…

Speaking of Nature

The Torah teaches the laws of liability for damages caused by one's animals using the scenario of one person's ox damaging another person's property. As Rashi explains, "Scripture speaks of the ordinary," and barring any specific reason for an exception, the same laws apply in all similar instances. In the case of property damage, for example, the same laws apply whether the damage was done by an ox or any other animal or bird.

Rashi's expression, "Scripture speaks of the ordinary," also conveys an important message about how we must view everything that transpires in the world.

It is easy to recognize and acknowledge G-d's influence over the world when we observe an unlikely turn of events or unnatural phenomena. Conversely, when things follow their regular patterns and everything seems predictable, we can easily make the mistake of thinking that the ordinary happenings are simply "natural" and automatic.

By saying "Scripture speaks of the ordinary," Rashi points out the fallacy in this way of thinking. Even the "ordinary," the most normal and predictable aspects of life, says Rashi, are brought about by "Scripture speaking"—by the words written in the Torah. As Chassidus teaches,[9] all of existence

---

9. See Tanya, Shaar Hayichud Veha'emunah.

is constantly recreated and animated by the words that G-d uttered to bring the world into existence, as described in the first chapter of Bereishis.

Rashi's words thus teach us that nothing is natural. "Scripture speaks of the ordinary": Because Scripture speaks, the ordinary happens.

—*Likkutei Sichos, vol. 6, p. 141*

23:25-26 | ‏כג:כה-כו‏

‏וַעֲבַדְתֶּם אֵת ה' אֱלֹקֵיכֶם... לֹא תִהְיֶה מְשַׁכֵּלָה וַעֲקָרָה בְּאַרְצֶךָ אֶת מִסְפַּר יָמֶיךָ אֲמַלֵּא‏

You shall worship Hashem, your G-d... There will be no bereaved or barren woman in your land; I will fill the number of your days.

It's Not All About You

The struggles people face in the worship of G-d, and the method with which they can overcome them, are alluded to in the Torah's blessing, "There will be no bereaved or barren woman in your land; I will fill the number of your days."

There will be no bereaved or barren woman:

We all strive to worship G-d with inner passion and devotion. It can happen, however, that we find ourselves *bereaved* or *barren*, meaning that the inspiration and passion we cultivate are short-lived, or that our efforts to develop genuine love and fear of G-d do not bear fruit at all.

In your land:

The next word in the verse, ‏בְּאַרְצֶךָ‏—"in your land," hints to the reason for this "barrenness." The word ‏בְּאַרְצֶךָ‏ alludes to the Hebrew word ‏רצון‏, which means "wish" or "desire."[10] ‏בְּאַרְצֶךָ‏ can thus be interpreted as "due to your wishes," i.e., due to the personal satisfaction that you derive from your worship of G-d.

The sense of fulfillment a person derives from his Divine service can ultimately hinder his inner devotion to G-d from

---

10. See Bereishis Rabbah 5:8.

flourishing. His feelings of satisfaction lead his Divine service to become contingent upon the degree to which it makes him feel happy and content. Eventually, instead of decisively fulfilling G-d's will and desire, he picks and chooses between the aspects of Divine service he relates to and those he does not. Understandably, genuine love and unconditional commitment to G-d cannot thrive in such an environment.

I will fill the number of your days:

The key to overcoming this pitfall is to internalize the message found at the end of the verse: "I will *fill* the number of your days." The days that G-d allots a person in this world are numbered: we are each given precisely enough time to achieve the goal for which we were born. Any moment that you do not properly utilize in the service of G-d, you are sabotaging the mission He intends for you to fulfill in this lifetime! One who contemplates this painful truth will quickly abandon any search for feelings of achievement, and devote his every living moment to realizing the potential for which G-d created him. And then, with no time to harp on his feelings and moods, his internal relationship with G-d will thrive.

—*Likkutei Sichos, vol. 16, pp. 273–274*

תרומה
Terumah

25:2 | כה:ב

דַּבֵּר אֶל בְּנֵי יִשְׂרָאֵל וְיִקְחוּ לִי תְּרוּמָה

Speak to Bnei Yisrael and have a contribution taken for Me.

Man's Highest Calling

The command to build the Mishkan, and Bnei Yisrael's donation of materials for its construction, took place immediately after the giving of the Torah, before the episode of the Golden Calf, according to one opinion in the Zohar. Because the Golden Calf was made from molten earrings[1] rather than from the plentiful supply of gold that Bnei Yisrael took from the Egyptians, we can deduce that they had already given most of their gold to the Mishkan.[2]

Per this chronology of events, when G-d commanded Bnei Yisrael to build the Mishkan they were in their most elevated,

---

1. Shemos 32:2–3.
2. Zohar 2:224a.

pure state, having just been spiritually cleansed at Mount Sinai.[3] Yet at that very point G-d instructed them to build a physical Mishkan, demonstrating that use of our mundane possessions to create a home for G-d is man's highest calling, even if he is already perfect in all other areas.

Moreover, according to this opinion, had Bnei Yisrael not already consecrated the bulk of their gold for a higher purpose—for use in the Mishkan—all that gold would have contributed toward their most grievous sin, the Golden Calf. This teaches us that only by wholly dedicating the *material* aspects of our lives to the goal of creating a home for G-d can we ensure that we will remain anchored in our righteousness.

—*Likkutei Sichos, vol. 6, pp. 153–155*

---

3. See Talmud, Shabbos 146a.

25:3–5 | ה-ג:כה

וְזֹאת הַתְּרוּמָה אֲשֶׁר תִּקְחוּ מֵאִתָּם... וַעֲצֵי שִׁטִּים
And this is the contribution that you shall take from them... and acacia wood.

Plant a Tree from Israel

How did Bnei Yisrael have acacia wood in the desert? Some commentaries suggest that it grew in nearby forests, or perhaps it was available for purchase from merchants they encountered in the desert.[4]

Rashi, on the other hand, maintains that Bnei Yisrael left Egypt with a supply of acacia wood intended for use in the Mishkan. The source for this is a Midrashic account that Rashi cites in the name of Rabbi Tanchuma: "Our forefather Yaakov foresaw with Ruach Hakodesh, Divine intuition, that Bnei Yisrael were destined to build a Mishkan in the desert. He therefore brought cedars to Egypt and planted them, and instructed his sons to take them along when they left Egypt."

Why did Yaakov go to the trouble of bringing trees with him from the Land of Israel and planting them in Egypt? Surely he knew that Bnei Yisrael would have other opportunities to obtain acacia wood. Why didn't he rely on Bnei Yisrael's simply buying the wood, or procuring it from a nearby forest? Evidently, Yaakov had additional reasons for bringing the wood with him.

Rashi alludes to these motives by citing the teaching in the name of Rabbi Tanchuma, whose name comes from the Hebrew word *tanchumin*—consolations.

---

4. See Ibn Ezra and Divrei David ad loc.

The acacia trees that Yaakov planted in Egypt were a *visible* symbol of his prophecy that one day G-d would free Bnei Yisrael from Egypt and command them to build a Mishkan for Him in the desert. In the most dark and difficult moments of their slavery, these trees served as a source of hope and comfort. Seeing the trees from the Land of Israel reminded and reassured Bnei Yisrael that they would not remain exiled forever; G-d would soon bring them home, back to the Land of Israel from which they—and the trees—originated.

Although he knew that Bnei Yisrael could obtain the acacia wood through other means, Yaakov bought them along from the Land of Israel to provide solace to his descendants throughout their bitter exile.

—*Likkutei Sichos, vol. 31, pp. 142–147*

25:15 | כה:טו

בְּטַבְּעֹת הָאָרֹן יִהְיוּ הַבַּדִּים לֹא יָסֻרוּ מִמֶּנּוּ

The poles of the Ark shall be in the rings; they shall not be removed from it.

Have Poles, Will Travel

To ensure that the Aron, the Holy Ark, is always ready for travel, its poles are not allowed to be removed. The Sefer Hachinuch elaborates:

> In the event that we'll need to urgently transport the Aron, and in the hurry of the moment we might not verify that the poles are properly secured, the Aron might, G-d forbid, slip from our hold... But if they are made with no intention of ever being removed, they will be firmly fastened in place.[5]

The Torah's concern for the Aron to be readily mobile teaches us an important lesson.

The Aron contained the Luchos, inscribed with the Ten Commandments, which our Sages explain comprise all 613 mitzvos.[6] Thus, the Aron, which housed the Luchos, is a metaphor for Torah study, through which one's mind and heart become a home for the Torah's wisdom.

To succeed in the study of Torah requires intense concentration, removing oneself entirely from outside distractions. This, too, is comparable to the Aron hidden away in the Kodesh Hakodashim, the holiest chamber in the Temple, off

---

5. Sefer Hachinuch, Mitzvah 96.
6. See Azharos of Rav Saadiah Gaon.

limits to everyone but the Kohen Gadol, **the high priest**—and even *he* could only enter once a year!

Nevertheless, the poles of the Aron **teach us** that even while wholly engrossed in Torah study, we **must always be** *readily mobile*. Our immersion in Torah must be accompanied by the awareness and willingness to embark at **any time, to any place,** to do whatever it takes to bring the Torah to another Jew.

—*Likkutei Sichos, vol. 16, pp. 334–335*

כה:טז | 25:16

וְנָתַתָּ אֶל הָאָרֹן אֵת הָעֵדֻת אֲשֶׁר אֶתֵּן אֵלֶיךָ

And you shall place into the Ark the testimony, which I will give you.

The People's Mishkan

The Talmud teaches that the Ark contained both the broken remnants of the first set of Luchos and the complete and unbroken second Luchos.[7]

The first Luchos were given to Moshe immediately after the revelation at Sinai, before Bnei Yisrael sinned and worshipped the Golden Calf. At that point, they were spiritually perfect;[8] thus, the remnants of the first Luchos represent the *tzaddik*—the Jew in his most perfect and elevated state.

The second set of Luchos were given to Moshe on Yom Kippur, after G-d pardoned Bnei Yisrael for the sin of the Golden Calf. These Luchos represent the *baal teshuvah*—a person who may have strayed from the Torah's ways in the past, but has since repented.

Both the *tzaddik* and the *baal teshuvah* were thus represented in the Aron, by the first and second Luchos, respectively. There is, however, a third possible state in which a Jew may find himself: having transgressed the Torah but not yet made amends. The first Luchos, the Luchos of flawlessness, no longer represent him. The second Luchos, the Luchos of repentance, do not yet represent him either. But this Jew,

---

7. Berachos 8b.
8. See Talmud, Shabbos 146a: "At the giving of the Torah, their filth departed."

too, is represented in the Aron—by *the broken state* of the first Luchos.

By representing all three categories of Jews in the Aron, the Torah highlights that the commandment to build a Mishkan—and likewise, the eternal lesson we learn from this mitzvah—applies to every Jew equally. Regardless of your current spiritual state, whether perfect or far from it, you must endeavor to elevate your material life to serve exclusively as a home for G-d.

—*Likkutei Sichos, vol. 6, pp. 156–157*

25:18 | כה:יח

וְעָשִׂיתָ שְׁנַיִם כְּרֻבִים זָהָב

You shall make two golden kerubim.

Baby Face

The faces of the two golden *keruvim* (cherubs) were fashioned to resemble the faces of infants.[9] Baal Haturim explains that this symbolized G-d's love and affection for the Jewish people, comparing it to one's love for his baby or small child.

Parents' love for their children is not related to or conditional upon the child's qualities or accomplishments. Parents are inherently one with their children, and therefore love them unconditionally. This is particularly evident by the way parents adore their infant children, well before the child's qualities and virtues can be seen.

Because the soul of every Jew is "a veritable part of G-d above,"[10] G-d holds us dear with an intrinsic, essential and unbreakable love, like the love parents have for their children. The *keruvim* therefore resembled babies, symbolizing that G-d's love for the Jewish people is not dependent on our accomplishments; it transcends the relationship we forge with Him by studying His Torah and observing His commandments.

—*Likkutei Sichos, vol. 26, p. 181*

---

9. See Rashi, Shemos 25:15.
10. Tanya, chapter 2.

27:1-8 | כז:א-ח

וְעָשִׂיתָ אֶת הַמִּזְבֵּחַ... וְצִפִּיתָ אֹתוֹ נְחֹשֶׁת.... נְבוּב לֻחֹת תַּעֲשֶׂה אֹתוֹ

You shall make the altar... and you shall coat it with copper... You shall make it hollow, out of panels.

Brazen as Brass, Soft as Soil

The altar that stood in the courtyard of the Mishkan was coated with a layer of copper. Rashi explains that copper is a metaphor for brazenness (see Yeshayahu 48:4), and the Mizbe'ach atoned for Bnei Yisrael's insolent behavior.

The copper coating also represented a positive form of brazenness and chutzpah, which is *demanded* of Bnei Yisrael: a Jew must be bold and unashamed about his Judaism, defiant and unfazed by anyone who might mock his worship of G-d.

Beneath its tough exterior, however, the Mizbe'ach was hollow. Wherever Bnei Yisrael erected the Mishkan, they filled the Mizbe'ach with earth, to symbolize that even while approaching a challenge with toughness and chutzpah, deep down we must always feel humble, like insignificant, trampled earth.

These two aspects of the Mizbe'ach, its copper coating and its hollow inside filled with earth, thus represent two opposite yet vital traits that are always required of a Jew.

—*Reshimos, no. 108*

תצוה
Tetzaveh

27:20 | כז:כ

וְאַתָּה תְּצַוֶּה אֶת בְּנֵי יִשְׂרָאֵל

And you shall command Bnei Yisrael.

Nameless

From the account of his birth at the beginning of the book of Shemos until his final monologue in the book of Devarim, Moshe is mentioned by name in every Torah portion with the exception of Tetzaveh. This notable absence hints to the timing of this portion's reading, which is always close to the 7th of Adar—the date of Moshe's passing.[1]

But why hint to Moshe's passing by erasing his name? Is not the name and legacy of a righteous person remembered even after his physical demise? In addition, it seems that Moshe is *more* present in this Parshah than in many others. Often Moshe is mentioned in the third person, as though he himself is absent. In Tetzaveh, however, Moshe is repeatedly

---

1. See Me'or Einayim, Tetzaveh.

addressed by G-d in the second person, beginning with the uncharacteristically direct reference "*You* shall command," emphasizing that he is indeed "present."

The Zohar teaches that a *tzaddik* who has passed on is "present in all the worlds—our physical world included—*even more* than during his lifetime."[2] For on the one hand, the *tzaddik's* physical passing reflects his soul's *ascent* to its spiritual essence, such that it utterly transcends visible manifestation in this physical world. On the other hand, in its heightened condition the *tzaddik's* soul is now fully accessible for all who wish to draw spiritual life and inspiration from it, even more so than during his physical lifetime. No longer confined to a body, the *tzaddik's* influence is far greater than when he was limited to what he expressed in words and thoughts.[3]

Accordingly, we can understand why Moshe's passing is hinted to in Tetzaveh by the absence of his name, even while referring to him directly in the second person. For a person's name is not his essential identity; it is merely the means by which he can be identified to others. The absence of Moshe's name in the Parshah, yet simultaneously his additional presence—"you shall command"—thus aptly represents the passing of Moshe on the 7th of Adar, when on the one hand Moshe's soul ascended from its *external* plane (i.e., his name), yet at the same time his nameless *essence*—"*you*"—became revealed in the world to an even greater degree than before.

—*Likkutei Sichos, vol. 26, pp. 204-206*

---

2. Zohar 3:71b.
3. See Tanya, Iggeres Hakodesh 27.

28:35 | כח:לה

וְנִשְׁמַע קוֹלוֹ בְּבֹאוֹ אֶל הַקֹּדֶשׁ לִפְנֵי ה' וּבְצֵאתוֹ וְלֹא יָמוּת

And its sound shall be heard when he enters the Holy before G-d and when he leaves, so that he will not die.

Sounds from a Distance

The hem of the Kohen Gadol's robe was adorned with golden bells that chimed as he moved about the Mishkan. The sound of these bells was of such significance that the Kohen Gadol's very life depended on it: "Its sound shall be heard when he enters the Holy... so that he shall not die."

What did the bells signify?

A person who senses his utter nothingness before G-d and serves Him with perfect humility can be aptly described as serving G-d with "silence"—a virtue and ideal to aspire to in the service of G-d.[4]

But what about the person who feels distant from G-d, whose passions are unholy, or whose very sense of himself as an independent being separated from the G-dly energy that animates him creates distance between himself and G-d? Like a drowning man facing the horror of imminent death, the "distant" Jew kicks and screams, trying to escape his current state of detachment from G-d—the Source of all life. This Jew's search for G-d is noisy and tumultuous.

The ringing of the bells reminded the Kohen Gadol that he was to represent *all* elements of Bnei Yisrael in his service, including those whose relationship with G-d is not yet at the

---

4. See I Melachim 19:11–12.

level of perfect "silence." By wearing the chiming bells on the lowermost hem of his robe, the Kohen Gadol symbolically "carries with him" even the furthest members of the Jewish community—those who relate to G-d not in silence, but with the thunderous rush of their scramble to return.

—*Likkutei Sichos, vol. 16, pp. 338–339*

כח:לה | 28:35

וְהָיָה עַל אַהֲרֹן לְשָׁרֵת וְנִשְׁמַע קוֹלוֹ בְּבֹאוֹ אֶל הַקֹּדֶשׁ לִפְנֵי ה' וּבְצֵאתוֹ וְלֹא יָמוּת

It shall be on Aharon when he performs the service, and its sound shall be heard when he enters the Holy before G-d and when he leaves, so that he will not die.

To Wear or to Serve?

After detailing the construction of the *ephod* (apron), *choshen* (breastplate) and *me'il* (cloak), three of the unique garments to be worn by the Kohen Gadol, the Torah warns that Aharon must wear these garments "so he shall not die." Rashi elaborates: "...If he is wearing them, he will not be liable to death; but if he enters lacking one of these garments, he is liable to death by the hands of Heaven."

At first glance, it would seem that this warning is superfluous. After all, later the Torah warns regarding *all* the priestly garments that are to be worn by any Kohen, "They shall be upon Aharon, and upon his sons... that they bear not iniquity, and die."[5] As Rashi comments there, "Thus you may learn that he who serves lacking the proper garments is liable to death [at the hands of G-d]."

A careful reading of Rashi, however, shows a difference between these two warnings. Whereas a Kohen who is missing one of his garments is liable to death only if he *serves* in the Temple, according to Rashi a Kohen Gadol who is not wearing the *ephod*, *choshen* or *me'il* is liable to death even if he merely *enters* the Sanctuary. As Rashi's words indicate, this warning

---

5. Shemos 28:43.

is unique to "these garments"—the three described by the Torah in the preceding verses, but not to the other garments of a Kohen or Kohen Gadol.

This distinction can be explained in light of the difference between the Torah's description of the *choshen, ephod* and *me'il*, and its description of the other garments. After describing each of the first three, the Torah gives a specific outcome that is achieved when the Kohen Gadol comes before G-d *wearing* them. Concerning the *ephod,* "Aharon shall carry their names before G-d upon his two shoulders as a remembrance;"[6] concerning the *choshen,* "Thus shall Aharon carry the names of Bnei Yisrael... as a remembrance before G-d at all times;"[7] concerning the *me'il,* "It[8] shall be upon Aharon... and its sound shall be heard when he enters the Holy before G-d."[9]

Regarding the other garments, however, after stating that wearing them initiates and sanctifies the Kohanim for the service,[10] the Torah simply says that by wearing all the garments, a Kohen can serve in the Temple without dying:[11] i.e., their *collective* purpose is to facilitate the Kohen's *service*. Hence, Rashi concludes that aside from the *choshen, ephod* and *me'il,* a Kohen is liable to death only if he *serves* without one of the garments, but not if he merely enters the Sanctuary without it.

—*Likkutei Sichos, vol. 21, pp. 181–187*

---

6. Shemos 28:12.
7. Ibid 28:29.
8. Ibid 28:35.
9. Though the Torah makes a similar statement regarding the *tzitz* (see Shemos 28:38), Rashi explains there that the *tzitz* serves its purpose even when the Kohen Gadol is not wearing it.
10. Ibid 28:41.
11. Ibid 28:43.

28:39 | כח:לט

וְאַבְנֵט תַּעֲשֶׂה מַעֲשֵׂה רֹקֵם

And you shall make a sash of embroidery.

Fasten Your Avnet

Each of the Kohanim's splendid garments adorned a specific part of their bodies. Each of the additional garments and ornaments worn by the Kohen Gadol served a defined purpose: the *choshen* was made of twelve stones corresponding to the Twelve Tribes, the *tzitz* atoned for sacrifices brought in a state of impurity, and so on.

The exception is the *avnet*, the sash or belt, which doesn't seem to have served any specific purpose. The other garments did not actually require a belt to hold them in place, and even the garments which might have benefited from a belt certainly did not need a 32-cubit long belt, which required the Kohen to wrap it around himself repeatedly![12]

The purpose of the *avnet* is simply to express the Kohen's "readiness" to serve before G-d (unlike the other garments, which are each associated with a particular mode and theme of Divine service, corresponding to a specific part of the body). This is akin to the Talmudic directive to wear a belt when praying,[13] in fulfillment of the words of Amos, "Prepare yourself to greet your G-d, O Israel,"[14] for girding your body signifies that you have completed the necessary preparations and are now mentally ready to stand before and serve the King of all kings.

---

12. See Mishneh Torah, Hil. Klei Hamikdash 8:19.
13. Shabbos 10a.
14. Amos 4:12.

In light of that, the *avnet*—more so than the other garments—represents the general sense of submission to G-d with which the Kohanim served in the Mishkan. Accordingly, we can understand why the *avnet* was so long, requiring the Kohen to wrap it around himself repeatedly. This symbolized the Kohen's absolute dedication to G-d: he girded himself not once, but again and again, until his sense of humble devotion before G-d was perfect and complete.

—*Likkutei Sichos, vol. 36, pp. 155–159*

30:1 | א:ל

וְעָשִׂיתָ מִזְבֵּחַ מִקְטַר קְטֹרֶת

You shall make an altar for burning incense.

The Altar of Anonymity

The Inner Mizbe'ach, the golden altar for incense that stood in the sanctuary of the Mishkan, is described at the conclusion of Parshas Tetzaveh. Its placement here is somewhat peculiar, considering that the construction of the Mishkan as well as the other holy vessels found in the sanctuary are described in the previous Parshah.

Another thing that stands out about this Mizbe'ach is that unlike the altar for animal offerings which stood in the courtyard, the Mizbe'ach for burning incense stood in the Sanctuary, hidden from the public eye. In fact, no one other than the Kohen offering the incense that day could be present in the Sanctuary or near its entrance when the incense was offered.[15] Moreover, according to the Talmud Yerushalmi, even the angels could not be present in the Mishkan at that time![16]

The offering of incense in the privacy and seclusion of the Sanctuary represents the good deeds we do "out of sight" of others—without publicity and fanfare. By describing the incense altar only *after* the commands regarding the Mishkan's structure and contents, and *after* describing the Kohanim's uniforms and inauguration, the Torah indicates that the offering of incense on this Mizbe'ach represents the ultimate form of Divine service performed in the Mishkan. The height

---

15. Mishneh Torah, Hil. Temidim Umusafim 3:3.
16. Talmud Yerushalmi, Yoma 5:2.

of Torah and mitzvah observance (and particularly charity) is when one merits that only he and G-d are aware of his great and many achievements.

—*Likkutei Sichos, vol. 1, pp. 171–172*

30:9 | ל:ט

לֹא תַעֲלוּ עָלָיו קְטֹרֶת זָרָה וְעֹלָה וּמִנְחָה וְנֵסֶךְ לֹא תִסְּכוּ עָלָיו

You shall not offer upon it any other incense, burnt-offering or flour-offering, and you shall pour no libation upon it.

Don't Sacrifice Your Heart

The Inner Mizbe'ach, the golden altar that stood in the sanctuary of the Mishkan, was used exclusively for offering *ketores*—incense. All other sacrifices, such as animal and grain offerings, were brought only on the Outer Mizbe'ach, the altar which stood in the courtyard.

These two altars, and their unique offerings, are likewise to be found in the spiritual Mishkan that we must each create within our lives.

The animal and grain offerings on the altar represent a Jew's efforts to elevate the mundane and physical aspects of life by infusing them with G-dly purpose. The incense offering, on the other hand, is more soul-centric,[17] and therefore symbolic not of elevating the mundane, but of cultivating a more profound spiritual relationship with G-d. Hence the word *ketores*, קטורת, akin to the Aramaic word קטר, "knot," alluding to the *internal* bond with G-d that a Jew nurtures within himself through holy and spiritual pursuits, such as the study of Torah, prayer, etc.

That is why *ketores* alone may be offered on the Inner Mizbe'ach.

---

17. See Talmud, Berachos 43b.

Chassidus explains that the Inner Mizbe'ach represents the "inner heart"—a sublime delight and profound sense of attachment that transcends the "outer heart"—the passion represented by the Outer Mizbe'ach.

The prohibition of offering the animal and grain sacrifices on the Inner Mizbe'ach teaches us that our true delight should never lie in mundane and material pursuits, even if we are directing them toward a higher goal. *Ketores*, however, is to be offered specifically on the Inner Mizbe'ach, symbolizing that endeavors that are exclusively holy must be pursued with total devotion and ecstasy.

—*Likkutei Sichos, vol. 6, pp. 185–187*

כי תשא
Ki Sisa

30:19 | ל:יט

וְרָחֲצוּ אַהֲרֹן וּבָנָיו מִמֶּנּוּ אֶת יְדֵיהֶם וְאֶת רַגְלֵיהֶם

Aharon and his sons shall wash their hands and feet from it.

Rinse Well Before Serving

Each morning, before the daily service, the Kohanim serving in the Mishkan would wash their hands and feet. Emulating this practice, we too wash our hands every morning upon awakening, to sanctify ourselves for a new day in the service of G-d.[1]

Strangely, however, the Rambam[2] writes that before the morning prayers, one must wash not only his hands (and feet), but *also his face*—something which was not even required before the daily service in the Mishkan! This implies that

---

1. See Rashba, cited in Beis Yosef, Orach Chaim 4.
2. Mishneh Torah, Hil. Tefillah 4:3.

our daily prayers, which replace the service in the Temple,[3] require even more preparation than was necessary for the service in the Mishkan and Beis Hamikdash.

This additional preparation reflects the unique challenges that a Jew faces in exile, in marked contrast to those faced by the Jews of Temple times.

Hands and feet serve as the body's primary means of physical activity. The face, in contrast, is home to our higher faculties and senses, such as sight, speech, etc. The face thus represents the things that we are involved in not only technically, but also mentally and emotionally.

In the times of the Mishkan and Beis Hamikdash, the Jewish people, particularly the Kohanim, were in an ideal spiritual state: they occupied their hearts and minds almost exclusively with holy pursuits. Their limited involvement with the mundane, material world (in order to sustain themselves physically) was only in deed, not in spirit. The Kohanim therefore needed only to rinse their hands and feet, metaphorically removing themselves from their mundane activities, and then they were ready to devote themselves to the sacred service in the Temple.

Under the stresses and confusion of exile, however, it is not uncommon that material concerns occupy a Jew's innermost thoughts and feelings. The preparations for prayer today therefore require washing even the face, according to the Rambam, in order to metaphorically wash away our internal engrossment in the material world and ready ourselves for focused service of G-d.

—*Likkutei Sichos, vol. 31, p. 189*

---

3. See Talmud, Berachos 26b.

31:18 | לא:יח

וַיִּתֵּן אֶל מֹשֶׁה כְּכַלֹּתוֹ לְדַבֵּר אִתּוֹ בְּהַר סִינַי שְׁנֵי לֻחֹת הָעֵדֻת

When He had finished speaking with him on Mount Sinai, He gave Moshe the two tablets of the testimony.

Positively Fulfilling the Negative Prohibitions

Rashi notes that here the Torah spells the word לֻחֹת, *luchos*, tablets—without the letter "ו" that emphasizes the plural—rendering the word readable as לֻחַת, *luchas*—a singular tablet. Rashi explains that the Torah employs this unusual spelling to highlight that the two Tablets were identical—as though they are one and the same.

Though the simple meaning of Rashi's explanation is that both Luchos were of equal size, his words can also be understood homiletically as alluding to the spiritual equivalence of the Tablets' contents.

Inscribed in the Luchos were the Ten Commandments, in the order they were said, five on each tablet. The first five commandments are principally positive commandments: faith in the existence of G-d, observance of Shabbos and honoring one's parents.[4] Conversely, the last five commandments are prohibitions: do not murder, do not commit adultery, etc.

---

4. See Sefer Hachinuch (Mitzvos 26–30), who explains that the second and third commandments, the prohibitions against making or worshipping idols and swearing falsely in G-d's name, are offshoots of the first commandment—the positive mitzvah to have faith in G-d's existence.

Accordingly, the Torah's spelling of the word *luchos* in singular form teaches us that refraining from that which the Torah prohibits is *equally as constructive* as fulfilling the positive commands. For the bond with G-d that we create with each mitzvah we fulfill is equal, whether we are observing that which He commands us to do, or abstaining from that which He prohibits us from doing.

In addition, equating the positive commands inscribed in the first Tablet with the prohibitions inscribed in the second Tablet highlights the *active* aspect of the mitzvos' fulfillment that is common to both the commands and the prohibitions—the study of their detailed laws as they are found in the Torah.

—*Sefer Hasichos 5751, vol. 1, pp. 369–370*

BOOK OF SHEMOS　　　　　　　　　　　　　　　　　KI SISA　**249**

32:32 | לב:לב

וְעַתָּה אִם תִּשָּׂא חַטָּאתָם וְאִם אַיִן מְחֵנִי נָא מִסִּפְרְךָ אֲשֶׁר כָּתָבְתָּ

*And now, if You forgive their sin—But if not,
erase me now from Your book that You have written.*

A Conflict of Interest

Moshe's life was defined by two passions: his passion for the Torah and his passion for Bnei Yisrael.

On the one hand, Moshe was "the lawgiver,"[5] the perfect conduit through whom G-d communicated His Torah to humanity. Hence the prophets' reference to the Torah as "Moshe's Torah."[6]

In his other role, Moshe was Bnei Yisrael's faithful shepherd. His devotion to his nation was such that Rashi writes, "Moshe is Yisrael, and Yisrael is Moshe."[7]

But when Bnei Yisrael rebelled against the Torah's most basic principle and worshipped the Golden Calf, Moshe's passions clashed. As a result of their transgression, G-d threatened to wipe Bnei Yisrael out and start a new nation from Moshe alone. But Moshe pleaded with G-d to spare Bnei Yisrael, ultimately demanding, "If You will not forgive them, erase me now from Your Torah"—i.e., his attachment to Bnei Yisrael ran even deeper than his attachment to the Torah.

With this demand, Moshe secured forgiveness for Bnei Yisrael and saved them from devastation. By expressing *his* unbreakable attachment to Bnei Yisrael, Moshe similarly

---

5. Devarim 33:21.
6. Malachi 3:22.
7. Bamidbar 21:21.

evoked *G-d's* affection for the Jewish people—an affection that transcends even His oneness with the Torah. By rekindling G-d's love for Bnei Yisrael, Moshe caused G-d to accept and forgive them—and grant them another opportunity to keep His Torah.

—*Likkutei Sichos, vol. 21, pp. 174–177*

לב:לב | 32:32

וְעַתָּה אִם תִּשָּׂא חַטָּאתָם וְאִם אַיִן מְחֵנִי נָא מִסִּפְרְךָ אֲשֶׁר כָּתָבְתָּ

And now, if You forgive their sin—but if not, erase me now from Your book that You have written.

Learned from the Pro

To the greatest degree possible for any human being, Moshe's identity and existence became one with the Creator. He surrendered himself to G-d to the extent that our Sages say, "The Shechinah (Divine Presence) spoke through Moshe's throat"[8]—i.e., he was G-d's veritable mouthpiece on this earth.

Accordingly, when Moshe demanded that his name be erased from the Torah if G-d would not forgive Bnei Yisrael for the sin of the Golden Calf, he was threatening to abandon much more than his own legacy. For considering Moshe's oneness with the Shechinah, to suggest erasing Moshe's "name" and association with the Torah would be to suggest erasing, in a sense, the Shechinah's association with the Torah!

Nevertheless, to save Bnei Yisrael, Moshe believed that such extreme measures were acceptable. Moshe learned this from the method by which the Torah tells us to examine a *sotah*, a woman accused of infidelity, who may not live with her husband until it is determined that she is innocent of sin. In order to restore their marriage, a portion of the Torah containing several mentions of G-d's name is erased into water which the *sotah* must drink. The water will affect her only if she is guilty. If it has no adverse effects on her, we consider

---

8. See Zohar 3:232a.

her innocent, and she may return to her husband. Of this process, the Talmud declares, "G-d says: Let My Name, written in sanctity, be blotted out in water to make peace between a man and his wife!"[9]

In the same vein, Moshe reasoned that it was right to demand that his name be erased if it meant Bnei Yisrael would be saved. Taking an example from G-d's willingness to "sacrifice" His name, allowing it to be erased in order to restore the relationship between a husband and wife, Moshe felt justified to compromise his name, his honor, and everything he represented, in order to restore the precious bond between G-d and the Jewish people.

—*Sefer Hasichos 5749, vol. 1, p. 290, fn. 68*

---

9. Shabbos 116a.

32:32 | לב:לב

וְעַתָּה אִם תִּשָּׂא חַטָּאתָם וְאִם אַיִן מְחֵנִי נָא מִסִּפְרְךָ אֲשֶׁר כָּתָבְתָּ

And now, if You forgive their sin—but if not, erase me now from Your book that You have written.

A Role Model

When Bnei Yisrael rebelled against the Torah's most basic principle and worshipped the Golden Calf, G-d threatened to wipe them out and to start a new nation from Moshe alone. But Moshe pleaded with G-d to spare them, ultimately demanding, "If You will not forgive them, erase me now from Your Torah." The reason behind Moshe's demand, Rashi explains, was "so that they will not say about me that I was unworthy of asking for mercy on their behalf."

Why was Moshe so concerned about the way future generations would view him? *This* is what worried him as he considered the possibility that G-d might not forgive Bnei Yisrael!

Clearly, Moshe was not simply worried about his own legacy. His concern was that if he did not insist on his name being erased from the Torah if the Jewish people weren't forgiven, future generations might reach mistaken conclusions about the extent to which a person must go in his love for his fellow Jew.

Moshe's love for Bnei Yisrael exceeded the Torah's command to "love your fellow as *yourself*."[10] Although the defining feature of Moshe's "self" was the Torah that he brought to

---

10. Vayikra 19:18.

this world—"Moshe's Torah"[11]—his love for Bnei Yisrael was such that he was ready to sacrifice his association with the Torah—his "self"—if G-d would not forgive Bnei Yisrael and spare them from devastation.

Moshe therefore asked that G-d erase his name from the Torah if He would not forgive Bnei Yisrael. He wanted to ensure that no one would ever mistakenly think that the reason he was unsuccessful in saving Bnei Yisrael was because his love for his fellow Jew did not exceed his love for "himself"—in his case, his connection to the Torah. He therefore insisted that his name be erased from the Torah if G-d would not forgive Bnei Yisrael, to serve as an example for all future generations that you must be willing to *sacrifice even "yourself"* out of love for your fellow Jew.

And how do you express that limitless love to your fellow Jew? Says the Mishnah:[12] by drawing them near to the Torah.

—*Likkutei Sichos, vol. 21, pp. 175–180*

---

[11]. Malachi 3:22.
[12]. Avos 1:12.

34:1 | ל״ד:א

וַיֹּאמֶר ה׳ אֶל מֹשֶׁה פְּסָל לְךָ שְׁנֵי לֻחֹת אֲבָנִים כָּרִאשֹׁנִים

G-d said to Moshe:
"Hew for yourself two stone tablets like the first ones."

When Broken Comes Before Whole

The Midrash relates that Moshe was distressed over having broken the Luchos, until G-d said to him, "Do not be pained over the first Tablets, which contained only the Ten Commandments. The second Tablets that I will give will be accompanied by *halachos*, *midrash* and *aggados*."[13] Implied is that the extensive and multifaceted Oral Torah—"*halachos*, *midrash* and *aggados*"—was gifted to Bnei Yisrael only as a result of Moshe's breaking the first Luchos.

How did such a negative event yield such positive results?

The Torah is Divine wisdom. Therefore, like G-d Himself, the wisdom of the Torah transcends any definition or limit. This infinitude is particularly evident in the Oral Torah. Whereas the Written Torah contains an exact amount of letters and words—even one extra letter renders a Torah scroll invalid—the Oral Torah is limitless: Aside from its myriad details, we are obligated to constantly extrapolate new details and applications of the law following the guidelines set out in the Torah, rendering the Oral Torah truly dynamic and endless.[14]

---

13. Shemos Rabbah 46:1.
14. See Shulchan Aruch Admor Hazaken, Hilchos Talmud Torah 2:2.

The human being, however, is fundamentally finite and limited. As such, to merit and be capable of absorbing G-d's inherently infinite wisdom, even as it is manifest in the comprehensible teachings of the Torah, a person must utterly remove his own limited identity from the equation. Simply put, he must rid himself of any sense of pride or ego—not only before G-d, but also before man. In the words of the Talmud, "If a man renders himself like a wilderness upon which everyone treads, his study will be retained by him; otherwise, it will not."[15]

Bnei Yisrael attained this sense of humility only after the humbling experience of the Golden Calf. When Moshe shattered the Luchos before their eyes, driving home the devastating reality of what they had done, they were utterly broken and humbled. Now, said G-d to Moshe, I can finally bestow upon them the limitless gift of the Torah. Now I can grant them the *halachos*, *midrash* and *aggados* of the Oral Torah that will accompany the Second Luchos.

—*Likkutei Sichos, vol. 26, pp. 249-253*

---

15. Eruvin 54a.

ויקהל
Vayakhel

35:1 | לה:א

וַיַּקְהֵל מֹשֶׁה אֶת כָּל עֲדַת בְּנֵי יִשְׂרָאֵל וַיֹּאמֶר אֲלֵהֶם אֵלֶּה הַדְּבָרִים אֲשֶׁר צִוָּה ה' לַעֲשֹׂת אֹתָם

Moshe assembled the entire community...
"These are the things that G-d commanded to be done."

Preoccupied

After prevailing upon G-d to wholeheartedly forgive Bnei Yisrael for the sin of the Golden Calf, Moshe descended from Mount Sinai, bringing with him the second set of Luchos. The following day,[1] Moshe assembled Bnei Yisrael and relayed G-d's command that they gather materials and construct the Mishkan.

Why did Moshe wait until the day *after* descending the mountain before informing Bnei Yisrael about this command?

Earlier, we read about the great eagerness for the study and observance of Torah that Bnei Yisrael felt after hearing

---

1. See Rashi, Shemos 35:1.

the Ten Commandments at Mount Sinai and receiving the first Luchos.[2] Their excitement upon receiving the second Luchos was therefore presumably just as great, if not greater, considering that the giving of the second Luchos represented that their relationship with G-d had been completely restored.

As a result, on the day that Moshe descended with the second Luchos, he and Bnei Yisrael were fully engrossed in the theme of the day—celebrating their forgiveness and enjoying the gift of the Torah. Their focus was likely the study of the Torah in and of itself, and not on action-oriented details and instructions, even the likes of building the Mishkan. Only the next day did it make sense for Moshe to reassemble them and get to work on "the things that G-d commanded *to be done.*"

The lesson for us is twofold. Firstly, Bnei Yisrael's "exclusive preoccupation" with receiving the second Luchos teaches us that the mitzvah to *engross ourselves* in Torah study cannot be substituted with tasks even as holy as building a Mishkan. During our set times for Torah study we must focus solely on our learning, and utterly detach ourselves from any other task or concern. At the same time, Moshe's haste to instruct Bnei Yisrael the very next morning regarding the Mishkan teaches us that our enthusiasm for Judaism must not end with studying the Torah. After "receiving the Torah" and delving into it, we must carry that same excitement into the task of making the world a Mishkan—a place where G-d's presence is revealed and manifest.

—*Likkutei Sichos, vol. 6, pp. 216–217*

---

[2]. See Shemos 19:8 and 24:3.

35:1 | לה:א

וַיַּקְהֵל מֹשֶׁה אֶת כָּל עֲדַת בְּנֵי יִשְׂרָאֵל

Moshe assembled the entire community of Bnei Yisrael...

Taking Donations from Children

Moshe assembled "the entire community of Bnei Yisrael" when he announced G-d's command to gather the materials necessary to construct the Mishkan. According to the Ohr Hachaim, the Torah's emphasis that Moshe assembled the *entire* community teaches us that Moshe also gathered the women and children for this announcement, for even children took part in contributing for the Mishkan.[3]

This represents a departure from the Torah's typical expectations of children under the age of majority, who are neither required nor held accountable for the fulfillment of any of the Torah's commands.

Why, then, were children included in the donation drive for the Mishkan?

One explanation is that the mitzvah to construct the Mishkan was a means for Bnei Yisrael to atone for their worship of the Golden Calf.[4] Though Jewish law never holds minors accountable for their actions, the sin of idolatry is an exception. We find this in the law of *ir hanidachas*, when all (or the majority) of the inhabitants of a particular city become idolaters, and as a result all residents of the city who are found guilty are

---

3. Ohr Hachaim ad loc.; see also Avos d'Rabbi Nosson 11:1.
4. See Shnei Luchos Habris, Torah Shebiksav, Vayakhel.

punished *along with their wives and children*.⁵ Likewise, in the story of Purim, the heavenly decree against the Jews was issued because they had succumbed to idolatry,⁶ resulting in the mortal decree issued by Achashveirosh to annihilate the *entire* Jewish nation, "young and old, children and women."⁷ Since the consequences of the Golden Calf affected all Bnei Yisrael, including the children, they too took part in rectifying the sin through the construction of the Mishkan.

—*Likkutei Sichos, vol. 3, pp. 930–931*

---

5. See Mishneh Torah, Hil. Avodah Zarah 4:6.
6. See Talmud, Megillah 12b.
7. Esther 3:13.

35:2 | לה:ב

שֵׁ֣שֶׁת יָמִים֮ תֵּעָשֶׂ֣ה מְלָאכָה֒ וּבַיּ֣וֹם הַשְּׁבִיעִ֗י יִהְיֶ֨ה לָכֶ֥ם קֹ֛דֶשׁ שַׁבַּ֥ת שַׁבָּת֖וֹן לַה׳

For six days work shall be done; on the seventh day you shall have sanctity, a Shabbos of complete rest to G-d.

The Shabbos Spell

The first time the Torah outlines the mitzvah of Shabbos is in the Ten Commandments: "Six days you shall work and perform all your labor, but the seventh day is a Shabbos to G-d, your L-rd."[8]

The Torah reiterates the mitzvah in Parshas Vayakhel, albeit with a number of differences. Most notably, in the Ten Commandments, the Torah says directly, "Six days you shall work," whereas in Vayakhel it says "For six days work shall be done"—as though the work in the six days happens on its own. In addition, unlike in the Ten Commandments, where the Torah calls the seventh day a "Shabbos to G-d," here the Torah refers to it as *"Shabbos Shabbason*—a Shabbos of Shabbos to G-d."[9]

These variations highlight the effects of Shabbos observance on the other six days of the week.

We rest on Shabbos to remember that G-d created the world in six days and rested on the seventh. Through this remembrance, "we ingrain in ourselves belief in the world's deliberate creation."[10] This acknowledgment and faith that

---

[8]. Shemos 20:9–10.
[9]. Literally, "a Shabbos of complete rest to G-d."
[10]. Sefer Hachinuch, Mitzvah 32.

G-d deliberately created the entire world and conducts all that transpires within it fundamentally affects the way we approach our work throughout the entire week. Knowing that G-d alone provides our sustenance, and the work we do serves merely as a conduit for His blessings, enables a person to remain emotionally unattached to his work so it does not consume his mind and heart. It becomes as though the work of the six weekdays happens passively—"For six days work *shall be done.*"

This, in turn, affects our Shabbos experience as well. For after six weekdays that pass under the spell of the previous Shabbos, the Shabbos that follows becomes *Shabbos Shabbason,* a "Shabbos upon Shabbos."

—*Sefer Hasichos 5749, vol. 1, pp. 297–298*

| 35:4 | לה:ד

וַיֹּאמֶר מֹשֶׁה אֶל כָּל עֲדַת בְּנֵי יִשְׂרָאֵל לֵאמֹר
זֶה הַדָּבָר אֲשֶׁר צִוָּה ה' לֵאמֹר

Moshe spoke to the entire community of Bnei Yisrael, saying: "This is the word that G-d has commanded."

The Mishkan Again?

The Torah's wording is concise, even cryptic at times; an extra word or letter is cause for discussion among the biblical commentaries. Seemingly, then, after the Torah's detailed record of all G-d instructions regarding the Mishkan and its parts, the account of the Mishkan's actual construction could have been summarized with one verse to the effect of "And Bnei Yisrael did as G-d had commanded Moshe." Instead, the Torah tells us that Moshe repeated G-d's commands to Bnei Yisrael, records all the materials that were donated, and finally gives an exhaustive depiction of the artisans' work. How is this not excessive?

We find, however, that such repetition is not entirely unprecedented. When Eliezer, Avraham's servant, goes to find a wife for Yitzchak, the Torah tells us about his experiences as they transpire, and then records the entire story again in the context of Eliezer's conversations. On that episode, Rashi exclaims, "The conversations of the servants of the fathers are more precious before G-d than the Torah of the sons! The section of Eliezer is told twice, whereas many principles of the Torah were given through clues."[11]

---

11. Bereishis 24:42.

Rashi's intention is not to contrast the servants of the forefathers with Bnei Yisrael, per se, but to point out the preciousness of some of their "conversations"—narratives that do not seem to convey any unique lesson. Rashi is saying that although the Torah is generally concise even when giving directives for Bnei Yisrael to follow, narratives that are particularly "enjoyable" to G-d, such as the marriage of Yitzchak and Rivkah, are related in detail and repeated, even though they may seem to be mere "conversation."

This explains why the Torah elaborates on the Mishkan's construction. G-d's command to build a Mishkan demonstrated His desire to dwell among Bnei Yisrael. This command was particularly significant in the aftermath of the Golden Calf, for "the Mishkan was testimony for Israel that G-d forgave them for the incident of the calf, as He caused His Shechinah to rest among them."[12] The Torah therefore savors, as it were, the details of this precious and pivotal moment in the relationship between G-d and His people, and excitedly repeats them.

—*Likkutei Sichos, vol. 16, pp. 458–461*

---

12. Rashi, Shemos 38:21.

35:26 | לה:כו

וְכָל הַנָּשִׁים אֲשֶׁר נָשָׂא לִבָּן אֹתָנָה בְּחָכְמָה טָווּ אֶת הָעִזִּים

All the women whose hearts uplifted them with wisdom spun the goat hair.

The Gifts of the Gifted

According to Rashi, the women spun goat hair into thread while it was still attached to the goats, a process entailing extraordinary talent. This extra effort was particularly remarkable considering that Bnei Yisrael had not been instructed to process the goat hair at all before donating it to the Mishkan. Nevertheless, these gifted women, "whose hearts uplifted them with wisdom," wanted their contribution to the Mishkan to be of the highest possible quality. They therefore spun the goat hair while it was still growing, when the fibers are most pliable and produce a better yarn. Only then did they donate it to the Mishkan.

The Torah's account of their donation teaches us an important lesson. The women who spun the goat hair recognized that their unique talent was a gift from G-d. They were therefore certain that this ability had been granted to them in order for them to utilize it in the construction of the Mishkan—the home we make for G-d in this world. As such, they specifically sought (and found) a way to enhance the Mishkan through their special talent, even though they had not been specifically commanded to do so.

The same is true for all the unique gifts that G-d grants us. We must recognize that being blessed by G-d with extraordinary abilities, whether an exceptional talent or abundant financial success, obliges us to *seek out* opportunities to contribute *extraordinarily* toward making this world a dwelling place for G-d.

—*Likkutei Sichos, vol. 16, pp. 451–456*

38:8 | לח:ח

וַיַּעַשׂ אֵת הַכִּיּוֹר נְחֹשֶׁת וְאֵת כַּנּוֹ נְחֹשֶׁת בְּמַרְאֹת הַצֹּבְאֹת

He made the copper washbasin and its copper base from the mirrors of the legions of women.

The Rearview Mirror

The Talmud contrasts Moshe with all the other prophets in history, saying, "All the prophets looked into a dim glass, but Moshe looked through an illuminated glass."[13] Chassidus explains that Moshe's perception of the Divine was comparable to a person looking through "an illuminated glass"—an instrument such as a telescope that enables us to see distances beyond the scope of the naked eye. In contrast, the other prophets' perception of the Divine was through a "dim glass," alluding to a mirror—a coated glass that expands our range of view to include angles that we could not view directly. Whereas through a telescope we see the distant objects themselves, in a mirror we see only the objects' reflections. Analogously, what the other prophets perceived was a reflection of the Divine, but Moshe was given a glimpse of Divinity itself.[14]

This explains why when the women offered their personal mirrors as a contribution to the Mishkan, Moshe hesitated to accept them because he viewed mirrors as instruments of lust and temptation. G-d, however, told Moshe to accept them, saying, "These are more precious to Me than all else,

---

13. Yevamos 49b.
14. See Torah Ohr, Mikeitz 33a.

because through them the women produced the legions (they gave birth to) in Egypt."[15]

The mirrors epitomized finding G-d in His reflection and shadow—discovering that even things that seem to be at odds with holiness can actually *reflect* the Divine. The women in Egypt "redirected" the mirrors from simple instruments of lust to agents of G-dly purpose, by utilizing them to bring about the birth of another generation of Jews in the most dire of times.

Moshe, however, hoped for the Mishkan to be a place where G-d's presence was perceived in the manner to which he was accustomed—manifestly and directly. Why blur the revelation in the Mishkan by incorporating in it aspects of life in which G-dliness—though present—is somewhat concealed?

Nevertheless, G-d told Moshe to accept the mirrors. For the unearthing of G-d's presence even where He is normally "out of sight" is the ultimate fulfillment of G-d's desire to dwell in the lowest elements of this world. Though the G-dly revelation therein is somewhat indirect, the Divine pleasure elicited by the challenge inherent in that discovery is "more precious to Me than all else."

—*Likkutei Sichos, vol. 6, pp. 197–199*

---

15. Rashi, Shemos 38:8.

פקודי
Pekudei

38:21 | לא:יח

אֵלֶּה פְקוּדֵי הַמִּשְׁכָּן מִשְׁכַּן הָעֵדֻת

These are the accounts of the Mishkan, the Mishkan of the Testimony.

The Collateral

Rashi notes the Torah's uncharacteristic repetition of the word *Mishkan* in this verse, and explains it based on the similarity between the word *Mishkan*, מִשְׁכָּן, and the word *mashkon*, מַשְׁכּוֹן, a security or collateral. "This [repetition] alludes to the Mikdash, the Temple," says Rashi, "which was taken as security by two destructions, due to Israel's sins." Meaning that near the conclusion of the Torah's discussion regarding the Mishkan, the verse hints to the first and second Batei Mikdash, the Holy Temples that would one day replace the Mishkan.

Notably, the verse hints not to the *construction* of the future Batei Mikdash, but to their being "taken as security" by two destructions! Paradoxically, in doing so, the Torah highlights the permanence and endurance of the future Batei Mikdash—despite their destruction.

The purpose of a security or collateral is merely to ensure the fulfillment of a pledge or the payment of a debt, after which *the security itself* is returned. Though it changes hands for the duration of the loan, the security remains intact until it is returned eventually to its owner.

Thus, by referring to the Batei Mikdash as collateral, the Torah is emphasizing their endurance. The Batei Mikdash embodied G-d's desire for a permanent presence among the Jewish people. The destruction did not mean that the existence of the Batei Mikdash no longer fulfilled this desire, but that due to outside causes—"Israel's sins," in Rashi's words—the Jewish people's access to the Batei Mikdash was temporarily taken away. From G-d's perspective, however, He merely took the first Temple, and likewise the second, as security, intending to return them and everything they represent when the time comes. May it be soon.

—*Likkutei Sichos, vol. 11, pp. 175–178*

38:21 | לח:כא

אֵלֶּה פְקוּדֵי הַמִּשְׁכָּן מִשְׁכַּן הָעֵדֻת

These are the accounts of the Mishkan, the Mishkan of the Testimony.

The Testimony

What is the "testimony" to which the Torah refers when calling the Mishkan "The Mishkan of the Testimony"? Rashi explains that the Divine Presence resting in the Mishkan was itself the testimony: "It served as testimony for the Jewish people that G-d forgave them for the incident of the Calf, as He caused His Shechinah to rest among them [in the Mishkan]."

A testimony makes known that which is otherwise unknown or hidden. Facts that are obvious and widely known do not require testimony; in Jewish law, even facts that are currently indefinite but will inevitably become known in the future do not need to be proven with testimony.[1]

Accordingly, inherent in the name "The Mishkan of the Testimony" are the two *novelties* to which the G-dly revelation in the Mishkan bore testimony.

First: the revelation was in a material structure, built by human effort. A revelation of G-dliness is not entirely novel or unexpected in a spiritual context. A revelation of the Divine within physicality, however, constitutes a "testimony" to a truth that is otherwise existentially hidden in this context.

In addition, the Torah calls the G-dly revelation in the Mishkan a "testimony" because it was an exposé of the

---

1. See Talmud, Rosh Hashanah 22b.

essentially unknown. Namely, the Mishkan served as the dwelling place for the essence of G-d that transcends revelation and is not manifest in any G-dly revelation or Divine influx found even in the spiritual realms.

—*Likkutei Sichos, vol. 1, pp. 198–199*

38:21 | לח:כא

אֵלֶּה פְקוּדֵי הַמִּשְׁכָּן מִשְׁכַּן הָעֵדֻת אֲשֶׁר פֻּקַּד עַל פִּי מֹשֶׁה

These are the accounts of the Mishkan, the Mishkan of the Testimony, as they were overseen by Moshe.

Mass-Energy Equivalence

The Torah records the total weight of the gold, silver and copper that Bnei Yisrael donated for the Mishkan. Notably, no mention of the value or quality of the precious metals is made, only their weight.

What is the difference between weight and worth? Whereas weight only measures an object's mass, value reflects its quality and distinct form as well.

In a spiritual sense, these two components exist in varying degrees in all our "contributions" toward "making a Mishkan"—our efforts to make a dwelling place for G-d in this world. The weight, or mass, of our contributions are our actions, such as our practical observance of a mitzvah. The quality and "character" of the contribution, on the other hand, is the intention and spirit of devotion with which we perform that mitzvah.

Now, one might assume that actions devoid of any conscious feelings or intent serve no purpose in making the Mishkan. After all, how can uninspired physical acts contribute toward making G-d manifest in our lives?

To dispel this notion, the Torah relates that Moshe specifically calculated the weight of the precious metals, meaning that he attributed significance not only to the worth of the donations but also to their weight. For even the mass—actual deed alone—was worthy enough in Moshe's eyes to count and record.

—*Likkutei Sichos, vol. 26, p. 279*

39:1 | לט:א

וַיַּעֲשׂוּ אֶת בִּגְדֵי הַקֹּדֶשׁ אֲשֶׁר לְאַהֲרֹן כַּאֲשֶׁר צִוָּה ה' אֶת מֹשֶׁה

They made Aharon's holy garments,
as G-d had commanded Moshe.

It's How You Wear It

In Parshas Vayakhel, Moshe conveys G-d's instructions regarding the Mishkan to Bnei Yisrael, and the craftsmen construct all the Mishkan's components. Parshas Pekudei then relates how the finished work was brought before Moshe, who assembled the Mishkan and initiated its service, whereupon "the glory of G-d filled the Mishkan."[2]

An exception to this pattern, however, is the account of the *bigdei kehunah*, the garments worn by the Kohanim while serving in the Mishkan. The crafting of the *bigdei kehunah* is not recounted in Vayakhel, where the Torah describes the other work done by the Mishkan's craftsmen, but in Pekudei, where the service is set into motion.

This anomaly draws attention to the distinction that the Rambam makes in his enumeration of the 613 mitzvos, where he includes *dressing* in the *bigdei kehunah* as one of the 613, but does not include crafting them.[3] Evidently, he views *crafting* the clothes merely as a means of facilitating the mitzvah of wearing them, but not a mitzvah of its own. Conversely, he lists *constructing* the other components of the Mishkan as a

---

2. Shemos 40:34.
3. See Sefer Hamitzvos, Positive Mitzvah 33.

mitzvah in and of itself,[4] independent of the mitzvos related to using them in the Mishkan's service.

Accordingly, Parshas Vayakhel, the theme of which is the construction of the Mishkan and its parts, discusses only the components of the Mishkan whose *construction* had independent "mitzvah significance." In contrast, the theme of Parshas Pekudei is the Divine response elicited by the Mishkan and its service *after it was operational*. The Torah therefore describes the fashioning of the *bigdei kehunah* in Parshas Pekudei, rather than in Vayakhel, for the garments achieve their "mitzvah significance" only through their actual utilization—when worn by the Kohanim for their service in a fully operational Mishkan.

—*Likkutei Sichos, vol. 3, p. 934, fn. 4*

---

4. Ibid, Positive Mitzvah 20.

40:17 | מ:יז

וַיְהִי בַּחֹדֶשׁ הָרִאשׁוֹן בַּשָּׁנָה הַשֵּׁנִית בְּאֶחָד לַחֹדֶשׁ הוּקַם הַמִּשְׁכָּן

And it came to pass in the first month,
in the second year, on the first day of the month,
that the Mishkan was erected.

Self-Construction

A seven-day training and initiation period for the Kohanim preceded the official erecting of the Mishkan on the first day of Nissan.[5] Each day that week, the Mishkan was successfully constructed, and then dismantled after the service was performed.[6]

On the day of the Mishkan's official construction, Bnei Yisrael brought the Mishkan to Moshe so he could erect it—*on his own*, in accordance with the singular tense of G-d's instruction to him, "And you shall raise the Mishkan."[7] However, as Rashi cites from the Midrash, "No human being could construct the Mishkan, because of the heaviness of the planks. Moshe said before G-d, 'How is it possible for a human being to raise it?' G-d replied, 'Apply your hands to it'; Moshe appeared to be raising it, but it arose by itself."[8]

This marked difference between the days of initiation and the day of the Mishkan's official construction reflects the distinction drawn in Chassidic teaching between a revelation of G-dliness that is "initiated from below"—elicited through

---

5. See Shemos, Chapter 29.
6. Rashi, Vayikra 9:23.
7. Shemos 26:30.
8. Shemos 39:33.

the efforts of mankind, and a G-dly influx that comes about independent of man's efforts—"initiated from above."

A revelation that is "initiated from below" has a particularly profound impact on its recipients, because they have made themselves worthy and capable of experiencing it. Nevertheless, finite human effort can elicit only a limited degree of revelation. Conversely, a spontaneous revelation that is "initiated from above" utterly transcends the limited efforts of humankind, and is therefore incomparably greater in its revelation of the Divine reality.

This contrast was reflected in the difference between the "preparatory" construction of the Mishkan in the seven days of training, and its official construction on the 1st of Nissan at G-d's explicit command.[9]

The erection of the Mishkan in the seven days of initiation and training did not cause G-d's presence to rest in the Mishkan. As mere *preparation* for the ultimate Divine revelation, the construction of the Mishkan in those days therefore came about through human effort alone.

On the 1st of Nissan, however, when G-d Himself would rest in the Mishkan upon its construction (at *His* command), "no human being could construct the Mishkan." Moshe merely applied his hands to it, and G-d caused it to rise on its own, reflecting the extraordinary revelation of the Divine presence in the Mishkan that could come about only through a spontaneous "initiation from above."

—*Likkutei Sichos, vol. 11, pp. 181–185*

---

9. See Shemos 40:2.

40:34-36 | מ:לד-לו

וַיְכַס הֶעָנָן אֶת אֹהֶל מוֹעֵד וּכְבוֹד ה' מָלֵא אֶת הַמִּשְׁכָּן...
וּבְהֵעָלוֹת הֶעָנָן מֵעַל הַמִּשְׁכָּן יִסְעוּ בְּנֵי יִשְׂרָאֵל בְּכֹל מַסְעֵיהֶם

The cloud covered the Tent of Meeting, and the glory of G-d filled the Mishkan... And when the cloud rose up from over the Mishkan, the children of Israel set out in all their journeys.

The Closing Pitch

After the construction of the Mishkan was completed, the Torah relates that a cloud covered the Mishkan, signifying that at last the Divine Presence had come to dwell within. The Torah adds that the cloud would remain above the Mishkan for as long as Bnei Yisrael were encamped at a particular location. When the cloud rose, it was a sign that it was time for them to proceed with their journey through the desert.

This detail about Bnei Yisrael's journeys in the desert seems to belong in the Book of Bamidbar—and is indeed repeated there—where the Torah describes their travel patterns in detail. Here, where the Torah relates that the Divine Presence finally dwelled in the Mishkan, this statement about the *ascent* of the Divine Presence from the Mishkan when it was time to travel seems entirely out of place!

Yet in truth, this mention of Bnei Yisrael's journeys serves as a perfect conclusion for the account of the Mishkan's construction, and indeed for the entire book of Shemos.

The book of Bereishis tells the story of the world's creation and the beginnings of humankind. The purpose of creation is announced in the book of Shemos: the Jewish nation is born, and they are given the Torah to guide them. Their task? To build a home on this earth where the Divine Presence can dwell and be manifest.

The construction of the Mishkan—a physical structure wherein G-d's presence was revealed—was the most obvious realization of this objective, and it is therefore the theme of the final portions of the Book of Shemos.

There remained, however, another detail that was necessary for the world's purpose to be realized. The final verses of the Book of Shemos discuss the journeys of Bnei Yisrael, which in a broader sense are symbolic of the exile of the Jewish people among foreign nations in lands where Torah and G-dliness were hitherto unknown. With this the Torah alludes that the Jewish people's ultimate goal is not only to reveal G-dliness in the Mishkan, but also "when Bnei Yisrael set out on all their journeys"—to reveal that even the lowliness and darkness of the world, beyond the confines of the Mishkan, can be transformed into a place wherein G-d's presence can be revealed.

—*Likkutei Sichos, vol. 16, pp. 475–479*

BOOK OF VAYIKRA

לחיזוק ההתקשרות לכ״ק אדמו״ר
ולזכות

שניאור זלמן
בן בת-שבע בינה

יהודית חיה
בת אלישבע

שיינא אסתר
בת יהודית חיה

שלמה אהרן
בן יהודית חיה

שיינא אסתר
בן יהודית חיה

מנחם מענדל
בן יהודית חיה

לוי יצחק
בן יהודית חיה

❦

ולזכות הוריהם

ר׳ דוד מיכאל
בן פייגע

בת-שבע בינה
בת ציפה

אחיו **מנחם מענדל**
בן בת-שבע בינה

אחותו **חנה פייגא**
בן בת-שבע בינה

להצלחה רבה ומופלגה בגו״ר בכל העניינים
מתוך בריאות טובה, נחת חסידותי ופרנסה בהרחבה
בטוב הנראה והנגלה

ויקרא
Vayikra

1:1 | א:א

וַיִּקְרָא אֶל מֹשֶׁה
And He called to Moshe

It's All in the Aleph

The letter א in the word ויקרא, "And He called," at the start of the Book of Vayikra, is laden with paradox.

On the one hand, the name of the letter א, *aleph*, is related to the Hebrew word *aluph*, "chieftain"—alluding to G-d, "Chieftain of the Universe."[1] In addition, the letter א is what distinguishes G-d's communication with Moshe from His communication with the gentile prophets, such as Bilaam; G-d's communications with Bilaam are introduced with the term ויקר, "And He happened upon,"[2] instead of ויקרא, "And He

---

1. Likkutei Torah, Tazria 23c.
2. Bamidbar 23:4.

called." As Rashi explains, the word ויקר denotes coincidence and impurity, whereas ויקרא denotes affection.[3]

On the other hand, despite its prominence, the א of ויקרא is written in smaller script than all the other letters, suggesting that this א is trifling and insignificant!

These conflicting implications can be understood in light of the message conveyed by the word ויקרא, *vayikra*—to call out. *Vayikra* is the mission that G-d asks of every Jew, to *call out* to others who may be distant, and draw them close to the Torah and its observance.

One must know that a person who accepts upon himself the holy task of ויקרא is imbued with an א, representing the "Chieftain of the Universe" who empowers him to act on His behalf. He therefore can—and must!—go about his G-dly mission with a spirit of strength, authority, and confidence in his ability to positively impact his environment.

At the same time, however, the person calling out recognizes that his strengths and accomplishments are not his own; they are his only by virtue of being an agent of the "Chieftain of the Universe." Thus, the presence of the *aleph* in his activities makes him modest and small.

To call attention to the *humility* imbued in the agent of *vayikra* through his empowerment by the "*Aluph*-Chieftain," the א of ויקרא is smaller than all the other letters in the Torah.

—*Sichos Kodesh 5741, vol. 2, pp. 615–619, 801*

---

3. Rashi, Vayikra 1:1.

| א:ב | 1:2

אָדָם כִּי יַקְרִיב מִכֶּם קָרְבָּן לַה'
A man who shall bring from you an offering to G-d...

Why Korbanos? That's Why

The significance the Torah attributes to animal sacrifice is mystifying. Why would the physical slaughter and burning of an animal be our primary form of Divine worship?[4] Would not a more spiritual exercise, in which the Jew's attachment to G-d is sensed and experienced, be more suitable as the focal point of the Temple service?

In truth, however, the significance of the sacrifices lies precisely in their seeming lack of spiritual experience. The Torah's word for sacrifice is *korban*, from the word *karov*, "close," indicating that the purpose of the sacrifices is to *arouse* and express the Jewish people's *inherent* "closeness" to G-d—a closeness that surpasses even the attachment we develop through observing His commands. As such, we can understand why the sacrifices atone for transgressions of the Torah: a sacrifice reveals the Jew's essential and unbreakable bond with G-d, thereby repairing any deficiency in their relationship caused by a breach of Torah observance.

This closeness could not be adequately expressed in a service that highlights the Jew's unique spiritual capacities, for this essential bond with G-d is not contingent on the Jew's efforts or spiritual awareness; it is purely the result of G-d's existential choice of His beloved nation. The unbreakable

---

4. See Avos 1:2; Yerushalmi, Taanis 4:1.

bond between the Jewish people and G-d is therefore best expressed through a Jew offering a *korban*, the *spiritual value* of which is not obvious, save for the fact that *G-d* has deemed it desirable for a Jew to offer a sacrifice to Him.

—*Likkutei Sichos, vol. 22, pp. 3–4*

מפני מה מתחילין לתינוקות בתורת כהנים, ואין מתחילין בבראשית? אלא שהתינוקות טהורין והקרבנות טהורין, יבואו טהורין ויתעסקו בטהורין (ויקרא רבה ז, ג)

Why do schoolchildren begin their learning with Toras Kohanim (the Book of Vayikra) and not with Bereishis? Since the children are pure and the sacrifices are pure, let the pure come and deal with the pure. (Vayikra Rabbah 7:3)

The Pure

Even before Jewish children are old enough to understand what it means to observe the Torah, their first studies of Jewish texts begin, according to age-old tradition, with the book of Vayikra. According to the Midrash, this is because Vayikra teaches the laws of sacrifices, and "since the children are pure and the sacrifices are pure, let the pure come and deal with the pure."

Remarkably, the only reference in the Torah to sacrifices being "pure" is with regard to those offered by Noach after the Flood: "Noach built an altar to G-d, and he took from all the pure animals and from all the pure fowl, and brought up burnt offerings on the altar."[5] The pure animals referred to there are the kosher animals, "which are destined to be pure for Israel."[6]

Noach's sacrifices predated not only G-d's command to the Jewish people "to distinguish between the impure and

---

5. Bereishis 8:20.
6. Rashi, Bereishis 7:2.

the pure"[7] and observe a kosher diet, but also the era of the patriarchs, of whom our Sages say, "They observed the entire Torah even before it was given."[8] Thus, by referring to the sacrifices as "the pure," the Midrash alludes to the potential of the sacrifices to reveal G-d's essential love for the Jewish people, a bond that "predates" and transcends even the attachment we develop by observing His Torah.

Accordingly, we can understand the tradition to introduce children to Torah study with the book of Vayikra. Children begin their school years long before they are of the age of responsibility to observe the Torah and mitzvos. Moreover, at that age they are too young even to digest the idea of obligation, or to be trained for the duties that they will have upon reaching the age of majority. Their early reading of the Torah therefore symbolizes a Jew's inherent connection to G-d and His Torah, a connection that transcends even the actual observance and study of the Torah and its laws. Since the sacrifices likewise reflect this pure and inviolable relationship with G-d, it is most appropriate that "the pure come and deal with the pure."

—*Likkutei Sichos, vol. 22, pp. 1–6*

---

7. Vayikra 11:47.
8. Kiddushin 82a.

2:1 | ב:א

וְנֶפֶשׁ כִּי תַקְרִיב קָרְבַּן מִנְחָה

And if one offers an offering of a minchah...

The Selfless Fuel of Sacrifice

The word *minchah* means "a grain offering," which makes the phrase *korban minchah*—"a grain offering offering"—seem redundant. The Midrash therefore interprets the additional word *korban* to allude to another genre of offerings that a person may donate and offer upon the altar,[9] namely stand-alone offerings of oil, wine, incense or wood, which are typically components of a (larger) *korban*, but which may also be offered individually.

The Midrash's view that wood is among the components of a sacrifice is somewhat puzzling. After all, the purpose of the wood is simply to fuel the altar's fire. Why does the Midrash regard it as part of the sacrifice?

In a certain sense, however, the wood accompanying the sacrifice represents the underlying theme of all sacrifices, even more so than the sacrifices' other components.

Ramban[10] explains that the objective of the sacrifices is to arouse the individual to offer himself—his inner qualities and character—to G-d. The animal he burns on the altar substitutes for him physically, but a spiritual offering is still expected of him.

In particular, each sacrifice draws attention to a unique aspect of the person's character that he must channel in the

---

9. See Toras Kohanim ad loc.
10. Ramban, Vayikra 1:9.

service of G-d. Common to all sacrifices, however, is the underlying readiness to offer yourself—ultimately, your entire being—to G-d.

This self-sacrifice required for every offering is represented by the one component that all the sacrifices have in common: the wood used to fuel the fire. And for good reason, because the firewood is the epitome of selflessness and abnegation.

Unlike the other components of the sacrifice, burning the firewood is not said to arouse "a pleasing fragrance for G-d."[11] Nevertheless, it is entirely burned and consumed in order to facilitate the arousal of that Divine delight—the credit for which will ultimately be attributed to "someone else."

Thus it is truly the firewood alone that meets the definition of *korban*, a sacrifice.

—*Likkutei Sichos, vol. 22, pp. 7–13*

---

11. Vayikra 1:9.

3:16 | ג:טז

כָּל חֵלֶב לַה׳

All fat is to G-d.

The Best and Finest

When an animal is offered as a sacrifice, its premium fats—the choicest parts of its flesh—are burned on the altar. The Rambam interprets this as a universal principle:

> The same applies to everything done for the sake of G-d—it must be of the finest and best. When one builds a house of prayer, it should be finer than his private dwelling. When he feeds the hungry, he should give them the best and sweetest from his table. When he clothes the naked, he should give him the finest of his garments. When consecrating an object to the Temple, he should give the finest of his possessions. And so it is written, "All the fat is to G-d."[12]

The Talmud teaches a similar principle, yet from a different source in the Torah, and with an entirely different set of examples:

> "This is my G-d, and I will beautify Him."[13] This means, beautify yourself before G-d in mitzvos. Make before Him a beautiful *sukkah*, a beautiful *lulav*, a beautiful *shofar*, beautiful *tzitzis* and a beautiful Torah scroll.[14]

While the Talmud speaks of beautifying *your* observance, the Rambam implies that by bringing an offering of superior

---

12. Mishneh Torah, Hil. Issurei Mizbeiach 7:11.
13. Shemos 15:2.
14. Talmud, Shabbos 133b.

quality, you enhance the value and effectiveness of the sacrifice itself.

The Talmud's principle is therefore applicable regardless of the status conferred on the object through its use in the performance of a mitzvah. The *sukkah, lulav, shofar, tzitzis* and Torah scroll are not "given" to G-d; they remain in your personal possession. Yet by performing G-d's commands in a beautiful manner, you bring additional splendor to G-d, whom you are serving.

The Rambam, however, speaks only of instances comparable to sacrifices, such as donations to the Beis Hamikdash or gifts to the poor, in which you are parting with the object itself and offering it to G-d. The emphasis is therefore on the object being consecrated. When "all the fat is to G-d"—i.e., your gifts are the choicest and finest possible—then not only is *your observance* beautiful, but the offering *itself* is more complete.

—*Likkutei Sichos, vol. 27, pp. 10–14*

5:17 | ה:י״ז

וְלֹא יָדַע וְאָשֵׁם וְנָשָׂא עֲוֺנוֹ

But he does not know; he is guilty and shall bear his transgression.

What Do You Crave?

Why does the Torah require a person to offer a sacrifice to atone for a sin he committed unknowingly, and in fact even if he is unsure that he transgressed at all?

Chassidus explains that even when one sins unintentionally, the very occurrence of the transgression is indicative of an internal spiritual weakness, for it is a person's subconscious attraction to the prohibited that causes him to sin even *inadvertently*.[15] He is therefore guilty for the choices he made in the past that developed this inner desire to transgress, which then manifests itself in actual—albeit inadvertent—wrongdoing. Conversely, regarding the righteous, Mishlei tells us, "No corruption shall *chance upon* the righteous."[16] The righteous person craves only G-dliness; he will therefore not stumble upon sin even unintentionally.

This explains why the Talmud's classic example of doubtful transgression regards a piece of animal fat. For example, Rashi explains the circumstances that warrant the sacrificing of a "pending guilt-offering":

> A piece of prohibited animal fat and a piece of permissible animal fat lay before someone, and, thinking that either was

---

15. See Tanya, Iggeres Hakodesh, Epistle 28.
16. Mishlei 12:21.

permissible, he ate one. He was later informed that one of those pieces was prohibited fat. As he doesn't know whether the one that he had eaten was indeed the prohibited one, he brings a "pending guilt-offering."[17]

Fat represents lusciousness and pleasure. Accordingly, the doubt whether one has indulged in forbidden fat or not is essentially the question that lies behind every possibility of unintentional sin: have you been drawn to lust the prohibited, or do you delight exclusively in the holy and permissible?

—*Likkutei Sichos, vol. 3, pp. 944–946*

---

17. Rashi, Vayikra 5:17.

צו
Tzav

6:2 | ו:ב

זֹאת תּוֹרַת הָעֹלָה הִוא הָעֹלָה עַל מוֹקְדָה עַל הַמִּזְבֵּחַ כָּל הַלַּיְלָה עַד הַבֹּקֶר

This is the law of the burnt offering, which is the burnt offering that burns on the altar all night until morning.

Limits and Permits

After an animal sacrifice is slaughtered and some of its blood is sprinkled on the altar, the Kohanim burn the choice fats of the animal (and in some instances, all its fats and limbs) on the altar. Though all of this should ideally take place during the daytime, the verse above teaches us that the sacrifice is still valid if the burning of the fats and limbs takes place over the course of the night, and is completed by dawn.

The Rambam, however, rules:

> As a precaution against inadvertent transgression [i.e., the sacrificial parts of the animal not being burned in time], our Sages declared that the fats and limbs of the burnt offerings should be offered on the fire of the altar only until midnight.[1]

---

1. Mishneh Torah, Hil. Maaseh HaKorbanos 4:2.

The Torah instructs and grants authority to the rabbis to create "fences" and boundaries, restricting what is otherwise permissible in order to protect the biblical laws from being transgressed.[2] As a rule, however, the rabbis do not place restrictions on conduct *explicitly sanctioned* by the Torah.[3] Considering that this verse specifically permits burning the sacrificial parts of the animal "all night until morning," how could the Sages require (according to Rambam) that everything be burned before midnight?

The burning of the animal parts on the altar serves two purposes. First, it is a component of the sacrificial service. In this capacity, burning the limbs and fats, like the other components of the service, should be done during the day. But burning these parts of the animal also serves a second purpose: it *prevents* them from being left over until morning, at which point they would be disqualified from being offered on the altar. When the fats and limbs are burned at night, the second objective is achieved, but not the first.

Accordingly, Rambam can explain that the Sages are "restricted from restricting" only when the Torah explicitly sanctions fulfilling a *positive* mitzvah in a particular manner. In instances like burning a sacrifice through the night, however, since the burning at that point is not a positive aspect of the service, but is merely to prevent the sacrifice from being left past its time, the Sages may indeed "limit the permit" granted by the Torah (to burn the sacrifice all night), and require that it be burned before midnight.

—*Likkutei Sichos, vol. 3, pp. 949–950*

---

2. See Vayikra 18:30; Yevamos 21a.
3. See Taz, Orach Chaim 588.

6:4 | ו:ד

וּפָשַׁט אֶת בְּגָדָיו וְלָבַשׁ בְּגָדִים אֲחֵרִים וְהוֹצִיא אֶת הַדֶּשֶׁן אֶל מִחוּץ לַמַּחֲנֶה

He shall then take off his garments and put on other garments, and he shall remove the ashes to outside the camp

Kohanim Without Borders

One of the daily tasks in the Mishkan was to clear the ashes from atop the altar and dispose of them outside the camp.[4]

Although this task was not an actual part of the Temple service, and the Kohen assigned to the job was required to change into clothes of lesser value (so that his priestly garments did not become soiled), no Kohen ever hesitated to do this job.[5]

The Jewish people are called "a kingdom of Kohanim,"[6] and our duties mirror the services performed by the Kohanim in the Temple. Their willingness to do any task, even if it required leaving the camp, teaches us that we must not differentiate between our responsibility to our fellow Jews "within the camp" and those who are "outside the camp." We must not say, "I will devote myself to the spiritual needs of those who are already living a Torah life, but the people who

---

4. In Temple times, outside Jerusalem.
5. See Mishneh Torah, Hil. Temidin U'Musafin 2:14.
6. Shemos 19:6.

are not yet Torah-observant I will leave to others who are more suited to the task."

The service in the Mishkan and the Beis Hamikdash teaches us that this approach is mistaken. The same Kohanim—indeed the very same Kohen[7]—who took part in the Temple service would happily take the ashes outside the camp. Like the Kohen, we must be ready and willing to change "garments," i.e., to engage a fellow Jew on his level, even if he is still a long way from living a life of Torah and mitzvos.

—Likkutei Sichos, vol. 37, p. 6, fn. 33

---

7. See Rashi, Vayikra 6:4.

6:4 | ו:ד

וּפָשַׁט אֶת בְּגָדָיו וְלָבַשׁ בְּגָדִים אֲחֵרִים וְהוֹצִיא
אֶת הַדֶּשֶׁן אֶל מִחוּץ לַמַּחֲנֶה

He shall then take off his garments and put on other garments, and he shall remove the ashes to outside the camp.

Dare to Prepare

The task of clearing the ashes from the altar was not an actual part of the Temple service; its purpose was simply to create more space for fresh wood on the altar. For this reason the Torah obligates the Kohanim to change into garments of lesser value while removing the ashes, so as not to soil their priestly garments.

Rashi explains, "The clothes worn by a servant while cooking a pot of food for his master, he should not wear when he mixes a glass of wine for his master." Just as cooking takes place behind the scenes, in preparation for actually serving the meal, clearing the ash was only a *preliminary* task, not on par with the other services in the Temple. Clearly, it would not be appropriate to wear garments dirtied by this preliminary task when you are actually serving "before the master."

Interestingly, the chore of clearing the ash from the altar, which *preceded* the actual service in the Temple, required only a different set of clothing, not a different servant. The very same Kohanim who performed the rest of the service would clear the ash too, for as true servants of G-d, their primary concern—and likewise that of every Jew, members of the "kingdom of Kohanim"[8]—was for G-d's desire to be fulfilled. With that focus, they made no distinction between roles that complete the mitzvah and those that merely *facilitate* its fulfillment, applying themselves to the preparative tasks as to the mitzvah itself.

—*Likkutei Sichos vol. 37, pp. 4–5*

---

8. Shemos 19:6.

6:6 | ו:ו

אֵשׁ תָּמִיד תּוּקַד עַל הַמִּזְבֵּחַ לֹא תִכְבֶּה

A constant fire shall burn upon the altar; it shall not be extinguished.

Cynical is Criminal

The Torah instructs us to maintain a constant fire burning on the Outer Mizbe'ach in the Temple courtyard. According to the Talmud Yerushalmi,[9] the Torah's emphasis that the fire must be "constant" informs us that even if the Kohanim responsible for the fire are in a state of ritual impurity, which would normally disqualify them from serving in the Temple, they are still obligated to maintain the fire on the altar.

The mitzvah to maintain a constant fire on the altar also applies to the spiritual "Mishkan" that the Torah bids each of us to create within ourselves. The altar represents the heart, and the fire symbolizes the passion and excitement that a Jew should feel toward everything G-dly.

Just as the Kohanim must maintain the fire on the altar even if they are ritually impure, we must never allow the G-dly fire burning in our souls to die, no matter how distant we feel from purity and holiness. By keeping that fire alive, we will ultimately purge ourselves of our "impurity." As the Maggid of Mezeritch explains, "'A constant fire shall burn upon the altar; it shall not be extinguished': When the fire

---

9. Yoma 4:6.

on the altar is constant, the 'not' (i.e., all things negative) will be extinguished."

—*Likkutei Sichos, vol. 1, p. 217*

6:6 | ו:ו

אֵשׁ תָּמִיד תּוּקַד עַל הַמִּזְבֵּחַ

A continuous fire shall burn upon the altar.

Burning Fats, Fueling Flames

In addition to the simple meaning of the verse, instructing us to maintain a constant fire on the altar, the Talmud sees the words "a continuous fire" as an allusion to the fire of the menorah, which is likewise called "a continual lamp."[10] Accordingly, the Talmud extrapolates that the flame used to kindle the Temple menorah must be taken from the fire on the altar.[11]

What is the significance of this requirement?

The light of the menorah symbolizes Torah study, as the verse in Mishlei states, "For a mitzvah is a lamp, and the Torah is light." Like the continuous burning of the menorah's flames, a Jew's obligation to study Torah is constant.

To succeed in Torah study, however, one must be prepared to sacrifice. As the Rambam writes, "He whose heart inspires him to fulfill this mitzvah in a fitting manner and to become crowned with the crown of Torah must remove the desires and pleasures of the times from his heart."[12] To maintain the level of dedication necessary to succeed in Torah study, one must utterly abandon his pursuit of material pleasure.

This principle is hinted at in the Torah's requirement that the fire for the menorah be taken from the Outer Mizbe'ach, upon which the blood and fats of the animal sacrifices were

---

10. Shemos 27:20.
11. Yoma 45b.
12. Mishneh Torah, Hil. Talmud Torah 3:6–9.

offered. This signifies that we "fuel" the fire of the menorah—our continuous fire of Torah study—when our "blood and fats"—our excitement, passion and delight—are completely "consumed" in the pursuit of G-dliness—the fire of the altar.

—*Reshimas HaMenorah, pp. 124-125*

7:31 | ז:לא

וְהִקְטִיר הַכֹּהֵן אֶת הַחֵלֶב הַמִּזְבֵּחָה וְהָיָה הֶחָזֶה לְאַהֲרֹן וּלְבָנָיו

The Kohen shall cause the fat to [go up in] smoke on the altar, and the breast shall belong to Aharon and his sons.

What does Joyful Judaism Mean?

After a sacrifice is slaughtered and some of its blood is sprinkled on the altar, the Kohanim burn the choice fats of the animal on the altar (with the exception of certain sacrifices that are burned in their entirety), and the remaining flesh is eaten. Although eating the sacrificial meat is a mitzvah in its own right, it may not be eaten before the sacrificial parts of the animal have been burned on the altar.

Ramban explains that the objective of the sacrifices is to arouse the individual to offer himself—his inner qualities and character—to G-d.[13] The fats of the animal represent lusciousness and pleasure. Burning the fats on the altar thus symbolizes that we must sacrifice our pursuit of pleasure and delight in order to come close to G-d.

We might assume that this refers only to enjoyment derived from physical delights, meaning that we should not indulge in material gratification. The requirement to sacrifice the fats to G-d even within the context of and *before doing the mitzvah* of eating the sacrificial meat teaches us, however, that even within the realm of holiness the "fat" of the mitzvah itself must be consecrated to G-d alone. In order to fulfill the

---

13. Ramban, Vayikra 1:9.

mitzvos and study the Torah properly, we must not taint these holy pursuits with personal gratification.

Of course, we must study Torah and fulfill the mitzvos with joy and excitement. Our delight, however, must not be a product of the physically enjoyable aspects of the mitzvos or even the intellectual stimulation that Torah study provides, but purely from the great merit that we have in fulfilling G-d's will and studying His wisdom.

—*Likkutei Sichos, vol. 3, p. 950*

שְׁמִינִי
Shemini

9:1-6 | ט:א-ו

וַיְהִי בַּיּוֹם הַשְּׁמִינִי... וַיֹּאמֶר מֹשֶׁה זֶה הַדָּבָר אֲשֶׁר צִוָּה ה' תַּעֲשׂוּ וְיֵרָא אֲלֵיכֶם כְּבוֹד ה'

It was on the eighth day... Moshe said, "This is what G-d has commanded that you do, and the glory of G-d will appear to you."

Drawing Down vs. Drawing Up

The Zohar compares Moshe and Aharon to the *shushvinin*, the groomsman and bridal escort respectively, in the celestial marriage between G-d and the Jewish people.[1] Moshe focused on bringing G-d to the Jewish people; Aharon focused on drawing the people to G-d. Moshe made G-d's wisdom, the Torah, known to the world, whereas Aharon "loved the people, and *drew them* to the Torah."[2]

---

1. See Zohar, Vayikra 53b, et al.
2. Avos 1:12.

While both these tasks are integral to the marriage between G-d and the Jewish people, ultimately Aharon's work is what completes and fulfills G-d's most important desire.

This idea is hinted to by the fact that the Shechinah, the Divine Presence, did not rest in the Mishkan throughout the seven days of its inauguration, during which Moshe assembled and took down the Tabernacle daily. This caused the Jewish people to feel humiliated, says Rashi, until Moshe told them, "My brother Aharon is more worthy and important than I. Through his offerings and his service, the Shechinah will dwell among you."[3] Aharon's service alone caused the Shechinah to dwell among the Jewish people, demonstrating that Aharon's life mission to elevate the Jewish people is what truly brings about G-d's ultimate delight. The goal of Moshe's work—to draw G-dly revelation from above—is to stimulate and facilitate Aharon's work, the Jewish people's ascent from below.

This lends even deeper significance to the Mishnah's directive, "Be of the disciples of Aharon… love the people [lit., creatures] and draw them near to the Torah." In addition to the obvious benefit this brings to those whom we draw near, by doing as Aharon did and drawing others to the Torah, we merit that the Shechinah will dwell in the work of our hands, as it did in Aharon's.

—*Likkutei Sichos, vol. 7, pp. 298–299*

---

3. Rashi, Vayikra 9:23.

10:2 | י:ב

וַתֵּצֵא אֵשׁ מִלִּפְנֵי ה' וַתֹּאכַל אוֹתָם וַיָּמֻתוּ לִפְנֵי ה'

Fire went forth from before G-d and consumed them, and they died before G-d.

Expectations

Why were Nadav and Avihu, the sons of Aharon, punished with sudden death? According to Rabbi Yishmael, they died because they entered the Mishkan under the influence of alcohol, as is evidenced by G-d's immediate warning to Aharon and his surviving sons to refrain from drinking wine before entering the Mishkan.[4]

To illustrate this explanation, the Midrash relates a parable of a king who once found his devoted domestic aide entering a tavern. The king executed him without a word, and appointed another aide in his place. "It might not have been obvious at first why the first aide was put to death," explains the Midrash, "but when the king instructed the new aide, 'Do not enter the doors of taverns,' the cause for the first aide's execution became evident."

Rashi[5] cites Rabbi Yishmael's above explanation and refers the reader to the Midrashic parable: "This is analogous to a king who had a domestic aide, etc., as taught in Vayikra Rabbah." Though he does not quote the parable in full, Rashi draws attention to its opening words, thereby addressing the most troubling issue raised by Rabbi Yishmael's explanation:

---

4. Vayikra Rabbah 12:1.
5. Vayikra 10:2.

How could G-d punish Nadav and Avihu for entering the Mishkan while intoxicated, if they had never been instructed otherwise? The warning not to drink wine before entering the Mishkan was told to Aharon immediately *after* their deaths, but not before!

To explain, Rashi emphasizes that the Midrashic parable likens Nadav and Avihu to the king's trusted aide—בן בית in Hebrew, a member of the king's household. Even though he was not warned, the aide is held accountable for his behavior because as a member of the king's household he should have intuitively sensed that his behavior was against the king's wishes.

The same is true of Nadav and Avihu, of whom G-d told Moshe, "Through *those nearest to Me* I will be sanctified."[6] Even if entering the Mishkan after drinking wine had not yet been explicitly forbidden, the appropriate mode of conduct should have come to Nadav and Avihu instinctively.

—*Likkutei Sichos, vol. 12, pp. 50-52*

---

6. Vayikra 10:3.

10:1-2 | י׳:א-ב

וַיִּקְחוּ בְנֵי אַהֲרֹן נָדָב וַאֲבִיהוּא אִישׁ מַחְתָּתוֹ וַיִּתְּנוּ בָהֵן אֵשׁ וַיָּשִׂימוּ עָלֶיהָ קְטֹרֶת וַיַּקְרִיבוּ לִפְנֵי ה' אֵשׁ זָרָה אֲשֶׁר לֹא צִוָּה אֹתָם: וַתֵּצֵא אֵשׁ מִלִּפְנֵי ה' וַתֹּאכַל אוֹתָם וַיָּמֻתוּ לִפְנֵי ה' (ויקרא י׳, א-ב)

Aharon's sons, Nadav and Avihu, each took his pan, put fire in them, and placed incense upon it, and they brought before G-d foreign fire, which He had not commanded them. Fire went forth from before G-d and consumed them, and they died before G-d.

No Instructions Necessary

The deaths of Nadav and Avihu were not a *punishment* for their actions, according to one explanation suggested by the Ohr Hachaim.[7] Rather, they died by "Divine kiss," in a manner akin to the deaths of Moshe and Aharon—i.e., they sensed G-d's closeness to the point that their souls expired from sheer ecstasy.

According to this interpretation, the Torah's characterization of the incense offered by Nadav and Avihu as "foreign fire, which He had not commanded them" must be understood not as criticism of their offering, but as praise of its virtue. It is called "foreign" because it wholly *surpassed* the fixed service in the Mishkan, for unlike the sacrifices that Aharon offered upon G-d's explicit command, Nadav and Avihu offered their incense without requiring instruction. Their union with G-d was so deep and so much a part of them that they instinctively sensed G-d's desire and acted accordingly.

---

7. Vayikra 16:1.

This explains why, after Aharon's sons' deaths, Moshe told him, "This is what G-d has said, 'I will be sanctified through those near to Me.'"[8] Based on the Midrash, Rashi explains that Moshe said to Aharon, "I knew that this House was to be sanctified through G-d's beloved ones, but I thought it would be either through me or through you. Now I see that they were greater than both of us!"[9] Nadav and Avihu, through their profound union with G-d, elicited a Divine response even greater than the G-dly revelation elicited by the sacrifices that Moshe and Aharon offered. Their *instinctive* worship of G-d, without requiring instruction, caused "the House to be—truly and *inherently*—sanctified."

—*Likkutei Sichos, vol. 32, pp. 98-102*

---

8. Vayikra 10:3.
9. Rashi ad loc.

11:17 | י:א׳

וְאֶת־הַחֲזִיר כִּי־מַפְרִיס פַּרְסָה הוּא וְשֹׁסַע שֶׁסַע פַּרְסָה וְהוּא גֵּרָה לֹא־יִגָּר טָמֵא הוּא לָכֶם

And the pig, because it has a cloven hoof that is completely split, but will not regurgitate its cud; it is unclean for you.

Act Now, Perfect Later

In the future, says the Ohr Hachaim, the pig will regurgitate its cud and will thereby become a fully kosher animal (since it already has split hooves.) This is alluded to in the words of the verse above, "the pig [is unkosher] because it has a cloven hoof *but* will not regurgitate its cud," which the Ohr Hachaim interprets to mean that it is unkosher only *so long as* it does not do so. Implied is that its nature and status is subject to change.[10]

Notably, the notion of a non-kosher animal being transformed in the future is unique to the pig, whose current "deficiency" is that it does not regurgitate its cud. Animals that regurgitate but lack split hooves will remain forbidden forever.

Why?

An animal that regurgitates its cud, thoroughly processing its food in order to make the food more digestible, symbolizes a person whose inner character is refined and up to par. In contrast, the pig does not process its food as thoroughly, but it bears the other sign of a kosher animal on the limbs with which it moves—it has split hooves. The pig thus represents a

---

10. This idea is mentioned in other Kabbalistic works as well. See Shnei Luchos Habris (Shaloh), Parshas Chayei Sarah; Me'orei Or, Ches, 6.

person whose inner character is unrefined but whose actions are nevertheless satisfactory.

In his current state, this person is deficient. In the future era of Moshiach, however, the entire universe will be elevated and refined, including the individual. Therefore, combined with his ample good deeds, this person will bear both spiritual qualities represented by the kosher signs, as is evidenced by the pig becoming fully kosher. Animals that only regurgitate their cud, however, will remain non-kosher even in the era of Moshiach, symbolizing that even exceptional inner refinement (such as that which the coming of Moshiach will bring) cannot compensate for a dearth of actual mitzvos performed and practical good accomplished.

—*Sefer Hasichos 5751, vol. 1, pp. 162–163, fn. 78*

11:9 | יא:ט

אֶת זֶה תֹּאכְלוּ מִכֹּל אֲשֶׁר בַּמָּיִם כֹּל אֲשֶׁר לוֹ סְנַפִּיר וְקַשְׂקֶשֶׂת בַּמַּיִם בַּיַּמִּים וּבַנְּחָלִים אֹתָם תֹּאכֵלוּ

From all that are in the water, you may eat any (living creature) that has fins and scales, whether it lives in the waters, seas or rivers; you may eat only these.

Fins and Scales

Two external features identify a kosher fish: a layer of scales that protect its body, and a set of fins that it uses to swim.

Fish symbolize Torah scholars. Like fish, which are always underwater, scholars are constantly immersed in the lifegiving waters of the Torah.[11] As such, the identifying features of a kosher fish also represent two qualities that are required of a Torah scholar, even when the "body" of his scholarship is undisputed.

The fish uses its fins to propel itself forward, quickly moving from one location to another. This represents the scholar's obligation to expound upon the Torah knowledge that he has received from others, to discover new layers of Torah interpretation and to explore novel approaches to its application.

But fins are only one of the requisite signs of a kosher fish; it must also be covered by a protective layer of scales. The Talmud compares the fear of G-d to a preservative, without which one's Torah study can spoil.[12] Similarly, the protective scales that identify a kosher fish represent the fear of G-d that must accompany one's Torah study.

---

11. See Berachos 61b.
12. Shabbos 31a.

This explains the spiritual significance of the Mishnah's statement that the presence of scales on a fish is an automatic proof that it is kosher, even though fins alone do not provide such proof. In the Mishnah's words, "Every fish that has scales also has fins, though there are some fish that have fins but have no scales."[13] This means that fear of G-d not only saves your Torah scholarship from spoilage and ensures that it will have the desired effect on your life; it also guarantees that you will ultimately make your own contribution to the chain of authentic Torah wisdom.

—*Reshimos, no. 39*

---

13. Niddah 6:9.

11:17 | יא:יז

וְאֶת הַכּוֹס וְאֶת הַשָּׁלָךְ וְאֶת הַיַּנְשׁוּף

The owl, the shalach and the little owl.

A Fish's Tale

What type of bird is the *shalach*, listed here among the non-kosher fowl?

"Our rabbis explained," says Rashi, "that it draws up fish from the sea." Its name, *shalach*, is similar to the Hebrew word for drawing out, *sholeh*, indicating that the manner in which this bird "draws out" is exceptional—it extracts its prey from deep within the water.

Rashi's words also hint to something else that the *shalach* extracts from the sea in addition to its prey.

The Talmud[14] relates that upon seeing a *shalach*, Rabbi Yochanan would proclaim, "Your judgments are vast depths!"[15] The commentaries explain that Rabbi Yochanan was referring to G-d's "judgment *in* the vast depths of the sea," whereby He sends the *shalach* to kill those fish whose time has come to die. This Talmudic passage supports the Baal Shem Tov's teaching that G-d's providence is not limited to humans; it extends to all wildlife, plant life, and even inanimate creations.

This extraordinary concept is hinted to in Rashi's words regarding the *shalach*. The Divine Providence that dictates every detail of creation hides beneath the veil of nature, like the vast and complex marine world that hides beneath the surface of the ocean. But Rabbi Yochanan's statement teach-

---

14. Chullin 63a.
15. Tehillim 36:7.

es us that the workings of nature are neither random nor spontaneous; even the lives and behavior patterns of fish and birds are precisely coordinated by Divine plan. Hence, what "our rabbis explained"—Rabbi Yochanan's insight about the *shalach* setting upon its prey as an emissary to carry out G-d's judgment—"draws up" what is hidden beneath the analogical "sea," extracting the Divine Providence found in the details of creation from beneath its veil.

—*Likkutei Sichos, vol. 7, pp. 60-64*

תזריע
Tazria

12:2 | יב:ב

אִשָּׁה כִּי תַזְרִיעַ וְיָלְדָה

If a woman conceives and gives birth...

Seeds of Rebirth

Parshas Tazria derives its name, "*Tazria*—she conceives," from the brief discussion about childbirth at its start.

The bulk of the Parshah, however, deals with the laws pertaining to *tzaraas*, a spiritual condition that affects a person's skin, clothing or home. Being afflicted with *tzaraas* is so miserable that the Talmud[1] likens it to death!

So how do these laws come under the name and banner of *Tazria*, which signifies birth and new life?

This unlikely name provides profound insight into the true objective of *tzaraas* and Divine retribution in general.

"*Tzaraas*," writes Maimonides,

---

1. Nedarim 64b.

is a sign and a wonder prevalent among the Jewish people to warn them against *lashon hara*, "undesirable speech." For when one speaks *lashon hara*, the walls of his house change color. If he repents, the house will become pure again. If, however, he persists in his wickedness until his house requires demolition, the leatherwear in his house upon which he sits and lies will change color.... If he persists in his wickedness until they require burning, the clothes he wears will change color.... If he persists in his wickedness until they require burning, his skin will change and develop *tzaraas*. He will be isolated and made known to the public until he ceases to engage in the talk of the wicked, namely mockery and *lashon hara*.[2]

The ordeal of *tzaraas* is thus essentially G-d's way of rehabilitating a person from habitually speaking *lashon hara*. Its purpose is to warn the affected to amend their speaking habits, or, when necessary, to force them into isolation in order to completely retrain them. The experience of *tzaraas* ultimately gives a person a new lease on life, freeing him from the wretched and pathetic life of a gossipmonger. Hence, the name of the Parshah, "*Tazria*—she conceives," because *tzaraas*, and likewise all the other punishments described in the Torah, are G-d's compassionate means of providing a sinner the seeds for renewal.

—*Likkutei Sichos, vol. 22, pp. 70–73*

---

2. Mishneh Torah, Hil. Tum'as Tzaraas 16:10.

12:2 | יב:ב

אִשָּׁה כִּי תַזְרִיעַ וְיָלְדָה זָכָר וְטָמְאָה שִׁבְעַת יָמִים

If a woman conceives and gives birth to a male, she shall be unclean for seven days.

The Hardest Thing to Change is Yourself

Parshas Tazria discusses several types of impurity associated with the human body, and teaches us how to purify ourselves from them. Rashi notes that this follows the previous Parshah's discussion concerning which animals are "pure" (kosher) and which are not. Quoting from the Midrash, Rashi explains: "Just as man's creation was after the creation of all animals, beasts and birds, likewise the Torah states the laws concerning the status of man after the laws regarding animals, beasts and birds."

Why indeed did G-d create man on the sixth day of creation, after everything else? The Midrash explains: "So that if he is not meritorious, we say to him, 'A gnat preceded you, a snail preceded you.'"[3] Man was created last to indicate that, in a certain sense, humankind is *inferior* to all the animals that preceded us in the order of creation. As explained in Tanya,[4] the inferiority the Midrash refers to is man's inherent ability to *desire* what G-d forbids—let alone actually disobey G-d's commands. Animals and beasts are incapable of defying the G-dly mission and purpose for which G-d created them;

---

3. Vayikra Rabbah 14:1
4. Likkutei Amarim, chapter 29.

only the human being is capable of being drawn to behavior that G-d despises and forbids. In this sense, the innate nature of the human being is lowlier than that of insects, beasts and fowl.

The laws of identifying kosher and non-kosher, pure and impure, represent the spiritual refinement of various aspects of creation through the guidance of the Torah. As a rule, the Torah gradually advances the learner from lighter topics and easier tasks to those that are more difficult to grasp and accomplish.[5] The final task that the Torah addresses is therefore the refinement of the coarse human body. Creation of man came after the creation of the animals, because man alone has the potential to directly oppose G-d's will, unlike any other creation. For that very reason, his "laws" and refinement are the most difficult task of all.

—*Likkutei Sichos, vol. 7, pp. 74–76*

---

5. See Mishnah, Avos 5:22; Talmud, Pesachim 68b, et al.

יג:ב | 13:2

אָדָם כִּי יִהְיֶה בְעוֹר בְּשָׂרוֹ שְׂאֵת אוֹ סַפַּחַת אוֹ בַהֶרֶת וְהָיָה בְעוֹר בְּשָׂרוֹ לְנֶגַע צָרָעַת

A person to whom shall occur in the skin of his flesh a se'eis or sapachas or baheres [patches of varying degrees of whiteness], and it be in the skin of his flesh the plague of tzaraas.

The Costly Effects of Cheap Talk

Tzaraas is, according to the Talmud,[6] G-d's supernatural method of deterring a person from *lashon hara*, speaking derogatorily about another person.

Yet when Rambam discusses the link between *tzaraas* and *lashon hara*, he also mentions other forms of undesirable speech. In his words:

> This is the pattern of the gatherings of the wicked scoffers: In the beginning, they speak excessively about empty matters.... Because of this, they come to speak negatively of the righteous.... Consequently, they will become accustomed to speaking against the prophets and casting aspersions on their words.... Ultimately, this leads them to deny G-d's existence entirely.... This is the speech of the wicked...[7]

By including all forms of undesirable speech in this discussion, the Rambam identifies and defines the essential pitfall of speaking *lashon hara*: the undesirable *speech* itself.

---

6. Arachin 16a.
7. Mishneh Torah, Hil. Tum'as Tzaraas 16:10.

The faculty of speech, despite being merely a tool of outward expression, is rooted deep within the soul; Jewish philosophers aptly categorize humankind as "the species that speaks." Consequently, even when *lashon hara* seems to bring no harm to the subject, nor does it stem from the evil character of the one speaking,[8] it has the potential to drag an otherwise righteous person towards actual evil. Negative speech *at any level*, the Rambam is telling us, can ultimately lead a person as far as heresy.

That is why the ailment of *tzaraas* is superficial: to symbolically warn those afflicted with it to change their speaking habits immediately, to prevent their ostensibly meaningless statements from resulting in profound flaws in their character.

—*Likkutei Sichos, vol. 22, pp. 66-68*

---

8. In fact, the classic example of someone afflicted with *tzaraas* for speaking *lashon hara* is Miriam, who was exceptionally righteous and intended no harm to Moshe when she spoke about him.

13:2 | יג:ב

נֶגַע צָרַעַת הוּא וְרָאָהוּ הַכֹּהֵן וְטִמֵּא אֹתוֹ

It is a lesion of tzaraas; when the Kohen sees it, he shall pronounce him unclean.

The Qualified Judge

A person afflicted with *tzaraas* can be deemed pure or impure only by a Kohen. "If the Kohen present does not know how to assess the skin discolorations [to determine if they meet the qualifications of *tzaraas*]," writes the Rambam, "a scholar observes them and instructs the Kohen: 'Declare, "You are impure,"' and the Kohen says: 'You are impure;' 'Declare, "You are pure,"' and the Kohen says: 'You are pure.'"[9]

This rule reflects the extreme sensitivity necessary when passing judgment on others, especially when the ramifications are as harsh as the impurity associated with *tzaraas*.

The Torah requires a person deemed impure with *tzaraas* to "dwell in isolation; his dwelling is outside the camp."[10] He is distanced from the entire community, even from others who are impure themselves! The Torah therefore insists that only a Kohen can declare someone impure, for a Kohen is "a man of kindness"[11] who "blesses the Jewish nation *with love*."[12] The Torah is certain that out of his love and genuine concern for his fellow Jew, the Kohen will spare no effort (within the guidelines of *halachah*) to try and find an angle from which

---

9. Mishneh Torah, Hil. Tum'as Tzaraas 9:2.
10. Vayikra 13:46.
11. Devarim 33:8.
12. From the blessing that the Kohanim recite before Birkas Kohanim.

to save a person from the isolation and misery that comes with the impurity of *tzaraas*.

The same is true anytime we see something unfavorable in another person, even if it is so bad that the person deserves to be distanced from the community. Before passing judgment on our fellow Jew, we must remember that only someone with a genuine sense of love and kindness toward his fellow (in addition to his knowledge of what the Torah deems right and wrong) can make such an important judgment call.

Like a Kohen, we must be certain that our sense of judgment is balanced with genuine love for our fellow Jew and sensitivity to his plight.

—*Likkutei Sichos, vol. 27, pp. 88–90*

13:14 | יג:יד

וּבְיוֹם הֵרָאוֹת בּוֹ בָּשָׂר חַי יִטְמָא

But on the day that live flesh is seen in it, he shall become unclean.

The Mitzvos of a Sinful Jew

Before a person afflicted with *tzaraas* is deemed impure, he must be examined by a Kohen to determine if his lesions indeed bear the signs of impurity. Only certain days are suitable for this examination, which the Talmud derives from the Torah's choice of the words "*On the day* that live flesh is seen in it," rather than, "*When* live flesh is seen in it."[13] For example, says Rabbi Yehudah, the lesions of a bridegroom are not examined during the seven days of his wedding celebration, and no lesions are examined during holidays. We do not disrupt the joy of observing the holidays or fulfilling the mitzvah of marriage with an examination for possible impurity.

The Torah's barring of examination for *tzaraas* on these days is remarkable.

"*Tzaraas*," writes Maimonides,

> is a sign and a wonder prevalent among the Jewish people to warn them against *lashon hara*, "undesirable speech." For when one speaks *lashon hara*, the walls of his house change color. If he repents, the house will become pure again. If, however, he persists in his wickedness until his house requires demolition, the leatherwear in his house upon which he sits and lies will change color.... If he persists in his wick-

---

13. Moed Katan 7b.

edness until they require burning, the clothes he wears will change color.... If he persists in his wickedness until they require burning, his skin will change and develop *tzaraas*. He will be isolated and made known to the public until he ceases to engage in the talk of the wicked, namely mockery and *lashon hara*.[14]

Evidently, the *tzaraas-* affected person whose mitzvah observance the Torah is accommodating is a repeat offender of the horrible sin of *lashon hara*! Yet his examination is delayed in order to allow him to properly celebrate his marriage or the holidays.

This illustrates the power of a Jew's observance of a mitzvah, regardless of his spiritual state: the holiness of his mitzvah can prevail over and even suspend the impurity caused by his otherwise sinful behavior.

—*Likkutei Sichos, vol. 37, pp. 37–41*

---

14. Mishneh Torah, Hil. Tum'as Tzaraas 16:10.

13:36 | יג:מו

כָּל יְמֵי אֲשֶׁר הַנֶּגַע בּוֹ... בָּדָד יֵשֵׁב מִחוּץ לַמַּחֲנֶה מוֹשָׁבוֹ

All the days the lesion is upon him... he shall dwell in isolation; his dwelling is outside the camp.

Preventive Medicine

The impurity of a *metzora*, a person afflicted with *tzaraas*, is unusually severe in that a *metzora*'s mere entry into a home conveys impurity to the home's contents.

Rabbi Yehudah[15] opines that this applies only when the *metzora* enters the house with permission, in which case the house is deemed "the *metzora*'s dwelling" and becomes impure. If the *metzora* enters without permission, however, Rabbi Yehudah says that "everything remains pure unless he stays long enough for a candle to be kindled."

What is the reasoning behind this leniency? According to Rabbi Yehudah, the home is deemed "the *metzora*'s dwelling" only if the residents of the home approve of his entry. As the people of the home might be preoccupied with something else when the *metzora* first enters, Rabbi Yehudah allows for the time it would take to light a candle before deeming them compliant. What is the significance of the time it takes to light a candle? The Sages based this allowance on the lighting of the Shabbos candles, which one may not interrupt before the *berachah* has been recited, and therefore one could not tell the *metzora* to leave.[16]

---

15. See Mishnah, Nega'im 13:11; Tosefta, Nega'im 7:11.
16. See Tiferes Yisrael, Nega'im ad loc.

That the lighting of Shabbos candles is the "standard" which determines how long the impurity of *tzaraas* can be kept at bay is a powerful indication of the importance of lighting Shabbos candles.

The purpose of the Shabbos candles, says the Talmud, is to promote *shalom bayis*, peace *in the home.* The light of the candles allows the people of the home to enjoy Shabbos by eliminating the discomfort caused by darkness and the discord it engenders. And just as the Shabbos candles save the home from physical distress, the light of this mitzvah also protects the home from any spiritual maladies—in this case, the impurity of *tzaraas*. Moreover, *tzaraas* is caused by *lashon hara*, derogatory speech, which "causes rifts between husband and wife or between man and his fellow."[17] It thus follows that the way to fend off the divisiveness and discord that is synonymous with *tzaraas* is the kindling of the Shabbos candles, which promote peace and harmony.

—*Likkutei Sichos, vol. 17, pp. 141-143*

---

17. Arachin 16a–b.

מצורע
Metzora

14:2 | יד:ב

זֹאת תִּהְיֶה תּוֹרַת הַמְּצֹרָע בְּיוֹם טָהֳרָתוֹ

This shall be the law of the metzora, on the day of his purification.

Skin Deep

The Talmud records a conversation between Eliyahu Hanavi and Rabbi Yehoshua ben Levi regarding the whereabouts of Moshiach. Eliyahu tells Rabbi Yehoshua that Moshiach can be found at the entrance to the city,[1] sitting among the poor and sickly.[2] According to Rashi, and as is implied elsewhere in the Talmud,[3] "the sickly" refers to people suffering from *tzaraas*, and Moshiach himself is also a *metzora*—a person afflicted with *tzaraas*.

Why is Moshiach said to be a *metzora*?

---

1. Rome, according to some variants of the text.
2. Sanhedrin 98a.
3. Ibid. 98b.

The Torah calls *tzaraas* an affliction *"in the skin of* his flesh,"[4] not a disease of the flesh itself. This indicates, says the Alter Rebbe,[5] that a person can develop *tzaraas* only when he has eradicated his deep internal character flaws, and his spiritual blemishes are solely skin-deep. Since the person has already refined himself entirely "from within," and his shortcomings are only superficial, G-d afflicts him with a supernatural skin condition to prompt him to perfect even these slight and uncharacteristic imperfections.[6]

Accordingly, we can understand why the Talmud identifies Moshiach as someone suffering from *tzaraas*. Moshiach's condition reflects the collective state of the Jewish people in the final days of our exile. Over the generations, the Jewish nation has been effectively refined, both in body and in soul; any remaining imperfections are largely only external. Therefore, in the final days before the redemption, Moshiach, the collective soul of the Jewish people, is comparable to a *metzora*, whose deficiencies are only slight and superficial. It is only a matter of moments until we perfect even these final details and merit our complete and final redemption.

—*Likkutei Sichos, vol. 22, pp. 75-79*

---

4. Vayikra 13:2.
5. Likkutei Torah, Vayikra 22b.
6. The Alter Rebbe thereby explains why *tzaraas* is virtually nonexistent nowadays—because people with no internal imperfections are difficult to find.

14:2 | יד:ב

זֹאת תִּהְיֶה תּוֹרַת הַמְּצֹרָע בְּיוֹם טָהֳרָתוֹ וְהוּבָא אֶל הַכֹּהֵן

This shall be the law of the metzora, on the day of his purification; he shall be brought to the Kohen.

Ready or Not

A *metzora*, a person afflicted with *tzaraas*, must remain outside the community encampment until his *tzaraas* heals. The isolation reflects his sorry spiritual state. *Tzaraas* is a punishment for *lashon hara*, speaking derogatorily about others, which causes strife and conflict.[7] Holiness, in contrast, is characterized by unity and harmony. The *metzora's* association with strife, the polar opposite of holiness, requires that he be separated and isolated from the rest of Bnei Yisrael's holy camp.

This gives even more depth to the Torah's statement that the *metzora* "will be brought to the Kohen." The verse is difficult to understand literally, for it is the Kohen who approaches the *metzora* and not vice versa, as the impure *metzora* may not enter the camp. Moreover, why does the verse specify that the *metzora* and not vice versa, "shall be brought," instead of saying that he will go on his own?

With these words, however, the Torah is hinting that the *spiritual* rehabilitation of the *metzora* is not merely a possibility, but an *eventuality*: "He shall be brought to the Kohen" whether he desires to be purified or not.

---

7. See Rashi, Vayikra 13:46.

The *metzora*, completely distanced from the Jewish camp, is also symbolic of a person so utterly removed from holiness that to willingly return to a Jewish lifestyle seems entirely unnatural for him. In fact, he may desire just the opposite. Nevertheless, the Torah foretells and guarantees that "he *shall* be brought to the Kohen"—even a person as distant as a *metzora* will ultimately do *teshuvah* and return to G-d and His ways. For, as is explained in Tanya,[8] before the coming of Moshiach, G-d will arouse a spirit of *teshuvah* in the heart of every single Jew, bringing him to the "Kohen," as it were, for purification, even if he is not on the level of seeking *teshuvah* on his own.

—*Likkutei Sichos, vol. 7, pp. 100–102*

---

[8]. Chapter 39.

יד:לד | 14:34

כִּי תָבֹאוּ אֶל אֶרֶץ כְּנַעַן... וְנָתַתִּי נֶגַע צָרַעַת בְּבֵית אֶרֶץ אֲחֻזַּתְכֶם

When you come to the land of Canaan... I will place a lesion of tzaraas upon a house in the land of your possession. (Vayikra 14:34)

Words of Worth

Rashi notes that the phrase "When you come to the land of Canaan... I will place a lesion of *tzaraas*..." implies that the future occurrence of *tzaraas* on the walls of Bnei Yisrael's homes would not be a misfortune, but in fact something to anticipate. Based on the Midrash, Rashi explains:

> For the Amorites (אמוריים) had hidden away golden treasures inside the walls of their houses throughout the forty years that the Jews were in the desert. As a result of a lesion, one would demolish his house and find [the treasures].

Although the verse speaks of *tzaraas* occurring on homes throughout the land of Canaan (which was inhabited by seven different nations), Rashi specifies that the hidden treasures were in the walls of the Amorite homes, thereby alluding to the unique association between *tzaraas* and what the Amorite nation represented.

According to Chassidus, each of the seven nations that Bnei Yisrael drove out of the land of Canaan represents a negative character trait that we must endeavor to eradicate from within ourselves. The Amorites represented the sins of speech and excessive chatter,[9] of which the verse in Mishlei

---

[9]. See Torah Ohr 102c.

says, "Where there is much talking, sin cannot be avoided."[10] This is hinted at in their name, אמורי, spelled with the same letters as the root word אמר, meaning "say" or "speak." Likewise, the occurrence of *tzaraas* was a punishment and warning to abstain from *lashon hara*, speaking derogatorily about others, and "from the talk of the wicked" in general.[11]

Therein lies the profound message conveyed by the presence of golden treasures specifically in the walls of the Amorite homes: Despite its pitfalls, speech has the ability to *reveal hidden resources and treasures* that may otherwise remain dormant within us. The ultimate goal is therefore not only to eliminate negative speech, but also to utilize the extensive power of speech for good, to share words of Torah and wisdom, or to speak positively about another Jew.

—*Likkutei Sichos, vol. 32, pp. 91–97*

---

10. Mishlei 10:19.
11. Rambam, Mishneh Torah, Hil. Tum'as Tzaraas 16:10.

14:34 | יד:לד

כִּי תָבֹאוּ אֶל אֶרֶץ כְּנַעַן... וְנָתַתִּי נֶגַע צָרַעַת בְּבֵית אֶרֶץ אֲחֻזַּתְכֶם

When you come to the land of Canaan... I will place a lesion of tzaraas upon a house in the land of your possession.

Treasure Land

When *tzaraas* appeared on a person's skin, its initial and most obvious effect was an impurity so severe that the person must "dwell isolated, outside the camp,"[12] separate even from other impure people. At the same time, however, Rambam explains *tzaraas* as a G-d-given "sign and wonder prevalent among the Jewish people, to warn them against *lashon hara*, undesirable speech," and to motivate them to repent from such behavior.[13] Hence, despite the lowliness of its impurity, *tzaraas* ultimately facilitated the great ascent of *teshuvah*, of which our Sages say, "Where penitents stand, even the wholly righteous do not stand!"[14]

In a similar vein, the occurrence of *tzaraas* on the walls of a person's home, which required the house to be demolished, signified the presence of both extraordinary spiritual filth *and* astonishing wealth. On the one hand, the Zohar attributes *tzaraas* to an exceedingly impure spirit brought upon the home by the idolatrous inhabitants who dwelled there previously.[15] G-d caused *tzaraas* to appear there, because only total

---

12. Vayikra 13:46.
13. Mishneh Torah, Hil. Tum'as Tzaraas 16:10.
14. Talmud, Berachos 34b.
15. Zohar 3:50a.

demolition of the house would drive away that particularly impure spirit. Yet paradoxically, Rashi writes,

> The Amorites had hidden away treasures of gold inside the walls of their houses throughout the forty years that the Jews were in the desert. As a result of a lesion of *tzaraas* [appearing on the walls of the home], one would demolish his house and find the treasures.[16]

Spiritually, this means that the houses most affected by idolatry were actually home to troves of *spiritual wealth* so abundant that it became manifest even in physical wealth—golden treasures that were discovered upon the homes' destruction.

These paradox-laden phenomena of *tzaraas* demonstrate that precisely in the lowest of situations lies the potential—through *teshuvah*—for the greatest heights.

—*Likkutei Sichos, vol. 27, pp. 107–110*

---

16. Vayikra 14:34.

14:36 | יד:לו

וְצִוָּה הַכֹּהֵן וּפִנּוּ אֶת הַבַּיִת בְּטֶרֶם יָבֹא הַכֹּהֵן לִרְאוֹת אֶת הַנֶּגַע וְלֹא יִטְמָא כָּל אֲשֶׁר בַּבָּיִת

The Kohen shall order that they clear out the house before the Kohen comes to look at the lesion, so that everything in the house should not become unclean.

Precious Possessions

When discolorations resembling *tzaraas* appear on the walls of a person's home, a Kohen is called to determine if these are signs of impurity or not. Until the Kohen declares otherwise, the home and everything inside of it remain pure. Therefore, before beginning his inspection, the Kohen instructs the owners of the home (and allows them time) to clear it of its contents.

The Mishnah[17] notes that even if the contents of the house would become impure, the loss would be minimal, for clothing, as well as metal and wooden utensils, can easily be restored to their pure status by immersion in a *mikvah*. The Torah's concern was solely for earthenware vessels, which cannot be purified, so the damage would be permanent if they were to become impure.

To put things in perspective: The supernatural occurrence of *tzaraas* on a person's home is a result of his indulgence "in the talk of the wicked—i.e., mockery and *lashon hara*."[18] Yet the Torah delays the examination of his house in order

---

17. Negaim 12:5, quoted in Rashi, Vayikra 14:36.
18. Mishneh Torah, Hil. Tum'as Tzaraas 16:10.

to save even the simplest of his personal possessions from being ruined.

This illustrates just how cherished every Jew is in the eyes of G-d, just by virtue of his inherent Jewishness. Despite the lowly level to which *metzora* has fallen, he and everything associated with him—even his most petty belongings!—forever remain G-d's top priority.

—*Likkutei Sichos, vol. 37, pp. 37–41*

15:16 | טו:טז

וְרָחַץ בַּמַּיִם אֶת כָּל בְּשָׂרוֹ

He must immerse all his flesh in water.

Keeping Your Head Underwater

The Torah's laws concerning ritual impurities and their means of purification are in the category of *chukim*—Divine decrees that transcend any reason or understanding. Nevertheless, writes Rambam, there is an important lesson in character development to be learned from one of the primary methods of ascending from ritual impurity: immersion in the waters of a *mikvah*.

> Just as one who intends to be purified becomes pure as soon as he immerses himself... so too, one who sets his heart on purifying himself from the filth that besets men's souls—namely, crooked ideals and negative traits—becomes clean as soon as he resolves in his heart to abandon those ideals, and immerses his soul in the waters of knowledge.[19]

But is this comparison accurate? In order for immersion in a physical *mikvah* to be effective, the entire body, including the head, must be submerged *beneath* the water's surface.[20] In the analogy, however, in which the spiritual purification occurs via "the waters of knowledge," it would seem that the

---

19. Mishneh Torah, Hil. Mikvaos 11:12.
20. In fact, the Sages determined the amount of water necessary to constitute a mikvah based on this very requirement—"it must be sufficient water for one's entire body to be covered therein" (Pesachim 109a).

objective should be to *unify* your mind with the knowledge, not to submerge your mind *beneath* it.

The Rambam's use of this analogy, however, is precise. By comparing spiritual purification and transformation to immersion in a *mikvah,* the Rambam is emphasizing that in order to purify yourself from the impurities of the soul, it is not enough to *fill* your mind with Torah wisdom; you must submerge and lower your head, as it were, so that the waters of Torah rise *above* you. Meaning that you must submit yourself entirely to the Torah's ideals, with a devotion that surpasses the extent of your understanding and intellect.

—*Igros Kodesh, vol. 5, p. 90;*
Toras Menachem, vol. 7, pp. 57–58

אחרי
Acharei

16:1 | א:טז

וַיְדַבֵּר ה' אֶל מֹשֶׁה אַחֲרֵי מוֹת שְׁנֵי בְּנֵי אַהֲרֹן בְּקָרְבָתָם לִפְנֵי ה'

G-d spoke to Moshe after the death of Aharon's two sons, when they drew near before G-d.

The Afterdeath

The first 34 verses of Acharei Mos discuss the holiest person, place, and time in the Jewish experience. They detail the service of the Kohen Gadol, the High Priest—who is "separated, to be sanctified as most holy [of people],"[1] in the Kodesh Hakodashim, the Holy of Holies in the Temple—the most sanctified space in the world, on Yom Kippur—the holiest day on the calendar.

Reading this Parshah annually encourages us too to likewise strive for holiness. The key to this quest for holiness lies in the name Acharei Mos.

---

1. I Divrei Hayamim 23:13.

The words *acharei mos* literally mean "after the death of," and refer to the circumstances in which G-d conveyed to Moshe the mitzvos recorded in this Parshah: after the deaths of Aharon's sons Nadav and Avihu. According to Chassidic teaching,[2] they died as a direct result of their ecstatic love of G-d, which became too intense for their bodies to handle. They truly "drew near before G-d,"[3] albeit to a fault. Thus the name Acharei Mos—"*After* the death [of the sons of Aharon]," implies that there is still something to strive for even after reaching the extraordinary heights Nadav and Avihu reached at their deaths.

How is this possible? We are told in the following Parshah, "You shall be holy, *because* I, Hashem, your G-d, am holy."[4] This means that a Jew has the ability to reach truly unlimited levels of holiness, mirroring the infinite holiness of G-d Himself, as the soul of every Jew is "a veritable part of G-d above."[5]

The Torah therefore categorizes the mitzvos given in this parsha as "*Acharei Mos*," after—or *beyond*—the "deaths of the sons of Aharon," to teach us that even if we have reached what seems to be the "spiritual ceiling" for a living human being, there is still more work to be done and greater holiness to attain.

—*Likkutei Sichos, vol. 12, pp. 92–93*

---

2. See also Ohr Hachaim, Vayikra 16:1.
3. Vayikra 16:1.
4. Vayikra 9:2.
5. Tanya, Likkutei Amarim, chapter 2.

טז:א | 16:1

וַיְדַבֵּר ה' אֶל מֹשֶׁה אַחֲרֵי מוֹת שְׁנֵי בְּנֵי אַהֲרֹן בְּקָרְבָתָם לִפְנֵי ה' וַיָּמֻתוּ

G-d spoke to Moshe after the death of Aharon's two sons, when they drew near before G-d and they died.

Business before Pleasure

The Parshah of Acharei Mos opens, "G-d spoke to Moshe after the death of Aharon's two sons, when they drew near before G-d and they died." The wording of this verse seems unnecessarily repetitive. Having established that this was taking place "after the death of the sons of Aharon," and explaining the circumstances in which they died—"when they drew near to G-d"—why repeat "and they died"?

According to an interpretation offered by Ohr Hachaim[6] regarding the cause of Nadav and Avihu's death, the words "and they died" can be understood not as repeating the fact that they died, but explaining *why* they died.

Nadav and Avihu died "by the kiss of G-d," says Ohr Hachaim. He explains this to mean that they sensed and delighted in the closeness of G-d to the point that their souls expired from sheer ecstasy.

Chassidus explains, however, that Nadav and Avihu's demise under such circumstances is regarded as sinful. Granted, a Jew must aspire to transcend the constraints of physicality in unbridled devotion to G-d, but at the same time it is imperative to acknowledge that G-d grants us physical life because

---

6. Or Hachaim, Vayikra 16:1.

He desires that we transform *this physical world* into a place where His presence is manifest. Our ultimate objective must therefore be not to escape mortal life, but to remain within and sanctify it. In contrast, the conduct of Nadav and Avihu, who allowed their spiritual rapture to reach a point of no return, is regarded as a "sin."

This is the meaning of the verse "After the death of the two sons of Aharon, when they drew near before G-d and they died." What brought about the death? Why was their conduct displeasing to G-d? Because "they drew near before G-d *and they died*" — i.e., they opted to delight in the closeness to G-d, to love G-d to death quite literally, at the expense of fulfilling their mission to infuse holiness into mortal life.

—*Likkutei Sichos, vol. 3, pp. 987–988*

16:6 | טז:ו

וְכִפֶּר בַּעֲדוֹ וּבְעַד בֵּיתוֹ

He will initiate atonement for himself and for his household.

Homeward Bound

One of the integral components of the Kohen Gadol's Yom Kippur service was the bull offering, the blood of which he sprinkled in the Kodesh Hakodashim, the Holy of Holies, to atone "for himself and for his household." "His household," explains the Mishnah,[7] refers to his wife. The Mishnah deduces from here that an unmarried Kohen Gadol was not suitable for the Yom Kippur service.

The requirement that the Kohen Gadol be married contrasts with the mistake made by Nadav and Avihu, whose deaths are mentioned at the beginning of this Parshah. They were punished, according to one opinion in the Midrash, because they never married, or according to another opinion, because they (consequently) never had children.[8] As Chassidus explains, Nadav and Avihu sought spiritual ecstasy and rapturous love of G-d to such an extent that they lost sight of G-d's desire that we all *sanctify our physical lives*, not abandon them. As a result, they neglected the Divine precept of marrying and building a family, opting instead for a more spiritual existence—a choice for which they were ultimately punished. Conversely, the Kohen Gadol must predicate his

---

7. Yoma 1:1.
8. See Vayikra Rabbah 20:8.

sublime spiritual service on a commitment to G-d's desire that we *fuse* our spiritual pursuits with our physical lives. His entry to the Holy of Holies is therefore not in contrast with his family life; his entry is contingent upon it.

The Kohen Gadol's synthesis of his extraordinary spiritual life and his more mundane family life serves as a lesson to us all. Our physical lives and our spiritual experiences must not be mutually exclusive; in our moments of inspiration—"in the Holy of Holies"—we must plan concretely how we will translate these spiritual highs into enhanced Torah observance in our mundane lives. At the same time we must imbue our families with the conviction that an increase in spiritual wealth, such as devoting additional time to prayer and Torah study, is not a cause for financial concern; on the contrary, this will bring us prosperity in our material lives as well.

—*Likkutei Sichos, vol. 3, pp. 989–993*

טז:כא | 16:21

וְהִתְוַדָּה עָלָיו אֶת כָּל עֲוֹנֹת בְּנֵי יִשְׂרָאֵל

He shall confess upon it all the willful transgressions of Bnei Yisrael...

The Insincere Vidui

One of the essential components of the Yom Kippur service—the Kohen Gadol's as well as the individual's—is *vidui*, to confess one's sins verbally before G-d and ask for His forgiveness.

> Obviously, confession alone is not enough. Per Rambam: One who confesses verbally without resolving in his heart to abandon [sin] can be compared to one who immerses [in a *mikvah*] while in his hand he holds a *sheretz*, the impure carcass of a crawling creature. His immersion is of no avail until he casts away the *sheretz*.[9]

The Rambam's analogy, however, seems to give the insincere "penitent" more credit than he deserves. Ostensibly, the singular value of confessing one's sins before G-d is the remorse that confession conveys. Absent of any intention to improve, of what worth is an admission of guilt? Accordingly, how can a person who has no remorse be compared to an impure person who *actually* immerses in a *mikvah* but remains impure only because additional sources of impurity stop his purification from taking effect? To recite *vidui* without remorse should be equivalent to not immersing at all!

Clearly, there is some value to *vidui* even when the confession is insincere.

---

9. Mishneh Torah, Hil. Teshuvah 2:3.

Our ability to communicate verbally is what defines us as human; Jewish philosophers aptly refer to the human being as "the speaker." That is why saying things that conflict with our conscience is naturally uncomfortable—because we are inherently sensitive to the words that we verbalize. As a result, verbal admission of guilt and stated remorse for one's past inevitably affect a person to some degree (including a sense of shame for his insincerity). The Rambam therefore intimates that although complete forgiveness requires that the penitent commit to long-term change, the *potential for teshuvah* lies even in the act of *vidui* alone.

—*Likkutei Sichos, vol. 27, pp. 211-213*

טז:כג | 16:23

וּפָשַׁט אֶת בִּגְדֵי הַבָּד אֲשֶׁר לָבַשׁ בְּבֹאוֹ אֶל הַקֹּדֶשׁ וְהִנִּיחָם שָׁם

He shall remove the linen garments that he had worn when he came into the Holy, and there he shall leave them.

Total Makeover

Regarding the words "and there he shall leave them," Rashi comments that the Kohen Gadol's Yom Kippur garments were single-use only; after the service they were stowed away and never used again, even for a future Yom Kippur.

This unique law reflects the essential theme of Yom Kippur: *teshuvah* — repentance and returning to G-d and His service. *Teshuvah* is reinvention. The penitent redirects the course of his life, reinventing himself and his character. In fact, Rambam writes that the penitent even changes his name, "as if to say, 'I am a different person, and not the same one who sinned.'"[10]

The ultimate Yom Kippur experience was that of the Kohen Gadol, and as representative of the entire Jewish nation, the Kohen Gadol's experience is the source from which all Jews draw the strength for their "Yom Kippur makeover"—a total transformation through *teshuvah*. After being in the Kodesh Hakodashim on Yom Kippur, the Kohen Gadol would emerge a new man, even in comparison to his "reinvention" on the Yom Kippurs of previous years. Reflecting the internal transformation that he is set to experience, the Kohen Gadol's Yom

---

10. Mishneh Torah, Hil. Teshuvah 2:4.

Kippur garments must be entirely new each year, not just a repeat of those he wore in the past.

—*Likkutei Sichos, vol. 28, pp. 224–225*

17:13 | יז:יג

אֲשֶׁר יָצוּד צֵיד חַיָּה אוֹ עוֹף אֲשֶׁר יֵאָכֵל וְשָׁפַךְ אֶת דָּמוֹ וְכִסָּהוּ בֶּעָפָר

He who traps a wild animal or fowl that is permissible for consumption, when he sheds its blood, he must cover the blood with dust.

Bloodless

The Torah instructs us to cover the blood of any fowl or non-domesticated animals that we slaughter. This obligation, known as *kisui hadam*, does not apply when slaughtering domesticated animals, such as sheep or cattle.

Ramban points out that the species which are exempt are those typically offered as sacrifices in the Temple. Whereas all types of domestic kosher animals are suitable for sacrifices, only two species of fowl (dove and turtledove) were offered on the *mizbei'ach*, and even then, they were not slaughtered in the regular manner. Non-domesticated animals were never offered as sacrifices.[11]

In a similar vein, only the blood of animals or fowl that are privately owned must be covered, but not the blood of animals or fowl that belong to *hekdesh* — the Temple treasury.[12] The limitation of *kisui hadam* to "non-*hekdesh*" and "non-sacrifice-worthy" animals indicates that the requirement to cover the blood is essentially due to that blood's unfitness to be offered on the *mizbei'ach*.

---

11. Vayikra 17:11
12. See Mishnah, Chullin 6:1.

This can be understood in light of what the Torah states earlier, "The soul of the flesh is in the blood, and I have therefore given it to you [to be placed] upon the altar, to atone for your souls."[13] Meaning that the ideal place for blood is on the altar. Accordingly, any blood not suitable for the altar should be covered.

As such, we can understand the inner meaning and lesson in the mitzvah of *kisui hadam*. Blood is synonymous with life and energy, symbolizing liveliness and enthusiasm. *Kisui hadam* reminds us that the ideal place for blood is on the *mizbei'ach*, meaning that we must sanctify our excitement, and direct them exclusively to activities that are overtly holy. Conversely, in aspects of our lives that are not plainly "sacrifice material," we are instructed to "cover the blood"—meaning, that physical enjoyment in fulfilling our material needs is "misplaced" and undesirable, and we are therefore to restrain it. Instead, our engagement with the material world must be *purely* for the sake of heaven.

—*Likkutei Sichos, vol. 37, pp. 52–53*

---

13. Vayikra 17:11.

קדושים
Kedoshim

19:2 | יט:ב

דַּבֵּר אֶל כָּל עֲדַת בְּנֵי יִשְׂרָאֵל וְאָמַרְתָּ אֲלֵהֶם קְדֹשִׁים תִּהְיוּ כִּי קָדוֹשׁ אֲנִי ה' אֱלֹקֵיכֶם

Speak to the entire congregation of Bnei Yisrael, and say to them, "You shall be holy, for I, Hashem your G-d, am holy."

The Motivation Behind It All

Rashi notes that G-d instructed Moshe to teach this passage to "the *entire* congregation of Bnei Yisrael," i.e., at an assembly of all the men, women and children. The need for publicity was, in Rashi's words, "because most of the fundamental teachings of the Torah are dependent on it." Although it is not the only portion containing many mitzvos, Parshas Kedoshim is unique because most of the Torah's teachings are "dependent on it": they hinge on the principle of holiness taught in its opening words, "You shall be holy, for I, Hashem your G-d, am holy."

Rashi's words also teach us the most effective method of motivating others and ourselves toward the service of G-d. Historically, one school of thought has been to focus on "shunning evil,"[1] through heightened awareness of Judaism's belief in Divine retribution. A different approach has been to highlight the value of Torah study and the beauty of its observance, and emphasize the Jew's distinction and good fortune in having been granted the opportunity to live a Torah life. Aversion to evil will follow automatically (for the most part, if not entirely).

The superiority of the second approach is evident from Rashi's words above. How did Moshe introduce "the fundamental teachings of the Torah" to the assembly of the entire Jewish people? By reiterating that through the observance of the Torah, "you shall be holy, because I, Hashem your G-d, am holy." Moshe conveyed to each of the men, women and children assembled that as a Jew, he or she has the potential to reach a level of holiness and sanctity comparable to the sanctity of G-d Himself! And as history has shown, communicating this positive message is what "most of the fundamental teachings of the Torah are dependent upon."

—*Sefer Hasichos 5748, vol. 2, pp. 433–434*

---

1. Tehillim 34:15.

BOOK OF VAYIKRA — KEDOSHIM

19:2 | יט:ב

דַּבֵּר אֶל כָּל עֲדַת בְּנֵי יִשְׂרָאֵל וְאָמַרְתָּ אֲלֵהֶם קְדֹשִׁים תִּהְיוּ

Speak to the entire congregation of the children of Israel, and say to them, "You shall be holy."

You Can Be Holy

The commentaries ask: what is the meaning of the command to "be holy" as a unique obligation? Is not the objective of every mitzvah, and of the entire Torah, for us to be sanctified?

Ramban[2] explains that the Torah's directive to "be holy," or in a broader sense to set ourselves apart, indeed refers to a distinct effort to sanctify ourselves—independent of the inherent sanctity that we achieve through the observance of the Torah's commands and prohibitions. Here the Torah warns us not to be "a hedonist with the Torah's permission," i.e. not to indulge excessively in the pleasures of the world even when they are technically permissible.[3] "Therefore," continues the Ramban, "after enumerating the things that it forbids entirely, the Torah adds the general directive: 'Be holy.' Constrain yourself and resist even that which is permissible."

Upon honest self-reckoning, however, one might assume that the Torah's directive to "be holy," to sanctify oneself even with that which is permitted, is directed at people who are already perfect in their observance of all the Torah's *explicit* commands and prohibitions. But can it be that a person who is still struggling to abstain from the things the Torah blatantly

---

2. Vayikra 19:2.
3. See also Talmud, Yevamos 20a.

prohibits is instructed to refrain even from indulging in the permissible?

G-d therefore prefaced His command with the somewhat unusual introduction, "Speak to *the entire congregation*," thereby emphasizing that *all* Jews, regardless of their weaknesses or spiritual struggles, are expected to—and therefore certainly have the capacity to—not only observe the Torah's laws, but sanctify themselves even beyond the letter of the law.

—*Likkutei Sichos, vol. 7, pp. 323–324*

19:15 | יט:טו

בְּצֶדֶק תִּשְׁפֹּט עֲמִיתֶךָ
You shall judge your fellow with righteousness.

The Power of Judging Favorably

This verse commands us to judge people justly and righteously. Rashi suggests an additional interpretation: "Judge your friend toward the scale of merit," meaning to judge others favorably.

Generally, "judging toward the scale of merit" refers to presuming a person's innocence before passing judgment.[4] Even if their conduct seems wrongful, consider the innocent or even virtuous intentions that may have motivated their behavior.

The Tanya, however, takes this a step further and says that even when you are *certain* that your friend has acted sinfully, you should not rush to condemn him. Rather, you should consider the difficult circumstances that may have led him to act in this manner, in light of which you can regard his behavior more forgivingly.[5]

The scenario addressed by the Tanya differs from the classic case of judging favorably (for in this instance you must concede that your fellow is indeed guilty). Still, by following the Tanya's approach and acknowledging his spiritually challenging circumstances, you not only diminish his degree of fault, you also "judge him toward the scale of merit" quite literally—you make him more meritorious. This is because

---

4. See Talmud, Shabbos 127b.
5. Likkutei Amarim chapter 30.

G-d certainly grants every person the necessary strength to overcome his set of challenges,[6] and by identifying and acknowledging another's struggle, we reveal the unique gifts and strengths he can use to overcome those challenges. In this way we tip him "toward the scale of merit," and bring out the best in him.

This idea is hinted at by the Rambam, who writes that a wise person "judges every person toward the scale of merit; he speaks of his fellow's praise, and never of his shame."[7] Upon recognizing someone's struggles, the wise man identifies and speaks about the unique strengths that that person has obviously been granted by G-d, thereby ensuring that ultimately there will be nothing shameful to say about that person at all.

—*Likkutei Sichos, vol. 27, pp. 164–165*

---

[6]. See Bamidbar Rabbah 12:3.
[7]. Mishneh Torah, Hil. De'os 5:7.

19:16 | יט:טז

לֹא תַעֲמֹד עַל דַּם רֵעֶךָ
You shall not stand by the blood of your fellow.

Knowing Means Doing

The Baal Shem Tov taught that from everything a Jew sees or hears, he must take a lesson in his service of G-d. This teaching is rooted in the Talmud: "Of all that G-d created in His world, He did not create a single thing without purpose."[8] Or, as the Mishnah says,[9] "Everything that G-d created in His world, He created only for His glory." Included in "everything that G-d created," taught the Baal Shem Tov, is your encounter with any particular object or situation: your very perception of it was created for you to apply its message toward your service of G-d.

This idea is hinted at in Rashi's commentary on the verse, "You shall not stand by the blood of your neighbor," which he interprets to mean "To see his death and you are able to save him." Rashi does not write the final clause tentatively, "*If* you are able to save him," but factually, "*And* you are able to save him," implying that your awareness of your friend's suffering is in and of itself an indication that you are able to save him! The proof is apparent: why would your friend's suffering be made known to you without purpose?

The same principle applies when your fellow is at risk of spiritual death, a life deprived of the life-giving teachings of the Torah, as unfortunately so many of our Jewish brothers

---

8. Shabbos 77b.
9. Avos 6:11.

and sisters are today. The Torah warns us that we may not stand idly by our brothers' blood; our very awareness of the spiritual threat facing our fellow Jews indicates that we are able and personally obligated to save them. How? By taking an active part in the dissemination of the Torah's wisdom and practices.

—*Likkutei Sichos, vol. 32, pp. 125–126*

19:18 | יט:יח

וְאָהַבְתָּ לְרֵעֲךָ כָּמוֹךָ

You shall love your fellow as yourself.

Love on Demand

The Torah's command to love your fellow Jew—to the same degree that you love yourself—raises a number of difficulties. How can we be commanded to experience an emotion? The average person can choose how he or she will *act*, but not necessarily how he or she *feels*! Moreover, is it even possible to love someone else to the same degree that you love yourself?

Rashi answers these questions by citing Rabbi Akiva's well-known saying, "'You shall love your fellow as yourself': This is a fundamental principle of the Torah."

Being that the mitzvah to "love your fellow like yourself" is a *principle*, it follows that your *actual* observance of this mitzvah is primarily through the concrete *details* that result from it—i.e., the numerous mitzvos in the Torah that direct your interactions with others. Those mitzvos can in fact be observed by any person, "on demand."

In addition, by citing Rabbi Akiva as the source for the great significance attributed to this mitzvah, Rashi hints to the way in which a person can truly come to love his fellow Jew as much as he loves himself.

Rabbi Akiva taught, "Beloved are Israel, for they are called children of G-d."[10] Moreover, the Talmud relates[11] that Rabbi

---

10. Avos 3:14.
11. Bava Basra 10a.

Akiva explained the virtue of providing for the Jewish poor with the following parable:

> Suppose an earthly king was angry with his son, and put him in prison and ordered that no food or drink should be given to him [analogous to the person whom G-d has destined to be poor], and someone went and gave him food and drink. If the king heard of it, would he not send him a gift? And we are called "children," as it is written, "You are children to Hashem your G-d."

Meaning that even if a Jew is deserving of Divine retribution, he is still G-d's child!

Considering that every Jew, without exception, is the child of G-d, it follows that we are all brothers and sisters in the full sense of the word.[12] When we reflect on this teaching of Rabbi Akiva, to love one another is only natural.

—*Likkutei Sichos, vol. 17, pp. 216-219*

---

12. See Tanya, chapter 32.

19:18 | יט:יח

וְאָהַבְתָּ לְרֵעֲךָ כָּמוֹךָ

You shall love your fellow as yourself.

Love in Two Dimensions

There are two well-known sayings of the Sages regarding the mitzvah to love your fellow Jew. Rabbi Akiva said, "You shall love your fellow as yourself—this is a fundamental principle of the Torah,"[13] meaning that this mitzvah is the underlying principle behind numerous other mitzvos in the Torah (namely, those that govern our interactions with others). A few generations earlier, Hillel said even more than that: "What is hateful to you, do not do to your neighbor. That is the entire Torah; the rest is simply commentary."[14]

These two sayings reflect two dimensions of the love you must have toward your fellow Jew, which in turn correspond to two different dynamics in the relationship between a Jew and the Torah.

The Midrash[15] tells us that in "G-d's thought" the Jewish people preceded everything, even the Torah itself. The Jewish soul, at its G-dly source, is rooted and attached to G-d to a degree that transcends even the G-dliness of the Torah.

Nevertheless, when the soul descends to this earthly world, its connection to G-d is specifically through the Torah. The Zohar thus states,[16] "The Jewish people attach themselves to

---

13. Sifra, Vayikra 19:18.
14. Shabbos 31a.
15. Bereishis Rabbah 1:4.
16. Vol. 3, p. 73a.

the Torah, and the Torah is attached to the Holy One, Blessed be He"—i.e., in *this* world, the soul's bond with G-d comes to the fore through the Jew's observance of His Torah.

These two dimensions of the Jewish soul and its relationship with the Torah are reflected in the teachings of our Sages cited above.

At its core, the basis of our love for our fellow Jew is the inherent unity of the Jewish people due to our common G-dly source, a source so high that indeed it *transcends* the Torah. Hillel therefore said that love for your fellow Jew *is the entire Torah*: The purpose of the entire Torah is to cultivate and reveal the Jew's *essential* connection to G-d, which is best achieved through our love for one another, whereby we reveal our mutual Divine source that transcends the Torah.

Rabbi Akiva, however, spoke of the mitzvah to love your fellow Jew as it must be observed practically in this physical world, where the Jewish people's connection to G-d is *through* our observance of the Torah. Accordingly, Rabbi Akiva could not say that this mitzvah *is* the entire Torah, because on this plane even your love for your fellow Jew must be observed as *a mitzvah among the mitzvos of the Torah*. He therefore said that loving your fellow as yourself is *a* fundamental principle in the Torah, but at the same time may not override your observance of the rest of the Torah.

—*Likkutei Sichos, vol. 17, pp. 219–224*

אמור
Emor

21:1 | כא:א

אֱמֹר אֶל הַכֹּהֲנִים בְּנֵי אַהֲרֹן וְאָמַרְתָּ אֲלֵהֶם לְנֶפֶשׁ לֹא יִטַּמָּא.

Speak to the kohanim, the sons of Aharon, and say to them: Let none [of you] defile himself for a dead person.

Warn and Shine

The words "Speak to the Kohanim... and say to them" seem repetitive. Having instructed Moshe to "speak to the Kohanim" about the special restrictions pertaining to them, why was it necessary to reiterate "and say to them"?

Rashi notes this redundancy and explains that the phrase "and say to them" alludes to a separate instruction which was conveyed to the Kohanim—that they must ensure that even their young children (who have not yet reached the age of personal responsibility) are in observance of the unique Kohen laws. In Rashi's words, the double expression is used in order "to caution the adults concerning the minors."

The Hebrew word Rashi uses for "to caution" is להזהיר, *l'hazhir*. This word can also be translated as "to make shine," like the Hebrew word זוהר, *zohar*, which means "gleam" or "shine." Rashi's words thus hint that the obligation of *l'hazhir*, cautioning others from negative conduct, is achieved primarily by focusing on their inherent goodness and nurturing it until you "cause them to shine" from within.

In addition, the word *l'hazhir* underscores that our concern to teach and caution others will cause us to shine as well. As the Talmud[1] says of someone who teaches his fellow Torah, "G-d enlightens the eyes of both of them."[2]

—*Likkutei Sichos, vol. 7, pp. 151-152; vol. 27, pp. 165-166*

---

1. Temurah 16a.
2. See Mishlei 29:13.

22:10-11 | כב:י-יא

וְכָל זָר לֹא יֹאכַל קֹדֶשׁ... וְכֹהֵן כִּי יִקְנֶה נֶפֶשׁ קִנְיַן כַּסְפּוֹ הוּא יֹאכַל בּוֹ.

No non-Kohen may eat the holy things… But if a Kohen acquires a person as a monetary acquisition, he [the slave] may eat of it.

Slave Rights

The Sages teach that one may not derive benefit from this world without first reciting a *berachah*—a blessing acknowledging G-d as the world's creator and owner. They compared partaking of this world without a *berachah* to the prohibition of deriving personal benefit from *hekdesh*, objects dedicated to the Temple.[3]

But how does the recitation of a *berachah* render benefit from G-d's world permissible? Does the *berachah* cause G-d to relinquish His ownership of the universe?

Though the *berachah* does not change the ownership of the item over which it was recited, it does change the status of the individual reciting it. And in their new reality, they may partake even from that which belongs to G-d alone.

For example, the Torah prohibits non-Kohanim from eating *terumah*, the share of agricultural produce that we give to the Kohanim. An exception to this rule, however, is a Kohen's servant, of whom the Torah says, "If a Kohen acquires a person as a monetary acquisition, he may eat of it." Similarly, there are select portions of the sacrificial meat that are off-limits

---

3. Berachos 35a.

to anyone other than a Kohen, yet a Kohen's servants may partake of them.[4]

We can likewise explain the significance of reciting a *berachah*. The text of the *berachah* affirms our acceptance of G-d as "*Elokeinu Melech ha'olam,* our L-rd, King of the universe." The *berachah* declares G-d's mastery of the entire universe, including the individual. Therefore, just as the servants of a Kohen may partake of foods that are ordinarily exclusive to their owner, so may those who recite a *berachah* enjoy the goodness of the world that is exclusively owned by G-d.

-*Sefer Hasichos 5751, vol. 2, p. 847*

---

4. See Talmud, Zevachim 55a.

22:32 | כב:לב

וְנִקְדַּשְׁתִּי בְּתוֹךְ בְּנֵי יִשְׂרָאֵל.

I shall be sanctified amidst the children of Israel.

Self-Sacrifice with a Capital "S"

The Torah's directive that we should cause G-d to be sanctified teaches us the obligation of *mesiras nefesh*, meaning that in certain situations we must sacrifice our lives in order not to disobey G-d's commands. When a Jew exhibits his commitment to G-d to the point that he is willing to surrender his life for Him, his devotion causes G-d to be revered and sanctified.

Now, from the verse in Tehillim "He declares *His* words to Yaakov, *His* rules and *His* ordinances to Yisrael,"[5] the Midrash understands that "All that G-d instructs the Jewish people to do, He Himself fulfills as well."[6] Accordingly, if G-d commands the Jewish people to sacrifice their lives for the fulfillment of a mitzvah, it must be that G-d, too, observes this commandment!

Where do we see this? In the mitzvah of examining a woman who is a *sotah*, a woman accused of immoral behavior, who is prohibited to her husband until she is proven innocent. In order to restore their marriage, the Torah provides a process in which a portion of the Torah, containing several mentions of G-d's name, is erased into water for the *sotah* to drink. The water will affect her negatively only if she is guilty. If it has no adverse effects on her, we consider her innocent and she may return to her husband.

---

5. 147:19.
6. Shemos Rabbah 30:9.

It can thus be said that G-d too sacrifices Himself,[7] as it were, for the fulfillment of a mitzvah. In the words of the Talmud, "G-d declares: My Name, written in sanctity, shall be blotted out in water in order to make peace between a man and his wife!"[8]

—*Sefer Hasichos 5749, vol. 1, p. 290, fn. 68*

---

[7]. Since "G-d is One and His name is One" (Zechariah 14:9).
[8]. Shabbos 116a.

22:32 | כב:לב

וְנִקְדַּשְׁתִּ֕י בְּת֖וֹךְ בְּנֵ֣י יִשְׂרָאֵ֑ל.
I shall be sanctified amidst the children of Israel.

The Ultimate Kiddush Hashem

The Torah's directive that "G-d shall be sanctified" teaches us the obligation of *mesiras nefesh*—to sacrifice our very lives for our faith (primarily, to choose death rather than transgressing the cardinal sins of idolatry, adultery or murder). When a Jew demonstrates his willingness to sacrifice his life in order not to abandon his faith, his devotion to G-d leads to G-d's being revered and sanctified.

Rashi makes a point of mentioning, however, based on the Midrash,[9] that "a person who surrenders his life [for the sanctification of G-d's name] must do so with complete willingness to die. Because if a person surrenders himself to die but is hoping for a miracle, a miracle will not be performed for him." This implies that the martyr's innermost intentions and true willingness to die are integral to the sanctification of G-d's name.

This is because, in Rashi's view, although our greatest act of sanctifying G-d is to willingly sacrifice of our lives for our faith, yet when a Jew dies a martyr it is not *G-d's* best publicity. On the contrary, when a Jew is harmed because of his religious beliefs, people deride the Torah and question G-d's existence.[10] The greatest possible glorification of G-d's name

---

9. Toras Kohanim, Vayikra 22:32.
10. See Tehillim 79:10: "Why should the nations say, 'Where is their G-d?'"

in this world is therefore when G-d miraculously *saves* those who surrender their lives for Him.

This ultimate sanctification of G-d's name is obviously beyond human effort and can be brought only about by G-d Himself, but it is subject to human interference—"if a person surrenders himself to die but is hoping for a miracle, a miracle is *not* performed for him." Rashi therefore cautions that when surrendering your life to sanctify G-d's name, you must do so with complete willingness to die in order *not to interfere* with the greatest sanctification of G-d's name, which only He can bring about—a miraculous deliverance from the threat to your life.

—*Likkutei Sichos, vol. 27, pp. 167–175, fn. 36*

23:10-14 | כג:י-יד

וַהֲבֵאתֶם אֶת עֹמֶר רֵאשִׁית קְצִירְכֶם אֶל הַכֹּהֵן... וְלֶחֶם וְקָלִי וְכַרְמֶל לֹא תֹאכְלוּ עַד עֶצֶם הַיּוֹם הַזֶּה.

You must bring the Omer, the beginning of your harvest, to the Kohen... You shall not eat bread, parched grain or fresh grain until this day.

Animals First

The Omer is an offering of barley flour that is brought in the Beis Hamikdash on the second day of Pesach. Until the harvesting and offering of the Omer, the Torah prohibits us from partaking of the new year's crops.

Most other flour offerings in the Temple involved wheat. In comparison to wheat, barley is regarded as animal food.[11] As such, the barley-flour offering represents the early stages of a person's spiritual development, when his internal "animal" is still untamed, and he must focus on "sacrificing" his inner "animal"—i.e., constraining his selfish or negative impulses.

In light of the above, we can understand why we may not partake of the new produce until we offer the Omer. Before deriving personal benefit from any grain of this year's crop, we must ensure that our "barley," our animalistic tendencies, are under control. By doing so at the start of the harvest, we make certain that even our mundane use of this year's grain

---

11. See Mishnah, Sotah 2:1.

will be "for the sake of Heaven," to further and facilitate our service of G-d.

—*Likkutei Sichos, vol. 32, pp. 136–137*

23:20 | כג:כ

וְהֵנִיף הַכֹּהֵן אֹתָם עַל לֶחֶם הַבִּכֻּרִים תְּנוּפָה לִפְנֵי ה' עַל שְׁנֵי כְּבָשִׂים.

The Kohen shall wave them with the bread of the first-fruits for a wave-offering before G-d, with the two lambs.

Sheepish Bread

The *shtei halechem* is a wheat-flour offering brought in the Beis Hamikdash on the holiday of Shavuos. Two loaves of bread made from the new crop of wheat, together with two sheep, are "waved" by the Kohanim. The sheep are offered as sacrifices, and the loaves are eaten by the Kohanim. After this, wheat from the new crop may be used in all other flour offerings too.

The bread of the *shtei halechem* is a metaphor for the study of Torah. Just as bread, the staple of human sustenance, becomes absorbed into the body's flesh and blood, G-d's wisdom is *absorbed* into man's mind and soul through intensive Torah study and comprehension.[12] The offering of sheep—a naturally weak and submissive animal—along with the bread symbolizes that our study of the Torah must be permeated with humility and *kabbalas ol* (complete submission to G-d's will), and acknowledgment that the Torah's inherent G-dliness transcends our limited human understanding.

These two elements of Torah study, and the need to combine them, are also hinted at in the two loaves themselves.

---

12. See Tanya, chapter 5.

According to the Zohar, the two loaves of bread represent the Written Torah and the Oral Torah.[13] The study of the Oral Torah is primarily an exercise of comprehension: one who reads the Oral Torah without understanding its meaning, has not fulfilled the mitzvah of Torah study. In contrast, since many parts of the Written Torah are inherently cryptic, a person who simply *reads* the words of Written Torah, even if he does not understand what he is reading, is observing the mitzvah of Torah study. As a result, the Divine origin of the Torah—and its transcendence of human understanding—is sensed more in the Written Torah than in the Oral Torah.

The symbolic unification of *both* parts of the Torah in the *shtei halechem* reminds us that we must infuse our understanding of the sound logic, typically found in the Oral Torah, with a submission to the Divinity of the Torah, akin to the humility that characterizes our reading of the Written Torah's cryptic words.

—*Likkutei Sichos, vol. 32, p. 137*

---

13. 1:260a.

בהר
Behar

25:1 | כה:א

וַיְדַבֵּר ה' אֶל מֹשֶׁה בְּהַר סִינַי לֵאמֹר.
G-d spoke to Moshe on Mount Sinai, saying.

A Little Big

The Midrash relates that the great mountains of the world all vied to be chosen as the site where G-d would give the Torah to Bnei Yisrael. Nevertheless, G-d selected the smallest of all the mountains, Mount Sinai, teaching us the value of humility.[1]

The question arises: Mount Sinai was indeed the smallest mountain, but it was still a mountain. If the Torah was to be given on a site that symbolized humility, why not choose a plain, or better yet, a valley? A valley is certainly more "humble" than even the smallest of mountains.

Evidently, humility was not the only quality sought for the site of the giving of the Torah; G-d desired to give the Torah on a mountain, albeit a small one.

---

1. Midrash Tehillim 68:17.

The paradoxical "small mountain" symbolizes that the Torah demands modesty, not meekness. Certainly, the primary criterion to receive the Torah is humility. This is emphasized in our Shmoneh Esrei prayers, where we precede the request for G-d to "open my heart in Your Torah" with the supplication "let my soul be like dust before all," i.e., humility is the key to success in Torah study. At the same time, we should be proud of our observance of G-d's will. As the Code of Jewish Law begins: "Do not be ashamed in the face of mockers."[2] Meaning that a Jew must be confident and determined in his observance of the Torah, not fazed in the slightest by scorn or adversity.

The Torah was therefore given on Mount Sinai, the smallest of the mountains, but not in a plain or a valley, to teach us that humility and pride are *both* necessary in order to receive and implement the Torah: we must regard ourselves with humility, while being staunchly proud of our Torah lifestyle and mitzvah observance.

—*Likkutei Sichos, vol. 1, pp. 276-278*

---

[2]. Shulchan Aruch Admor Hazaken, Orach Chaim 1:1.

25:2-4 | כה:ב-ד

כִּי תָבֹאוּ אֶל הָאָרֶץ אֲשֶׁר אֲנִי נֹתֵן לָכֶם וְשָׁבְתָה הָאָרֶץ שַׁבָּת לַה'. שֵׁשׁ שָׁנִים תִּזְרַע שָׂדֶךָ... וּבַשָּׁנָה הַשְּׁבִיעִת שַׁבַּת שַׁבָּתוֹן יִהְיֶה לָאָרֶץ.

When you come to the land that I am giving you, the land shall rest a Shabbos to G-d. For six years you may sow your field... but in the seventh year, the land shall have a complete rest.

Goal-Oriented

The seven-year agricultural cycle observed in the Land of Israel begins with six years of work, followed by a year of Shemittah, a Sabbatical year. Yet when the Torah introduces the commandment of Shemittah, it opens with the statement "When you come to the land... the land shall rest a Shabbos to G-d," which gives the impression that the year of rest is at the start of the seven-year cycle, even before the six years of work begin.

The Alter Rebbe explains that the Torah writes it this way to teach us that the upcoming Shemittah year must be the underlying motivation during the first six years of work.[3] In other words, we must establish our six years of working the land on the ideal that our ultimate goal is the seventh year, which is "Shabbos to G-d," when our freedom from agricultural labor will allow us devote our time to purely holy pursuits, such as extensive Torah study. This awareness must pervade our attitude and conduct throughout the years of work, and

---

3. Likkutei Torah, Behar 40d.

will thereby ensure that our seventh year is *truly* sanctified, and provided for by G-d (in advance) with an abundance of material blessing, too.

The Shemittah cycle that Bnei Yisrael began observing when they settled the Land of Israel serves as a model for the individual "lands" we each establish—i.e., the homes we build and the families we raise. Jewish parents might spend the bulk of their day doing tasks that seem mundane—identical to those performed in a non-Jewish home. Nevertheless, the mitzvah of Shemittah teaches us that from the very get-go, when a child is born, the goal in a Jewish home must be to raise this child to be "Shabbos-like," free to grow and thrive in Judaism and holiness, with no concern for the material. As a result, even the everyday tasks of parenthood will not be the same. Our "Shabbos objective" will be evident in every aspect of how we raise our families, and we will merit that our children will grow up to be truly "Shabbos-like"— devoted entirely to G-d, and provided for by Him with abundant goodness and prosperity.

—*Likkutei Sichos, vol. 12, pp. 247-250*

25:20-21 | כה:כ-כא

וְכִי תֹאמְרוּ מַה נֹּאכַל בַּשָּׁנָה הַשְּׁבִיעִת הֵן לֹא נִזְרָע וְלֹא נֶאֱסֹף אֶת תְּבוּאָתֵנוּ. וְצִוִּיתִי אֶת בִּרְכָתִי לָכֶם בַּשָּׁנָה הַשִּׁשִּׁית וְעָשָׂת אֶת הַתְּבוּאָה לִשְׁלֹשׁ הַשָּׁנִים.

And if you should say, "What will we eat in the seventh year? We will not sow, and we will not gather in our produce!" I will command My blessing for you in the sixth year, and it will yield produce for three years.

Give Me Your Tired

Once every seven years we observe a year of Shemittah in the Land of Israel, during which we refrain from working the land and growing new produce. For our sustenance in the Shemittah year, G-d promises that in the sixth year the earth will yield much more produce than it normally does, providing enough food to last for two and a half years, until new crops are ready for harvest in the ninth year.

The tremendous output that G-d promises for the sixth year utterly defies the earth's natural ability. The sixth year's crop would naturally be smaller and weaker than that of the previous years, as the nutrients in the soil are somewhat depleted after five consecutive years of planting. In fact, this is one of the reasons suggested for the observance of Shemittah in the seventh year: to ensure that the nutrients in the earth will have a chance to replenish.[4] Nevertheless, G-d promises that specifically the produce of the sixth year will be greater than the crop of any other year.

---

4. See Moreh Nevuchim 3:39.

This promise is reflected in our efforts to bring about the coming of Moshiach and the long-awaited Redemption. The Talmud compares our history to the seven-year Shemittah cycle. After six thousand years of human effort to develop G-d's world, the seventh millennium will be a sabbatical era, holy and sanctified to G-d—namely, the era of Moshiach.[5]

Like in the sixth year of the Shemittah cycle, the question of "what will we eat in the seventh year?" is strongest in the sixth millennium. For with every passing generation, our sensitivity to holiness has only become duller in comparison to the generations that preceded us. How can it be that our impoverished deeds will succeed at bringing about the coming of Moshiach, if theirs did not?

To this G-d responds with the guarantee, "I will command My blessing to you in the sixth year": it is precisely your simple loyalty despite the weariness of thousands of years of exile that will elicit the extraordinary blessings of the era of Moshiach.

—*Likkutei Sichos, vol. 27, pp. 189–190*

---

[5]. Sanhedrin 97a.

כה:מז | 25:47

וּמָךְ אָחִיךָ עִמּוֹ וְנִמְכַּר לְגֵר תּוֹשָׁב עִמָּךְ אוֹ לְעֵקֶר מִשְׁפַּחַת גֵּר.

...And your brother becomes destitute with him, and is sold to a resident non-Jew among you, or to an idol of the family of a non-Jew.

A Jew's Red Line

The Talmud[6] views the series of laws discussed in Parshas Behar as depicting the downward spiral—both spiritual and financial—of a person who is not careful in his observance of the Torah's laws. At the beginning of the Parshah, the Torah admonishes us to observe the laws of Shemittah, to rest from agricultural work every seventh year. Then the Torah talks about the laws of selling property, then about loans, and then about selling oneself as a slave. The Torah is warning us, says the Talmud, that should one not refrain from agricultural pursuits during the Shemittah year, he will eventually be forced to sell his personal belongings, then his inherited land, and even his home, and then to borrow on interest. If he still does not repent, he will eventually be forced to sell himself as a slave—first to a fellow Jew, then to a gentile, and then even worse, "to an idol of the family of a non-Jew."

Notably, Rashi interprets selling oneself "to an idol," the lowest link in this chain of descent, to mean selling oneself to be an attendant for idolatry—"*not* [to serve the idol] as a deity, but to chop wood and draw water [for its service]."[7]

---

6. Kiddushin 20a–b.
7. Rashi in his commentary on the Talmud, as well as on Vayikra 25:27.

Rashi's negation of that possibility supports the Alter Rebbe's assertion in Tanya[8] that at the core of every Jew is a suprarational attachment to G-d, due to which even the crassest sinners "sacrifice their lives for the sanctity of G-d's Name and suffer harsh torture rather than deny G-d's unity… without any knowledge or reflection, but as though it were absolutely impossible to renounce the one G-d." In truth, says the Alter Rebbe, if a Jew were conscious of his soul's indomitable desire to cleave to G-d, he would never be willing to sever himself from G-d and defy His will by transgressing any mitzvah whatsoever. It is only that this aspect of the soul "is *dormant* in the wicked"—never absent, merely inactive—"as long as their knowledge and understanding are preoccupied with mundane pleasures. But, when they are confronted with a test of faith… touching the very soul… it 'stirs from its sleep' and exerts its influence… to withstand the test of faith in G-d."

Rashi therefore asserts that even a person so spiritually debased that he could sell himself as a slave to an idol-worshipper (against the Torah's wishes[9]), or even as an attendant for idolatry, would never go a step further and worship an idol for pay—even only outwardly.

—*Likkutei Sichos, vol. 17, pp. 300–301*

---

8. Chapters 18–24.
9. Mishneh Torah, Hil. Avadim 1:3.

25:55 | כה:נה

כִּי לִי בְנֵי יִשְׂרָאֵל עֲבָדִים עֲבָדַי הֵם אֲשֶׁר הוֹצֵאתִי אוֹתָם מֵאֶרֶץ מִצְרָיִם.

For the children of Israel are servants to Me; they are My servants, whom I took out of the land of Egypt.

Out of Control

Why does the verse repeat itself, saying "Bnei Yisrael are servants to Me; they are My servants whom I took out of the land of Egypt"? Would it not have been enough to say only once, "Bnei Yisrael are My servants, whom I took out of the land of Egypt"?

This double expression reflects the twofold nature of Bnei Yisrael's servitude to G-d. One degree of servitude is the obedience to G-d's will to which they committed themselves on their own; the other is an inescapable debt of servitude—a condition on which G-d redeemed them from Egyptian bondage.

Before the giving of the Torah, Bnei Yisrael said of their own accord, "*na'aseh v'nishma*, we will obey and we will listen," emphatically announcing their readiness to obey G-d's will even before (and not conditional upon) "listening" and understanding what He would expect of them. This pledge stemmed from their profound eagerness to be His servants and to carry out His wishes, whatever they may be. G-d acknowledges this pledge in the Torah, saying, "For the children of Israel are servants to Me"—they have committed themselves to Me.

However, since the declaration of *na'aseh v'nishma* expressed the *people's* choice to accept G-d's sovereignty, their pledge hinges on and reflects the "participation," as it were, of those making the commitment. The servitude generated thereby is thus not entirely independent of their will and desire. This personal and mortal commitment to G-d does not contain the *limitlessness* of Bnei Yisrael's "inescapable" debt of servitude owed to G-d for redeeming them from Egypt.

That is what the verse adds by saying, "They are My servants, whom I took out from the land of Egypt," after already noting our acceptance of G-d as our master—"Bnei Yisrael are servants to Me." The debt we owe to G-d for redeeming us from Egypt is independent of any pledge of ours, giving our obligation to Him an element of "inescapability." This "compulsory" servitude to G-d, which was revealed at the giving of the Torah when G-d said, "I am Hashem your G-d who took you out of Egypt,"[10] is what makes Bnei Yisrael "My servants"—infinitely committed to G-d, with an unnatural devotion that transcends all circumstances.

—*Toras Menachem, Sefer Hamaamarim Melukat, vol. 3, pp. 357–358, fn. 32*

---

10. Shemos 20:2.

26:1-2 | כו:א-ב

לֹא תַעֲשׂוּ לָכֶם אֱלִילִם... אֶת שַׁבְּתֹתַי תִּשְׁמֹרוּ... אֲנִי ה'.

You shall not make idols for yourselves...
You shall keep My Sabbaths... I am G-d.

Well Paid

The final verses of Parshas Behar caution us in the observance of a number of mitzvos stated previously in the Torah. Rashi explains that the Torah directs these warnings at the person discussed in the preceding verses—a Jew who has sold himself into slavery to a gentile. He might assume, says Rashi, "Since my master has illicit relations... worships idols... desecrates the Shabbos, I may also be like him." The Torah therefore warns that despite his subjugation to a non-Jew, he must still observe the mitzvos. The Parshah then concludes, "I am G-d"—"Who is faithful to give reward";[11] i.e., the slave's devotion to the Torah despite his circumstances will not go unrewarded.

Though every person who observes the mitzvos elicits a Divine response, the Torah specifically mentions that G-d will reward this slave, because the slave might otherwise suspect that in his current situation he is incapable of receiving Divine compensation.

To explain:

Everything we have comes from G-d: our rains and our crops, our health and our livelihood. Still, the "G-dliness" of our blessings, i.e., the degree to which their Divine source is revealed, varies.

---

11. Rashi ad loc.

During the Shemittah year, for example, when agricultural work in the Land of Israel is prohibited, the survival of the Jewish people living in Israel is distinctly and recognizably supernatural. In truth, a Jew's needs are *always* provided for supernaturally—just as the Jewish nation has been miraculously preserved by G-d throughout history. But in the non-Shemittah years, when G-d instructs us, "Six years you shall sow your field, and six years you shall prune your vineyard," our *truly supernatural* blessings come to us through a natural vehicle—our physical toil and the workings of nature.

The garb through which G-d provides for non-Jews, however, is even more concealing, and their sustenance more subject to the limited forces of nature.[12] As such, since the Jewish slave of a non-Jew is dependent upon his gentile master to provide for him—provisions that are indeed subject to the forces of nature—he might assume that though his observance of the mitzvos surely generates a Divine reward, he is (currently) incapable of receiving the reward for observing Shabbos and refraining from idol-worship—rewards which certainly outstrip any natural disguise whatsoever.

The Torah therefore reiterates that G-d Himself—"Who is faithful to give reward"—has given the commandments, and He can and will fully compensate all who observe the mitzvos, regardless of their current circumstances.

—*Likkutei Sichos, vol. 7, pp. 183–187*

---

12. See Devarim 4:19. A non-Jew is thus more prone to believe that the forces of nature determine his sustenance, and that they are not merely carrying out the will of G-d. See Rema, Orach Chaim 156:1; Toras Menachem, Sefer Hamaamarim Melukat, vol. 1, pp. 321–324.

בחוקותי
Bechukosai

26:3 | כו:ג

אִם בְּחֻקֹּתַי תֵּלֵכוּ וְאֶת מִצְוֹתַי תִּשְׁמְרוּ וַעֲשִׂיתֶם אֹתָם.

If you follow My statutes, and observe My commandments and perform them.

When the Going Gets Tough

Rashi wonders about the meaning of the phrase "If you follow My statutes." We might assume it refers to mitzvah observance, but that is mentioned in the next phrase, "and observe My commandments." What, then, is the meaning of the command to "follow G-d's statutes"? Rashi concludes that it must refer to the study of Torah—"to toil in Torah."

Rashi's assertion that following G-d's statutes requires not only studying the Torah, but also *toiling* in it, is supported by the verse's unusual reference to Torah study with the term *bechukosai*, "in My statutes."

The Torah generally uses the term *chok*, "statute," in reference to mitzvos that have no logical explanation. The observance of these commandments is naturally toilsome on an emotional level, as it takes great sacrifice for a logical person to act in a manner that defies rationality and explanation. As such, the term *chok* is virtually synonymous with challenge and difficulty.

So, when used in the context of Torah study, Rashi understands the term *chok* as a reference to Torah study that is challenging and toilsome, such as devotedly studying Torah even when we do not derive satisfaction and enjoyment from our studies. For to "follow My statutes" means to not only study the Torah, but "to toil in Torah."

—*Toras Menachem, vol. 25, pp. 292-293*

כו:ג | 26:3

אִם־בְּחֻקֹּתַי תֵּלֵכוּ וְאֶת־מִצְוֹתַי תִּשְׁמְרוּ.
If you follow My statutes and observe My commandments.

The Art of Carving

The term *chok*, statute, has a number of meanings. In the context of Torah study, Rashi interprets the phrase "If you follow my statutes" as a requirement to *"toil* in Torah." Generally, however, the Torah uses the term *chok* in reference to mitzvos that have no logical explanation. As well, the word *chok* is associated in Likkutei Torah[1] with the Hebrew word for engraving, חקיקה, *chakikah*.

These three definitions are related. One of the obvious differences between writing and engraving is that writing requires minimal physical effort, whereas carving in stone (or other hard surfaces) is physically strenuous. Engraving is therefore a metaphor for observing the mitzvos that defy logic, which is naturally a greater challenge than adhering to the commandments whose purpose we do understand. Similarly, in the context of Torah study, the term *bechukosai*, "in My statutes," refers to *laboring* in the study of Torah—in Rashi's words, "to toil in Torah."

The metaphor of engraving also encapsulates the impact that laboring in the study of Torah has on the individual. Just as a hard surface, such as stone, can be engraved with persistent toil, even the most unmoved and hardened heart

---

1. Bechukosai 45a.

can be softened and inspired through diligent Torah study. As Rabbi Akiva famously remarked upon observing a stone that had been gouged by the consistent dripping of water, "If soft water can carve solid stone, how much more can the iron word of G-d penetrate the fleshy human heart."[2]

—*Likkutei Sichos, vol. 17, pp. 318–319*

---

2. Avos D'Rabbi Nasan, chapter 6.

26:4 | כו:ד

וְנָתַתִּי גִשְׁמֵיכֶם בְּעִתָּם.
I will give your rains in their time.

Timing

In Parshas Bechukosai, G-d declares that if the Jewish people will observe His commandments and follow His statutes—meaning, they will "toil in the study of Torah"[3]—they will be blessed with prosperity, peace and security, and they will multiply and flourish.

Among the blessings detailed in the Torah is G-d's promise that not only will the Land of Israel have rain, but the rains will also fall "in their time." As Rashi explains, the distinctive blessing in this verse is not just the rain but the timing of the rainfall—"at a time that people do not usually go out."[4] Meaning that the rains of blessing will not be inconvenient or disruptive.

The blessing of rain, in its broader sense, is a reference to overall material bounty. (Hence the Hebrew word for physicality, *gashmius*, from the word *geshem*, rain.) Accordingly, the distinctive blessing of rain falling "in its time" also applies to the general blessing of material prosperity. If we follow His statutes and observe His commandments, G-d will not only bless us with material wealth, He will grant it in a manner that will not distract us from our primary pursuits, Torah study and Divine worship; it will serve only to bolster and strengthen them.

—*Toras Menachem, vol. 2, p. 117*

---

3. Rashi, Vayikra 26:3.
4. Vayikra 26:4.

כו:ד | 26:4

וְעֵץ הַשָּׂדֶה יִתֵּן פִּרְיוֹ.
And the tree of the field will give forth its fruit.

The Messianic Age: Out of This World?

The Torah's reference here to "trees of the field"—as opposed to trees planted in an orchard—denotes non-fruit-bearing trees, according to the Midrash.[5] Thus the promise that "the tree of the field will give forth its fruit," says the Midrash, refers to the era of Moshiach, when even non-fruit-bearing trees will grow fruit.

This Midrashic teaching seems to contradict the position taken by the Rambam: "Do not presume that in the messianic era any aspect of the natural order will be nullified, or that there will be innovations in the work of creation. Rather, the world will continue according to its pattern."[6] How can the Rambam reconcile this position with the Midrash's teaching that even non-fruit-bearing trees will bear fruit when Moshiach comes?

A similar issue with the Rambam's stance is presented by one of the cardinal principles of Jewish faith, the belief that the dead will one day be resurrected, which will take place in the messianic era.[7] The resurrection of the dead is obviously a huge breach of nature!

---

5. Toras Kohanim, cited by Rashi, Vayikra 26:4.
6. Mishneh Torah, Hil. Melachim 12:1.
7. According to Rambam. Others contend that the resurrection will take

We must conclude that even the Rambam agrees that there will be changes to the natural order of the world after the coming of Moshiach.[8] He maintains, however, that these supernatural changes are not components of the actual event of Redemption—whose purpose is for the Jewish people to be able to serve G-d without hindrance or challenge, and to observe all the Torah's laws in their entirety—and therefore might not take effect immediately upon Moshiach's arrival. The Rambam regards as *definitive* components of the Moshiach-led redemption only the restoration of the Jewish kingdom, an end to war and hunger, and the removal of similar disturbances that might stand in the way of devoting ourselves entirely to Torah study and mitzvah observance.

In contrast, the supernatural events prophesied in the Torah, such as the resurrection of the dead and non-fruit-bearing trees giving fruit, might not occur immediately upon Moshiach's arrival but at a later phase, depending on the merits of the Jewish people.[9] Certainly, however, with the freedom to limitlessly engage in Torah and mitzvos that the coming of Moshiach will bring, we will eventually merit those supernatural blessings and experiences as well.

—*Likkutei Sichos, vol. 27, pp. 191–206*

---

place in the post-messianic era known as "the world to come." See Mishneh Torah, Hil. Teshuvah 8:2, and commentaries ad loc.
8. Iggeres Techiyas Hameisim, sec. 6.
9. See Talmud, Sanhedrin 98a.

כו:ט | 26:9

וּפָנִיתִי אֲלֵיכֶם.
I will turn towards you.

Chores or Passions?

After stating that if you follow G-d's statutes and observe His commandments, G-d will grant you prosperity, security and peace, the Torah adds that G-d will also "turn towards you" and grant you additional blessings as well. Rashi comments on the words "I will turn towards you," and interprets this to mean, "I will turn away from all My preoccupations to pay your reward."

The expression "I will turn away from all My preoccupations"—not "from My *other* preoccupations," but from "My preoccupations" in general—implies that the payment of additional reward described here is *not* among G-d's preoccupations or chores. Why not? What is it then?

In addition, the placement of this promise after the verse has already enumerated some of G-d's other promised rewards implies that there are two degrees of reward promised here: the earlier blessings are indeed among G-d's preoccupations, while the latter blessings are not. What does this mean?

The term "(My) preoccupations," or עסקי in Hebrew, denotes tasks that occupy your mind but are essentially "outside of you," imposing on and distracting from your internal desires and interests. These "preoccupations" represent a descent from your truest and most natural self. "Turning away from all your preoccupations" thus means that you are now concentrating on an expression of your truest self—the essence of who you are.

We can now understand the two degrees of reward that G-d promises for toiling in Torah study and observing His commandments. One degree of reward is for fulfilling the mitzvos to the extent required of you; the other is for devoting yourself to the fulfillment of G-d's will *beyond* what the law requires.

By going beyond the law's demands, such as toiling in the study of Torah more than is required, you demonstrate that this is not merely a duty or chore, but your truest passion. Commensurately, G-d's reward for such devotion emanates not, as with the blessings enumerated in the earlier verses here, from a level of Divine effluence that is a "descent" from His essence—analogous to a "preoccupation" or "chore"—but from the Divine essence itself!

—*Likkutei Sichos, vol. 17, pp. 324–329*

כז:לג | 27:33

וְלֹא יְמִירֶנּוּ וְאִם הָמֵר יְמִירֶנּוּ וְהָיָה הוּא וּתְמוּרָתוֹ יִהְיֶה קֹּדֶשׁ.
And he shall not substitute for it. If he shall exchange it, then it will be, and its exchange will be, holy.

Exchange Rate

According to the teachings of Kabbalah, the twelve possible configurations of the four letters of G-d's name Yud-Hey-Vav-Hey each represent a distinct Divine revelation, and are each alluded to by a verse in the Torah.

One of these combinations derives from the verse in the Torah that prohibits substituting an animal consecrated as a sacrifice with a different (unconsecrated) animal. If one attempts to do so, the animals must both be offered as sacrifices, as the Torah states, "If he shall exchange it, then it will be, and its exchange will be, holy." The first letter of each of the four words, "הָמֵר יְמִירֶנּוּ וְהָיָה הוּא—he shall exchange it, then it will be," spell out one of the twelve configurations of G-d's name.[10]

The suggestion that these four words are a distinct phrase that formulates a name of G-d seems to contradict the actual meaning of the verse. The context of this verse is the *prohibition* of making such exchanges. These four words on their own, however, form a phrase that implies that such an exchange is permissible and even obligatory: "He shall exchange it, then it will be!"

The unlikely use of these four words as an independent phrase teaches us a remarkable lesson. The prohibition of

---

10. Siddur HaArizal, Kavanas Rosh Chodesh.

exchanges, as it relates to each of us spiritually in our service of G-d, refers to the substitution of our own spiritual growth with efforts to transform the mundane world outside of us into holiness. Under normal circumstances, "exchanges" are prohibited: one may not leave the shelter of a holy Torah environment, risking his own spiritual sensitivity, in an attempt to confer sanctity on the outside world.

There are times, however, when such exchanges are not a sin but a virtue, and the Torah in fact instructs us, "He shall exchange it!" Namely, when so many of our fellow Jews are at risk of assimilation and spiritual devastation, we are obligated to compromise the security we feel when staying within a Torah environment, and instead to go out and find those whose spiritual lives are at risk and draw them towards the lifegiving waters of the Torah.

And what of your own spirituality? To this, the Torah guarantees (in the final words of this four-word phrase), "then it will be!"—you will succeed not only in revealing holiness in others, but even your own spirituality "will *be*"—it will remain as strong as ever.

—*Likkutei Sichos, vol. 26, pp. 90-92*

במדבר
BOOK OF BAMIDBAR

לחיזוק ההתקשרות לכ"ק אדמו"ר
ולזכות

שניאור זלמן
בן בת-שבע בינה

יהודית חיה
בת אלישבע

שיינא אסתר
בת יהודית חיה

שלמה אהרן
בן יהודית חיה

שיינא אסתר
בן יהודית חיה

מנחם מענדל
בן יהודית חיה

לוי יצחק
בן יהודית חיה

❧❧

ולזכות הוריהם

ר' דוד מיכאל
בן פייגע

בת-שבע בינה
בת ציפה

אחיו מנחם מענדל
בן בת-שבע בינה

אחותו חנה פייגא
בן בת-שבע בינה

להצלחה רבה ומופלגה בגו"ר בכל העניינים
מתוך בריאות טובה, נחת חסידותי ופרנסה בהרחבה
בטוב הנראה והנגלה

במדבר
Bamidbar

1:2 | א:ב

שְׂאוּ אֶת רֹאשׁ כָּל עֲדַת בְּנֵי יִשְׂרָאֵל

Take the sum of all the congregation of the children of Israel.

Numbers that Matter

In the first thirteen months after their exodus from Egypt, the Jewish people were counted three times.[1] Rashi explains the significance of all this counting: "Because of their dearness to Him [G-d], He counts them all the time."

The significance of all the counting is not for G-d to determine the precise number of individuals within the Jewish nation—as G-d surely knows their number without conducting an actual census—but, in Rashi's words,[2] "to make their dearness known." In spiritual terms, this means that the cen-

---

1. See Shemos 12:37; ibid. 30:12–16; and Bamidbar, chapters 1–3.
2. Shemos 1:1.

sus revealed within the Jewish people themselves the *nature* of their endearment to G-d.

How so? Because in a census, the value that each individual adds to the count is the same; every person counts as no less and no more than one. This means that the count highlights a quality common to all Jews, regardless of their background, education or spiritual sophistication: the "Jewish spark"—the essential Jewishness of the soul of every Jew. This "Jewish spark" manifests as a sense of unbreakable attachment to G-d, due to which every Jew, regardless of their level of Jewish knowledge or observance, is capable of surrendering their very life for their faith in order not to separate from the one G-d in whom they intrinsically believe.

This indomitable "Jewish spark," common to all Jews, is the Jewish people's greatest source of "dearness" before G-d. By taking a simple count of the number of people that make up the Jewish nation, G-d "made their dearness known," revealing within them (and in fact, to the entire world) the essential Jewish spark possessed by every single Jew.

—*Likkutei Sichos, vol. 8, pp. 3–4*

| 1:2 | א:ב

שְׂאוּ אֶת רֹאשׁ כָּל עֲדַת בְּנֵי יִשְׂרָאֵל

Take the sum of all the congregation of the children of Israel.

Just a Number?

If a foreign substance falls into a mixture and is minute in comparison to the rest of the mixture, according to Jewish law we may disregard the foreign substance to some degree, and treat the entire mixture homogeneously. For example, if one piece of non-kosher food lands among several pieces of kosher food and cannot be identified, we treat the entire mixture as kosher.[3]

There are certain items, however, which are inherently significant and can never be nullified, even when they are lost among thousands of others. These include: a living animal, a complete creature (as opposed to a piece of one), and any *davar sheb'minyan* (object that is counted)—an item that is sold by unit rather than by weight or volume. When we reckon each unit as an individual article of sale, we establish that each unit is independently significant. We therefore may not ignore the presence of even one such unit, despite the mixture containing thousands more that seem identical.

This was the purpose, says the Shaloh,[4] of the census that G-d instructed be taken of the Jewish people. The count itself

---

[3]. At times, a greater degree of nullification is required, such as with a liquid mixture, in which a ratio of 60:1 (or more) is necessary in order to discount the prohibited food.
[4]. Shnei Luchos Habris, Torah Shebichsav, Bamidbar.

revealed the prominence of each individual Jew. As a result, the specialness of a Jew's identity became an unignorable reality, despite the Jewish people being only a tiny minority among the nations of the world.

In addition, the prominence of a *davar sheb'minyan* is unique even in comparison to the other possible forms of "halachic prominence" mentioned above (live animal, complete creature). Whereas those articles of distinction are noticeably special, the importance of the counted object might not be observable at all—the only indicator of its significance is its being counted. Similarly, the count of the Jewish people brought to the fore the inner specialness of the Jew that is not contingent on his qualities or actions, but due simply to being chosen as a member of G-d's nation.

Since the time that the Jewish people were counted, not only is the Jew capable of maintaining his unique identity regardless of his surroundings, his surroundings can recognize and be influenced by his specialness as well.

—*Likkutei Sichos, vol. 4, pp. 1019–1020; vol. 18, p. 25*

1:2 | א:ב

שְׂאוּ אֶת רֹאשׁ כָּל עֲדַת בְּנֵי יִשְׂרָאֵל לְמִשְׁפְּחֹתָם לְבֵית אֲבֹתָם
Take the sum of all the congregation of the children of Israel, by their families, by their fathers' houses.

The Differences We Have in Common

The census taken in the beginning of the Book of Bamidbar seems paradoxical. On the one hand, a tally of the entire nation, in which each person counts as no more and no less than *one*, means that each person is counted and valued equally. A count of this nature highlights the qualities that are common to every person in the census.

On the other hand, the Torah states that Bnei Yisrael were counted "by their families, by their fathers' houses." As Rashi explains[5] (and as is apparent from the Torah's accounting of each tribe separately), the members of each tribe were counted individually, and then the sum total of all the tribes was tallied. Counting each tribe individually implies that each tribe represents a unique unit whose qualities *differ* from the others, warranting an individual census.

The conflicting features of this count—its emphasis on the distinct qualities of each individual tribe, but at the same time every individual being of equal value, symbolizing the similarity of all members of Bnei Yisrael—are not actually a contradiction.

---

5. Bamidbar 1:2.

The Torah's emphasis on the distinctiveness of each tribe (some thriving in Torah study, others in business, etc.,[6] corresponding to each tribe's unique path in the service of G-d) is not to highlight their differences, but to express how all their unique features *equally* contribute to the beautiful tapestry that is the Jewish nation. The tribes were therefore first counted separately, and then the totals were combined, with each person holding equal value in the sum total, to teach us that the unique qualities each Jew brings to the table are equally crucial to the nation as a whole.

—*Likkutei Sichos, vol. 23, pp. 6–7*

---

6. See Bereishis 49:3–27.

ג:ח | 3:8

וְשָׁמְרוּ אֶת כָּל כְּלֵי אֹהֶל מוֹעֵד וְאֶת מִשְׁמֶרֶת
בְּנֵי יִשְׂרָאֵל לַעֲבֹד אֶת עֲבֹדַת הַמִּשְׁכָּן

They shall guard all the vessels of the Ohel Moed, the charge of Bnei Yisrael, to perform the service of the Mishkan.

You Must Be a Levi Too

The Rambam writes that the extraordinary sanctity that G-d conferred upon the tribe of Levi is not exclusive to biological descendants of that tribe. Rather, "any individual whose spirit motivates him and whose wisdom guides him to set himself apart and stand before G-d to serve Him and worship Him… behold, that person is sanctified…."[7]

One might assume, however, that the ability to "be sanctified" to serve G-d, to genuinely and entirely devote oneself to carrying out the Divine mission of making this entire world a "dwelling place" for Him—i.e., the very purpose of Creation—is not for everybody. After all, the Rambam describes the person who can achieve this sanctity as an individual "whose spirit motivates him and whose wisdom guides him." If I am not yet at that level of inspiration and understanding, who is to say that I can be "sanctified like a Levi," to truly devote myself exclusively to the service of G-d?

The Torah removes this doubt when it says, "They shall guard all the vessels of the Ohel Moed, the charge of Bnei Yisrael, to perform the service of the Mishkan,"[8] which means,

---

7. Mishneh Torah, Hil. Shemittah V'Yovel 13:13.
8. Bamidbar 3:8.

as Rashi explains, that although this service is actually the duty of Bnei Yisrael, "the *Levi'im* serve in their stead, as their agents."

One of the principles of the laws of agency is that one cannot commission an agent to act as his legal proxy if the commissioner himself is not legally allowed to perform that task.[9] But the Torah states that the Levites' responsibility to sing in the Mishkan, and to transport it from place to place when Bnei Yisrael traveled, were in essence "the charge of Bnei Yisrael"—the responsibility of the entire Jewish nation. It is only that "the *Levi'im* serve in their stead, as their agents." Since one can empower the Levi to act as his proxy only if he can potentially do the service himself, evidently every Jew has the innate ability "to stand before G-d to serve Him."[10]

Accordingly, though the actual service in the Temple has been delegated to the tribe of Levi, the Levi-like ability to wholly devote oneself to bringing about the Divine purpose of creation is still within reach of every single Jew.

—*Likkutei Sichos, vol. 13, p. 15*

---

[9]. See Talmud, Kiddushin 23b.
[10]. Devarim 10:8.

3:29 | ג:כט

מִשְׁפְּחֹת בְּנֵי־קְהָת יַחֲנוּ עַל יֶרֶךְ הַמִּשְׁכָּן תֵּימָנָה

The families of the sons of Kehas shall camp to the south side of the Mishkan.

Choose Your Neighbors Carefully

The families comprising the tribe of Levi camped on all four sides of the Mishkan. Around them, the other twelve tribes camped, three tribes on each side. Rashi notes that the tribe of Reuven was particularly influenced by the Levite family of Kehas (of which the rebellious Korach was a member), next to whom they camped. In Rashi's words:

> Woe is to the wicked and woe is to his neighbor. This is why Dasan, Aviram and two hundred and fifty others (of the tribe of Reuven) were smitten along with Korach and his band: they were drawn with them into the dispute.

The Midrash makes a similar observation, saying, "Woe to the wicked, and woe to his neighbors!... Korach's neighbors in the south were lost along with him in his rebellion."[11] But unlike Rashi, who emphasizes that many Reuvenites *joined* Korach's rebellion, the Midrash implies that they were merely punished alongside him. In other words, according to the Midrash, the effects of a wicked neighbor are definite but limited. An evil person could cause his innocent neighbor to be punished alongside him by association, or at most to

---

11. Tanchuma, Bamidbar 12.

be dragged along to participate in his criminal acts, but he does not necessarily cause the innocent neighbor to become an evil person himself.

Concerning a good neighbor, however, even the Midrash agrees that the benefits are more than incidental. As our Sages taught, "any quality is more powerful when it is used for good than when it is used for evil."[12] Thus, the Midrash observes that "Moshe, along with Aharon and his sons, encamped in the east, and next to them were Yehudah, Yissachar and Zevulun. On this basis it was said: 'How fortunate is the righteous, and how fortunate are his neighbors!' This refers to these three tribes, who were adjacent to Moshe and Aharon, and who became great in Torah." These tribes were impacted by their close proximity to the righteous in a meaningful and life-altering way; in the words of the Midrash, the tribes of Yehudah, Yissachar and Zevulun themselves "became great in Torah."

— *Likkutei Sichos, vol. 33, pp. 10–15*

---

12. Sotah 11a.

4:5-6 | ד:ה-ו

וּבָא אַהֲרֹן וּבָנָיו בִּנְסֹעַ הַמַּחֲנֶה וְהוֹרִדוּ
אֶת פָּרֹכֶת הַמָּסָךְ וְכִסּוּ בָהּ אֵת אֲרֹן הָעֵדֻת:
וְנָתְנוּ עָלָיו כְּסוּי עוֹר תַּחַשׁ וּפָרְשׂוּ בֶגֶד
כְּלִיל תְּכֵלֶת מִלְמָעְלָה

*When the camp is about to travel,
Aharon and his sons shall come and take down
the dividing curtain, and they shall cover the Ark of
the Testimony with it. They shall place upon it a
covering of tachash skin, and on top of that they shall
spread a cloth of pure blue wool.*

Hide and Go

One of the tasks of the Kohanim was to prepare the vessels of the Mishkan for travel by covering them with specially designated covers and sacks. The Aron, says the Torah, was wrapped in three distinct coverings. First, they draped the *paroches* (the dividing curtain that hung before the Kodesh Hakodashim) over it. Over that, they placed a covering of *tachash* skin. Lastly, the Aron and all its coverings were placed in a blue woolen sack.

Like the Aron in transit, the holy soul imbued in every Jew—"a veritable part of G-d Above"[13]—is subjected in this world to numerous layers of concealment and suppression. The soul strives to live an exclusively G-dly life, yet its physical body has a never ending list of needs and demands that must be met. In addition, the G-dly soul is competing against the

---

13. Tanya, chapter 2.

"animal soul"—our natural tendencies based on ego and lust. If that weren't enough, the Jew is surrounded by unholy outside influences that obscure his perspective of right and wrong, placing yet another obstacle in the way of his G-dly soul's goal.

Considering all the disadvantages that the G-dly soul faces, one begins to wonder: what purpose is there to this virtually impossible task?

The Torah answers this question with its description of how the Aron traveled. When Bnei Yisrael camped, the Aron stood in the Mishkan in all its glory. Yet no less than three coverings concealed it when it was time to *travel*, to advance and ascend toward its ultimate home in the Promised Land. Similarly, the blockages that our G-dly souls encounter are actually opportunities for us to climb and soar in our union with G-d. As such, we must never despair over our challenges, but instead view them as a way to attain an even greater degree of G-dliness than we have ever enjoyed before.

—*Likkutei Sichos, vol. 8, pp. 18-20*

נשא
Naso

4:22 | ד:כב

נָשֹׂא אֶת רֹאשׁ

Take a headcount.

By a Raise of Heads

The command נשא את ראש at the beginning of Parshas Naso means to take a census.

However, the literal translation of this phrase is "raise the heads." This peculiar expression alludes to a fundamental and guiding principle of Jewish life.

The Mishna instructs us: "Be bold as a leopard... to do the will of your Father in heaven!"[1] This means to be unashamed in the face of scorn.[2] This directive is the principle with which the Alter Rebbe opens his Shulchan Aruch, his Code of Jewish Law.

Practically, how do we fulfill this mandate? Through נשא את ראש.

---

[1]. Avos 5:20.
[2]. Tur, Orach Chaim 1:1.

When confronted by ridicule, the Torah advises us to "raise our heads," i.e., to arouse within ourselves a spirit of *exaltedness*, enabling us to rise above and be utterly unmoved by scoffers and skeptics. To realize our Divine mission in this world, we must "raise our heads": we must be proud, courageous, and utterly unfazed by ridicule from outside or cynicism from within.

—*Toras Menachem 5743, vol. 3, p. 1612*

5:7 | ה:ז

וְהִתְוַדּוּ אֶת חַטָּאתָם אֲשֶׁר עָשׂוּ
They shall confess the sin they committed.

Holistic Healing

The Rambam writes in Sefer Hamitzvos:

> The 73rd mitzvah is that we are commanded to verbally acknowledge the sins we have committed before G-d, exalted be He, when we repent from them... As the Torah states, "They shall confess the sin they committed."

The Rambam mentions *teshuvah*, repentance, as the circumstance under which one can fulfill the mitzvah of verbal confession, but he does not enumerate *teshuvah* as a mitzvah unto itself. The absence of *teshuvah* from the Rambam's list caused the later commentaries to wonder if repentance is actually an obligation. Does one fulfill a mitzvah by repenting, and neglect a mitzvah if he does not repent? If it *is* a mitzvah, why does the Rambam not list it among the 613?

One explanation is that although *teshuvah* is indeed a mitzvah, it is a general recommitment to all of G-d's other commands. Since it does not entail any unique activity that is not included in the other mitzvos, the Rambam does not list it among the 613.

This idea reflects the inner meaning of *teshuvah* and its relationship with the other mitzvos. Our Sages explain that the 248 commandments and 365 prohibitions correspond to the 248 limbs and 365 sinews in the human body.[3] Chassidus

---

3. See Talmud, Makkos 23b; Zohar 1:170b.

explains that the soul comprises 613 spiritual "limbs" or faculties, each corresponding to a particular mitzvah.[4] Any lack in the fulfillment of the one of the mitzvos causes a deficiency in the corresponding "limb" in one's soul.[5]

Through *teshuvah*, however, the deficient limbs of the soul can be repaired. This is because *teshuvah*, which is motivated and characterized by a profound desire to reconnect with G-d, draws from the very essence of the soul, the source from which the individual limbs of the soul extend. *Teshuvah* thus breathes new life into *all* the limbs of the soul, restoring them to their proper "health." Accordingly, it can be suggested that only mitzvos corresponding to a specific limb in the soul are enumerated in the 613, but not *teshuvah*, which stems from the essence of the soul and enlivens them all.

—*Likkutei Sichos, vol. 38, pp. 18-23*

---

4. Tanya, chapter 4.
5. Likkutei Torah, Nitzavim 45c.

5:9 | ה:ט

וְכָל תְּרוּמָה לְכָל קָדְשֵׁי בְנֵי יִשְׂרָאֵל
אֲשֶׁר יַקְרִיבוּ לַכֹּהֵן לוֹ יִהְיֶה

*Every raised-offering of all the holy things
that the children of Israel bring to the Kohen,
it shall be his.*

How to Give

Rashi explains that this verse teaches us that the Bikkurim are given to the Kohen. Elsewhere,[6] the Torah instructs us to bring Bikkurim, the first fruits of the season, to the Beis Hamikdash, the Holy Temple, but does not state what shall be done with the fruit afterward. The Torah tells us now, "to the Kohen, it shall be his"—the Bikkurim are divided among the Kohanim.

The Torah's portrayal of Bikkurim as a two-step process, first requiring us to bring the new fruits to the Beis Hamikdash and then instructing us to leave them for the Kohanim, teaches us the approach we should adopt when it comes to giving *tzedakah*.

Bikkurim must be brought from fruits of the highest quality,[7] whose cultivation requires great effort and patience. The mitzvah to bring the very first of these fruits to the Temple demonstrates that when we chance upon an opportunity to give to charity, we must not hesitate to part with it as we consider how difficult it was for us to earn. Rather, we should

---

6. Shemos 23:19.
7. See Mishneh Torah, Hil. Bikkurim 2:3.

readily give the first and finest of our earnings to a G-dly purpose—*tzedakah*.

The ultimate challenge, however, is not in contributing toward a holy or communal cause, but in giving the first of our earnings to the poor, for their personal benefit. We can rightfully argue: why is the next person more entitled to the first fruits of my labor than I am? I, too, am needy and deserving!

The mitzvah of Bikkurim shows us how to surmount this inner struggle: by bringing the new fruits to the Temple *before* giving them to the Kohen. Figuratively, this means to regard the first of our earnings as funds that already belong to charity. The process begins with "bringing the fruits to the Temple," because the struggle of parting with our hard-earned money in favor of giving it to someone else exists only so long as we are parting with *our* possessions. Once we regard the funds as belonging to charity, giving them away becomes much easier.

—*Likkutei Sichos, vol. 8, pp. 39–40*

5:12 | ה:יב

אִישׁ אִישׁ כִּי תִשְׂטֶה אִשְׁתּוֹ וּמָעֲלָה בוֹ מָעַל

A man whose wife strayed and was unfaithful to him.

Returning Shortly

A *sotah* is a married woman who is suspected of adultery and prohibited from being with her husband until she proves her innocence. The term *sotah* means "woman who strays," and comes from the verse in the Torah, "A man whose wife strays (*sisteh*) and was unfaithful to him." The word *shtus*, meaning foolishness or irrationality, stems from the same root. By using a term synonymous with foolishness to describe the *sotah*'s sin, the Torah teaches us that it is simply inconceivable that a Jew would transgress the Torah's laws unless he or she is not thinking rationally.[8]

The Torah's allusion to this principle in the context of the laws of a *sotah* also teaches us that, like a *sotah*, a Jew who is distant from G-d through "foolish" transgressions is in this state only temporarily. A *sotah* is not necessarily guilty of adultery; she is deemed a *sotah* simply because she behaved in a manner that allowed for suspicion. Such conduct is, in and of itself, immodest for a Jewish woman, and temporarily bars her from her normal married life. Once she drinks the miraculous "*sotah* waters," however, and establishes her innocence, she returns to her husband and they continue living together. In fact, the Torah promises that her marriage will now be even more blessed than it was previously.[9] If she was barren, she

---

8. See Talmud, Sotah 3a.
9. See Bamidbar 5:28.

will now conceive; if she gave birth painfully, she will now give birth with ease; if she used to give birth to unattractive children, she will now give birth to beautiful children.[10]

The same is true concerning the distance we put between ourselves and G-d when we sin. The Jewish people as a whole are regarded as G-d's "wife," which is why our conduct is of such significance to Him. Yet even when the foolishness of the *yetzer hara*, the evil inclination, gets the better of us, our distance from G-d is only temporary. Ultimately, every Jew will certainly do *teshuvah* and be cleared from sin, and our relationship with G-d will be renewed and enhanced.

—*Likkutei Sichos, vol. 2, pp. 313-314*

---

10. See Talmud, Sotah 26a; Talmud Yerushalmi, Sotah 3:4.

6:8 | ו:ח

כֹּל יְמֵי נִזְרוֹ קָדֹשׁ הוּא לַה'

All the days of his separation, he is holy to G-d.

I am Holy, Therefore I Am Different

A *nazir* is an individual who chooses to dedicate himself to G-d, by vowing to abstain (usually for a limited period of time) from wine or any grape products, from cutting his hair, and from defiling himself with the ritual impurity contracted from the dead.

The Torah emphasizes, however, that being a *nazir* is not just a matter of abstinence. Rather, "all the days of his separation, he is holy to G-d"—the *nazir*'s vow is a pledge of holiness, in the context of which he undertakes certain restrictions.

This understanding of the laws of *nazir* teaches us a valuable lesson. The Torah demands that we conduct ourselves in a manner that far exceeds society's ethical and moral standards. In addition, we are encouraged to distance ourselves from even a faint brush with the Torah's prohibitions. Now, one way to approach these expectations is from a place of fear and frailty: a person regards himself (correctly or incorrectly) as spiritually or morally weak, and therefore accepts that he must take extra precautions to prevent himself from succumbing to corruption, sin and immorality.

The ideal and correct approach, however, is one of distinction and pride. Like the *nazir* who is "holy, *therefore* abstains," a Jew must approach the Torah's high standards and expectations with the attitude that "I have been set apart by

G-d to be distinguished and sanctified; would it befit me to behave otherwise? Considering my illustrious lineage—I am a descendant of Avraham, Yitzchak, Yaakov, Sarah, Rivkah, Rachel and Leah—how can I compare myself to the rest of society? G-d selected *me* to receive the Torah. It therefore behooves me to be different, and to take the high road in all areas of sanctity and morality."

—*Toras Menachem, vol. 44, pp. 75-79*

7:3 | ג:ז

וַיָּבִיאוּ אֶת קָרְבָּנָם לִפְנֵי ה' שֵׁשׁ עֶגְלֹת צָב וּשְׁנֵי עָשָׂר בָּקָר עֲגָלָה עַל שְׁנֵי הַנְּשִׂאִים וְשׁוֹר לְאֶחָד

They brought their offering before G-d: six covered wagons and twelve oxen, a wagon from each two princes and an ox from each one.

Where More is Less

Bnei Yisrael's generosity when they donated materials for the construction of the Mishkan was extraordinary. As the craftsmen told Moshe, "The people are bringing very much, more than is enough for the labor of the articles which G-d had commanded to make."[11] In contrast, when the Mishkan was later dedicated, the princes of the tribes jointly gave what seems to be a very meager gift: "six covered wagons and twelve oxen, a wagon from each two princes and an ox from each one." Each of the princes sponsored only *half* a wagon, instead of donating a full wagon of his own!

This is even more troubling considering the purpose the wagons would serve—to assist the *Levi'im* in transporting the Mishkan and its parts. Knowing the many items requiring transportation, why did the princes limit their donation to a mere six wagons, barely enough to do the job?

As components of the holy Mishkan, every wagon in its entirety needed to be critical to the Mishkan's service. The Mishkan would be a dwelling place for G-d, wherein the G-dliness and Divine purpose inherent in all of creation would

---

11. Shemos 36:7.

be revealed and manifest. Indeed, our Sages taught, "In all of G-d's creation, He did not create even one thing for naught."[12] Certainly, then, in the Mishkan itself, if any of its components were unnecessary or underutilized, the integrity of the entire Mishkan would be compromised.

The princes' donation was therefore limited to six wagons—no less, but also no more. Since the task *could* be completed with six wagons, to spread the load over more than six would mean that each of the wagons was not being used to its fullest potential.

The same is true of the "Mishkan" that we each create within our own lives. Only when all our talent and potential is fully utilized for the purpose for which it was created—"I was created only to serve my Creator"[13]—is the home we make for G-d truly complete.

—Likkutei Sichos, vol. 28, pp. 40-48

---

12. Shabbos 77b.
13. Kiddushin 82a.

בהעלתך
Beha'aloscha

8:2 | ח:ב

בְּהַעֲלֹתְךָ אֶת הַנֵּרֹת
When you ignite the lamps.

Step Up

When the Torah mentions igniting the lamps of the menorah, the term used for "when you ignite" is *beha'aloscha*, which literally means "when you cause to ascend." From this the Sages understood that there was a step in front of the menorah, which the Kohen ascended while preparing the lamps.[1]

The kindling of the menorah is also a metaphor for kindling the G-dly flame in the "lamp of G-d" which is the "soul of man"[2]—i.e., to cause the soul to shine brightly with the light of Torah and mitzvos.[3]

---

1. See Rashi, Bamidbar 8:2.
2. Mishlei 20:27.
3. See also Mishlei 6:23.

Accordingly, the step that stood before the menorah teaches us that when a person ignites the G-dly spark in his fellow Jew, the igniter himself has an "ascension" as well. Like the Kohen who would ascend a step in order to prepare the lamps of the menorah, a person who takes upon himself to kindle the soul of his fellow Jew is elevated spiritually in every aspect of his life. And from his elevated state, he will certainly succeed in his mission to ignite the lamps of the spiritual menorah.

—*Sefer Hasichos 5748, vol. 2, pp. 486–487*

8:2 | ח:ב

דַּבֵּר אֶל אַהֲרֹן וְאָמַרְתָּ אֵלָיו בְּהַעֲלֹתְךָ אֶת הַנֵּרֹת אֶל מוּל פְּנֵי הַמְּנוֹרָה יָאִירוּ שִׁבְעַת הַנֵּרוֹת

Speak to Aharon and say to him, "When you ignite the lamps, the seven lamps shall cast their light toward the face of the menorah."

Lamps and Flames

The Talmud regards the menorah as a symbol of Torah study. Hence our Sages taught, "One who wants to become wise should turn to the south [when praying]… Your sign for this is… the menorah stood to the south [in the Mishkan]."[4]

Why, then, did G-d command Aharon to kindle the menorah, and not Moshe, through whom the Torah was given?

The menorah was kindled specifically by Aharon to teach us that for the Torah to have its desired effects, Torah study alone is not enough. Torah study alone is like the *lamps* of the menorah, which did not give off any light until Aharon kindled their *flames*. Likewise, a person might study and comprehend the Torah, but his soul will still not be "ignited" by his Torah study if his menorah is lacking flames.

Flames are caused by the combustion of fuel. The flames of the menorah thus represent prayer, during which one contemplates "the greatness of G-d and the lowliness of man."[5] By contemplating our own insignificance, and thereby appreciating the great opportunity that G-d has given us to approach

---

4. Bava Basra 25b.
5. Rema, Orach Chaim 98:1.

Him through prayer, our egos are "consumed," allowing for the creation of a flame.

Why is prayer associated with Aharon?

The Zohar compares Moshe and Aharon to *shushvinin*, the ushers who escort a bride and groom to the *chupah*.[6] In the analogy, Moshe is the escort of the groom (G-d) and Aharon is the escort of the bride (the Jewish nation). Moshe revealed G-d's wisdom to the world, but Aharon focused on elevating Bnei Yisrael, drawing them closer to G-d. Elevating ourselves and drawing ourselves closer to G-d is likewise the focus of prayer. G-d therefore commanded Aharon to ignite the menorah, for it is our service of prayer, represented by Aharon, which enables our Torah study to illuminate our lives.

—*Toras Menachem, vol. 40, pp. 108-112*

---

6. See Zohar 3:53b, et al.

9:7 | ט:ז

לָמָּה נִגָּרַע לְבִלְתִּי הַקְרִיב אֶת קָרְבַּן ה׳ בְּמֹעֲדוֹ

"Why should we be deprived, that we may not bring the offering of G-d in its appointed season?"

Searching for Connection

The mitzvah of Pesach Sheni, the second opportunity to offer the Pesach sacrifice, is somewhat of an anomaly among the other mitzvos of the Torah. All the other mitzvos are characterized by obedience: we dutifully follow whatever G-d instructs. Pesach Sheni, however, came about through the insistence of a few people who were restricted from offering the Pesach sacrifice in its proper time due to ritual impurity. They approached Moshe and begged not to be deprived of offering this sacrifice.

Seemingly, what basis was there for their request? If G-d had not communicated a desire that they bring the Pesach offering at a later occasion, they were obviously not obligated to do so! Yet, in response to their demand, G-d gave the Jewish people a *new* mitzvah—the observance of Pesach Sheni.

From here we learn that when a Jew senses that he is being deprived of an opportunity associated with Torah and mitzvos, he must not simply accept that G-d has not yet obligated him in this area. He must demand, "Why should I be deprived?" As the Talmud declares, "Everything is in the hands of heaven except the fear of heaven."[7] G-d waits for the individual to pursue a relationship with Him, but when a person demonstrates

---

7. Berachos 33b.

a genuine desire to connect with G-d through the Torah and mitzvos, G-d graciously grants him additional opportunities to find the connection he seeks.

—*Toras Menachem 5744, vol. 3, pp. 1679–1682*

9:1-2 | ט:א-ב

וַיְדַבֵּר ה' אֶל מֹשֶׁה בְמִדְבַּר סִינַי בַּשָּׁנָה הַשֵּׁנִית לְצֵאתָם מֵאֶרֶץ מִצְרַיִם בַּחֹדֶשׁ הָרִאשׁוֹן לֵאמֹר: וְיַעֲשׂוּ בְנֵי יִשְׂרָאֵל אֶת הַפָּסַח בְּמוֹעֲדוֹ

G-d spoke to Moshe in the Sinai Desert, in the second year of their exodus from the land of Egypt, in the first month, saying: "Bnei Yisrael shall make the Pesach sacrifice in its appointed time."

Fight for Your Rights

In Parshas Beha'aloscha, the Torah recounts the one occasion when Bnei Yisrael offered a Pesach sacrifice in the desert. This took place in the month of Nissan, a month prior to the events that are related eight chapters earlier at the start of the Book of Bamidbar. Rashi explains that the Torah does not document these events in chronological order, so as not to begin the Book of Bamidbar with a source of shame for the Jewish people, for in the 40 years that they were in the desert, this was the only Pesach offering they brought.

But what was the shame in not offering the Pesach sacrifice in the desert? Besides for the one offered in Egypt, G-d commanded that the yearly Pesach offering be observed "when you come into the land that G-d shall give to you."[8] As Rashi explains, "The Torah makes this mitzvah contingent upon their entry into the Land. In the desert, they were obligated to offer the Pesach sacrifice only once, in the second year, and that was by explicit Divine mandate." If G-d had not com-

---

8. Shemos 12:25.

manded them to do so, why is their lack of Pesach offerings in the desert a source of shame?[9]

The explanation is that, unlike other mitzvos whose obligation is exclusive to the Land of Israel, the Pesach sacrifice was indeed offered one time in the desert—albeit upon explicit Divine mandate. Hence, its fulfillment was not *inherently* contingent on arrival in the Land. Moreover, we know that the insistence of a few individuals who were restricted from offering the sacrifice (in the desert) brought about the mitzvah of Pesach Sheni—a replacement holiday for those who could not offer the first Pesach sacrifice in its proper time.

Therein lies the shame in the Jewish people's lack of Pesach offerings during their time in the desert. If G-d accepted the plea of a handful of individuals, certainly He would have granted an entire nation's demand not to be deprived of this mitzvah. Knowing the possibility of offering a Pesach sacrifice in the desert, how is it that for 39 years no one requested the opportunity?

To hide this shameful fact, the Book of Bamidbar begins instead with G-d's instruction to count Bnei Yisrael, demonstrating nonetheless the Jewish people's preciousness before G-d.

—*Likkutei Sichos, vol. 23, pp. 65–70*

---

9. See Tosafos, Kiddushin 37b.

9:22 | ט:כב

אוֹ יֹמַיִם אוֹ חֹדֶשׁ אוֹ יָמִים בְּהַאֲרִיךְ הֶעָנָן עַל הַמִּשְׁכָּן לִשְׁכֹּן עָלָיו יַחֲנוּ בְנֵי יִשְׂרָאֵל וְלֹא יִסָּעוּ וּבְהֵעָלֹתוֹ יִסָּעוּ

Whether it was for two days, a month or a year that the cloud lingered over the Mishkan, the children of Israel would encamp and not travel, and when it departed, they traveled.

Not Just a Stopover

Each of Bnei Yisrael's journeys and encampments in the desert was by Divine bidding. When it was time to travel, the miraculous cloud that covered the Mishkan would depart, at which point Bnei Yisrael would travel, the cloud leading the way. "And in the place where the cloud came to rest, there the Bnei Yisrael encamped. At the commandment of G-d the Bnei Yisrael journeyed, and at the commandment of G-d they encamped."[10]

Some of their encampments lasted for a year or more, but in some locations their stay was only one night, or a day or two. Upon their arrival at each location, the Levi'im would reassemble the entire Mishkan, and then dismantle it when the cloud indicated that it was time to go. Since "at G-d's bidding they would encamp, and at G-d's bidding they would travel,"[11] there was obviously a G-dly reason to assemble the Mishkan in that particular place at that particular time. And since G-d and His will transcend time and space, the importance of any particular encampment was not determined by the length of

---

10. Bamidbar 9:17–18.
11. Bamidbar 9:23.

time spent there. The Mishkan was therefore assembled in each location where they camped, regardless of how long or short their stay would be.

As Jews, we know that our *every* step is determined by G-d's providence (and not only in the desert, where it was plain to see). Recognizing that our journeys in life are planned by G-d, who transcends time and space, we must "create a Mishkan" within every situation, for however long G-d determines that moment will last. Whether a circumstance seems long-term or only temporary, it is an opportunity to unite with the infinite G-d and His infinite will in a union that transcends all time and space.

—*Likkutei Sichos, vol. 2, p. 687*

10:35 | י:לה

קוּמָה ה' וְיָפֻצוּ אֹיְבֶיךָ וְיָנֻסוּ מְשַׂנְאֶיךָ מִפָּנֶיךָ

Arise, O G-d, may Your enemies be scattered, and may those who hate You flee from You.

Your Honor

Rashi explains that Moshe's entreaty to G-d, "May those who hate You flee from You," refers to those who hate the Jewish people. "For anyone who hates the Jewish people hates the One who spoke and the world came into being."

Why did Moshe pray that G-d cause *His* enemies to flee, merely *alluding* to the enemies of the Jews, instead of asking directly that G-d cause the enemies of the Jewish people to flee?

In this way, Moshe asked that G-d save the Jewish people even if they are deficient in their worship and unworthy of salvation on their own merit. Moshe demanded that even so, their enemies should be forced to flee because they are G-d's enemies. For the enemies of the Jews are not concerned with the extent of the Jewish people's devotion to the Torah and mitzvos, and will not attribute the Jews' suffering to their misdeeds. They do know, however, that the Jewish people are called the children of G-d. Therefore, Moshe insinuated, if they succeed at harming the Jews, and G-d does not save them, Heaven forfend, this will cause disgrace to G-d Himself. To avoid this disgrace to Your holy name, prayed Moshe, protect the Jewish people even if they are not worthy on their own accord. "Because anyone who hates the Jewish people hates the One who spoke and the world came into being"—it is Your own honor, G-d, that must be protected.

—*Likkutei Sichos, vol. 23, p. 79*

שלח
Shelach

13:30 | יג:ל

וַיַּהַס כָּלֵב אֶת הָעָם אֶל מֹשֶׁה וַיֹּאמֶר עָלֹה נַעֲלֶה וְיָרַשְׁנוּ אֹתָהּ כִּי יָכוֹל נוּכַל לָהּ

Calev silenced the people regarding Moshe, and he said, "We shall surely go up and take possession of it, for we can indeed overcome it."

Telling Priorities

Moshe sent spies to the Land of Israel. Upon their return, they reported: "We came to the land to which you sent us, and indeed it is flowing with milk and honey, and this is its fruit. However, the people who inhabit the land are mighty, and the cities are extremely huge and fortified…"[1]

At that point Calev interrupted them. He silenced the nation and assured them, "We shall surely go up and take possession of it [the Land], for we can indeed overcome it."

Why did Calev interrupt the spies' report? Up until that point, they had spoken only about the richness of the land

---

1. Bamidbar 13:27–28.

and the strength of its inhabitants—precisely what Moshe had asked them to investigate! What did Calev see in their words that already put him on the defensive?

What Calev noticed was that they did not report their findings in the same order as Moshe's directives to them. In this slight deviation Calev sensed a fundamental difference of priorities between the spies and Moshe.

Moshe said, "See the land, what is it: are the people who inhabit it strong or weak? Are they few or many? And what of the land they inhabit: is it good or bad?"[2] The first thing he asked about was the strength of the land's inhabitants, because his primary concern was how to go about fulfilling G-d's instruction to conquer the land. The quality of the land was only of secondary significance to him.

The spies, however, spoke first about the benefits of the Land—"it flows with milk and honey, and this is its fruit"—and only afterward about the challenging task of conquering it that lay before them.

Calev realized immediately that they were making a dreadful mistake. When a person is doing G-d's will, but is primarily focused on the reward he will receive, his dedication to the task is determined by the benefit it will yield: does the reward justify going to great lengths to fulfill this particular mitzvah or not? And when mitzvos become defined by the degree of difficulty they entail, it isn't long before a person wrongly concludes that some of G-d's commands are simply impossible.

As such, even before the spies finished sharing the conclusions they had garnered from their visit, Calev knew he had to protest.

—*Likkutei Sichos, vol. 4, pp. 1313–1314*

---

2. Bamidbar 13:18–19.

13:31 | יג:לא

לֹא נוּכַל לַעֲלוֹת אֶל הָעָם כִּי חָזָק הוּא מִמֶּנּוּ

"We are unable to go up against the people, for they are stronger than we are."

Manufacturer's Instructions

Moshe sent spies to the Land of Israel, instructing them, "See the land, what is it: are the people who inhabit it strong or weak? Are they few or many? And what of the land they inhabit: is it good or bad? And what of the cities in which they reside: are they in camps or in fortresses?"[3]

When the spies returned, they reported, "The people that dwell in the land are strong, and the cities are fortified and very great."[4] Thus, concluded the spies, "We are unable to go up against the people, for they are stronger than we are."[5] Their report caused the people to weep, insisting that they would rather return to Egypt than enter the land. As a result, G-d delayed Bnei Yisrael's entry into Israel for an additional thirty-nine years, and the ten spies were punished and died from a plague.

But what was the spies' actual crime? Had Moshe not instructed them to investigate those exact details?

The spies' offense was not in their report, per se, but in the mistaken conclusions they drew based on their findings. Seeing the natural challenges that they would face, the spies

---

3. Bamidbar 13:18–19.
4. Bamidbar 13:28.
5. Bamidbar 13:31.

concluded that fulfilling G-d's command was simply beyond Bnei Yisrael's abilities.

Moshe, on the other hand, asked about the land and its inhabitants, but only for tactical purposes—in order to chart the most feasible route for a natural victory. If it would ultimately require miracles, Moshe trusted that G-d would intervene. He was certain that G-d's instruction to conquer the land would be realized; it was only a question of the best way to make it happen.

The story of the spies and their tragic mistake underscores the importance of taking Moshe's approach when we encounter any mitzvah that seems too difficult, or even impossible, for us to fulfill. The logic is simple: If even a human being would not instruct someone to perform a task that he knew the other person was incapable of performing, certainly the Creator, who knows the precise abilities with which He created each of us, and before whom there are no miscalculations, gives only commands that are unquestionably within our reach.

—*Likkutei Sichos, vol. 13, pp. 39–40*

13:33 | יג:לג

וְשָׁם רָאִינוּ אֶת הַנְּפִילִים בְּנֵי עֲנָק מִן הַנְּפִלִים

There we saw the Nephilim, sons of the giant, who descended from the Nephilim.

Where the Angels Failed

The Midrash[6] relates that when the early humans took to worshipping idols, two angels, Shamchazai and Azael, suggested before G-d that they could replace humankind in fulfilling the world's purpose. G-d replied, "It is known and revealed to Me that if you dwelled upon the earth, the evil inclination would dominate you; in fact, you would be even worse than the sons of man." But they insisted, so G-d allowed them to descend to earth. Sure enough, they immediately became corrupted.

Years later, when Moshe sent spies to the Land of Israel, the spies returned and reported that in addition to the "natural" giants that they saw in the Land,[7] they also encountered giant Nephilim. These Nephilim were the descendants of the corrupted angels. As Rashi[8] explains, the word Nephilim shares a common root with the Hebrew word *nafal*, fallen, for the Nephilim descended from Shamchazai and Azael, who "fell" from heaven.

With their report about the Nephilim, the spies intended not only to frighten Bnei Yisrael with regard to the brute strength of the Land's inhabitants, but also to terrify them about the spiritual risks that entering the Land entailed. As

---

6. Yalkut Shimoni, Bereishis 44.
7. See Bamidbar 13:28.
8. Bamidbar 13:33.

explained in Likkutei Torah,[9] the spies wanted to remain in the desert, where all their physical needs were automatically (miraculously) provided. They feared that the burden of material concerns awaiting them in the Land would preclude them from enjoying the spiritual life they had become accustomed to in the desert. The spies' mention of the Nephilim, whose interaction with the material world led to their corruption, was meant to validate their claim.

But the spies were mistaken. As Yehoshua and Calev insisted, "If G-d desires us, He will bring us to this land."[10] Where angels failed, a Jew can succeed. For "G-d desires us": His greatest source of delight is the Jew who serves Him from within the physical constraints of this world. Therefore, a Jew's ability to be spiritually sensitive even while engaging with the material world is incomparably greater than that of an angel. Moreover, a Jew can ultimately transform the material world, and make it a place of holiness.

—*Likkutei Sichos, vol. 28, pp. 91–92*

---

[9]. Shelach 37a.
[10]. Bamidbar 14:8.

15:20-21 | טו:כ-כא

רֵאשִׁית עֲרִסֹתֵכֶם חַלָּה
תָּרִימוּ תְרוּמָה... תִּתְּנוּ לַה' תְּרוּמָה

The beginning of your dough you shall separate as challah... a gift to G-d.

The Theory of Dough

The mitzvah of *challah* obligates us to separate a portion of every (large) batch of dough that we bake, and give it as a gift to the Kohen. The Midrash notes that immediately following this commandment comes a portion in the Torah regarding someone who worshipped idols. "This teaches us," says the Midrash, "that one who fulfills the mitzvah of *challah* is as though he has abolished idolatry; while one who does not fulfill the mitzvah of *challah* is as though he maintained idolatry."[11]

How is the simple act of separating a piece of dough associated with the cardinal sin of idolatry?

At its core, idolatry is not just the worship of a deity other than the one true G-d, but also the mistaken belief that any power, such as nature, functions independently of Him. Moreover, even the belief that any entity exists independently of G-d runs contrary to our belief that "there is nothing beside Him."[12]

The Midrash therefore compares the observance of *challah* to the abolition of idolatry, and the failure to separate *challah* to maintaining idolatry.

---

11. Vayikra Rabbah 15:6.
12. Devarim 4:35.

From planting the grain to baking the dough, the making of bread involves a great degree of human involvement and skill. So, on a broader scale, dough represents our effort to provide for our needs through what seems to be a natural process, in which our returns seem directly influenced and controlled by our toil. However, when the first thing we do with our dough is to separate a portion of it as a gift to G-d, we are acknowledging that all of our human efforts don't even begin to generate our income. Rather, it is G-d's blessing that ensures our sustenance and success.

Moreover, the separation of *challah* as a gift to G-d acknowledges that since G-d brings the entire world into existence anew at every moment, all of existence truly belongs to Him. We are therefore giving Him the dough that is truly His own.

Thus, by separating *challah* we abolish the mistaken theory of idolatry, by declaring to the world that neither the powers of nature nor the efforts of man exist apart from G-d.

—*Likkutei Sichos, vol. 18, pp. 183–185*

15:32 | טו:לב

וַיִּהְיוּ בְנֵי יִשְׂרָאֵל בַּמִּדְבָּר וַיִּמְצְאוּ אִישׁ מְקֹשֵׁשׁ עֵצִים בְּיוֹם הַשַּׁבָּת

*When Bnei Yisrael were in the desert,
they found a man gathering wood on the Shabbos day.*

Intentions Alone Won't Do

The Torah tells of a man who gathered wood in violation of Shabbos, and whom G-d instructed be put to death. According to the Midrash,[13] the wood-gatherer had noble motives. After the incident of the spies, it was decreed that the Jews of that generation would not enter the Land of Israel. As a result, some of the people erroneously believed that they were no longer obligated to keep the mitzvos. In order to demonstrate—through his liability—that the commandments were still in full effect, the wood-gatherer publicly violated Shabbos.

According to this explanation, the wood-gatherer did not truly desecrate Shabbos, for only deliberate and purposeful work constitutes *melachah*—labor that is biblically prohibited on Shabbos. Hence, Rabbi Shimon rules in the Mishnah[14] that one is not liable for performing on Shabbos "labor that is not needed for itself." An example would be if a person carried objects from his home to the public domain, but his objective was not the transfer to the public domain, but the removal of unwanted objects from his home. Similarly, the wood-gatherer's objective was not the actual task he was performing (gathering wood), but the demonstration that the Shabbos laws were still in effect. Accordingly, he should not have been liable!

---

13. Cited in Tosafos, Bava Basra 119b.
14. Shabbos 93b, et al.

Nevertheless, G-d instructed that he be punished, because his motives did not have any discernible impact on the manner in which he did the prohibited labor, and therefore cannot be taken into halachic consideration.

The wood-gatherer's liability thus refuted the notion that mitzvos were not obligatory after the incident of the spies. As explained in Likkutei Torah,[15] the spies wanted to remain in the desert, where Bnei Yisrael's chief occupation was the study of the Torah, instead of entering the Land of Israel, where their primary task would be actual observance of the mitzvos. Therefore, when G-d decreed that they would remain in the desert for forty years, the people reasoned that their generation was indeed not ready for a service of G-d that emphasized action. For them, a service of G-d involving the mind alone was sufficient.

The wood-gatherer demonstrated, however, that even in the laws of Shabbos, where thought plays such a significant role, intentions that have no bearing on one's actions are irrelevant. Likewise, even in the desert, a Jew's union with G-d is primarily achieved through practical observance of the mitzvos.

—*Likkutei Sichos, vol. 28, pp. 94–97*

---

15. Shelach 38b.

טו:לט | 15:39

וְהָיָה לָכֶם לְצִיצִת וּרְאִיתֶם אֹתוֹ וּזְכַרְתֶּם
אֶת כָּל מִצְוֹת ה' וַעֲשִׂיתֶם אֹתָם

It shall be a fringe for you, that you may look upon it and remember all the commandments of G-d and do them.

Committed Clothing

Rashi explains how the *tzitzis*, ritual fringes, remind us of all the mitzvos. The numerical equivalents of the letters that spell the word *tzitzis*, ציצית, total 600. Add 8 for the number of threads on each corner and 5 for the number of knots tied on each fringe, and you have 613. Seeing the *tzitzis* thus reminds us of the 613 commandments.

Yet if the fringes alone remind us of the mitzvos, why does the fulfillment of this mitzvah require that the fringes be attached to a garment, a *tallis*? This requirement indicates that there is more to remembering the mitzvos than simply calling to mind the number 613.

Unlike the food we eat, which becomes absorbed into our flesh and blood, the clothing we wear envelops us but remains separate from our bodies. Clothing is therefore a metaphor for that which transcends understanding and cannot be absorbed by the human mind.

That is why the mitzvah can be fulfilled only when the *tzitzis* are strung on a garment. When the fringes extend from a garment, they symbolize that all 613 mitzvos stem from G-d's *will*, which utterly transcends human understanding, and likewise our commitment to their observance must transcend reason. Without this recognition, symbolized by the *tallis*, the fringes alone do not represent the 613 mitzvos at all.

—*Likkutei Sichos, vol. 2, pp. 324–325*

קרח
Korach

16:1 | ‏טז:א‏

וַיִּקַּח קֹרַח

Korach set [himself] apart.

In Memoriam: Korach

"The mention of a righteous man shall be a blessing, but the name of the wicked shall rot."[1] The Talmud[2] interprets the latter part of this verse as a directive to not name your child after an evil or corrupt person, so that the wicked person's name will be put out of circulation.

But surprisingly, a portion in the Torah is named Korach, perpetuating the memory of a man who led a rebellion against Moshe—the greatest leader of all time! If we shouldn't name our child Korach, why give a Torah portion his name?

---

1. Mishlei 10:7.
2. Yoma 38b.

Evidently, despite Korach's serious wrongdoing, at the root of his rebellion lay a kernel of truth— a virtue we must aspire to emulate.

Korach wanted to replace Aharon as the Kohen Gadol, the high priest. The attraction of this position was the extraordinary sanctity that came with it, which enabled the Kohen Gadol to stand in perfect union with G-d and to serve Him constantly. Therefore, at its essence, Korach's aspiration was commendable. In fact, the Midrash relates that when Korach and his associates told Moshe what they wished for, Moshe said, "I, too, desire the same!"[3] We therefore title the Parshah using Korach's name, paying tribute to his admirable quest for holiness.

Nevertheless, the first word of the Parshah, *vayikach*, is not included in its title. *Vayikach Korach* means "Korach set himself apart," emphasizing the rebellion against Moshe, who at G-d's behest appointed only Aharon as Kohen Gadol. The word *vayikach* is therefore omitted from the title, because Korach's deplorable actions and the strife he caused are not what we seek to memorialize.

Korach's name, however, is enshrined in Jewish tradition, for his lofty dreams are an inspiration for all time.

—*Likkutei Sichos, vol. 18, pp. 190–191;*
Sefer Hasichos 5748, vol. 2, pp. 500–501

---

3. See Rashi, Bamidbar 16:6.

16:3 | ג:טז

כִּי כָל הָעֵדָה כֻּלָּם קְדֹשִׁים וּבְתוֹכָם ה'
וּמַדּוּעַ תִּתְנַשְּׂאוּ עַל קְהַל ה'

"The entire congregation are holy, every one of them, and G-d is in their midst. So why do you raise yourselves above the assembly of G-d?"

Protecting Your Information

Korach challenged Moshe, "If a house is full of Torah scrolls, what is the law? Does it need a *mezuzah* on its doorpost or not?"

Moshe replied, "It is obligated."

Said Korach: "The entire Torah, all 275 chapters, is not enough to absolve this house of its obligation, but the two chapters in the *mezuzah* do absolve it? G-d did not command you these laws; you have invented them yourself!"[4]

The house full of Torah scrolls in Korach's challenge also alludes to the Torah scholar who has lined his mind with the Torah's wisdom. And, as is evident from his response, Moshe informed Korach that even a scholar who is a virtual storehouse of Torah is in need of the *mezuzah*'s protection.

The *mezuzah* represents our obligation to develop a conscious and personal relationship with G-d, including both love and trepidation before Him. These emotions are highlighted in the two chapters contained in the *mezuzah*. The first chapter, *Shema*, instructs: "You shall love Hashem, your G-d, with all your heart, with all your soul and with all your

---

4. Midrash Tanchuma, Korach 2.

might." The second chapter, *Vehayah im Shamoa*, outlines the rewards for fulfilling G-d's commandments, and warns of the consequences for neglecting them. Hence, the focus of this chapter is to instill in us fear and awe of G-d's Omnipotence.

Moshe's statement that even a house full of Torah scrolls requires a *mezuzah* teaches us that the study of Torah alone is insufficient. The Torah scholar needs the protection of a *mezuzah* i.e., to develop within himself genuine feelings of awe and love for G-d. For in the words of the Mishnah, "One whose fear of sin takes precedence over his wisdom, his wisdom endures. But one whose wisdom takes precedence over his fear of sin, his wisdom does not endure."[5]

—*Likkutei Sichos, vol. 2, p. 329*

---

5. Mishnah, Avos 3:9.

16:5 | טז:ה

בֹּקֶר וְיֹדַע ה' אֶת אֲשֶׁר לוֹ וְאֶת הַקָּדוֹשׁ וְהִקְרִיב אֵלָיו

*In the morning, G-d will make known who is His,
and who is holy, and He will draw [them] near to Him.*

Separate is Better than Equal

Korach fought for equality, which he believed to be the key to Jewish unity. "The entire congregation is all holy,"[6] he argued. Why single out the Kohanim—and particularly the Kohen Gadol—as superior to everyone else?

But instead of going down in history as a great unifier, the Torah regards Korach as the quintessential instigator of conflict and divisiveness, whom we are cautioned not to emulate.[7]

What made Korach's case for unity the textbook example of disunity? The answer is hinted at in Moshe's warning to Korach and his followers, "In the morning, G-d will make known who is His." According to the Midrash, Moshe compared the allocation of roles within the Jewish people to the division of day and night. Moshe said, "G-d assigned boundaries to His world. Are you capable of transforming morning into evening? Such is the possibility of undoing this."[8]

In this way, Moshe illustrated that peace can be achieved only by respecting the boundaries inherent in creation, not by abolishing them. G-d created the world with diversity. Each day consists of both morning and evening, but individually, each of these periods serves a distinct purpose. The same

---

6. Bamidbar 16:3.
7. See Talmud, Sanhedrin 110a.
8. See Rashi, Bamidbar 16:5.

is true of all G-d's creations. He created every being with a unique identity and a specific role that it must fill. When its energies are devoted to the purpose it serves best, not wasted on a task intended for another part of creation, then the world functions in harmony, instead of chaos and discord.

In order to achieve Jewish unity, explained Moshe, the Divinely ordained distinctions of Kohen, Levi and Yisrael must not be annulled—they must be maintained and protected. Like the limbs and organs in the human body that function differently but cohesively, when a Jew thrives within his intended role in the service of G-d, his unique service complements his fellow Jews' unique roles as well, and theirs in turn enhance his.

—*Likkutei Sichos, vol. 18, pp. 203-207*

16:5 | ט״ז:ה

בֹּקֶר וְיֹדַע ה' אֶת אֲשֶׁר לוֹ

In the morning, G-d will make known who is His.

Same but Different

Korach and his followers took issue with Moshe's authority. They acknowledged that G-d communicated the Torah directly to Moshe, and that Moshe was therefore superior to the rest of the nation in his understanding of G-d's wisdom. In actual observance of the mitzvos, however, every Jew is equally capable. If so, argued Korach, considering that our primary purpose in this world is to observe the mitzvos in *practice*, what makes Moshe so much greater than "the entire congregation," which is "all holy"?[9]

The answer to Korach's question is hinted to in Moshe's response, "In the morning, G-d will make known who is His." With these words the Torah implies that even in the performance of a mitzvah there can be vast differences.

A mitzvah is comparable to a diamond. If a diamond is not clean, instead of dispersing light brilliantly, the filth on its surface obscures light. The same is true of mitzvos. When a wicked person observes mitzvos, he temporarily draws additional energy into the negative forces of *kelipah* that animate his life at that time.[10] Likewise, if a person's observance of a mitzvah makes him conceited, his ego and self-regard prevent the light of G-d's infinite presence from being revealed. (When

---

9. Bamidbar 16:3.
10. See Shulchan Aruch Admor Hazaken, Hil. Talmud Torah 4:3.

this person later repents, the mitzvos he previously fulfilled are "reclaimed" by the forces of holiness.)

The mitzvos Moshe performed, however, were not clouded by ego or insincerity. He therefore responded to Korach, "In the morning, G-d will make known": G-d's will is fulfilled equally no matter who performs the mitzvah, but only mitzvos that shine like the morning reveal G-dliness in the world around them.

Granted, we are obligated to fulfill the mitzvos regardless of our spiritual state. Ultimately, however, the home that G-d desires in this world is not only a place where He will "be," but also where He will be felt. This was the uniqueness of the mitzvos performed by Moshe, whose spiritual greatness made even his practical mitzvah observance superior to that of the rest of Bnei Yisrael. His mitzvos shone brightly, like the morning; they refined him and illuminated his life with G-dliness, bringing light to the world around him.

—*Likkutei Sichos, vol. 4, pp. 1049–1055*

16:5 | טז:ה

בֹּקֶר וְיֹדַע ה' אֶת אֲשֶׁר לוֹ וְאֶת הַקָּדוֹשׁ וְהִקְרִיב אֵלָיו

In the morning, G-d will make known who is His, and who is holy, and He will draw them near to Him.

A Morning Person's Teshuvah

Korach and his followers contested Moshe's authority, and his appointment of Aharon as the Kohen Gadol, the High Priest. In response, Moshe challenged them to come the next morning and offer *ketores*, incense, one of the most sacred services in the Mishkan. Moshe warned them that in the morning G-d Himself would make known "who is holy, and He will draw them near to Him." Rashi explains that Moshe delayed the showdown until the next morning, hoping that in the meantime they might rethink and retract their complaints.

Moshe's delay also hinted to the ideal manner of *teshuvah*, repentance, which he hoped they would do. To be sure, a person's sins can be atoned for through one moment of sincere regret, even if the remorse is motivated solely by fear of Divine retribution for his transgressions. This form of repentance, however, does not necessarily transform the individual; his fear of punishment is simply another form of his egocentric fixation on self-preservation and survival.

The ideal *teshuvah* is repentance that is not motivated by any personal gain, but which stems simply from a pure love for G-d and a yearning to cleave to Him. This *teshuvah* refines and transforms the penitent's life. His sincere observance of G-d's commandments is no longer obscured by personal pride or satisfaction, and he now radiates G-dly light to the world around him.

When Moshe told Korach and his followers to wait until morning, he was expressing his hope that not only would they retract, but that their repentance would be inspired and "morning-like"—*teshuvah* that would illuminate their lives.

—*Likkutei Sichos, vol. 4, pp. 1053–1054*

16:24-25 | טז:כד-כה

דַּבֵּר אֶל הָעֵדָה לֵאמֹר הֵעָלוּ מִסָּבִיב לְמִשְׁכַּן קֹרַח דָּתָן וַאֲבִירָם: וַיָּקָם מֹשֶׁה וַיֵּלֶךְ אֶל דָּתָן וַאֲבִירָם וַיֵּלְכוּ אַחֲרָיו זִקְנֵי יִשְׂרָאֵל

"Speak to the congregation, saying, 'Withdraw from the dwelling of Korach, Dasan and Aviram.'" Moshe arose and went to Dasan and Aviram, and the elders of Israel followed him.

To Save Those You Love

The fate of Dasan and Aviram, the ringleaders in Korach's revolt against Moshe, was sealed. Moshe had tried to warn them to abandon their rebellion, but they shunned his messengers. Now G-d instructed Moshe to tell Bnei Yisrael to distance themselves from Dasan and Aviram's tents, lest they be punished along with them. Moshe had no choice but to immediately oblige.

The Torah notes, however, that when Moshe went to warn the people gathered near Dasan and Aviram to leave, he did not simply "go." Rather, he "arose" and went, with an entourage of revered elders, making a stately and regal public appearance. For although he could not engage Dasan and Aviram directly at this point, he hoped that his impressive presence alone might arouse feelings of regret and repentance, saving them from their doom. As Rashi notes, "He thought that perhaps they would act toward him in deference, but they did not."

Moshe's conduct teaches us the extent to which we should go to fulfill the mitzvah of loving our fellow Jews. Even after G-d forbade anyone from approaching Dasan and Aviram to caution them to repent, Moshe still dreamed and conspired of ways to save them.

If this was Moshe's approach toward those who *rebelled* against G-d, certainly we are obligated to go to any length to save those whose only sin is their ignorance, often not due to any fault of their own, but because they were never given a proper Jewish education. With determination and creativity, we must seek and pursue every means possible to touch the heart of every Jew and draw them nearer to G-d and His Torah, the true source of life.

—*Likkutei Sichos, vol. 28, pp. 101–103*

חקת
Chukas

19:2 | יט:ב

זֹאת חֻקַּת הַתּוֹרָה אֲשֶׁר צִוָּה ה' לֵאמֹר דַּבֵּר אֶל בְּנֵי יִשְׂרָאֵל וְיִקְחוּ אֵלֶיךָ פָרָה אֲדֻמָּה

This is the decree of the Torah that G-d commanded to say: Speak to Bnei Yisrael, and have them take to you a red heifer.

Irrational Judaism

The Torah commands us to use the ashes of a *parah adumah*, a red heifer, to ritually purify people or articles that have contracted impurity from a human corpse. The mitzvah of *parah adumah* is classified by the Torah as a *chok*, a decree that transcends reason. Indeed, King Shlomo, wisest of men, said, "All of the Torah's commandments I have comprehended. But the chapter of the red heifer, though I have examined, questioned and searched, 'I thought to be wise [in it], but it is distant from me.'"[1]

---

1. Koheles 7:23; Bamidbar Rabbah 19:5.

This mitzvah is characterized by its uniqueness as the ultimate *chok*, yet the Torah introduces its laws with the words "This is the decree of the Torah," thereby associating the entire Torah with this single inexplicable commandment. In doing so, the Torah teaches us that the inexplicableness that characterizes the mitzvah of *parah adumah* is actually common to *all* the mitzvos, which are, in essence, expressions of G-d's will—what G-d wills simply because He so wills. Their relevance is therefore not defined by logic and reason—even Divine reason. Granted, G-d desired that some of the mitzvos should also "descend" to the realm of reason, and He therefore gave them rational significance as well. At their core, however, even the rational mitzvos are *chukim*, decreed by G-d's will; their ultimate purpose transcends all reason.

This explains why G-d did not reveal the reason for the *parah adumah* even to the wisest of men. If every aspect of the Torah were logically explicable, then the always-rational Jew would be at a loss when the fulfillment of a mitzvah would require self-sacrifice—a demand that is inherently irrational. The mitzvah of *parah adumah* is deliberately inexplicable, and at the same time associates the entire Torah with its mysteriousness, because the *chok* element of *parah adumah* serves as the basis for our uncalculated devotion to all the Torah's commands.

—*Likkutei Sichos*, vol. 18, pp. 230–232

יט:ב | 19:2

וְיִקְחוּ אֵלֶיךָ פָרָה אֲדֻמָּה תְּמִימָה

They shall take to you a perfectly red heifer.

Is Death Final? Depends Whom You Ask

The Torah commands us to use the ashes of a *parah adumah*, a red heifer, for the ritual purification of people or articles that have contracted impurity from a human corpse. The Torah assigns this mitzvah to Moshe, emphasizing that Bnei Yisrael must bring the red heifer to him, even though the ashes were actually prepared by Elazar. Similarly, the Midrash states that Moshe alone understood the true purpose of this mitzvah.[2]

Moshe's devotion to G-d was characterized by permanence—nothing in the world could cause his commitment to G-d to waver or weaken. As a result, everything associated with Moshe is everlasting.[3] For example, the Mishkan that Moshe built was hidden away, and was never destroyed by enemy hands. Even regarding Moshe himself, the Talmud states matter-of-factly, "Moshe never died. It is written, 'Moshe died there,' and elsewhere it is written, 'He was there with G-d.' Just as in the latter passage Moshe was standing and serving, so does the former mean that he is standing and serving."[4] Likewise, according to the Midrash, the ashes of Moshe's *parah adumah* outlasted all the others. When ashes of a new *parah*

---

2. See Tanchuma, Chukas 8.
3. See Talmud, Sotah 9a.
4. Sotah 13b.

adumah were made in later generations, the Kohen involved in their preparation would first be purified using ashes from Moshe's *parah adumah*.[5]

This explains why the mitzvah of *parah adumah*, more so than any other mitzvah, is attributed to Moshe. In order for the *parah adumah* to remove the impurity caused by a human corpse, it must undo, to some degree, the cause of the impurity—death itself. This purification was therefore intrinsically connected to Moshe, who represents permanence, perpetuity and immortality.

—*Likkutei Sichos, vol. 33, pp. 127–130*

---

5. Tanchuma, ibid.

19:2 | יט:ב

וְיִקְחוּ אֵלֶיךָ פָרָה אֲדֻמָּה תְּמִימָה

They shall take to you a perfectly red heifer.

The Cow and the Calf

The ashes of the *parah adumah* were used for the ritual purification of people or things that had contracted impurity from a human corpse. In order to remove this impurity, the *parah adumah* must undo, to some degree, the root cause of the impurity—death itself.

The Midrash teaches that the offering of the *parah adumah* atones for the sin of the Golden Calf: "Let the cow come and atone for the calf."[6] The commentaries explain that at the giving of the Torah, Bnei Yisrael were "freed from the clutches of the angel of death,"[7] but their immortality was taken from them when they worshipped the Golden Calf. Accordingly, by atoning for the sin that caused death, the *parah adumah* also undoes the impurity that death imparts.[8]

This explains why, in his Laws of Parah Adumah, the Rambam records the number of red heifers ever used for spiritual purification, emphasizing that the one prepared by Moshiach will be the tenth.[9]

The number ten in Jewish thought symbolizes completeness and perfection.[10] The Rambam thus hints that the com-

---

6. Tanchuma, Chukas 8.
7. See Shemos Rabbah 32:1.
8. See Kli Yakar and Alshich, Bamidbar 19:2.
9. Mishneh Torah, Hil. Parah Adumah 3:4.
10. See Ibn Ezra, Shemos 3:15.

pleteness of this mitzvah will be achieved only in the era of Moshiach, when the sin of the Golden Calf will be entirely forgiven, and "death will be swallowed up forever."[11] As such, the tenth and final *parah adumah* will purify us not only from the effects of death, but from death itself.

—*Likkutei Sichos, vol. 33, pp. 127–128*

---

11. Yeshayahu 25:8.

| 19:2 | יט:ב

וְיִקְחוּ אֵלֶיךָ פָרָה אֲדֻמָּה תְּמִימָה

They shall take to you a perfectly red heifer.

Living on Edge

The Rambam's compendium of Jewish law, the Mishneh Torah, is famous for its precise wording and organization. It is therefore surprising and most unusual that in the midst of a discussion on the laws of the *parah adumah*, the ashes of the red heifer that were used for ritual purification, the Rambam interrupts with a prayer for the immediate revelation of Moshiach.

In the Laws of Parah Adumah, the Rambam writes:

> Nine red heifers were offered from the time that they were commanded to fulfill this mitzvah until the destruction of the Second Temple. The first was brought by Moshe. The second was brought by Ezra. Seven others were offered until the destruction of the Temple. And the tenth will be brought by the King Moshiach, may he speedily be revealed. Amen, so may it be G-d's will.[12]

What place is there for a wishful prayer in the middle of a text on Jewish law? Moreover, it is not written into a discussion about the laws relating to the coming of Moshiach, but in the midst of an entirely different topic!

Evidently, with his "spontaneous" prayer the Rambam intended to teach us yet another law, the fulfillment of which is expressed by such spontaneity.

---

12. Mishneh Torah, Hil. Parah Adumah 3:4.

In his Laws of Kings the Rambam writes that belief in the future redemption of the Jewish people through Moshiach, as well as constantly longing for his arrival, is a fundamental principle of Jewish faith.[13] The obligation to yearn for Moshiach, not only conceptually but also emotionally, means that a Jew must sense that the redemption is a critical need: without it, his life is severely lacking. He therefore anxiously awaits the coming of Moshiach, so much so that the mere mention of the topic is deeply emotional.

This explains why the Rambam inserted the prayer for the immediate revelation of Moshiach specifically in the midst of an entirely unrelated set of laws, merely upon the mention of the word Moshiach. In this way, the Rambam demonstrated that our intense yearning for the Redemption must be such that the mere mention of Moshiach triggers heartfelt prayers for his immediate arrival—may he speedily be revealed. Amen, so may it be G-d's will.

—*Likkutei Sichos, vol. 28, pp. 135–136*

---

13. Mishneh Torah, Hil. Melachim 11:1.

20:29 | כ:כט

וַיִּבְכּוּ אֶת אַהֲרֹן שְׁלֹשִׁים יוֹם כֹּל בֵּית יִשְׂרָאֵל

The entire house of Israel wept for Aharon for thirty days.

How I Really Feel about You

The Torah emphasizes that Aharon's passing was mourned by the entire Jewish nation. The Midrash explains that Aharon was particularly beloved by the people because he was active in restoring peace between disputing parties and quarreling families.[14]

How did Aharon initiate peace between parties in a dispute? He approached each of the parties separately and said, "Have you seen how your friend is berating himself, saying how ashamed he is to see you after what he's done to you?" He would thereby instill feelings of reconciliation in each of them. When the two would later meet, they would be ready to overlook their disagreements and reestablish their friendship.

Aharon's conduct is often cited as an example of the Talmudic teaching[15] that one may modify the truth in the interest of peace. Notably, the Talmud only says that one may *modify* the truth, not that one may speak falsely, for the Torah prohibits saying something inherently false even for the sake of peace. But this raises a question about Aharon, who told each party that the other was remorseful and seeking reconciliation, when in fact they were not!

---

14. Avos d'Rabbi Nasan 12:3.
15. Yevamos 65b.

The answer is that although Aharon's words may have seemed like a misrepresentation of the facts, they were not inherently untrue.

Proof for this can be found in the Rambam's ruling in the Laws of Divorce, where he says that when a husband is halachically obligated to divorce his wife, the court may use physical force to prevail upon him to agree to give his wife a *get*, a bill of divorce, even though a *get* is valid only if given *willingly*.[16] This is not a contradiction because, as the Rambam explains, the genuine desire of every Jew is to observe all the mitzvos and to refrain from the prohibitions. Therefore, when he agrees under pressure to do a mitzvah, he is actually just acknowledging his *true* will and desire.

If this is true regarding any mitzvah, then it is certainly so with regard to the mitzvah to love one's fellow Jew, "a fundamental principle of the Torah."[17] Accordingly, when Aharon spoke of the love between two Jews as an obvious reality, even though outwardly they behaved otherwise, it was perhaps an *embellishment* of the truth, but it was certainly far from being entirely false.

—*Sichos Kodesh 5741, vol. 4, pp. 439-440*

---

16. Mishneh Torah, Hil. Geirushin 2:20.
17. Rashi, Vayikra 19:18.

21:7 | כא:ז

וַיָּבֹא הָעָם אֶל מֹשֶׁה וַיֹּאמְרוּ חָטָאנוּ כִּי דִבַּרְנוּ
בַה' וָבָךְ... וַיִּתְפַּלֵּל מֹשֶׁה בְּעַד הָעָם

The people came to Moshe and said, "We have sinned, for we have spoken against G-d and against you…" So Moshe prayed on behalf of the people.

When Moshe Forgives

Bnei Yisrael spoke against G-d and Moshe, and were attacked by venomous snakes. Nevertheless, Moshe prayed on their behalf. "From here we learn," says Rashi, "that one who is asked to forgive should not be cruel about pardoning."

In the Talmud, however, it seems that this principle is learned from a much earlier source—Avraham's prayers to heal Avimelech and his household from their punishment for abducting Sarah. The Mishnah remarks, "From where do we learn that one who is asked to forgive should not be cruel? As it is written,[18] 'Avraham prayed to G-d; and G-d healed Avimelech.'"[19]

This raises a question on Rashi. If we have already learned this ethic of forgiveness from Avraham, what more can we learn here? Evidently, according to Rashi, Moshe's conduct teaches us something that Avraham's conduct does not.

The difference lies in the Torah's emphasis that Moshe prayed *"on behalf of* the people."

Avraham forgave Avimelech to the extent that he was willing to pray that Avimelech not be punished for his actions.

---

18. Bereishis 20:17.
19. Bava Kamma 8:7.

Moshe, however, forgave Bnei Yisrael so wholly that he was able to pray for their general wellbeing, as if they had never wronged him at all.

G‑d's response to Moshe's prayers likewise reflected this degree of forgiveness. He instructed Moshe to place a bronze serpent upon a pole, and all who gazed upon it would be healed. As Rashi explains, "Does a snake cause life or death? Rather, when Israel looked heavenward [toward the serpent] and subjected their hearts to their Father in heaven, they would be healed."[20] Hence, commensurate with Moshe's concern for Bnei Yisrael, the brass serpent not only removed their immediate punishment, it fully rehabilitated them and caused them to change their conduct for the long term.

Rashi therefore learns from Moshe that "we should not be cruel about pardoning"—even our pardoning should be generous, not begrudging. We should harbor no resentment whatsoever toward those who ask for our forgiveness, and even actively seek their wellbeing.

—*Likkutei Sichos, vol. 28, pp. 138-144*

---

20. Bamidbar 21:8.

בלק
Balak

23:10 | כג:י

מִי מָנָה עֲפַר יַעֲקֹב

Who has counted the dust of Yaakov?

Outnumbering

When Bilaam attempted to curse Bnei Yisrael, G-d caused him to bless and praise them instead. Extolling their impressive merit and endearment to G-d, Bilaam said, "Who has counted the dust of Yaakov?"

What does this mean?

According to one interpretation, Bilaam was saying: Even the mitzvos they observe with dust are innumerable! For example, says Rashi, the Jewish people may not harness an ox and a donkey together when plowing the earth,[1] nor may they plant a mixture of seeds together.[2]

---

1. Devarim 22:10.
2. Vayikra 19:19.

These two examples emphasize another nuance in Bilaam's praise. The Talmud identifies several mitzvos that the Torah demands not only of the Jewish people, but of all of humankind, including the prohibition against crossbreeding animals and the prohibition of grafting different species of trees together. Still, as the Talmud notes, only limited forms of these hybrids are forbidden for gentiles. "They are permitted to… sow diverse seeds together; they are forbidden only to hybridize animals and to graft trees of different kinds."[3] The Torah prohibits a non-Jew only from direct and active mutation of nature, such as crossbreeding animals or grafting one species of tree upon another. A Jew, however, may not even place two different types of animals under one yoke, or plant a mixture of seeds in which the hybridization happens on its own.

By citing these specific prohibitions, Rashi highlights the fact that even in the mitzvos incumbent upon all of humanity, the Jews' obligations—and therefore merits—far outnumber those of all others.

—*Likkutei Sichos, vol. 38, p. 96, fn. 50*

---

[3]. Sanhedrin 56b.

23:10 | כג:י

מִי מָנָה עֲפַר יַעֲקֹב
Who has counted the dust of Yaakov?

Uncountable Mitzvos

Bilaam's plan to curse the Jewish people was foiled when G-d forced him to bless and praise them instead. Describing the Jewish people's endearment to G-d, Bilaam said, "Who has counted the dust of Yaakov?" According to one interpretation brought by Rashi, Bilaam was saying, "Even merely the mitzvos they observe that involve dust are innumerable!" For example, says Rashi, the Jewish people are commanded not to harness an ox and a donkey together when plowing the earth,[4] not to sow their fields with a mixture of seeds,[5] to use the dust-ashes of the red heifer for purification,[6] and to use dust in the examination of a *sotah,* a woman suspected of infidelity.[7]

The Midrashim enumerate many more mitzvos associated with dust, yet Rashi names these four in particular. In doing so, Rashi hints that the mitzvos involving dust are not only numerous, but that to a certain degree they are actually *innumerable.*

Rashi's first two examples are agricultural prohibitions. The Jewish people's primary occupation in biblical times was farming. Accordingly, their fulfillment of the laws related to

---

4. Devarim 22:10.
5. Vayikra 19:19.
6. See Bamidbar, chapter 19.
7. See Bamidbar 5:11–31.

plowing and planting was constant, each time they plowed or planted in the permissible manner.

In the same vein, the mitzvos involving the ashes of the *parah adumah* and the dirt used to examine the *sotah* contain an element of immeasurability: their fulfillment was not a one-time occurrence. For in addition to using the ashes to maintain the purity of Bnei Yisrael, we are commanded to set aside a portion of the ashes "as a keepsake for the congregation of Israel."[8] Hence, the fulfillment of this mitzvah continues as long as some ashes remain in existence. The same is true of the dirt used in the examination of the *sotah*. Its significance as "mitzvah-dust" extends throughout the duration of its use, and for as long as it is effective. This includes the effects of the *sotah*-waters on the woman's future—"she is cleansed and she will bear seed"[9]—i.e., the dust of the *sotah*-water restores her marriage and infuses it with continuous blessing.

Considering the Jewish people's "incalculable" observance of these innumerable mitzvos, said Bilaam, no curse could possibly affect them.

—*Likkutei Sichos, vol. 38, pp. 93–96*

---

8. Bamidbar 19:9.
9. Bamidbar 5:28.

23:24 | כג:כד

הֶן עָם כְּלָבִיא יָקוּם וְכַאֲרִי יִתְנַשָּׂא

Behold, a people that rises like a lioness,
and raises itself like a lion.

Live Prey

Bilaam compared the Jewish people to lions. The Midrash explains that the comparison hints to the vigor with which the Jewish people recite the Shema—like a lion pouncing on its prey. "They arise from their sleep like lions, seize the recitation of Shema and proclaim the Almighty's kingship."[10]

Why is the recitation of Shema compared specifically to a lion's attack on its prey, as opposed to any other animal?

The Shema begins with a declaration of G-d's Oneness: "Hashem is our G-d, Hashem is One." As Chassidus explains, this means that everything in existence is truly an extension of the Divine energy that creates it and continuously maintains its existence. It follows that even the *yetzer hara*, man's self-serving and negative inclination, has a G-dly purpose. The Shema therefore continues with the command to love Hashem "with all your heart," which, our Sages explain,[11] means that all of your heart's passions and desires, even those which stem from the *yetzer hara*, should be directed toward your devoted service of G-d. In the words of Rabbi Yochanan, "Invest in Torah the very same energies" that you used until now for wrongdoing![12]

---

10. Tanchuma, Balak 14.
11. Mishnah, Berachos 9:5.
12. Bava Metzia 84a.

This explains why Bilaam compared the recitation of Shema to a lion seizing its prey. According to the Talmud,[13] the lion eats its victim while it is still alive, unlike other animals, which first kill their prey and then eat it. This is analogous to the message of the Shema: the ultimate service of G-d is not to drain the *yetzer hara* of its energy, but to "eat it alive," to absorb and channel its passion into your service of G-d.

—*Igros Kodesh, vol. 1, pp. 156–157*

---

[13]. Bava Kamma 16b.

24:5 | כד:ה

מַה טֹּבוּ אֹהָלֶיךָ יַעֲקֹב

How beautiful are your tents, Yaakov!

Beauty is in Detail

What was the beauty that Bilaam saw in Bnei Yisrael's tents?

According to the Talmud,[14] Bilaam observed that the Jewish people arranged their tents so that the entrances did not line up, and they did not peer into each other's homes. This demonstrated their dedication to maintaining privacy.

Recognizing their modest conduct and the purity it engendered, Bilaam exclaimed, "These people are worthy of having the Divine Presence rest upon them!"[15] This, says Rashi,[16] is what caused Bilaam to reconsider his plans to curse them, and he blessed them instead.

The Torah's ethic of *tznius*—not exposing those aspects of life intended to be private—clearly involves much more than not peering into another person's tent. Yet Bilaam reconsidered his curses upon noticing this seemingly minor detail of the Jewish people's conduct. From here we see that adherence to the *details* of *tznius* (and not sufficing with the general laws alone) has the power to transform even the worst curses into blessings.

Moreover, Bilaam's reference to Bnei Yisrael's *tents* highlights that they maintained this high standard of modesty even when they were in a temporary setting. This teaches us

---

14. Bava Basra 60a.
15. Ibid.
16. Bamidbar 24:2.

that adherence to the Torah's standards of *tznius* not only in our regular environments, but also in temporary and short-term settings, is truly our most beautiful feature and our greatest source of blessing.

—*Likkutei Sichos, vol. 13, pp. 83–84*

24:14 | כד:יד

לְכָה אִיעָצְךָ אֲשֶׁר יַעֲשֶׂה הָעָם הַזֶּה לְעַמְּךָ בְּאַחֲרִית הַיָּמִים

Come, I will advise you what this people will do to your people at the end of days.

Radical Blessings

Fearing that the Jews would wage war against him and conquer his land, Balak, the king of Moav, summoned the prophet Bilaam and asked him to curse them. Bilaam, however, knew that Balak had nothing to fear, for as a prophet he certainly knew that G-d had commanded Bnei Yisrael, "Do not distress Moav, and do not provoke them to war, for I will not give you any of their land as an inheritance."[17]

Nevertheless, Bilaam made no attempt to reassure Balak, because he himself was eager to harm Bnei Yisrael and was excited by this opportunity to curse them. As Rashi notes, "Bilaam hated them more than did Balak."[18] Whereas Balak hated the Jews because he felt threatened by them, Bilaam hated the Jews fundamentally and irrationally—pure, simple, baseless hatred.

Despite Bilaam's enthusiasm, things did not go to plan. "...Hashem, your G-d, did not want to listen to Bilaam. So Hashem, your G-d, transformed the curse into a blessing for you, because Hashem, your G-d, loves you."[19] Not only did G-d force Bilaam to bless the Jews instead of cursing them, He transformed the curses themselves into blessings. And

---

17. Devarim 2:9.
18. Rashi, Bamidbar 22:11.
19. Devarim 23:6.

since Bilaam had hoped to unleash his unfounded hatred in his curses, the blessings G-d forced him to bestow were extraordinary, reflecting G-d's fundamental and unconditional love for His people.

This explains why Bilaam's blessings also foretell the future and final redemption of the Jewish people. The Talmud[20] says that Moshiach's arrival will be *b'hesech hadaas*, which literally means "in absence of cognizance." On a simple level, this means that the precise moment of the Redemption cannot be known in advance, so Moshiach's arrival will automatically catch us off guard. According to the teachings of Chassidus,[21] this Talmudic statement also means that the era of Moshiach will be characterized by an absence of *daas*—knowledge and cognizance. This will not be due to a lack of knowledge, but because a deep-seated, fundamental and suprarational connection to G-d will be revealed in the conscious mind of every Jew. It is therefore most fitting that the suprarational era of Moshiach is foretold in the radical blessings of the irrational Bilaam.

—*Likkutei Sichos, vol. 38, pp. 88–89*

---

20. Sanhedrin 97a.
21. Tanya, Iggeres Hakodesh 4.

24:17 | כד:יז

אֶרְאֶנּוּ וְלֹא עַתָּה אֲשׁוּרֶנּוּ וְלֹא קָרוֹב דָּרַךְ כּוֹכָב מִיַּעֲקֹב

I see him, but not now; I behold him, but not near. A star shoots forth from Yaakov.

Moshiach and You

Many early sources interpret Bilaam's prophecy, "A star shoots forth from Yaakov," as a reference to Moshiach, the future redeemer of the Jewish people.[22] According to the Sages of the Talmud, however, it refers to every Jew.[23]

The two interpretations of this verse, either as a reference to even the simplest Jew or as a hint to Moshiach, the redeemer of the Jewish people, are not contradictory. In fact, according to the Baal Shem Tov, they are one and the same.

The Baal Shem Tov taught that the soul of Moshiach is the collective soul of the Jewish people. The complete revelation of the soul of Moshiach is therefore dependent on every Jew "preparing and repairing" the aspect of Moshiach's soul that relates specifically to him.[24] This is the meaning of the prophet Yeshayahu's words, "He bears our illness; he suffers our pain."[25] The completeness of Moshiach's identity is dependent on the individual input of every single Jew, and he "suffers" when our work is deficient.

Similarly, the Rambam writes: "A person must see himself and the world as equally balanced on two ends of the

---

22. See Ramban and other commentaries *ad loc.*
23. See Talmud Yerushalmi, Maaser Sheni 4:6.
24. See Me'or Einayim, Pinchas.
25. Yeshayahu 53:4.

scale... By doing one good deed, he tips the scale and brings for himself and the entire world salvation,"[26] for it is truly in the hands of every individual to complete the soul of Moshiach and bring about his revelation.

Bilaam's prophecy is thus equally attributable to the aspect of Moshiach entrusted to the individual Jew as it is to our future redeemer himself.

—*Toras Menachem, vol. 31, pp. 122–125*

---

26. Mishneh Torah, Hil. Teshuvah 3:4.

פנחס
Pinchas

25:11 | כה:יא

פִּינְחָס בֶּן־אֶלְעָזָר בֶּן־אַהֲרֹן הַכֹּהֵן הֵשִׁיב אֶת־חֲמָתִי מֵעַל בְּנֵי־יִשְׂרָאֵל בְּקַנְאוֹ אֶת־קִנְאָתִי בְּתוֹכָם וְלֹא־כִלִּיתִי אֶת־בְּנֵי־יִשְׂרָאֵל בְּקִנְאָתִי׃

Pinchas, the son of Elazar, the son of Aharon the Kohen, has turned My anger away from Bnei Yisrael by zealously avenging Me among them, so that I did not destroy Bnei Yisrael because of My zeal.

Grassroots Initiative

A deadly plague was spreading among Bnei Yisrael, killing thousands of people.

Meanwhile, Zimri, the leader of the tribe of Shimon, publicly took a Midianite princess into his tent. Moshe, Elazar and the elders of Bnei Yisrael all witnessed Zimri's brazen act, but were at a loss how to respond.

Pinchas was neither a leader nor an elder of Bnei Yisrael (up until that point), but he remembered what Moshe had taught as the correct response to a situation like this. He brought the law to Moshe's attention, and Moshe urged him to fulfill it: "Let the one who reads the letter be the agent to carry it out,"[1] he said. Pinchas entered Zimri's tent, witnessed him sinning with the non-Jewish woman and killed him, whereupon the plague miraculously stopped. G-d rewarded Pinchas for his zealousness with an eternal covenant of goodwill, and *kehunah* (priesthood) for him and all his descendants.

Commenting on this episode, Rashi remarks: "At the incident of the Golden Calf, Moshe successfully confronted six hundred thousand people... and here he was so helpless? Rather, this happened so that Pinchas would come and take what was suited for him."[2]

The story of Pinchas teaches us that there are times when we cannot look solely to our leaders for instruction. In this instance, the leaders' lack of clarity was Divinely orchestrated in order to allow Pinchas to take "what was suited for him." Likewise, when something on which you can have a positive impact comes to your attention, you must step up to the plate and get involved. The inaction of those responsible and the silence of the regular sources of inspiration are not an indication that you too can stand by idly. For every person is charged with a unique spiritual mission—part of the Divine plan that no one else in the world can fulfill. The inaction of others may be G-d's way of urging you to claim the moment that is rightfully yours.

—*Likkutei Sichos, vol. 2, pp. 342-343*

---

1. Rashi, Bamidbar 25:7.
2. Ibid. 25:6.

25:11 | כה:יא

פִּינְחָס בֶּן אֶלְעָזָר בֶּן אַהֲרֹן הַכֹּהֵן הֵשִׁיב אֶת חֲמָתִי מֵעַל בְּנֵי יִשְׂרָאֵל בְּקַנְאוֹ אֶת קִנְאָתִי בְּתוֹכָם וְלֹא כִלִּיתִי אֶת בְּנֵי יִשְׂרָאֵל בְּקִנְאָתִי

Pinchas, the son of Elazar, the son of Aharon the Kohen, has turned My anger away from Bnei Yisrael by zealously avenging Me among them, so that I did not destroy Bnei Yisrael because of My zeal.

A Legacy of Love

A deadly plague broke out among Bnei Yisrael, punishing them for sinning with the daughters of Moav and worshipping their gods. Meanwhile, Zimri, the leader of the tribe of Shimon, publicly took a Midianite princess into his tent. Moshe and the elders were stunned. Pinchas, remembering what Moshe had taught about a situation like this, entered Zimri's tent, caught him sinning with the Midianite woman and killed him, whereupon the plague miraculously stopped.

What caused Pinchas, more than anyone else present at the time, to remember the law and implement it correctly?

The Torah explains by highlighting Pinchas's ancestry at the very beginning of the Parshah.[3]

Aharon, as we know, excelled in his love for his fellow Jews and persistently concerned himself with their wellbeing. Aharon "pursued peace and promoted love between disputing parties."[4] When Moshe and Aharon stood before Pharaoh and daringly demanded that he free the Jewish people from Egypt,

---

3. Bamidbar 25:7.
4. Rashi, Bamidbar 20:29.

Aharon did most of the persuading.[5] Later, Aharon took the blame for the sin of the Golden Calf in an attempt to spare the people from G-d's wrath.[6] And it was in Aharon's merit that the Clouds of Glory protected Bnei Yisrael in the desert.[7]

As Aharon's grandchild, Pinchas inherited his love for his fellow Jews and his devotion to their wellbeing. As the plague took one Jewish life after another, Pinchas frantically searched for a way to stop it. His desperate desire to save his fellow Jews led him to recall a law that everyone else had forgotten, and motivated him to risk his life to implement that law in order to stop the plague.

The Torah therefore reiterates that Pinchas was "the son of Elazar, the son of Aharon the Kohen." For the source of Pinchas's profound love for his people, which dictated his thinking process and drove him to absolute self-sacrifice, was his direct lineage from Aharon.

—*Toras Menachem 5748, vol. 4, pp. 71-75*

---

5. See Shemos 6:27 and 7:1-2, and Rashi ad loc.
6. See Rashi, Shemos 32:5.
7. See Rashi, Bamidbar 20:1.

25:11 | כה:יא

פִּינְחָס בֶּן אֶלְעָזָר בֶּן אַהֲרֹן הַכֹּהֵן הֵשִׁיב אֶת חֲמָתִי מֵעַל בְּנֵי יִשְׂרָאֵל בְּקַנְאוֹ אֶת קִנְאָתִי בְּתוֹכָם וְלֹא כִלִּיתִי אֶת בְּנֵי יִשְׂרָאֵל בְּקִנְאָתִי

Pinchas, the son of Elazar, the son of Aharon the Kohen, has turned My anger away from Bnei Yisrael by zealously avenging Me among them, so that I did not destroy Bnei Yisrael because of My zeal.

An Eternal Reward

Pinchas's heroic actions averted G-d's anger from Bnei Yisrael. In reward, G-d granted Pinchas *kehunah* (priesthood) "for him and his descendants after him."[8]

Moshe, too, protected Bnei Yisrael from G-d's wrath on numerous occasions, but we do not find that Moshe was rewarded with any similar "hereditary" reward. In fact, even when Moshe requested that his children inherit his position, he was explicitly refused by G-d.[9] Why, then, was Pinchas's reward so great? What was so unique about his actions?

Moshe saved the Jewish people by beseeching G-d to forgive their sins and to retract the harsh punishments that they faced. In contrast, Pinchas saved the Jewish people through his actions. He heroically killed the sinful prince of Shimon, and by sanctifying G-d's name before all of Israel (and inspiring them to repent), he stopped the deadly plague. Whereas Moshe saved the Jewish people by intervening on high, Pinchas saved them through his efforts to elevate them "from below."

---

8. Bamidbar 25:13.
9. See Rashi, Bamidbar 27:16.

In the same vein, Moshe put his spiritual life on the line to save the Jewish people: he challenged G-d to forgive the people, and "if not, erase me now from Your book which You have written."[10] Pinchas, however, risked his physical life in order to stop the plague. He exposed himself to mortal risk, entering the encampment of the tribe of Shimon and killing their beloved leader.

The underlying uniqueness of Pinchas's efforts was his focus not on assistance and illumination "from above," but on transforming and elevating the darkness itself—in himself, by harnessing even his physical body as a "chariot" to the Divine will; and in others, by inspiring them to transform their lives and return to G-d in repentance. In this way, Pinchas not only saved the Jewish people in that moment of wrath, he brought about permanent and lasting change in the Jewish people and their relationship with G-d.

Accordingly, since his efforts were uniquely "grounded" in their nature and in their effects, his reward too was an *eternal* covenant, firmly established "for him and his descendants after him" for all time.

—*Likkutei Sichos, vol. 18, pp. 344–347*

---

10. Shemos 32:32.

25:13 | כה:יג

וְהָיְתָה לּוֹ וּלְזַרְעוֹ אַחֲרָיו בְּרִית כְּהֻנַּת עוֹלָם תַּחַת אֲשֶׁר קִנֵּא לֵאלֹקָיו

An eternal covenant of kehunah (priesthood) shall be for him and for his descendants after him, because he was zealous for his G-d.

A Breach of Nature

Zimri, the leader of the tribe of Shimon, sinned with a Midianite princess. Pinchas, knowing the law that Moshe had taught regarding such a situation, courageously entered Zimri's tent and killed him. G-d rewarded Pinchas with *kehunah* (priesthood) for himself and his future descendants.

The Torah states that Pinchas was rewarded so greatly "because he was zealous for his G-d." As Rashi explains, this means that "he raged G-d's rage and avenged G-d's vengeance."[11] This implies that the sin Pinchas avenged is considered an affront to G-d Himself—more so than any other transgression. Why?

Chassidus explains that when a Jew transgresses any of the Torah's commandments, the soul-faculties that he employs in committing that sin are in a state of "exile," vested against their will in an act defying G-d's will. This exile of the soul is even greater when one sins with his reproductive abilities, since reproduction draws from the very fabric of human life and the essence of the living soul. Even so, the sinner remains a Jew, and his G-dly energies remain holy—albeit in a state

---

11. Bamidbar 25:11.

of exile and captivity until he repents. Even if a child is born from that prohibited union, the illegitimate child (whose soul draws its life from the souls of those who conceived it) is still Jewish—provided the child's mother is Jewish.

A child born from a non-Jewish woman, however, is not a Jew. Hence, a sin such as Zimri's causes the essential material of a Jewish body and soul to lose its Jewishness entirely, breaching the inherent distinction that G-d created between Jew and gentile.

This explains why G-d rewarded Pinchas with *kehunah* (priesthood). *Kehunah* is a reality of nature; Rashi compares it elsewhere to the unchangeable realities of day and night.[12] Because Pinchas was zealous for G-d, avenging Zimri's attempt to breach nature's distinction between Jew and gentile, G-d rewarded him commensurately with a breach of nature as well—He granted him *kehunah*.

—*Likkutei Sichos, vol. 8, pp. 153–157*

---

12. See Rashi, Bamidbar 16:5.

26:9-11 | כו:ט-יא

הוּא דָתָן וַאֲבִירָם קְרִיאֵי הָעֵדָה אֲשֶׁר הִצּוּ עַל מֹשֶׁה וְעַל אַהֲרֹן בַּעֲדַת קֹרַח בְּהַצֹּתָם עַל ה': וַתִּפְתַּח הָאָרֶץ אֶת פִּיהָ וַתִּבְלַע אֹתָם וְאֶת קֹרַח... וּבְנֵי קֹרַח לֹא מֵתוּ.

They were Dasan and Aviram, the chosen of the congregation who incited against Moshe and Aharon in the assembly of Korach, when they incited against G-d. The earth opened its mouth and swallowed them and Korach... but Korach's sons did not die.

Just a Thought

After naming the families of the tribe of Reuven that would enter the Land of Israel, the Torah mentions that Dasan and Aviram (who were also from the tribe of Reuven) perished along with Korach when they incited the rebellion against Moshe. The Torah then notes (seemingly incidentally) that the sons of Korach did not die in that episode. As Rashi explains, although the earth swallowed Korach's sons together with him, "an elevated area was set apart for them underground, and they stayed there."[13] Eventually, they were allowed to leave and rejoin the community.[14]

Rashi adds that while Korach's sons had in fact been among the original instigators of the rebellion, they were spared from death because during the conflict they inwardly regretted what they had done—"they contemplated repentance in their hearts."

---

13. Bamidbar 26:11.
14. See Rashi, Bamidbar 16:7.

How do we know that Korach's sons were so involved in the conflict? Because it would seem logical for the Torah to note that they survived when it names the descendants of Korach among the *Levi'im* who would enter the Land.[15] But instead the Torah comments "Korach's sons did not die" immediately alongside the account of Dasan and Aviram's leading role in the rebellion, thereby indicating that Korach's sons, too, played a crucial role in inciting the conflict.

Nevertheless, the Torah states that the sons of Korach were not punished like the others, because they ultimately repented—at least internally.

This illustrates the remarkable power of *teshuvah* (repentance). Korach's sons not only took part in his dispute, they were among its original conspirators. Even upon acknowledging their wrongdoing, they did not openly abandon the rebellion—they merely "contemplated repentance in their hearts." Yet their thoughts of remorse alone were sufficient to save them from dying with the other instigators, and their families ultimately merited to enter the Land of Israel.

—*Likkutei Sichos, vol. 33, pp. 172–175*

---

15. See Bamidbar 26:58.

27:8-9 | כז:ח-ט

אִישׁ כִּי יָמוּת וּבֵן אֵין לוֹ וְהַעֲבַרְתֶּם אֶת נַחֲלָתוֹ לְבִתּוֹ: וְאִם אֵין לוֹ בַּת וּנְתַתֶּם אֶת נַחֲלָתוֹ לְאֶחָיו

If a man dies and has no son, you shall transfer his inheritance to his daughter. If he has no daughter, you shall give his inheritance to his brothers.

Don't Forget Your Father

If a person dies with no children, the next in line to inherit his estate is his father. If his father predeceased him, then his estate goes to his brothers. Yet when the Torah outlines the laws of inheritance, the verse ignores the possibility of a living father, and simply states, "If he has no daughter, you shall give his inheritance to his brothers."

According to the Talmud, "The wicked, even in their lifetime, are called dead."[16] The Zohar takes this a step further and says, "One who falls from his rung in Divine service is called dead."[17] Accordingly, the Torah's omission of a scenario where a person died during his father's lifetime can also be interpreted as an insight into the nature of spiritual death.

The Alter Rebbe explains in Tanya that a Jew who is conscious of his G-dly soul's intrinsic desire to cleave to G-d would never willingly transgress any mitzvah whatsoever. For essentially, by breaching any of G-d's commandments one is severing and denying his relationship with G-d. This is akin

---

16. Berachos 18b.
17. Zohar 3:135b.

to idol worship, which a Jew would go to any extent—even sacrificing his life—to avoid.[18]

This suprarational attachment to our Father in heaven, and our inability to consider separating ourselves from Him, is the G-dly soul's highest faculty, from which all the other faculties of the G-dly soul evolve. It is therefore called the "father" of the soul's diverse capacities.

We can thus understand why the instances of death addressed by the Torah are scenarios in which the deceased's father has already passed away—i.e., he was no longer an active presence in his life. Because if not for the absence of one's "father"—meaning, if one would always remember his G-dly soul's fundamental and unwavering attachment to G-d—he would never allow himself to succumb to spiritual death.

—*Likkutei Sichos, vol. 17, pp. 297-299*

---

18. Tanya, chapter 19.

מטות
Matos

30:2 | ל:ב

וַיְדַבֵּר מֹשֶׁה אֶל רָאשֵׁי הַמַּטּוֹת לִבְנֵי יִשְׂרָאֵל

Moshe spoke to the heads of the tribes of Bnei Yisrael.

Tough Staff

Here the Torah refers to the tribes of Bnei Yisrael as *matos*; each individual tribe is called a *mateh*. Elsewhere, the tribes are called *shevatim*, with each tribe known as a *shevet*. *Mateh* and *shevet* both mean "wooden branch" or "stick," and their use in reference to the Jewish people denotes that the tribes are all branches of a single tree.

What is the difference between a *shevet* and a *mateh*?

A *shevet* is a moist, freshly cut branch, or one still attached to the tree, at its most pliable. On the other hand, the term *mateh* is used in reference to a branch that has lost its moisture and become hard and tough.

In spiritual terms, the tree here represents the common Divine source from which every Jew's G-dly soul extends. Accordingly, *mateh* and *shevet* allude to two different phases experienced by the G-dly soul in its relationship with its Divine source.

The term *shevet* refers to the soul when its connection to its source is fresh and evident. In a general sense, this refers to the G-dly soul before its descent into this lowly world to be clothed in a physical body. The dry *mateh*, on the other hand, alludes to the G-dly soul while it is within the human body, when its connection to the Divine source is not as obvious.

These two branches likewise represent different eras in Jewish history. The "fresh branch" would best describe the Jewish people in the era of the Beis Hamikdash, the Holy Temple that stood in Jerusalem, when they were constantly aware of G-dliness. In contrast, the dry *mateh* alludes to the state of the Jewish people ever since the destruction of the Beis Hamikdash and the ensuing exile which has sapped us of our spiritual sensitivity.

Yet the term *mateh*, or *matos*, as this Parshah is called, also expresses the benefit engendered by this spiritual dryness: the harsh and bitter exile has uncovered the Jewish people's intense resolve to observe the Torah even in the most trying of circumstances. Indeed, the challenges and adversity we face in exile have revealed the soul's unyielding determination to obey G-d's will, like a firm staff that does not break or bend under pressure.

—*Likkutei Sichos, vol. 28, pp. 281-283*

30:3 | ל:ג

אִישׁ כִּי יִדֹּר נֶדֶר... לֹא יַחֵל דְּבָרוֹ

If a man makes a vow... he shall not violate his word.

No Ordinary Matter

The Torah expresses the prohibition of violating one's vows with the words לֹא יַחֵל דְּבָרוֹ. Rashi explains that the Hebrew word יַחֵל is akin to the word יְחַלֵּל, and should be understood to mean "he shall not *desecrate* his word." This means, Rashi continues, "One shall not treat his words mundanely." Meaning that the law of vows is more than simply an obligation to stand by one's verbal commitments; it is a recognition of the inherent sanctity in one's words, and hence a duty to honor them.

The Hebrew word דבריו, "his words," used by Rashi in the phrase "one shall not treat his words mundanely," can also be translated as "his matters." The phrase would thus mean "one shall not treat his matters mundanely." This too mirrors the above ideal, for the sanctity the Torah attributes to our vows illustrates the potential we have to infuse all our "matters" with holiness and G-dly purpose. The weight that the Torah ascribes to our ordinary words reminds us of the capacity for holiness innate in every aspect of our lives, and our personal duty to reveal it.

—*Likkutei Sichos, vol. 13, p. 108*

30:3 | ל:ג

אִישׁ כִּי יִדֹּר נֶדֶר לַה'

A man who makes a vow to G-d.

To Abstain or Not to Abstain

"Vows are the safeguard of restraint," says the Mishnah.[1] By prohibiting yourself (through vows) from indulging in even that which the Torah permits, you can effectively fulfill the Torah's command to "sanctify yourself [even] with that which is permitted to you."[2]

Conversely, the Rambam writes:[3]

> Our Sages directed man to abstain only from those things that the Torah denies him, and not to forbid himself from partaking in permitted things by taking vows and oaths. Rhetorically they asked, "Is that which the Torah prohibited not sufficient for you? [Why] must you add further prohibitions?"

Which is the correct path? Should we vow to abstain from physical indulgence, or are we not to prohibit ourselves from partaking in the permissible pleasures of the world?

The correct approach depends on the spiritual state of the individual. A verse in Koheles describes the two possible states of man with the words "G-d made man upright, but they have gone in search of many schemes."[4] To the "upright man" who does not pursue any selfish desire, the Sages said,

---

1. Avos 3:13.
2. See Ramban, Vayikra 19:2; Talmud, Yevamos 20a.
3. Mishneh Torah, Hil. De'os 3:1.
4. Koheles 7:29.

"Is that which the Torah prohibited not sufficient for you? Must you add further prohibitions?" On the contrary, you must endeavor to utilize as many aspects of the material world as possible in the service of G-d, thereby elevating them to a higher purpose.

"Gone in search of many schemes," by contrast, refers to the person who does not view subservience to G-d's will as the only objective in life, but who seeks out opportunity and justification to indulge in the material world. For this person, the delights of the material world are not opportunities for elevation; enjoying them will only make him more self-indulgent. The Torah therefore encourages him to eliminate the risk of further decline by taking vows—"the safeguard to restraint."

—*Likkutei Sichos, vol. 4, p. 1076*

30:3 | ל:ג

אִישׁ כִּי יִדֹּר נֶדֶר לַה' אוֹ הִשָּׁבַע שְׁבֻעָה לֶאְסֹר אִסָּר עַל נַפְשׁוֹ לֹא יַחֵל דְּבָרוֹ כְּכָל הַיֹּצֵא מִפִּיו יַעֲשֶׂה

A man who vows to G-d or takes an oath placing a prohibition upon himself, he shall not violate his word; according to whatever came out of his mouth, he shall do.

Tapping into the Sanctity Line

A person who declares, "This shall be prohibited unto me like a sacrifice" about an otherwise permissible object is legally bound to abide by his vow. Just as a person can consecrate an animal as a sacrifice, thereby conferring sanctity upon it and prohibiting any personal benefit from it, a vow equating a permissible object with a sacrifice can prohibit the one taking the vow from using that object for personal benefit.

In contrast, if a person declared, "This object shall be prohibited unto me like the flesh of a swine," his vow is meaningless.[5] This is because the flesh of the swine is inherently non-kosher and prohibited by G-d—not due to its consecration by any individual. It therefore cannot serve as a model for the vow one takes upon himself to make something personally prohibited.

This distinction reflects the true purpose of vows according to the Torah.

Ideally, G-d wants us to utilize all permissible aspects of the material world in our service of Him.[6] But if a person finds

---

5. See Talmud, Nedarim 14a.
6. See Talmud Yerushalmi, Nedarim 9:1.

that instead of elevating the material world, he is being drawn *into* it, he may take a vow of abstinence to protect himself from succumbing to lust and temptation.

This is also why many things which were biblically permissible were later prohibited by rabbinic decree as a "fence" for the Torah. Increased challenges in terms of living a sanctified life warrant taking additional precautions.[7]

The power of these vows and prohibitions, however, lies not only in minimizing our contact with temptation. Rather, through these measures we draw additional sanctity upon ourselves, giving ourselves the strength to overcome any obstacles to our Divine mission.

Accordingly, we can understand why only a vow based on a comparison to a sacrifice is effective, and not a vow based on a comparison to something inherently prohibited. For like a sacrifice, which the Torah prohibits for personal use due to its extraordinary sanctity, the purpose of a vow is to obtain additional sanctity and strength to help us battle the ever-present spiritual darkness.

—*Likkutei Sichos, vol. 4, pp. 1076–1077, fn. 12*

---

[7]. See Likkutei Torah, Rosh Hashanah 57a.

___
32:33 | לב:לג

וַיִּתֵּן לָהֶם מֹשֶׁה לִבְנֵי גָד וְלִבְנֵי רְאוּבֵן וְלַחֲצִי שֵׁבֶט ׀ מְנַשֶּׁה בֶן־יוֹסֵף אֶת־מַמְלֶכֶת סִיחֹן מֶלֶךְ הָאֱמֹרִי וְאֶת־מַמְלֶכֶת עוֹג מֶלֶךְ הַבָּשָׁן

Moshe gave to the descendants of Gad and the descendants of Reuven and half the tribe of Menasheh, the son of Yosef: the kingdom of Sichon, king of the Amorites, and the kingdom of Og, king of Bashan.

Greater Israel

The tribes of Reuven and Gad approached Moshe and requested the pasture-rich territories east of the Jordan as their inheritance, instead of a portion in the land of Canaan alongside the other tribes. Initially, Moshe was reluctant, comparing them to the spies who loathed the Promised Land.[8] But he later agreed to their request on condition that they take part in, and even lead, the battles Bnei Yisrael would have to wage in order to conquer the land of Canaan. Moshe ultimately not only agreed to these two tribes' request, he even gave some of the land east of the Jordan to half the tribe of Menasheh as well.

Despite their arrangement with Moshe, their preference to dwell outside the official borders of Israel was frowned upon. Of this arrangement it was said,[9] "An inheritance may be acquired hastily in the beginning, but its end will not be blessed."[10]

___

8. Bamidbar 13.
9. Mishlei 20:21.
10. See Bamidbar Rabbah 22:9.

In contrast, the tribe of Menasheh received the land east of the Jordan on *Moshe's* initiative—obviously, for positive reasons.

Moshe's decision to allocate land to the tribe of Menasheh beyond the official borders of the Land can be said to represent his participation in (and initiation of) the expansion of Israel's borders that will take place in the future. As the Torah foretells, regarding the final Redemption, "...Hashem, your G-d, will expand your boundaries, as He swore to your forefathers, and He will give you all the land of which He spoke..."[11] This refers to the land of the Kenites, Kenizzites and Kadmonites, which G-d promised to Avraham in addition to the land of Canaan.[12]

Why did Moshe select the tribe of Menasheh for this unique honor and privilege? As is evident from the story of the daughters of Tzelafchad, who were from the tribe of Menasheh and who defied all norms when they approached Moshe to beg for a portion of the Land,[13] the tribe of Menasheh loved the Land of Israel *distinctively*. Therefore, unlike the tribes of Reuven and Gad, who requested and received their inheritance *entirely* outside of Israel's borders, Menasheh received *two* portions of land: one in the Land of Israel proper, and one beyond its official borders, symbolizing (not a rejection of the Land of Israel, but) the *expansion* of the Land of Israel in the era of the future Redemption.

—*Likkutei Sichos, vol. 28, pp. 210–215*

---

11. Devarim 19:8.
12. Bereishis 15:19.
13. See Bamidbar 27:1-11.

32:41 | לב:מא

וְיָאִיר בֶּן־מְנַשֶּׁה הָלַךְ וַיִּלְכֹּד אֶת־חַוֹּתֵיהֶם וַיִּקְרָא אֶתְהֶן חַוֹּת יָאִיר

Yair, the son of Menasheh, went and conquered the villages, and called them "the villages of Yair."

The Villager

The tribes of Reuven and Gad, and half the tribe of Menasheh, took their portion of the land from the pasture-rich territories that Bnei Yisrael conquered east of the Jordan (outside of the land of Canaan). The Torah relates that Yair, from the tribe of Menasheh, conquered a large swath of land there and named the villages in his territory "Chavos Yair"—the Villages of Yair.

Elsewhere[14] we read that Yair's territory actually included a full 60 cities and their surrounding villages. Why did Yair place more emphasis on the surrounding villages (even naming them the Villages of Yair!) than the rest of the area he conquered?

One of the reasons the tribes requested to settle in the lands east of the Jordan, writes Rabbeinu Bechayei,[15] was to prevent these desirable areas from being repopulated by idolaters, and to ensure that the cities and towns were not rededicated to their deities. We thus find that Bnei Yisrael renamed a number of cities in this area which previously bore pagan names,[16] highlighting the tribes' true objective in occupying these cities: to "reinvent" them, as it were, eliminating

---

14. Devarim 3:4–5, 14; Yehoshua 13:30.
15. Bamidbar 32:3.
16. See Bamidbar 32:38 and Rashi ad loc.

the idolatry that was once prevalent there, and to fill them instead with the service of G-d.

In light of the above, the Torah's emphasis on the *villages* that Yair conquered can be understood as a metaphor for the transformation Yair engendered there.

The Talmud[17] contrasts the reactions of an urbanite and a village dweller upon seeing the king. For the city dweller, the king and his entourage are a common sight; for the village dweller, who is unaccustomed to seeing royalty, the sight of the king is novel and exciting.

The Torah therefore highlights that Yair conquered "villages" and called them "the Villages of Yair," for Yair's line of work was marked by the excitement and novelty of the villagers discovering "the king": he made the King of Kings known and revealed in places where He had previously been relatively unknown and unseen.

—*Likkutei Sichos, vol. 38, pp. 117–121*

---

17. Talmud, Chagigah 13b; see Rashi ad loc.

מסעי
Masei

33:1 | לג:א

אֵלֶּה מַסְעֵי בְנֵי יִשְׂרָאֵל אֲשֶׁר יָצְאוּ מֵאֶרֶץ מִצְרָיִם

These are the journeys of the children of Israel who left the land of Egypt.

What Goes Down

In Parshas Masei, the Torah recounts the details of Bnei Yisrael's travels as they journeyed through the desert from Egypt to the Promised Land. Citing the Midrash, Rashi compares the Torah's account to "a king whose son was ill, so he took him to a faraway place to heal him. As they returned home, the father recounted all the stages of their journey, saying to him, 'This is where we slept; here we were cold; here your head ached; etc.'" In the same vein, Moshe now reminds Bnei Yisrael of their journeys and struggles over the past 40 years in the desert.

Chassidus likens Bnei Yisrael's desert travels to the journeys of the Jewish people in exile in the "desert of the nations,"[1] with the mission to elevate the spiritually barren world and prepare it for the coming of Moshiach.

These journeys force our G-dly souls to descend from their lofty source On High to face conditions and circumstances which, like a desert, appear to be "uninhabited" by G-dliness. But just as the king and his son's travels were for the purpose of renewed health and healing, the hindrances faced by the soul are ultimately for its own benefit. For not only does the *world* benefit when a Jew turns it into a home for G-d, but the soul too reaches its greatest spiritual potential as a result of this difficult work. Nevertheless, until that benefit is realized, these hindrances are sources of pain and grievance for the soul—in Rashi's words, "here we were cold; here your head ached…"

Upon their return, however, the Midrash implies that the king and his son *revisit* the landmarks they passed on their original journey. In the journey of the G-dly soul through the "desert of nations," the return trip refers to the time of Moshiach, at which time we will revisit and ascend each step of our journey through exile. When Moshiach comes, not only will we enjoy the ultimate benefit for which the exile was necessary, we will realize how the very descents and sufferings that the soul experienced in exile were truly part of its climb to the highest heights.

—*Likkutei Sichos, vol. 18, pp. 392-395*

---

1. Yechezkel 20:35.

33:1 | לג:א

אֵ֚לֶּה מַסְעֵ֣י בְנֵֽי־יִשְׂרָאֵ֔ל אֲשֶׁ֥ר יָצְא֖וּ מֵאֶ֣רֶץ מִצְרָ֑יִם

These are the journeys of the children of Israel who left the land of Egypt.

Journeys with the King

In Parshas Masei, the Torah gives a summarized account of all the journeys of Bnei Yisrael as they traveled through the desert from Egypt to the Promised Land. The Midrash explains the idea behind this narrative:

> This is analogous to a king whose son was ill, so he took him to a faraway place to heal him. As they returned home, the father recounted all the stages of their journey, saying to him, 'This is where we slept; here we were cold; here your head ached.' Similarly, G-d said to Moshe: Recount for them all the places where they angered Me.

What is the meaning of this parable? What is the purpose of stopping throughout the journey home to revisit and identify all the places where "you angered Me" during the original trip?

With this parable, the Midrash is explaining that Bnei Yisrael's journeys and experiences in the desert are regarded in a different light on the return home—i.e., after the purpose of their travels was achieved. For Bnei Yisrael did not make these journeys on their own. Rather, as in the parable, "the King" accompanied and *took them* on all these journeys, specifically with their benefit in mind—"to heal him [the son]." It is therefore certain that what may have originally been a struggle, or even a source of grievance, was at its core a step towards their ultimate goal.

Even when "they angered Me," meaning that the particular journey represents Bnei Yisrael in a state of failure due to their transgression of G-d's will, this too was by Divine design.[2] It was, in essence, a step toward G-d's ultimate desire that their repentance, fueled by the painful pangs of distance, lead them to a new, greater and more profound relationship with Him.

—*Likkutei Sichos, vol. 18, pp. 393–396*

---

2. Although one's decision to transgress G-d's will is not *influenced* by G-d's knowledge and plans (the reason he is held accountable for his sins, which he commits of his own volition), nevertheless, his profound longing to return, resulting from his failed state, is indeed part of G-d's plan.

לד:ב | 34:2

צַו אֶת בְּנֵי יִשְׂרָאֵל וְאָמַרְתָּ אֲלֵהֶם כִּי אַתֶּם בָּאִים אֶל הָאָרֶץ כְּנָעַן זֹאת הָאָרֶץ אֲשֶׁר תִּפֹּל לָכֶם בְּנַחֲלָה אֶרֶץ כְּנַעַן לִגְבֻלֹתֶיהָ

Command Bnei Yisrael and say to them: When you arrive in the land of Canaan, this is the land that will fall to you as an inheritance, the land of Canaan according to its borders.

Reciprocating the Gift of the Land of Israel

Rashi explains that Moshe told Bnei Yisrael the exact boundaries of the Land of Israel for religious purposes: "Since many mitzvos apply to the Land of Israel and not outside of it, it was necessary to chart the outer limits of its boundaries from all sides, to inform you that those mitzvos apply anywhere within these borders."

How does Rashi conclude that Moshe outlined the borders of the Land for any reason other than informing Bnei Yisrael exactly which parts G-d intended for them to conquer?

Rashi derives this from the words "that will fall to you," which the Torah adds in the verse "this is the land that will fall to you as an inheritance." The borders could have been introduced with the words "This is your inheritance in the land of Canaan according to its borders." Why was it relevant to mention that the Land "will fall to you"?

These additional words indicate that the emphasis here is not on the conquest of the Land through Bnei Yisrael's efforts and warfare, but on the fact that the Land of Israel "will fall to you"—it will be delivered by G-d as though without effort on their part. Presumably, then, the borders are not outlined here solely to guide Bnei Yisrael's efforts at conquering the Land, but also for reasons related to what G-d desires from the Land. Namely, the mitzvos that will be observed there—our obligations toward G-d, who will cause this land to fall into our hands with ease. As Rashi explains, "Since many mitzvos apply to the Land of Israel and not outside of it, it was necessary to chart the outer limits of its boundaries from all sides, to inform you that those mitzvos apply anywhere within these borders."

—*Likkutei Sichos, vol. 13, pp. 122–124*

לה:יג | 35:13

שֵׁשׁ עָרֵי מִקְלָט תִּהְיֶינָה לָכֶם

Six cities of refuge shall serve for you.

24-Hour Security

The Sefer Hachinuch lists six mitzvos that are constantly obligatory: "their obligation does not depart from the person for a single moment throughout his lifetime."

1) To believe in G-d.
2) Not to believe in any power other than Him.
3) To acknowledge His oneness.
4) To love Him.
5) To fear Him.
6) Not to stray after the thoughts of our hearts and the sight of our eyes.

"These six are symbolized," says the Sefer Hachinuch, "by the verse 'Six cities of refuge shall serve for you.'"

Like all aspects of the Torah, even this mnemonic is laden with meaning.

The six cities of refuge provide protection for a person who accidentally caused someone's death. As long as he is within their borders, he is safe from those who wish to avenge the deceased's blood.

The avenger of the deceased's blood is a metaphor for the *yetzer hara*. For as the Talmud[3] teaches, the *yetzer hara*, our evil inclination that incites us to sin, and the *malach hamaves*, the angel of death that avenges the sin, are one and the same.

---

3. Bava Basra 16a.

It follows, then, that the protection provided by the cities of refuge represents our means of protecting ourselves from the *yetzer hara*.

Now, all the mitzvos that we perform provide us with the spiritual enrichment necessary to grapple with the *yetzer hara*. Most mitzvos, however, are obligatory only at specific times; hence the protection they provide is also limited. Yet the *yetzer hara*'s efforts to tempt man to sin are not limited to any specific time or place: "The impulse of man's heart is evil from his youth,"[4] i.e., nonstop. As such, in order to assist us in our constant struggle, G-d gave us six mitzvos that must be observed constantly. Their observance serves as the "cities of refuge" that provide us with 24-hour shelter from the *yetzer hara*'s constant threat.

—*Sefer Hasichos 5747, vol. 2, pp. 492-493*

---

4. Bereishis 8:21.

לה:כה | 35:25

וְיָשַׁב בָּהּ עַד מוֹת הַכֹּהֵן הַגָּדֹל

He shall remain there until the death of the Kohen Gadol.

One Nation, One Soul

A person who inadvertently caused someone's death is exiled to a city of refuge, where he must remain until the passing of the Kohen Gadol (during whose term he was sentenced). If he leaves the city of refuge earlier, he risks being killed by "the avengers of the blood"—the relatives of the deceased.

What changes with the passing of the Kohen Gadol? One explanation is that until then the inadvertent killer's sin is not completely atoned for, so if he leaves the city of refuge, the relatives of the deceased may still avenge their relative's blood. The passing of the righteous, however, serves as atonement for all the Jewish people.[5] Therefore, the passing of the Kohen Gadol fully atones for the sin of the inadvertent killer.

Why is the atonement for this sin specifically through the passing of the Kohen Gadol, and not any other righteous person living at that time? The answer to this question lies in the words of Rashi,[6] who says that "the Kohen Gadol should have prayed that such a misfortune should not befall Israel during his lifetime." The Kohen Gadol bears some degree of responsibility for this accident, since his prayers could have prevented the tragedy from ever occurring. As such, it is spe-

---

5. See Rashi, Bamidbar 20:1.
6. Bamidbar 35:25; cf. Talmud, Makkos 11a.

cifically *his* passing that completes the inadvertent killer's atonement.

This association between the inadvertent killer and the Kohen Gadol demonstrates the extraordinary inherent bond between one Jew and another. The Kohen Gadol is the one selected from among all Jews "to be distinctly holy of holies."[7] On the opposite end of the spectrum is the person who has caused someone's death, whose crime is so awful that he is sentenced to (and deserving of) exile, a punishment comparable to death itself.[8] Nevertheless, the bond between Jews is so strong that the passing of one, the righteous Kohen Gadol, brings atonement for the other. Moreover, Rashi teaches us that the Kohen Gadol's attachment to his fellow Jews was so great that he would (typically) intercede on behalf of even the lowest elements of society, to save them from sin.

—*Likkutei Sichos, vol. 33, pp. 206-212*

---

[7]. I Divrei Hayamim 23:13.
[8]. Sefer Hachinuch, mitzvah 410.

35:29 | לה:כט

וְהָיוּ אֵלֶּה לָכֶם לְחֻקַּת מִשְׁפָּט לְדֹרֹתֵיכֶם בְּכֹל מוֹשְׁבֹתֵיכֶם

These shall be for you a statute of justice for all your generations, in all your dwelling places.

Local Judge, Distant Sentence

A person who accidentally caused someone's death would be exiled by the court to one of the six cities of refuge, where he would be safe from potential avengers of the deceased's blood. The Sifri notes that the cities of refuge that guarantee such protection are established only in the Land of Israel. Thus, if a person accidentally killed someone outside of Israel, his trial and sentencing would take place in a local court outside of the Land;[9] his exile, however, would be to a city of refuge within the Land of Israel.[10]

This distinction between the place of the trial and the place of the exile can be explained as follows:

The struggle to abide by the Torah's commands is much greater outside the Land of Israel than it is within the Holy Land, where one can sense that "the eyes of Hashem your G-d are always upon it."[11] Therefore, a person who committed a crime outside the Land of Israel must be tried before local judges, who understand the realities and challenges faced by the one they are judging, and sentence him accordingly.

If the court finds the defendant guilty, however, he must be exiled to a city of refuge in the Land of Israel. This sentence is

---

9. See Sifri Zuta, Masei 35:29.
10. See Sifri, Masei 35:13.
11. Devarim 11:12.

not a punishment, but a method of rehabilitation. Complete rehabilitation requires the person who committed the crime to not only regret his past deeds, but to also be steadfast in his resolve to conduct himself differently in the future. Now, the Midrash associates the name Eretz Yisrael, the Land of Israel, to the Hebrew words *ratz*, "running," and *ratzon*, "will": "Why is it called *Eretz*? Because it runs *(ratz)* to do the will *(ratzon)* of its Master."[12] So, for a complete rehabilitation, the person who accidentally committed such a grievous crime cannot remain outside of the Land. He must relocate to Eretz Yisrael, so that "running to do the will of his Master" will become second nature.

—*Likkutei Sichos, vol. 2, pp. 380-382*

---

12. Bereishis Rabbah 5:8.

דברים
BOOK OF DEVARIM

לזכות
שלום דובער
בן חנה
חי'ה
בת חנה
אברהם משה
בן חנה
שמואל
בן חנה
מאשע רבקה
בת חנה

להצלחה בכל המצטרך להם
בגשמיות וברוחניות בבריאות הנכונה
ומתוך שמחה וטוב לבב

לעילוי נשמת
איסר
בן יצחק דוד
שרה
בת ישראל
רבקה יהודית
בת ר' אשר אנשיל
אברהם יוסף
בן ר' משה

נדבת משפחת
ליבליך

דברים
Devarim

1:1 | א:א

אֵלֶּה הַדְּבָרִים אֲשֶׁר דִּבֶּר מֹשֶׁה אֶל כָּל יִשְׂרָאֵל

These are the words that Moshe spoke to all Israel.

Filtered, Not Altered

Although the Book of Devarim is the word of G-d just as the other four books of the Torah are, we are told that Moshe transmitted it differently to Bnei Yisrael. In the first four books, "Moshe spoke on behalf of the Almighty," but in the book of Devarim, "Moshe spoke in his own name"—"by Divine inspiration."[1]

This means that in the first four books, Moshe served merely as a messenger to transcribe G-d's words and convey them to Bnei Yisrael as he received them.[2] Due to the Torah's inherent transcendence of creation[3]—the finite, mortal mind

---

1. Megillah 31b; see Tosafos ad loc.
2. See Rashi, Megillah ibid.
3. See Bereishis Rabbah 8:2.

included—if G-d had transmitted all of the Torah in this manner, then anything we might ever grasp from the Torah would at best *reflect* the Divine truth, but inherently could not be the essential Divine wisdom, which transcends the created being.

In the Book of Devarim, however, G-d communicated His word to Moshe in a manner that Moshe could internalize, and Moshe in turn "spoke in his own name," conveying the Divine wisdom that his mind had perceived. Thereby, the Divine wisdom of the Torah itself became graspable by the human mind.

The Book of Devarim is called "*Mishneh Torah*—the repetition of the Torah,"[4] because it is a review of the previous four books. Since the book of Devarim has the dual quality of being the word of G-d yet "descending" into the realm of human comprehension, by extension, every other part of the Torah has this quality as well.

In addition, since Moshe's role was to connect *every* member of the Jewish community with G-d,[5] this became the reality of Torah study for every Jew. By virtue of the Book of Devarim (which "Moshe spoke in his own name," but is still the word of G-d like the other books of the Torah), any Jew, regardless of his spiritual state or level of comprehension, by studying and comprehending *any* part of the Torah, can ingest the very word of G-d—its divinity neither tainted nor diminished.

—*Likkutei Sichos, vol. 19, pp. 9-12*

---

4. Devarim 17:18.
5. See Devarim 5:5.

1:5 | ה:א

בְּעֵבֶר הַיַּרְדֵּן בְּאֶרֶץ מוֹאָב הוֹאִיל מֹשֶׁה
בֵּאֵר אֶת הַתּוֹרָה הַזֹּאת לֵאמֹר

On the other side of the Jordan, in the land of Moav, Moshe began explaining this teaching, saying...

War of Words

Before his passing, Moshe began to prepare Bnei Yisrael for their entry into the Land of Israel by recounting all that they had experienced during their 40 years in the desert. The Torah adds that, as part of this address, Moshe "explained this teaching." Rashi interprets this to mean that he taught Bnei Yisrael the Torah in 70 languages.

Why did Moshe translate the Torah at this point? Bnei Yisrael were about to begin their conquest of the land of Canaan, a process that would involve seven years of battle and another seven years dedicated to dividing and settling the land. Why did Moshe find it necessary to translate the Torah specifically now, as Bnei Yisrael prepared to enter this phase?

By translating the Torah, Moshe was carrying out a crucial component of Bnei Yisrael's conquest of the seven nations who occupied the Land of Israel. For everything in the physical world has a spiritual source, and any change that takes place on the physical plane must first be executed in a spiritual sense. According to Kabbalah, the seven nations who occupied the land of Canaan represented the 70 original nations of humanity and contained their spiritual source. Moshe's translation of the Torah, which breached the language barrier between the Torah and the 70 nations, constituted a spiritual victory for the Torah over any opposition it faced from the other nations of the world. Only once Moshe had achieved a spiritual victory over the nations could Bnei Yisrael succeed in defeating them physically.

—*Sichos Kodesh 5730, vol. 1, pp. 358–359*

1:6 | א:ו

ה' אֱלֹקֵינוּ דִּבֶּר אֵלֵינוּ בְּחֹרֵב לֵאמֹר רַב לָכֶם שֶׁבֶת בָּהָר הַזֶּה

Hashem, our G-d, spoke to us in Chorev, saying, "Your stay at this mountain has been much for you."

Being Productive isn't Enough

As Bnei Yisrael prepared to enter the Land of Israel, Moshe recounted the experiences that had brought them to that point. He began by reminding them that if not for the episode of the spies, G-d would have brought them into the Land of Israel 39 years earlier: "Hashem, our G-d, spoke to us at Chorev (Mount Sinai), saying, 'Your stay at this mountain has been plenty for you. Turn away and journey… Go in and possess the land that G-d promised to your fathers.'"

Rashi explains that the phrase "Your stay has been much" can be understood literally. That is to say, "Not only has your stay been sufficient, it has already been excessive."[6] In other words, G-d so strongly desired to hasten Bnei Yisrael's arrival at the Land of Israel that He regarded their stay at Mount Sinai as *too long*.

Granted, their eleven months at Mount Sinai were not wasted. In addition to receiving the Torah and growing in their knowledge and understanding of its precepts throughout their stay, their very residence at the foot of the mountain reminded them constantly of the extraordinary Divine revelation they had witnessed there. Nevertheless, G-d's desire for them to

---

[6]. See Rashi's comments on Bamidbar 16:3 regarding a similar phrase.

proceed to the Promised Land was so great that He regarded any additional time spent at Sinai as excessive.

From here we understand the extent to which the Torah demands constant advancement in our service of G-d. "Your stay has been much!" No matter how admirable our current spiritual state may be, for a Jew to "stay put" is unnecessary and undesirable; even the slightest pause in growth is already too much.

—*Likkutei Sichos, vol. 24, pp. 14–18*

1:8 | א:ח

רְאֵה נָתַתִּי לִפְנֵיכֶם אֶת הָאָרֶץ בֹּאוּ וּרְשׁוּ אֶת הָאָרֶץ אֲשֶׁר נִשְׁבַּע ה' לַאֲבֹתֵיכֶם לְאַבְרָהָם לְיִצְחָק וּלְיַעֲקֹב לָתֵת לָהֶם וּלְזַרְעָם אַחֲרֵיהֶם

See, I have given the land before you; come and possess the land that G-d swore to your forefathers, to Avraham, to Yitzchak and to Yaakov, to give them and their descendants after them.

Jewish Nationality

Moshe reminded Bnei Yisrael that if not for the episode of the spies, G-d would have brought them into the Land of Israel 39 years earlier. "Hashem, our G-d, spoke to us at Chorev (Mount Sinai), saying, 'Your stay at this mountain has been much for you. Turn away and journey… Come and possess the land that G-d promised to your fathers.'"

According to one explanation offered by Rashi, the phrase "Your stay at this mountain has been much for you" alludes to the spiritual wealth that Bnei Yisrael accumulated at Mount Sinai.

> "Your residence at this mountain has brought you significant greatness and reward. You built the Mishkan, the menorah and other furnishings; you received the Torah; you appointed a Sanhedrin for yourselves…

This explanation complements the simple meaning of the phrase, which is that G-d regarded Bnei Yisrael's continued stay at Mount Sinai as excessive because He was eager for them to advance and enter the Promised Land. For unlike other nations, which are formed when a group of people take possession of a particular territory and inhabit it, Jewish nationality is defined by our spiritual identity as "a holy nation,"[7] in reward for which G-d grants us the Land of Israel. Thus, the spiritual "much" that Bnei Yisrael amassed at Mount Sinai led directly to G-d's eagerness to bring them into the Land.

Moreover, the verse continues, "Come and possess the land!" As Rashi explains, this means, "No one will contest the matter, and you will not need to go to war."[8] For in the words of the Midrash, "G-d chose the Land of Israel as His portion… and the Jewish people as His portion… It is befitting that His portion inherit in His portion."[9] Therefore, having established themselves as a holy nation through the spiritual wealth they acquired at Mount Sinai, Bnei Yisrael were ready to enter the Land unopposed, and to easily take possession of the land that was essentially theirs.

—*Likkutei Sichos, vol. 24, pp. 14–19*

---

7. Shemos 19:6.
8. Devarim 1:8.
9. Tanchuma, Re'eh 8.

1:8 | א:ח

רְאֵה נָתַתִּי לִפְנֵיכֶם אֶת הָאָרֶץ בֹּאוּ וּרְשׁוּ אֶת הָאָרֶץ אֲשֶׁר נִשְׁבַּע ה' לַאֲבֹתֵיכֶם לְאַבְרָהָם לְיִצְחָק וּלְיַעֲקֹב לָתֵת לָהֶם וּלְזַרְעָם אַחֲרֵיהֶם

See, I have given the land before you; come and possess the land that G-d swore to your forefathers, to Avraham, to Yitzchak and to Yaakov, to give them and their descendants after them.

Incontestably Yours

Moshe told Bnei Yisrael that when they were yet at Mount Sinai, G-d had expressed His desire to bring them into the Land of Israel immediately. Moreover, G-d assured them at that time that their conquest of the Land would be swift and uncontested: "See, I have given the land before you; come and possess the land that G-d promised to your forefathers." As Rashi explains, "No one will contest the matter, and you will not need to go to war."

With these words Rashi identifies two distinct points that were included in G-d's declaration that the Land was already given to Bnei Yisrael.

Firstly, G-d assured Bnei Yisrael that none of the nations would contest their right to the Land on legal grounds. For as Rashi explains, this takeover was legal and legitimate: "All of the earth belongs to G-d. He created it [the Land of Israel], and gave it to whomever He saw fit. By His will He gave it to them, and by His will He took it from them and gave it to us."[10]

---

10. Bereishis 1:1.

Moreover, even nations that descended from Avraham and Yitzchak, who might consider themselves equal heirs to the land that G-d promised to the forefathers, would have no legal claim. As Bnei Yisrael would (eventually) tell the Edomites, the descendants of Eisav: "You have no right to contest our inheritance of the Land of Israel, since you did not pay the debt [of exile that was decreed upon Avraham's heirs]."[11]

Even with the legal issue settled, however, Bnei Yisrael might have been concerned that the nations living in the Land would not willingly abandon their homes without a fight. G-d therefore reassured them, "I have given the Land before you" in this aspect as well. "You will not need to go to war," for the nations will leave on their own, and you will take possession of the Land unopposed.

—*Likkutei Sichos, vol. 34, pp. 6–7*

---

11. Rashi, Bamidbar 20:17.

1:8 | א:ח

רְאֵה נָתַתִּי לִפְנֵיכֶם אֶת הָאָרֶץ בֹּאוּ וּרְשׁוּ אֶת הָאָרֶץ אֲשֶׁר נִשְׁבַּע ה' לַאֲבֹתֵיכֶם לְאַבְרָהָם לְיִצְחָק וּלְיַעֲקֹב לָתֵת לָהֶם וּלְזַרְעָם אַחֲרֵיהֶם

See, I have given the land before you; come and possess the land that G-d swore to your forefathers, to Avraham, to Yitzchak and to Yaakov, to give them and their descendants after them.

War? What For?

As Bnei Yisrael prepared to begin their conquest of the land of Canaan, Moshe reminded them that if not for the episode of the spies, G-d would have brought them into the Land 39 years earlier. Moreover, G-d had assured them at that time that their conquest of the Land would be swift and uncontested: "See, I have given the land before you; come and possess the land that G-d promised to your forefathers." According to Rashi, this means, "No one will contest the matter, and you will not need to go to war; if they had not sent spies, they would not have needed weapons."

A careful reading of Rashi shows that he first asserts that G-d was ready to bring Bnei Yisrael into the Land of Israel without war, but then he concludes by saying that they would not have needed weapons. With his conclusion, Rashi is not simply reiterating that the nations would not oppose Bnei Yisrael's conquest of the Land; he is describing the extraordinary manner in which this would take place—without the need for weapons. Not only would the nations living in the Land leave without a fight, they would do so without Bnei

Yisrael even displaying any military might. The usual tactics of intimidation would not be necessary, for G-d would miraculously cause them to flee on their own.

Rashi adds, however, that Bnei Yisrael would have merited this miracle only if they hadn't sent the spies at all. Merely rejecting the spies' report about the dangers of entering the Land of Israel would not have been enough. The very sending of the spies demonstrated that Bnei Yisrael believed it was necessary to strategize how to conquer the land with military force. This indicated that they lacked conviction in G-d's promise that He would deliver the Land into their hands without any effort on their part. Consequently, they lost the opportunity for G-d to miraculously cause the inhabitants of the land to flee without even the threat of war.[12]

—*Likkutei Sichos, vol. 34, pp. 7–8*

---

12. Still, had Bnei Yisrael rejected the spies' report, they would have needed only to bear arms, but not actually go to war.

ואתחנן
Va'eschanan

5:19 | ה:יט

אֵת הַדְּבָרִים הָאֵלֶּה דִּבֶּר ה' אֶל כָּל קְהַלְכֶם בָּהָר מִתּוֹךְ הָאֵשׁ הֶעָנָן וְהָעֲרָפֶל קוֹל גָּדוֹל וְלֹא יָסָף

G-d spoke these words to your entire assembly at the mountain out of the midst of the fire, the cloud, and the thick darkness, with a great voice, which did not cease.

The Unstoppable Sound

The Midrash[1] describes several aspects of G-d's "great voice... which did not cease" at the giving of the Torah. Among them, that it had no echo.

How does the lack of an echo imply greatness? Ostensibly, the mightier a sound, the greater its reverberation!

At the giving of the Torah, however, the lack of resonance was not a sign of weakness, but of strength. And in fact, this lack of echo was not *despite* nature; it was the world's most natural reaction to the infinitely powerful sound of G-d's voice.

---

1. Shemos Rabbah 28:4.

When sound waves encounter a barrier they can neither pierce nor penetrate, they bounce back and resonate, creating what we call an echo. Naturally, more powerful sounds resound with louder echoes. But if a sound meets no barriers, because anything it encounters either absorbs it or is powerless to prevent it from passing, what will cause it to reverberate and echo?

This explains what took place at the giving of the Torah. When G-d proclaimed, "I am Hashem, your G-d, who took you out of Egypt...," the mighty sound pierced and penetrated all of existence. The great voice of G-d traveled without obstruction, and therefore naturally "did not cease" or bounce back with an echo. Every part of creation, from the spiritual to the inanimate, sensed the infinite power of G-d's voice and absorbed its eternal message.

—*Likkutei Sichos, vol. 4, pp. 1092–1096*

6:4 | ו:ד

שְׁמַע יִשְׂרָאֵל ה' אֱלֹקֵינוּ ה' אֶחָד

Hear, O Israel: Hashem is our G-d, Hashem is one.

The One and Only Word Echad

This verse expresses Judaism's cardinal principle: belief in the singular existence of G-d. The deeper meaning of this "oneness" is not only that is there no deity other than G-d, but that G-d is the one and only true existence: nothing exists outside of Him. Since G-d's will is the cause of any and all existence, the true identity of every being is the will of G-d that is continuously causing it to exist.[2]

This idea is hinted to by the Hebrew word *echad*, "one," spelled אחד. The numerical values of its three letters are one, eight and four, respectively. The ח, equaling eight, is symbolic of the seven heavens and one earth.[3] The ד, equaling four, represents the four directions—north, south, east and west. The א, which equals one, represents our singular G-d, who is Master over all that exists in heaven and earth and in all four directions.[4]

This demonstrates the difference between Lashon Hakodesh—the sacred language of the Torah—and all other languages. The ten utterances with which G-d created the world[5] were stated in Lashon Hakodesh.[6] Hence, words in

---

2. See Tanya, Shaar Hayichud Veha'emunah, at length.
3. Sefer Mitzvos Katan, sec. 2.
4. Shulchan Aruch, Orach Chaim 61:6.
5. Mishnah, Avos 5:1.
6. Rashi, Bereishis 2:23.

Lashon Hakodesh are not arbitrary: each word reflects the Divine energy animating the particular object it refers to, and captures the essential character of that object. In contrast, all other languages form by human consensus; the words do not reflect the essential nature of the articles or ideas to which they refer.[7]

This is evident in the Aramaic translation of the word one, *chad*, as rendered by Targum Onkelos on this verse. The word *chad* contains a ח and a ד, representing all of creation, as explained above, but it is missing the א, which represents G-d. Though the meaning of the word *chad* is "one," and in this context expresses the idea of G-d's singular existence (just as the word *echad* does), the truth of this oneness is not as obvious and revealed in the Aramaic word as it is in Lashon Hakodesh.

—*Toras Menachem 5743, vol. 1, p. 264*

---

7. See Shnei Luchos HaBris (Shaloh), Toldos Adam, Bayis Acharon.

6:5 | ו:ה

וְאָהַבְתָּ אֵת ה' אֱלֹקֶיךָ בְּכָל לְבָבְךָ וּבְכָל נַפְשְׁךָ וּבְכָל מְאֹדֶךָ

You shall love Hashem, your G-d, with all your heart, with all your soul and with all your might.

The Martyr's Shema

Our Sages explain the commandment to "love G-d... with all your soul" to mean, "even if He takes your soul," i.e., to devote yourself to G-d even at the cost of your life.

The Talmud relates:

> When they [the Romans] took Rabbi Akiva out for execution, it was the time for the recitation of Shema. As they combed his flesh with iron combs, he was accepting upon himself the kingship of Heaven [reciting the Shema]. His disciples said to him, "Our teacher, even to this extent?" He replied, "All my days I have been distressed by the verse 'with all your soul,' which means 'even if He takes your soul.' I said, 'When shall I have the opportunity to fulfill this?' Now that I have the opportunity, shall I not fulfill it?"[8]

The students of Rabbi Akiva were men of great stature in their own right. Certainly, they were not surprised that the saintly Rabbi Akiva could suppress his physical pain and fulfill the mitzvah of reciting the Shema even during his execution. But the Shema proclaims G-d's Oneness, which means that nothing exists outside of Him: the true identity of all of existence is the will of G-d that is causing it to exist. Rabbi Akiva's

---

8. Berachos 61b.

students therefore understood that by reciting Shema at that moment, Rabbi Akiva was declaring that he recognized G-d's Oneness even within the torture he was suffering for studying Torah! This caused them to wonder, "Even to this point?" Could Rabbi Akiva identify G-d's singular existence even in this blasphemous attack on G-d and His Torah?

Rabbi Akiva, however, did not view his execution as a challenge to G-d's Oneness. On the contrary, in Rabbi Akiva's eyes, G-d's Oneness in this world meant that even experiences (that were not assisting in his worship of G-d directly) were enhancing his relationship with G-d indirectly—by allowing him to commit to G-d *in spite of them*. In fact, all his life, Rabbi Akiva had yearned to fulfill the mitzvah of dedicating himself to G-d to the point of *ultimate* sacrifice. Now that the Romans were offering him that "opportunity," he found the Oneness of G-d even in their cruelty.

—*Likkutei Sichos, vol. 6, p. 126, fn. 35*

6:8 | ו:ח

וּקְשַׁרְתָּם לְאוֹת עַל יָדֶךָ וְהָיוּ לְטֹטָפֹת בֵּין עֵינֶיךָ

You shall bind them as a sign upon your hand, and they shall be a reminder between your eyes.

The Tefillin Line of Attack

Our Sages teach that the mitzvah of *tefillin* frightens away the enemies of the Jewish people. The Talmud declares, "It is written: 'All the peoples of the earth will see that the name of G-d is called upon you, and they will fear you'[9]... This refers to the *tefillin* of the head."[10] Even if our enemies do attack, G-d forbid, we are told that the merit of the mitzvah of *tefillin* will give our soldiers remarkable strength in battle: "By fulfilling the mitzvah to wear the *tefillin* [on the arm and on the head], those going to war will see the fulfillment of [Moshe's blessing to the warriors of Gad,[11]] 'May he tear off the arm [of his enemy] as well as his head.'"[12]

Interestingly, when saying that the *tefillin* will scare off our enemies before they attack, the Talmud mentions only the *tefillin* of the head.[13] In contrast, when describing the power of *tefillin* in the event that our enemies *do* attack, the *tefillin* of the arm and head are said to be *individually* effec-

---

9. Devarim 28:10.
10. Berachos 6a.
11. Devarim 33:20.
12. Rabbeinu Asher, Laws of Tefillin 15.
13. In this context, the function of the *tefillin* of the arm is that it facilitates the donning of the *tefillin* of the head. See Tzafnas Pa'aneach, Hilchos Tefillin 4:4.

tive, helping those at battle "tear off the arm [of the enemy] as well as his head."

This explains the difference between the way the mitzvah of *tefillin* is related in the Book of Shemos[14] and in the Book of Devarim.[15] In Shemos, the Torah describes the *tefillin* of the arm and of the head as two components of one unit: "It shall be to you as a sign upon your hand and a remembrance between your eyes." In Devarim, however, the Torah states, "You shall bind them as a sign upon your hand, *and they shall be* a reminder between your eyes"—distinguishing them as two separate acts and obligations.

The reason for this difference is that in Shemos, the conquest of the Land of Israel was still intended to be led by Moshe, in which case the two *tefillin* together would have had a single effect: the nations would have been afraid to go to war against them. As Bnei Yisrael sang at the Splitting of the Sea, "All the inhabitants of Canaan melted..."[16] In Devarim, however, Moshe knew that the conquest of the Land would be led by Yehoshua, and would require going to battle. Accordingly, he ascribed to the *tefillin* of the head and the hand two distinct mitzvos and merits.

—*Likkutei Sichos, vol. 9, pp. 55–56*

---

14. Shemos 13:9 and 13:16.
15. Devarim 6:8 and 11:18.
16. Shemos 15:15.

6:8 | ו:ח

וּקְשַׁרְתָּם לְאוֹת עַל יָדֶךָ וְהָיוּ לְטֹטָפֹת בֵּין עֵינֶיךָ

You shall bind them as a sign upon your hand, and they shall be a reminder between your eyes.

Controlling Your Mind and Heart

The Torah commands us to wear *tefillin shel yad* on the arm and *tefillin shel rosh* on the head. The Torah's wording indicates that the mitzvah to wear the *tefillin shel yad* is observed actively—"you shall bind them... upon your arm," whereas the mitzvah to wear *tefillin shel rosh* is observed passively—"they shall be between your eyes" (on your head). This implies that while the observance of the mitzvah of *tefillin shel rosh* is fulfilled continuously, i.e., for as long as the *tefillin* are upon the person's head, the mitzvah of *tefillin shel yad* is defined by, and its fulfillment thus limited to, the singular *act* of binding.

This distinction reflects the two intended effects of *tefillin* on the person wearing them.

The Shulchan Aruch states:

> With the donning of *tefillin*, one should contemplate that G-d commanded us... to place the arm *tefillin* near the heart, and the head *tefillin* over the brain... and he shall submit to G-d his soul that is in the brain, and his heart that is the seat of his desires and thoughts.[17]

The average person is capable of controlling and deter-

---

17. Shulchan Aruch, Orach Chaim 25:5.

mining the ideas that will occupy his mind. In contrast, most people are not capable of dictating which desires will occupy their hearts. Granted, they can refrain from *acting* on their impulses, but, with the exception of *tzaddikim*—the perfectly righteous—the average person has limited influence in determining what he or she will desire. As the Tanya explains: "One's mind is under his control, and with it he can meditate as he pleases, on any subject.... [But] it is not a 'very near thing' to change one's heart from worldly desires to a sincere love of G-d."[18] To constantly feel drawn toward that which is holy, and be repulsed by anything unholy, is not within the average person's reach.

Accordingly, we can understand why wearing the *tefillin shel yad* close to our hearts is a mitzvah of *action* (we are commanded to *bind* the tefillin upon our arms). Since we cannot determine what our hearts will desire, we have no choice but to *actively* wage war with our negative impulses. The mitzvah of *tefillin shel rosh*, however, is for the tefillin to "be" upon our heads, because its desired effect of the *tefillin shel rosh* is something that we are capable of maintaining. Since we can choose which ideas we will contemplate and which we will not, we can keep our minds consistently and continuously devoted to G-d.

—*Likkutei Sichos, vol. 39, pp. 24–28*

---

18. Chapter 17.

6:9 | ו:ט

וּכְתַבְתָּם עַל מְזֻזוֹת בֵּיתֶךָ וּבִשְׁעָרֶיךָ

You shall inscribe them upon the doorposts of your house and upon your gates.

Mezuzah: Protecting the Citizens of Israel

Our Sages teach that affixing *mezuzos* to the doorposts of our homes brings security and protection for the house and all its inhabitants.[19] The Zohar[20] takes this a step further, saying that through the *mezuzah* "G-d will watch your going out and your coming in, from now and to eternity."[21] The *mezuzah* protects a person not only when he is at home, but even when he is away.[22]

Moreover, since all Jews are connected and accountable for one another, one person's good deeds bring merit to all his fellow Jews as well. As such, one Jew's observance of the mitzvah of *mezuzah* provides additional safety and security even for others who might not have a *mezuzah* themselves (though they are obviously not exempt from fulfilling this *mitzvah* on their own).

The mitzvah of *mezuzah* and the protection that it provides have particular significance in the Land of Israel, as is evident from the law taught in the Talmud: "One who rents a home outside of Israel is exempt from affixing a *mezuzah*

---

19. See Talmud, Avodah Zarah 11a.
20. Zohar 3:263b.
21. Tehillim 121:8.
22. Zohar 3:263b.

for the first 30 days; from then on, he is obligated. But one who rents a home in the Land of Israel must affix a *mezuzah* immediately, for the sake of *yishuv Eretz Yisrael*, settling the Land of Israel."[23] (Rashi explains that since it is considered improper for a Jew to remove his *mezuzah* when he leaves his home,[24] the renter will not rush to move out and incur the cost of acquiring new *mezuzos*. Even if he does move out, the home will soon attract another Jewish renter, because it is already equipped with a *mezuzah*.)

This unique law demonstrates that the mitzvah of *mezuzah* is particularly connected to *yishuv Eretz Yisrael*, which in its truest sense means not only dwelling there technically, but also living there in comfort and security.[25]

This highlights the importance of ensuring that every Jew has a *mezuzah* on his doorpost. Through this mitzvah, particularly in the Land of Israel, we help create peace and security for ourselves and for the entire Jewish nation.

—*Likkutei Sichos, vol. 13, pp. 212–216*

---

23. Menachos 44a.
24. Bava Metzia 102a.
25. See Vayikra 26:5: "וִישַׁבְתֶּם לָבֶטַח בְּאַרְצְכֶם, you will live securely in your land."

עקב
Eikev

7:13 | ז:יג

וּבֵרַךְ פְּרִי בִטְנְךָ וּפְרִי אַדְמָתֶךָ דְּגָנְךָ וְתִירֹשְׁךָ וְיִצְהָרֶךָ שְׁגַר אֲלָפֶיךָ וְעַשְׁתְּרֹת צֹאנֶךָ

He will bless the fruit of your womb and the fruit of your soil, your grain, your wine, and your oil, the offspring of your cattle and the choicest of your flocks.

The Greatest Reward of All

The compensation one receives for fulfilling any given task generally reflects the value and significance of the job at hand. This raises the question: how could any reward possibly constitute adequate compensation for observing the mitzvos? It goes without saying that the material prosperity the Torah promises those who observe the mitzvos is not commensurate with the intrinsic value of fulfilling G-d's will—an achievement far more valuable than any amount of grain or cattle. And even the spiritual delights we will enjoy in the World to Come cannot be regarded as adequate reward, considering that "a single moment of repentance and good deeds in this world is greater than the entire World to Come"![1]

The answer lies in the Mishnah's teaching: "The reward for a mitzvah is a mitzvah."[2] One interpretation of this statement is that the true reward for observing a mitzvah is the bond that one creates with G-d through fulfilling His will, illustrated by the similarity between the words מצוה—*mitzvah* and צוותא—*tzavsa*, which means "attachment" or "companionship" in Aramaic. Alternatively, the Mishnah's statement can be understood to mean that the reward for observing one mitzvah is the observance of another. Both interpretations essentially make the same point: the ultimate reward for observing a mitzvah is that through it we merit to attach ourselves to G-d—through that mitzvah itself, and through the additional mitzvos that we merit fulfilling in its wake.

In view of that, we can understand that the material prosperity and physical wellbeing that the Torah promises those who observe the mitzvos is not the reward itself, but a means of facilitating the ultimate reward. Namely, if we fulfill the mitzvos, G-d will provide us with the material blessings needed to continue observing them even more comfortably, thereby rewarding us in fact with the greatest prize of all—mitzvah observance itself. In the words of the Rambam:

> If we observe it [the Torah] joyfully and happily... all obstacles that could prevent us from fulfilling it, such as sickness, war or famine, will be removed. G-d will grant us all the

---

1. Avos 4:17.
2. Avos 4:2.

good that will reinforce our fulfillment of the Torah, such as satiety, peace, and abundance of silver and gold, so that we should not need to devote our days to physical needs, but will instead be free to study wisdom and perform the mitzvos...[3]

—*Sefer Hasichos 5749, vol. 2, pp. 642-644*

---

[3]. Mishneh Torah, Hil. Teshuvah 9:1.

8:16 | ח:טז

הַמַּאֲכִלְךָ מָן בַּמִּדְבָּר אֲשֶׁר לֹא יָדְעוּן אֲבֹתֶיךָ לְמַעַן עַנֹּתְךָ

...[the One] who fed you with manna in the desert, which your ancestors did not know, in order to afflict you.

The Faith Diet

The Talmud[4] interprets the verse above quite literally—the manna was a food that left one feeling hungry and afflicted. According to one explanation, this was because it could not be saved from one day to the next, and one had to constantly rely on its falling anew. Therefore, even after eating their fill of manna, the people still felt vulnerable and wanting.

In terms of spiritual qualities, however, the manna's lack of normal shelf life or endurance reflected its transcendence of physical reality. One of the basic characteristics of physicality is that it is defined by and exists within the framework of time. The manna, on the other hand, due to its inherently transcendent nature, did not have a natural "lifespan," as all other created beings do. Additionally, in keeping with its transcendence of nature, the manna was visibly reliant on G-d's bringing it into existence each day, unlike the rest of creation, whose continued existence appears natural and spontaneous.

The manna was thus a food of paradoxes. For those seeking a sense of self-sufficiency and independence, the manna caused anxiety and affliction. For humble men of faith, however, receiving nourishment from the manna was the greatest source of delight, for in the manna they could constantly sense

---

4. Yoma 74b.

G-d's influence. In addition, through their humility they became worthy and capable of being sustained by the *limitless* goodness contained in the manna, which infinitely exceeded the limited benefits found in natural forms of sustenance.

This explains the Talmud's assertion that Moshe composed the text of the first blessing of Birkas Hamazon when G-d gave the manna to the Jewish people.[5] One might ask: the blessings of Birkas Hamazon are recited in fulfillment of the biblical command, "[When] you will eat and be *satisfied*, you shall bless G-d."[6] But if the manna left people feeling hungry, how could eating it be the basis for a blessing that is recited upon feeling satisfied?

In light of the above, however, we can understand how the manna provided the satisfaction required for the recitation of Birkas Hamazon. Indeed, the *truest* satiation came from the manna, for through it one sensed clearly that his sustenance was entirely from G-d, and thereby became a worthy recipient of G-d's infinite benevolence.

—*Toras Menachem, Sefer Hamaamarim Melukat,*
vol. 4, p. 186

---

5. Berachos 48b.
6. Devarim 8:10.

ט:יז | 9:17

וָאֶתְפֹּשׂ בִּשְׁנֵי הַלֻּחֹת וָאַשְׁלִכֵם מֵעַל שְׁתֵּי יָדָי וָאֲשַׁבְּרֵם לְעֵינֵיכֶם

So I grabbed hold of the two tablets, cast them out of my two hands, and broke them before your eyes.

To the Exclusion of All Others

The commentaries discuss why it was necessary for Moshe to "grab hold" of the Luchos before he broke them, considering that he was already holding them as he descended the mountain.[7]

One explanation is that Moshe did so for legal reasons—to establish his exclusive ownership of the Luchos before acting on his decision to break them. Although the Torah states that G-d "gave" Moshe the Luchos,[8] and the Talmud interprets this verse to mean that the Torah was given to Moshe as a gift,[9] Moshe had not intended to keep the Luchos for himself, but to confer their ownership on the entire Jewish nation. Moshe therefore "grabbed hold" of the Luchos before breaking them, to reestablish outright ownership over them and avoid the possibility of damaging (or stealing) property that did not belong to him exclusively.

Alternatively, Moshe's repossession of the Luchos before breaking them stemmed from his extraordinary devotion to the Jewish people. By claiming exclusive ownership, Moshe sought to ensure that the guilt of shattering the holy Luchos

---

7. See Ohr HaChaim, Devarim 9:17.
8. Shemos 31:18.
9. Nedarim 38a.

would lie squarely on his shoulders, and not on the Jewish people, whose behavior caused him to do so.

—*Likkutei Sichos, vol. 34, pp. 51–56*

| יא:יט | 11:19

וְלִמַּדְתֶּ֥ם אֹתָ֛ם אֶת־בְּנֵיכֶ֖ם לְדַבֵּ֣ר בָּ֑ם

You shall teach them to your children to speak with them.

First Words

This verse is the source from which we learn that a father is obligated to teach his children Torah. As the Alter Rebbe writes:

> A father is obligated to teach his young son Torah… as it is written, 'You shall teach them to your sons to speak about them.' From when is he obligated to teach him? From when he begins to speak, he should teach him *Torah tzivah lanu Moshe…*, as well as the first verse of Shema Yisrael.[10]

Earlier, the Torah instructs us, "These words that I command you today… you shall teach them thoroughly to your children."[11] That command, however, speaks of a more advanced level of learning—when the child is capable of *thoroughly* grasping and retaining the Torah that he is taught. In addition, our Sages interpret the word "children" in that verse as a reference to students, one's spiritual children. The mitzvah to "teach them thoroughly to your children" is the obligation upon the learned to teach the Torah to all who desire to study—even those who are not their biological offspring.[12]

---

10. Shulchan Aruch Admor Hazaken, Hil. Talmud Torah 1:1.
11. Devarim 6:6–7.
12. See Sifri, Eikev 34.

In contrast, the mitzvah given here, "You shall teach them to your children *to speak with them*," refers to a very early stage in a child's education, when he is just beginning to speak. As Rashi explains, this verse is meant quite literally: "From the moment your son knows how to speak, teach him [the verse] *Torah tzivah lanu Moshe*. Let him learn to speak with this."[13] This training obviously begins at home, long before the child is old enough to be sent to school. Clearly, then, this verse refers to a parent's personal mitzvah to teach the Torah to his child—an obligation that goes into effect as soon as the child begins to talk.

—*Likkutei Sichos, vol. 9, p. 33, fn. 3;*
Sichos Kodesh 5737, vol. 2, pp. 387–388

---

13. Devarim 11:19.

11:19 | יא:יט

וְלִמַּדְתֶּם אֹתָם אֶת־בְּנֵיכֶם לְדַבֵּר בָּם בְּשִׁבְתְּךָ בְּבֵיתֶךָ וּבְלֶכְתְּךָ בַדֶּרֶךְ וּבְשָׁכְבְּךָ וּבְקוּמֶךָ׃

You shall teach them to your children, to speak with them, when you sit in your house and when you go on the way, when you lie down and when you rise.

What's On Your Mind?

Sforno explains the verse "You shall teach them to your children to speak with them when you sit in your house…" to mean that one must teach his children to engage constantly in the words of the Torah—in the morning and at night, and under all circumstances.[14] On a more literal level, however, one can understand this verse as an instruction to be constantly educating our children—"You shall teach them to your children… when you sit in your house and when you go on the way, when you lie down and when you rise."

Practically, this means that providing a proper Jewish education to your children—and by extension, to all Jewish children whom you can reach and affect—must constantly be on your mind. You must think about their education, and be active in ensuring it, not only "when you sit in your house"—i.e., when you focus on your family life—but even as you "go on the way"—as you go about your daily affairs. Even when you relax and wind down at the end of the day, your thoughts "when you lie down" to sleep should be about the

---

14. Devarim 11:19.

importance of providing the next generation with a proper Torah education.

Moreover, the verse continues, "You shall teach them to your children... when you rise up." In the very first moments after you wake up, along with your recitation of Modeh Ani, thanking G-d for restoring your soul for another day, your first thoughts must be, "How will I best fulfill my duty to teach the Torah to my children today?"

—*Sichos Kodesh 5737, vol. 2, pp. 388–389*

11:22 | יא:כב

לְאַהֲבָה אֶת ה' אֱלֹקֵיכֶם לָלֶכֶת בְּכָל דְּרָכָיו וּלְדָבְקָה בּוֹ

To love Hashem, your G-d, to walk in all His ways, and to cleave to Him

Speak as G-d Speaks

How does one walk in all G-d's ways? The Sifri interprets this as a commandment to emulate the virtues that the Torah attributes to G-d:

> G-d is called 'merciful and gracious'[15]—so too, you should be merciful and gracious… G-d is called 'righteous,' as it says, 'G-d is righteous in all His ways and kind in all His deeds'[16]—so too, you should be righteous.[17]

In light of this teaching, it can be suggested that we are also obligated to emulate another feat attributed to G-d—namely, just as G-d's speech alone causes things to exist,[18] we too must ensure that our words are effective.

How? By following two strategies taught by our Sages:

Rule one: Be sincere. "Words spoken from the heart enter the heart."[19]

---

15. Shemos 34:6.
16. Tehillim 145:8.
17. Sifri, Eikev 49.
18. See Bereishis Rabbah 44:22.
19. See R. Moshe ibn Ezra, Shiras Yisrael, p. 156.

Rule two: Fear G-d. "Anyone who has fear of Heaven, his words will be heeded."[20] If you live a G-d-fearing life, not only will your sincere words "penetrate your listeners' hearts," but they will be acted upon as well.

In this way, you too can speak as G-d speaks.

—*Igros Kodesh, vol. 15, p. 112*

---

[20]. Berachos 6b.

ראה
Re'eh

12:3-4 | יב:ג-ד

וְנִתַּצְתֶּם אֶת מִזְבְּחֹתָם... לֹא תַעֲשׂוּן כֵּן לַה' אֱלֹקֵיכֶם

You shall demolish their altars...
You shall not do so to Hashem your G-d.

Under Renovation

The Torah commands us to destroy the altars used for idol worship, and warns, "Do not do so to Hashem your G-d"—i.e., do not destroy the Beis Hamikdash, the Holy Temple.

Now, from the verse "He declares *His* words to Yaakov, *His* rules and *His* ordinances to Yisrael,"[1] the Midrash learns that "All that G-d instructs the Jewish people to do, He Himself fulfills as well."[2] Meaning, that G-d Himself "observes," as it were, all the commandments and prohibitions of the Torah. This raises the question: how could G-d allow the destruction of the Beis Hamikdash—and even send agents to carry

---

1. Tehillim 147:19.
2. Shemos Rabbah 30:9.

it out[3]—in violation of the prohibition[4] of demolishing even one of its stones?

There is one instance, however, in which such demolition is permissible—if done in order to make improvements to the Beis Hamikdash. For, as the Rambam emphasizes, one is liable for causing damage to the Beis Hamikdash only if he does so "with destructive intent."[5] To enhance the structure itself, however, demolition is permissible.[6]

Accordingly, we can understand the "permissibility" of G-d's sending of agents to destroy of the first and second Batei Mikdash.

The Midrash states:

> The *aryeh*, lion [Nevuchadnetzar, king of Babylon],[7] rose, in the *mazal* of Ari [in the constellation of Leo—i.e., in the month of Av,] and destroyed Ariel [the Beis Hamikdash],[8] **in order that** the Lion [G-d][9] come during the *mazal* of Ari and reconstruct Ariel.[10]

As we see from the words of the Midrash, the destruction of the Temple was "in order that"—i.e., provisional upon and for the sake of the third Beis Hamikdash being built by G-d. As such, the destruction of the first and second Batei Mikdash was not "with destructive intent," but for the sake of upgrading and improving the Temple itself. Whereas the first

---

3. See Yirmiyahu 25:9 and 7:14.
4. Mishneh Torah, Hil. Yesodei Hatorah 6:7, and Hil. Beis Habechirah 1:17.
5. Ibid.
6. See Kesef Mishneh ad loc.; Taz, Orach Chaim 151:3.
7. Yirmiyahu 4:7.
8. Yeshayahu 29:1.
9. Amos 3:8.
10. Yalkut Shimoni, Yirmiyahu 259.

two were temporary structures built by man, the third Beis Hamikdash will be an eternal edifice built by G-d Himself.[11] Hence, by halachic standards, the demolition of the Batei Mikdash was not an act of destruction, but actually the start of their restoration.

—*Likkutei Sichos vol. 29, pp. 11–14*

---

11. See Zohar 3:221a.

12:20-23 | יב:כ-כג

כִּי יַרְחִיב ה' אֱלֹקֶיךָ אֶת גְּבֻלְךָ כַּאֲשֶׁר דִּבֶּר לָךְ וְאָמַרְתָּ אֹכְלָה בָשָׂר כִּי תְאַוֶּה נַפְשְׁךָ לֶאֱכֹל בָּשָׂר בְּכָל אַוַּת נַפְשְׁךָ תֹּאכַל בָּשָׂר... רַק חֲזַק לְבִלְתִּי אֲכֹל הַדָּם

When Hashem, your G-d, expands your borders, as He has spoken to you, and you say, "I will eat meat," because your soul desires to eat meat... However, be strong in not eating the blood.

Let Them Eat Meat

According to one opinion in the Talmud,[12] during their years in the desert the only meat Bnei Yisrael were permitted to consume was that of the sacrifices. It was therefore necessary for Moshe to tell them that when G-d "expands your borders," i.e., when they will arrive in the Land of Israel, they will be allowed to eat meat whenever "your soul desires to eat meat," even from an animal that was not brought as a sacrifice.

The permission to consume non-sacrificial meat upon entering the Land of Israel reflects the shift of spiritual focus that accompanied Bnei Yisrael's transition from the desert to the Land.

Upon entering Israel, Bnei Yisrael would begin engaging with the world on a natural level, working the land and settling it. Their Divine mission would be to elevate the material world by imbuing it with G-dly purpose.

In the desert, however, G-d had provided all their material needs, allowing them to devote themselves entirely to spiritual development and the study of Torah. There was therefore no

---

12. Chullin 16b.

justification for eating "mundane" meat in the desert, for the job of elevating the mundane had not yet begun. Animals were to be offered to G-d as sacrifices, and only in that holy context was the consumption of meat permissible.

Non-sacrificial meat became permissible for consumption only when Bnei Yisrael entered the Land of Israel. Now they were permitted to partake of the physical world—even beyond that which is obviously sacred (as the sacrifices were), for they now had the ability (and responsibility!) to infuse even their mundane desires with G-dly purpose.

The Torah warns, however, "Be strong in not eating the blood." Blood is a metaphor for energy, enthusiasm and passion. The Torah's admonition to eat meat only if it has been drained of its blood means that when we utilize what the world has to offer for a G-dly purpose, we must do so without "blood"—i.e., without excitement or lust for physical pleasure.

—*Likkutei Sichos, vol. 4, pp. 1108–1110*

16:1 | טז:א

שָׁמוֹר אֶת חֹדֶשׁ הָאָבִיב וְעָשִׂיתָ פֶּסַח לַה' אֱלֹקֶיךָ כִּי בְּחֹדֶשׁ הָאָבִיב הוֹצִיאֲךָ ה' אֱלֹקֶיךָ מִמִּצְרַיִם לָיְלָה

Safeguard the month of spring and offer a Pesach to Hashem, your G-d; for in the month of spring, Hashem, your G-d, brought you out of Egypt at night.

What Spring Teaches Us about Winter

The Torah commands us to structure the calendar in a manner that ensures that the 15th of Nissan—the day Pesach begins—falls in the spring. The emphasis placed on the timing of this holiday highlights the uplifting message conveyed by springtime.

During the months of winter, there are almost no visible signs of thriving plant life. When winter concludes, however, the processes of growth that lay dormant in the earth suddenly spring to life, and it becomes evident that the lack of growth we witnessed throughout the winter was only a temporary pause, to allow for nature's rejuvenation. Now a fresh crop of vegetation can blossom and thrive.

The exodus from Egypt contains a very similar message. Bnei Yisrael suffered bitterly in Egypt, oppressed in both body and spirit. It was revealed only later that the exile had in fact refined them,[13] enabling them to receive the Torah—the very word of G-d—a short 50 days after leaving Egypt.

---

13. See Devarim 4:20 and Rashi ad loc.

The same is true for us, as individuals. If ever we experience a period in life that seems to be barren, with no signs of productivity or growth, we must realize that this barrenness is almost certainly not our permanent reality. It is merely a temporary break so we can rejuvenate, and ultimately blossom and flourish again.

—*Igros Kodesh, vol. 4, pp. 267–268*

16:14 | טז:יד

וְשָׂמַחְתָּ בְּחַגֶּךָ

You shall rejoice in your Festival.

Appreciating the Joy of Yom Tov

The obligation of *simchas Yom Tov*, rejoicing on the holidays, is described by the Alter Rebbe:

> For all seven days of Pesach, eight days of Sukkos, and the holiday of Shavuos, a person is obligated to be happy and in good spirits—he, his children, his wife, the members of his household and all who depend on him. This rejoicing is a positive commandment in the Torah, as it is written, "You shall rejoice in your festival." How are they caused to rejoice? To children, one gives roasted kernels and nuts; for women, one buys clothes and jewelry according to his means; men, in the times of the Beis Hamikdash, they would eat the meat of the *shelamim* offering. Nowadays, in absence of the Beis Hamikdash, they fulfill their obligation to rejoice only by drinking wine.[14]

The Alter Rebbe's wording indicates that by enjoying physical treats one genuinely fulfills the mitzvah to be joyous on Yom Tov. Granted, he notes that the ideal joy for men was achieved in Temple times by eating sacrificial meat, but in its absence, drinking wine fulfills this mitzvah as well.

In contrast, the Rambam suggests that the joy we are obligated to feel on the holidays is primarily spiritual—the joy of offering and eating the *shelamim* sacrifice—and the physical

---

14. Shulchan Aruch Admor Hazaken, Orach Chaim 529:6–7.

aspects of rejoicing are merely secondary. Thus, the Rambam writes:

> Even though the rejoicing mentioned here refers to the *shelamim* offering... included in this joy is to make himself, his children and the members of his household joyous, each one accordingly. How so? To children, one gives...[15]

This debate between the Rambam and the Alter Rebbe mirrors the discussion surrounding the delight in Divine revelation that we will experience in the future, in the era of reward, known as Olam Haba, the World to Come. The Rambam writes that in Olam Haba "there is no body or physical form, only the souls of the righteous alone, without a body."[16] The Alter Rebbe, however, follows the opinion that since the observance of the mitzvos is intended to refine and elevate even our physical bodies, the reward in Olam Haba will likewise be experienced only after the soul is restored to a physical body at the time of *techiyas hameisim*, the resurrection.[17]

Accordingly, the Alter Rebbe rules that both body and soul must equally partake in the Mitzvah and experience the joy of Yom Tov.

—*Likkutei Sichos, vol. 33, pp. 62-70*

---

15. Mishneh Torah, Hil. Shevisas Yom Tov 6:17–18.
16. Ibid., Hil. Teshuvah 8:2.
17. See Likkutei Torah, Tzav 15c.

טז:טו | 16:15

שִׁבְעַת יָמִים תָּחֹג לַה' אֱלֹקֶיךָ ... וְהָיִיתָ אַךְ שָׂמֵחַ

Seven days you shall celebrate the Festival to Hashem, your G-d... and you will be only happy.

The Holiday that was Left Out

The Torah commands us to be exceedingly joyous during the seven-day festival of Sukkos. The obligation to rejoice on Shemini Atzeres, the eighth day of the holiday, however, is not stated explicitly. Rather, the Talmud[18] derives this obligation from the extra words stated at the conclusion of the commandment to rejoice on Sukkos, "והיית אך שמח—and you will be only happy." As Rashi explains, "From here it is derived that the evening of the last day of the festival is included in the obligation of rejoicing."[19]

The methodology of this Talmudic teaching is unusual. Generally, the Torah's use of the word אך, "only," in the context of any particular mitzvah, denotes an *exception* to the obligation stated there.[20] Yet here the Talmud interprets the words "והיית אך שמח—you will be *only* happy" as *extending* the obligation to rejoice on Sukkos to include an additional day—Shemini Atzeres!

In doing so, the Talmud hints that not only should our joy on Shemini Atzeres be equal to our joy on the other holidays, it should truly be exceeded.

How so?

---

18. Sukkah 48a.
19. Devarim 16:15.
20. See Talmud Yerushalmi, Berachos 9:7.

The obligation to rejoice on the festivals has limits. In fact, the religious authorities are obligated to appoint patrolmen on the holidays to see that the drinking and festivities do not get out of control.[21]

Accordingly, the phrase "You will be only happy," which indicates an *exception* to the rule, teaches us that there is a holiday when our joy must be *excluded* from the typical limited joy of the holidays—i.e., our celebration of this holiday must exceed our constrained celebration of the other holidays. Which one? Says the Talmud: Shemini Atzeres.

As such, the custom of *hakkafos*, dancing with the Torah scrolls, which has no parallel in any other holiday, is observed specifically on Shemini Atzeres (and Simchas Torah, in the Diaspora). For the holiday of Shemini Atzeres is to be celebrated not only in a manner equivalent to the other holidays, but with a joy that is truly boundless.

—*Sefer Hasichos 5749, vol. 2, pp. 661-662*

---

21. See Shulchan Aruch, Orach Chaim 529:4.

16:10–17 | ט״ז:י׳-י״ז

מִסַּת נִדְבַת יָדְךָ אֲשֶׁר תִּתֵּן... אִישׁ כְּמַתְּנַת יָדוֹ כְּבִרְכַּת ה' אֱלֹקֶיךָ

According to the generosity with which you will give... Each man according to his ability to gift, consistent with the blessing of Hashem, your G-d.

Expectations

The Torah instructs us here about two different types of giving: one is described as stemming from a sense of "generosity," and the other is "according to your ability to gift."

These correspond to two different approaches toward charity, which often reflect the financial means of the individual. First, the Torah addresses a person who is not particularly wealthy, and who could easily justify using all his earnings for his own needs and the needs of his dependents. In this case the Torah appeals to his generosity, telling him to be benevolent and give even more than can be expected of him.

With the instruction to give "according to your ability to gift," however, the Torah demands more than generosity. Here the Torah addresses one who is affluent and is aware that G-d has blessed him with wealth well beyond his needs. Presumably, this person also knows that G-d provides sustenance for all humanity; some have the good fortune of earning it on their own, and some must rely on the generosity of others in order to receive the sustenance intended for them. He therefore understands that G-d has not only provided him wealth to support himself, He has also appointed him custodian over funds intended for others, and it is therefore only logical for him to be charitable. In this instance, it is not necessary for the Torah to demand that he be generous—for he already knows that the money is intended for charity, and does not even regard it as his own. Instead, the Torah addresses the *cordiality* with which he gives, and instructs him not to give grudgingly, but "according to his ability to *gift*"—with the warmth and friendliness of a person giving a gift to a friend.

With the sequence in which the verse addresses these two types of donors, the Torah hints that one type of charitableness will lead to the other. If you give to charity when it requires a spirit of generosity—i.e., even when your funds are limited—G-d will bless you to be in a position where you no longer require a command to be generous. You will be blessed with such prosperity that your charitableness will be self-understood. Moreover, G-d will also grant you a noble spirit of "gifting," rousing you to donate to charity warmly and happily.

—*Likkutei Sichos, vol. 9, pp. 288-290*

שפטים
Shoftim

16:18 | ט״ז:י״ח

שֹׁפְטִים וְשֹׁטְרִים תִּתֶּן לְךָ בְּכָל שְׁעָרֶיךָ

You shall set up judges and law-enforcement officials for yourself in all your cities.

Counseling Law

The Torah instructs us to set up court systems in every city where Jews live, comprising judges who determine the law and officials who enforce the judges' rulings. We find, however, that regarding the era of the future Redemption, G-d says, "I will restore your judges as at first, and your counselors as in the beginning."[1] The verse makes no mention of law-enforcement officials, only judges who will determine the law and counselors who will advise the people how to conduct their lives.

---

1. Yeshayahu 1:26.

This is because in the era of the Redemption all evil will be annulled,[2] including the *yetzer hara*, the negative inclination we have within us, thereby eliminating the need for police to enforce the law. Instead, counselors, whose task will be not to enforce laws or give orders but to advise, will complement the judges' authority.

Advice, by definition, is *offered*—i.e., it is a suggestion, not a command. The person advising speaks as though to an equal, in a manner that the recipient does not feel compelled, but can come to understand that this advice is truly in his best interest.

This will be the role of the "counselors" in the era of Moshiach: they will help people recognize the value of adhering to the Torah's laws on their own. Consequently, in the time of Moshiach we will not only observe the laws of the Torah (taught by the judges) obediently, we will do so with inner drive.

—*Sefer Hasichos 5751, vol. 2, pp. 780-785*

---

2. Zechariah 13:2.

17:15 | יז:טו

שׂוֹם תָּשִׂים עָלֶיךָ מֶלֶךְ

You shall appoint a king over you.

The Real King

From a historic and halachic perspective, it seems that a basic component of every new king's inauguration involved anointing the king with oil.[3] Yet, surprisingly, though the Torah explicitly outlines in detail how the mitzvah of appointing a new king is to be carried out, the verse makes no mention of the anointment with oil.

Moreover, the first Jewish king anointed with oil was Shaul, who was appointed by the prophet Shmuel.[4] We know, however, that Yehoshua had the halachic status of a king,[5] yet he received his appointment through *semichah*—by Moshe's "leaning his hands upon him."[6] Granted, the authority to transmit the Torah is conferred through *semichah*,[7] but the authority to rule the nation is conferred through anointment. So why did Moshe not anoint Yehoshua with oil?

The Rambam defines the purpose of the Jewish monarch:

> His purpose and intent shall be to elevate the true faith and to fill the world with justice, destroying the power of the wicked and waging the wars of G-d. For the entire purpose of appointing a king is to execute justice and wage wars.[8]

---

3. Mishneh Torah, Hil. Melachim 1:7–12.
4. I Shmuel 10:1.
5. See Mishneh Torah ibid. 1:3.
6. Bamidbar 27:18–23.
7. Mishneh Torah, Hil. Sanhedrin 4:1.
8. Ibid., Hil. Melachim 4:10.

As is evident from the Rambam's words, the Jewish king's role is not only to govern and lead the nation's material affairs, but *primarily* to promote the ways of the Torah. As such, though the king's reign over the nation is his exclusively, at the same time the monarchy is in essence an extension of the Sanhedrin—the body of authority entrusted with transmitting the Torah.

Yet the monarchy and the Sanhedrin remain distinct branches of government, and each is conferred its power differently and independently.

The reign of Yehoshua was the exception. On the one hand, Yehoshua exclusively was tasked with transmitting the Torah to his generation[9]—a power normally granted to the Sanhedrin (as a group). At the same time, Yehoshua was also king, charged with implementing the Torah's teachings within the capacity of his kingship.

It was therefore unnecessary for Yehoshua to be anointed with oil. Since Yehoshua held both branches of Jewish leadership exclusively, the *semichah* that endowed him with his spiritual authority—*of which the monarchy is merely an extension*—was sufficient to establish his kingship as well.

Accordingly, we can understand why the Torah does not explicitly mention the requirement of anointing a new king with oil. For the Torah's ideal form of monarchy, as embodied by Yehoshua, is one in which the king is the Torah authority as well, in which case anointing with oil is unnecessary.

—*Likkutei Sichos, vol. 23, pp. 190-197*

---

9. See Avos 1:1.

20:8 | כ:ח

מִי הָאִישׁ הַיָּרֵא וְרַךְ הַלֵּבָב יֵלֵךְ וְיָשֹׁב לְבֵיתוֹ
וְלֹא יִמַּס אֶת לְבַב אֶחָיו כִּלְבָבוֹ

"Is there anyone [here] who is fearful and fainthearted? Let him go and return to his house, lest he cause his brothers' hearts to melt like his heart."

A Little Remorse, A Lot of Merit

Just before a Jewish army goes out to battle, the leaders announce that anyone who is afraid should return home, lest their anxiety spread to their fellow fighters.

The Sages of the Talmud[10] debate the nature of the "fearful and fainthearted" addressed here. Some interpret this as reference to those who fear because of their sins —i.e., they recognize their shortcomings in Torah observance, and fear they are thus unworthy of G-d's protection during battle. According to this opinion, all who were simply fearful of the battle presumably returned home earlier, when the Kohen addressed the soldiers, saying: "Let your hearts not be faint; you shall not be afraid, and you shall not be alarmed..."[11]

Rabbi Akiva, however, insists that this final announcement addresses those "who cannot stand in the closed ranks of battle and look upon a drawn sword." As the battle draws nearer, even those who felt confident earlier might now be overcome with fear, and are encouraged (again) to return home.

Rabbi Akiva's rejection of the alternative explanation indicates that those who "fear because of their sins" can in fact

---

10. Sotah 44a.
11. Devarim 20:3

still go to war with confidence, and therefore do not pose any risk to the army's morale.

What was Rabbi Akiva's reasoning?

The Talmud states elsewhere[12] that out of his immense love for his fellow Jews, Rabbi Akiva always sought angles from which the Jewish people would be judged favorably and meritoriously. Now, a person who "fears because of his sins" recognizes that his conduct was objectionable, believes that G-d can and will hold him accountable, and hopes to be spared that Divine retribution. Thus, even if he lacks the inner strength to actually implement change in his behavior, he still regrets the sinful ways that brought him to this point, and in Rabbi Akiva's view, this "contemplation of repentance" alone makes him worthy! Rabbi Akiva therefore held that he can go off to battle with confidence, assured of Divine protection and deliverance.

—*Likkutei Sichos, vol. 9, pp. 128–129*

---

12. Sanhedrin 110b.

20:19 | כ:יט

כִּי הָאָדָם עֵץ הַשָּׂדֶה
Is then man the tree of the field...?

Planting Smart

According to its simple meaning, this verse rhetorically questions the logic of wantonly destroying a fruit tree when you are waging war against a city's inhabitants: "Is man the tree of the field, such that the tree too is your enemy?" The Talmud,[13] however, interprets this verse as a matter of fact: indeed, man is like the tree of the field.

This comparison teaches us an important lesson regarding the significance of how we educate our children in their formative years, which can be compared to caring for a tree in its earliest stages. An injury in a fully grown tree is not ideal, but it is unlikely to significantly impact the tree's future. A developed tree is strong enough to recover from the damage, and can continue to grow healthily and fruitfully. In a seed or young sapling, however, even the smallest scratch can be devastating, and possibly ruin the prospects of the tree ever growing straight and tall.

The same is true of our children: compromised standards are undesirable even for adults, but compromise in the education of children can be absolutely devastating! In order to nurture and raise a generation of Jews who are spiritually fit, we must ensure that our children receive a healthy and

---

13. Taanis 7a.

undiluted Jewish education, especially during their early, formative years.

—*Likkutei Sichos, vol. 1, p. 82; Igros Kodesh, vol. 2, p. 82*

20:19 | כ:יט

כִּי הָאָדָם עֵץ הַשָּׂדֶה

Is then man the tree of the field...?

Love what You Learn

The Talmud[14] interprets this verse not as a question, but as a matter of fact: indeed, man is like the tree of the field. Particularly, according to the Talmud, the man compared to a fruit tree is a *talmid chacham*—a Torah scholar.

The Talmud's association of fruit trees with Torah scholarship—and not with, for example, excellence in fulfillment of the mitzvos—highlights the unique nature of man's relationship with G-d through Torah study in contrast with other aspects of Divine Service.

A central component of mitzvah observance is sacrifice: surrendering your personal interests in order to obey G-d's commands and fulfill His expectations.

The objective of Torah study, however, is to absorb G-d's wisdom with your mind. Although the ultimate form of Torah study is when a person studies with no sense of ego or self-importance, surrender of self is not the objective of the studying itself. Rather, the goal of Torah study is to grasp G-d's wisdom with your own understanding, making it a part of your own identity.

Given this emphasis on the individual, as opposed to the surrender of self that characterizes mitzvah observance, we can understand why the Talmud states, "One should always

---

14. Taanis 7a.

study the area of Torah which his heart desires."[15] Since the objective of Torah study is not to deny your identity, but to make the Torah a part of it, you must consider your personal preferences when choosing which area of Torah to study, so that it will be personally gratifying and enjoyable!

The Talmud therefore compares a Torah scholar to a fruit tree. What sets fruit apart from grain or any other produce? Whereas grain primarily provides sustenance, fruit is also a source of pleasure. By specifically comparing Torah scholars to fruit trees, the Talmud is emphasizing that, more so than in other aspects of religious observance, you must study the Torah not only as a duty, but also as a passion.

—*Toras Menachem, Sefer Hamaamarim Melukat, vol. 2, pp. 412–415*

---

15. Avodah Zarah 19a.

21:7 | כא:ז

וְעָנוּ וְאָמְרוּ יָדֵינוּ לֹא שָׁפְכוּ אֶת הַדָּם הַזֶּה וְעֵינֵינוּ לֹא רָאוּ

They shall announce and say, "Our hands did not shed this blood, nor did our eyes see…"

Equipped for Life

If a person is found murdered outside of a city, and the killer is unknown, the Torah mandates a process known as *eglah arufah* to atone on behalf of the city's inhabitants for the occurrence of this murder. The purpose of this much-publicized ritual, led by the city's elders, is to make the public aware of the tragic incident, in order to prevent, or decrease the likelihood of, such occurrences in the future. In addition, by making the public aware of the crime, the likelihood of finding the murderer increases.[16]

As part of the process, the elders and judges make a disclaimer that "our hands did not shed this blood, nor did our eyes see." As the Talmud explains, this means, "We did not see him and knowingly let him depart without food or escort,"[17] implying that had they known this person was setting off on a precarious journey, the elders themselves would have ensured that he was well equipped for the road.

"You who cleave to Hashem, your G-d, are alive," says the Torah.[18] Accordingly, the law of the corpse found outside the city also alludes to someone who has died a spiritual death— i.e., he does not cleave to G-d and His Torah. It follows that if

---

[16]. See Sefer Hachinuch, Mitzvos 530–531.
[17]. Sotah 45b.
[18]. Devarim 4:4.

the Torah expects the elders to save all who pass through their town from risk of mortal danger, certainly they are required to save them from any threat of spiritual death!

How must they do so?

Before any Jewish boy or girl sets off on their life's journey, the leaders of the community must ensure that they are "accompanied" and well stocked with "provisions" for the way. The "elders" must see to it that every Jewish child in their community begins their journey equipped with an education in Torah study (Torah is compared to food),[19] and trained in mitzvah observance (mitzvos are compared to clothing).[20] By doing so, the community ensures the child's survival in the face of any spiritual dangers he or she may encounter along life's path.

—*Likkutei Sichos, vol. 30, p. 223*

---

[19]. See Tehillim 40:9.
[20]. See Rashi, Bereishis 3:7.

כי תצא
Ki Seitzei

21:10 | כא:י

כִּי תֵצֵא לַמִּלְחָמָה עַל אֹיְבֶיךָ וּנְתָנוֹ ה' אֱלֹקֶיךָ בְּיָדֶךָ וְשָׁבִיתָ שִׁבְיוֹ

When you go out to war against your enemy, then Hashem, your G-d, will deliver him into your hands, and you will take his captives.

Just Go Out

The Torah introduces the laws concerning prisoners of war by stating assuredly, "When you go out to war against your enemy, then Hashem, your G-d, will deliver him into your hands, and you will take his captives."

This verse also alludes to the battles we wage against our internal spiritual enemies—the physical desires of the body and the selfish tendencies of the animal soul, which constantly challenge our devotion to G-d. The goal is not to destroy these enemies, but to redirect their energy and passion toward fulfilling our G-dly mission in this world. Yet this effort is also a war, for the body and animal soul fiercely resist such transformation.

Despite the difficulty of this battle, the Torah guarantees us certain victory—even before we enter the thick of the war. "If you go out to war," says the Torah, meaning, "If you set yourself to the task and 'go out' on the mission to transform your inner enemy," you are guaranteed that "Hashem, your G-d, will deliver him into your hands." And not only will you vanquish your enemies (and not be vanquished by them, G-d forbid), you will even "take their captives." By redirecting the energies of the body and animal soul toward your G-dly mission, you will succeed in extracting the sparks of Divine purpose that lie dormant in the physical world to an even greater degree than you were capable of previously.

—*Likkutei Sichos, vol. 2, p. 384*

22:8 | כב:ח

כִּי תִבְנֶה בַּיִת חָדָשׁ וְעָשִׂיתָ מַעֲקֶה לְגַגֶּךָ וְלֹא תָשִׂים דָּמִים בְּבֵיתֶךָ כִּי יִפֹּל הַנֹּפֵל מִמֶּנּוּ

When you build a new house, you shall make a guardrail for your roof, so as not to cause blood in your house when the faller will fall from it.

Beware of Heights

The mitzvah to erect a *maakeh*, a guardrail around the roof of a house, can be interpreted as a lesson on the importance of humility. The rooftop represents pride and self-importance, and the requirement to place a guardrail around it means that we must limit and contain our pride, for pride and arrogance are the root of all spiritual deterioration.

Moreover, the Sifri states that even the roof of the Heichal, the Temple sanctuary, requires a *maakeh*. In spiritual terms, this means that we must be cautious of pride even when it stems from spiritual achievement, for it is equally as harmful as the pride caused by material success.

Certainly, we should be confident about our devotion to G-d and His Torah. At the same time, we must be careful not to allow this to develop into feelings of arrogance. For even upon the roof of the Heichal—i.e., even at the height of spiritual achievement—there is a risk of spiritual downfall if our pride is not contained.

—*Likkutei Sichos, vol. 24, pp. 141–142*

22:8 | כב:ח

כִּי תִבְנֶה בַּיִת חָדָשׁ וְעָשִׂיתָ מַעֲקֶה לְגַגֶּךָ וְלֹא תָשִׂים דָּמִים בְּבֵיתֶךָ כִּי יִפֹּל הַנֹּפֵל מִמֶּנּוּ

When you build a new house, you shall make a guardrail for your roof, so as not to cause blood in your house when the faller will fall from it.

Don't Put Others at Risk

The Torah instructs us that upon building a new home we must erect a *maakeh*, a guardrail around the roof, to prevent others from falling.

In addition to its literal meaning, this command also refers to G-d's blessing and mandate that each Jew "build a new home"—i.e., take initiative to create an environment in which Judaism flourishes. The "homes" built by others do not exempt us from building our own home, i.e., positively influencing those who have been led specifically to *you* by Divine Providence.

The Torah warns us, however, that we must limit and enclose the "rooftops" of the new homes that we build. The roof represents pride and self-importance, and the requirement to place a guardrail around it means that we must limit and contain our pride. For "the faller will fall from it"—our pride can place those who seek shelter in our "new homes" at risk of spiritual downfall.

This is because "words spoken from the heart enter the heart."[1] If our efforts to draw others closer to Torah observance

---

[1]. See R. Moshe ibn Ezra, Shiras Yisrael, p. 156. See also Shnei Luchos Habris, Shaar HaOsios, Lamed, quoting Sefer HaYashar by Rabbeinu Tam.

are pure and altruistic, we will certainly succeed. But if our words are tainted with the pursuit of self-aggrandizement or other personal agendas, we have no such guarantee. Worse yet, our self-pride—even if it stems from spiritual achievements—can distance from our "homes" those who depend on them for spiritual shelter.

This is the inner meaning of the mitzvah of *maakeh*: by curbing our self-pride, we can succeed at creating environments in which all who seek spiritual shelter will thrive.

—*Likkutei Sichos, vol. 24, pp. 142-144*

23:21 | כג:כא

לַנָּכְרִי תַשִּׁיךְ וּלְאָחִיךָ לֹא תַשִּׁיךְ

You may lend at interest to a gentile, but to your brother you shall not lend at interest.

Collecting Dues

Charging interest on a loan is fair and reasonable. The borrower knowingly accepts this fee in exchange for the temporary use of the money, thereby compensating the creditor for the "inactivity" of his money while it is on loan. That is why the Torah permits collecting interest from a gentile (though we are repeatedly commanded to lend money to our fellow Jews free of interest). The Rambam writes, however, that not only is it permitted to lend to a non-Jew with interest, it is actually a positive mitzvah to collect interest on loans to an idolater.[2] Why?

The Baal Shem Tov taught that the money G-d places in a Jew's possession contains "sparks of holiness" that relate specifically to his soul and therefore depend on him for their elevation. Since money has the natural potential to generate more money when it is loaned, it follows that the permissible interest your money generates is related to your soul just as the principle is. Thus the Torah's directive to know G-d "in *all* your ways,"[3] meaning to utilize every aspect of your life to come closer to G-d, also applies to the potential interest that your money can generate.

---

2. Mishneh Torah, Hil. Malveh v'Loveh 5:1.
3. Mishlei 3:6.

Therefore, when lending to an idolater, from whom it is permissible to collect interest, collecting the justly earned interest is actually a mitzvah. For his requirement for a loan indicates that the interest he will owe on it is money whose elevation depends on the lender, who will extract it and reveal its Divine purpose to the best of his ability.[4]

—*Likkutei Sichos, vol. 12, pp. 118–119*

---

[4]. Nevertheless, the Torah obligates us to lend money to our fellow Jews free of interest. In this instance, the potential interest is elevated in the opposite fashion—by the lender refraining from collecting it, like other prohibited objects that are elevated through our restraint.

24:1 | כד:א

כִּי יִקַּח אִישׁ אִשָּׁה
When a man takes a wife.

Holy Matrimony

This verse teaches us the mitzvah of *kiddushin*—that a man must betroth his wife before they begin living together as a married couple. In the words of the Rambam:

> Once the Torah was given, the Jews were commanded that when a man desires to marry a woman, he must acquire her as a wife in the presence of witnesses, and only then does she become his wife. This is stated in the verse "When a man takes a wife."[5]

The effect of the *kiddushin* is twofold: it designates the woman to be married to this man, and simultaneously "prohibits her to the rest of the world."[6]

The relationship between G-d and the Jewish people, which is often compared to a marriage in the scriptures and teachings of Chazal, likewise contains both aspects of *kiddushin*.[7] The first aspect of this *kiddushin* is to devotedly strive to cleave to Him; the second is to distance ourselves from anything that could distract us from this relationship—namely, mundane passions and desires. Just as both components of the *kiddushin* between man and woman are interdependent, and one cannot exist without the other, so is it with the *kid-*

---

5. Mishneh Torah, Hil. Ishus 1:1.
6. See Talmud, Kiddushin 2b.
7. See Kesser Shem Tov, sec. 10.

dushin between G-d and the Jewish people. In order for our love and attachment to G-d to be complete, we must truly separate ourselves from any other lusts or passions. In the words of the Chovos HaLevavos, "It is impossible to implant love of G-d in our hearts while love of this world still resides within us."[8]

—*Likkutei Sichos, vol. 19, pp. 217–218*

---

8. Shaar Ahavas Hashem.

24:19 | כד:יט

כִּי תִקְצֹר קְצִירְךָ בְשָׂדֶךָ וְשָׁכַחְתָּ עֹמֶר בַּשָּׂדֶה לֹא תָשׁוּב לְקַחְתּוֹ לַגֵּר לַיָּתוֹם וְלָאַלְמָנָה יִהְיֶה לְמַעַן יְבָרֶכְךָ ה' אֱלֹהֶיךָ בְּכֹל מַעֲשֵׂה יָדֶיךָ

When you reap your harvest in your field and forget a bundle in the field, you shall not go back to take it; it shall be for the stranger, the orphan, and the widow, so that Hashem, your G-d, will bless you in all that you do.

Being Kind by Accident

The Torah promises that in the merit of fulfilling the mitzvah of *shikchah*, leaving any forgotten sheaves of grain for the poor, "Hashem, your G-d, will bless you in all that you do." Rashi observes that the Torah promises this great reward for a mitzvah whose fulfillment came about *unintentionally*! "It can hence be said," Rashi concludes, "that if a *sela* [coin] dropped from one's hand, and a poor man found it and was sustained by it, then he who lost the coin will be blessed on its account."

The significance of a mitzvah performed without conscious intent can be understood in light of the Rambam's ruling regarding the laws of divorce, that when a husband is halachically obligated to divorce his wife, the court may use physical force to prevail upon him to agree to give his wife a *get*, a bill of divorce, even though a *get* is valid only when given willingly.[9] The Rambam explains that this *get* is still valid because the genuine desire of every Jew is to observe all the mitzvos and

---

9. Mishneh Torah, Hil. Gerushin 2:20.

to refrain from the prohibitions. Therefore, when he agrees under pressure to do a mitzvah, he is simply acknowledging his true will and desire.

The same is true whenever a person fulfills a mitzvah. Even if he seems to do so out of habit, or for ulterior motives, what truly motivates him is the "sincere desire of every Jew to observe all the mitzvos."[10] Moreover, this desire to obey G-d's will is rooted in the essential nature of the soul that transcends even the conscious mind. It can thus influence a person's actions without his knowledge at all.

As such, when a Jew unknowingly drops a coin, it is possible that his subconscious desire to fulfill the mitzvah of *tzedakah* is what caused him to drop the coin, in the hope that a poor person will ultimately find it. He is therefore credited with this mitzvah, which stemmed from the innermost desire of his soul, even though he is entirely "unaware" of the mitzvah that he fulfilled.

—*Toras Menachem, Sefer Hamaamarim Melukat,*
vol. 1, p. 243

---

[10]. Ibid.

כי תבוא
Ki Savo

26:1-2 | כו:א-ב

וְהָיָה כִּי תָבוֹא אֶל הָאָרֶץ אֲשֶׁר ה' אֱלֹקֶיךָ נֹתֵן לְךָ נַחֲלָה וִירִשְׁתָּהּ וְיָשַׁבְתָּ בָּהּ וְלָקַחְתָּ מֵרֵאשִׁית כָּל פְּרִי הָאֲדָמָה

It will be, when you come into the land which Hashem, your G-d, gives you for an inheritance, and you possess it and settle in it, that you shall take of the first of all the fruit of the ground...

Your Happiness is My Happiness

The Torah instructs us in the mitzvah of Bikkurim—the obligation to bring the first-ripened fruits of each year's crop to the Beis Hamikdash, whereby we declare our gratitude to G-d for all He has done for us. The Torah emphasizes, however, that observance of this mitzvah is to begin only once Bnei Yisrael have conquered and divided the entire Land of Israel.[1]

Ultimately, it took seven years to conquer the Land and another seven until every family received their portion, but during

---

1. Rashi, Devarim 26:1.

all that time, even those who had already received and begun settling their land were not required to bring Bikkurim.

Why were the individuals who were already settled not obligated to bring Bikkurim until everyone else was settled as well? Since bringing Bikkurim expresses our gratitude for the Land of Israel and its fruit, it would seem that the requirement to bring Bikkurim should have begun for each person individually, as soon as he received his portion of land and began to benefit from it.

But unlike other offerings of thanksgiving, the Bikkurim express our gratitude specifically for the gifts that G-d gives us *in the fullest measure*. We thus find that Bikkurim are offered only from the Seven Species with which the Land of Israel is exceptionally blessed; "standard" fruits or vegetables do not warrant this unique offering. In the same vein, the declaration that accompanies the offering of Bikkurim is said only at times of joy,[2] and only once a year,[3] since the joy that we express in the offering of Bikkurim must be complete on every level.

The offering of Bikkurim was therefore not possible until every Jewish family had received a portion of the Land. Until that was complete, even those families who had already established themselves could not possibly feel entirely happy and blessed, knowing that some of their fellow Jews were still unsettled. For a Jew's blessings and happiness are complete only when he knows that G-d has granted happiness to his fellow Jew as well.

—*Likkutei Sichos, vol. 9, pp. 154–156*

---

2. Rashi, ibid. 26:11.
3. Rashi, ibid. 26:3.

26:3 | כו:ג

וּבָאתָ אֶל הַכֹּהֵן אֲשֶׁר יִהְיֶה בַּיָּמִים הָהֵם
וְאָמַרְתָּ אֵלָיו הִגַּדְתִּי הַיּוֹם לַה' אֱלֹקֶיךָ כִּי בָאתִי אֶל
הָאָרֶץ אֲשֶׁר נִשְׁבַּע ה' לַאֲבֹתֵינוּ לָתֶת לָנוּ׃

You shall come to the Kohen who will be in those days, and say to him, "I extol today Hashem, your G-d, for I have come to the land that G-d swore to our forefathers to give to us."

Earn your Keep

We are commanded to bring Bikkurim, the first-ripened fruits of the year, to the Beis Hamikdash, to express our gratitude to G-d for all He has done for us. The Torah instructs that before presenting the Bikkurim, the one offering must declare, "I extol today Hashem, your G-d, for I have come to the land that G-d swore to our forefathers to give to us."

The person offering the Bikkurim states, "I extol *today*... for I have come to the Land," even if he has lived in the Land of Israel his entire life. In fact, even if hundreds of years have passed since his ancestors arrived in the Land!

In doing so, the person offering the Bikkurim acknowledges that residence in the Land of Israel is unlike that of any other land. The Torah warns us, "Let the land not vomit you out for having defiled it, as it vomited out the nation that preceded you."[4] This means that a person must continuously earn his stay in the Land of Israel: each day of one's residence in the Holy Land must be granted by G-d.

---

4. Vayikra 18:28.

The person can therefore truly say, "I declare today... that I have come to the Land," for his residence in the Land of Israel today is not due simply to his arrival there a few years back, or his ancestors' arrival in the Land of Israel hundreds of years ago. It is something he has merited on this very day.[5]

—*Likkutei Sichos, vol. 19, p. 521*

---

[5]. Moreover, if not for G-d's promise to our ancestors, our merits alone would be insufficient to earn our stay. Hence, "I have come to the Land that G-d swore *to our forefathers* to give to us."

כו:ה | 26:5

וַיֵּרֶד מִצְרַיְמָה וַיָּגָר שָׁם

He went down to Egypt and sojourned there...

Don't Make Yourself Too Comfortable

The Passover Haggadah elaborates on this verse, and asserts that Yaakov descended to Egypt against his will: "'He went down to Egypt'—forced by Divine decree."

This statement is somewhat perplexing. Yaakov, as we know, was devoted to G-d with all his being. If he knew that G-d desired he move to Egypt, how could he hesitate to oblige? Moreover, G-d had assured him, "I will go down with you to Egypt, and I will bring you up—you will also ascend."[6] This made it clear that the descent to Egypt was only temporary, and that the heights he would reach because of it would be extraordinary. With a future so promising, Yaakov should have been thrilled to make the trip! Why does the Haggadah say that he felt forced?

Although Yaakov was happy to do G-d's bidding, his descent to the debased environment of Egypt was a constant source of angst. Despite the benefit that his move would ultimately yield, Yaakov never made peace with the enormous spiritual risk it posed to him and his family. Even if its impact would be temporary, he was perpetually uncomfortable, "reluctant" as it were, to be in the Egyptian environment. It was this discomfort, however, that ensured that his children

---

6. Bereishis 46:4.

were not entirely consumed by their surroundings, and the purpose of their exile was ultimately realized.

We, too, are destined by Divine Providence to be at times in situations and environments that are devoid of holiness. Like our ancestor Yaakov, we must recognize the Divine mission that we have been assigned, and happily devote ourselves to infusing our surroundings with holiness and meaning. Nevertheless, in order to successfully elevate our surroundings while ensuring that the environment does not negatively influence *us*, we must keep in mind that such surroundings constitutes a "descent to Egypt," a place where a Jew is inherently uncomfortable, and only because Divine decree has compelled us to be.

—*Likkutei Sichos, vol. 4, pp. 1218–1220*

כו:ז | 26:7

וַנִּצְעַק אֶל ה' אֱלֹקֵי אֲבֹתֵינוּ וַיִּשְׁמַע ה' אֶת קֹלֵנוּ וַיַּרְא אֶת עָנְיֵנוּ וְאֶת עֲמָלֵנוּ וְאֶת לַחֲצֵנוּ

So we cried out to Hashem, G-d of our fathers, and G-d heard our voice and saw our affliction, our toil, and our oppression.

Raising Children: The Hardest Job of All

The offering of Bikkurim, the first-ripened fruits of the year that we bring to the Beis Hamikdash, is accompanied by a proclamation thanking G-d for His kindness that has brought us to this day. We mention in particular that He heard our voices when we were slaves in Egypt, and saved us from "our affliction, toil and oppression."

Commenting on this verse, the Sifri states: "'Our toil'—these are the sons, as it is written, 'Every son that is born you shall cast into the river, and every daughter you shall keep alive,'"[8] meaning that the words "our toil" allude in particular to the suffering we endured in Egypt with regard to our children.

It is worth noting that the Sifri demonstrates that there was a particularly evil decree targeting the Jewish children, but does not provide proof or explain how the words "our toil" allude specifically to children.

The Sifri's omission of any proof that "our toil" refers to our children indicates that such proof is superfluous. For it is

---

8. Shemos 1:22.

self-evident that raising children to grow on the proper path takes hard work—not only "effort," but also what the Torah deems "toil," difficult labor. It therefore goes without saying that our "toil" is our children.

The same is true with regard to educating and nurturing students, whom the Torah likewise refers to as "your children."[9] You have not fulfilled your most basic duties as an educator until you have invested yourself to the point of "toil."

—*Likkutei Sichos, vol. 1, pp. 113-114*

---

9. See Devarim 6:7 and Rashi ad loc.

כו:יח | 26:18

וַה' הֶאֱמִירְךָ הַיּוֹם לִהְיוֹת לוֹ לְעַם סְגֻלָּה כַּאֲשֶׁר דִּבֶּר לָךְ

G-d has set you apart this day to be His treasured people, just as He spoke concerning you...

The King's Hidden Treasures

What is the meaning of G-d setting the Jewish people apart as His *am segulah*, His "treasured nation"?

Rashi (elsewhere) explains:

> [*Segulah* means] a cherished treasure... costly vessels and precious stones, which the kings stow away. Likewise, you will be treasured by Me more than the other nations.[7]

The distinctiveness of a king's precious treasures is that they are stowed away, not intended for use. These "costly vessels and precious stones" do not fund the king's domestic programs or military campaigns, nor do they add beauty to his crown or palace. They are collected and saved for no purpose other than their very being—for the king to own them and delight in them. In fact, the king's possession of national treasures amassed simply for him to enjoy owning them is part of what makes him a king—it contributes to his personal sense of kingship and eminence.

This is the significance of G-d setting apart the Jewish people as His "treasured nation"—their preciousness transcends the "purpose" they serve. Certainly, through the observance of G-d's commands, the Jewish people reveal G-d's reign throughout the world, thereby expanding His "kingdom."

---

7. Shemos 19:5.

The essential identity of a Jew, however, is not the purpose he serves, but the delight that he brings G-d simply by his existence. Like the hidden treasures of a king, a Jew's very existence is a source of delight for G-d, even prior to his fulfilling G-d's demands.

—*Likkutei Sichos, vol. 24, p. 162–164*

29:3-8 | כט:ג-ח

וְלֹא נָתַן ה' לָכֶם לֵב לָדַעַת וְעֵינַיִם לִרְאוֹת וְאָזְנַיִם לִשְׁמֹעַ עַד הַיּוֹם הַזֶּה: וָאוֹלֵךְ אֶתְכֶם אַרְבָּעִים שָׁנָה בַּמִּדְבָּר ... וּשְׁמַרְתֶּם אֶת דִּבְרֵי הַבְּרִית הַזֹּאת

Yet until this day, G-d did not give you a heart to know, eyes to see, and ears to hear. I led you through the desert for forty years... You must safeguard the words of this covenant.

Graduation

Based on the Talmud,[10] Rashi explains the sequence of these verses.

> One cannot fathom the depths of his teacher's mind or the wisdom of his teachings until 40 years. Hence, said Moshe to Bnei Yisrael, "G-d was not strict with you until this day; but from now on He will be strict with you"; therefore, "Safeguard the words of this covenant..."

Now, Moshe had not taught the entire Torah ("the words of this covenant") solely during the first year in the desert, but over the course of 40 years. Similarly, many of the events that Moshe warned the people here to take heed of took place at the end of the 40 years. Yet Moshe told Bnei Yisrael that they would now be held responsible to observe *all* the teachings and to pay heed to *all* the lessons, even though 40 years had not yet passed from the later teachings and events.

Evidently, the Talmud's assertion (based on Moshe's words) that one cannot fathom the depths of his teacher's mind until

---

[10]. Avodah Zarah 5b.

40 years does not mean that it takes 40 years to understand any teaching one heard from his teacher. Rather, this means that after 40 years of diligently studying the words of one's teacher, the teacher's unique method of study—meaning, the discipline and approach that pervades all his ideas—becomes the student's approach as well. When the student first begins studying from his teacher, he understands only the actual ideas that he is being taught. After 40 years, however, the thinking that lies beneath all the teacher's ideas becomes the student's thought process as well, enabling the student to see the world as his teacher does.

Moshe was thus telling Bnei Yisrael that after 40 years of being educated by G-d, they could now truly sense what lay beneath everything that G-d had taught and shown them throughout their 40 years in the desert. Consequently, G-d now fully expected them to "safeguard the words of this covenant."

—*Likkutei Sichos, vol. 34, pp. 163–165*

נצבים
Nitzavim

29:9-11 | כט:ט-יא

אַתֶּם נִצָּבִים הַיּוֹם כֻּלְּכֶם לִפְנֵי ה' אֱלֹקֵיכֶם רָאשֵׁיכֶם שִׁבְטֵיכֶם זִקְנֵיכֶם וְשֹׁטְרֵיכֶם כֹּל אִישׁ יִשְׂרָאֵל: טַפְּכֶם נְשֵׁיכֶם וְגֵרְךָ אֲשֶׁר בְּקֶרֶב מַחֲנֶיךָ מֵחֹטֵב עֵצֶיךָ עַד שֹׁאֵב מֵימֶיךָ: לְעָבְרְךָ בִּבְרִית ה' אֱלֹקֶיךָ...

You are standing today, all of you, before Hashem your G-d: the leaders of your tribes, your elders and your officers, every man of Israel; your young children, your women, and your convert who is within your camp, your woodcutters and your water-drawers, so that you may enter the covenant of Hashem your G-d.

Solid Backing

The purpose of this covenant was to enlist every Jew as a guarantor that his fellow Jews will observe the Torah.[1] As our Sages taught, "All of Israel are guarantors for one another,"[2]

---

1. See Ohr Hachaim, Devarim 29:9; see also Rashi, ibid. 29:28.
2. Shevuos 39a.

meaning that every Jew bears personal responsibility for his fellow.

A guarantor is presumably in a better position than the person he is backing, which is what makes him more dependable than the person behind whose commitment he stands. For example, a wealthy person could serve as a guarantor for a poor person's loan, but not vice versa. Hence, if "all of Israel are guarantors for one another," it is evident that each and every Jew, from "the leaders of your tribes" down to "your water-drawers," has a unique strength that qualifies him as a guarantor for the others.

This can be understood in light of the Alter Rebbe's teaching that the Jewish nation is "one complete figure," comparable to a human body, in which every limb and organ completes and complements the other.[3] The head and brain are ostensibly "superior" to the other parts of the body, yet the legs support and give mobility to the entire body, including the head. Similarly, every single Jew has a quality with which he, and only he, can serve as the guarantor for the rest of the Jewish nation, due to his extraordinary strength in that particular area.

—*Likkutei Sichos, vol. 4, pp. 1140–1141*

---

3. Likkutei Torah, Nitzavim 44a.

29:9-11 | כט:ט-יא

אַתֶּם נִצָּבִים הַיּוֹם כֻּלְּכֶם לִפְנֵי ה' אֱלֹקֵיכֶם רָאשֵׁיכֶם שִׁבְטֵיכֶם זִקְנֵיכֶם וְשֹׁטְרֵיכֶם כֹּל אִישׁ יִשְׂרָאֵל: טַפְּכֶם נְשֵׁיכֶם וְגֵרְךָ אֲשֶׁר בְּקֶרֶב מַחֲנֶיךָ מֵחֹטֵב עֵצֶיךָ עַד שֹׁאֵב מֵימֶיךָ: לְעָבְרְךָ בִּבְרִית ה' אֱלֹקֶיךָ...

You are standing today, all of you, before Hashem your G-d: the leaders of your tribes, your elders and your officers, every man of Israel; your young children, your women, and your convert who is within your camp, your woodcutters and your water-drawers, so that you may enter the covenant of Hashem your G-d.

The Pact

Every year we read Parshas Nitzavim on the Shabbos before Rosh Hashanah. Implied is that Parshas Nitzavim addresses the themes of Rosh Hashanah, and reading it enables us to experience the holiday properly.

In the first verses we read that the entire Jewish nation assembled to enter a covenant with G-d. The Torah mentions specifically that from the leaders to the water-drawers, all of Israel stood united as one—"all of you."

What is the purpose of a covenant? If two friends are concerned that their relationship might sour at some point, they may enter into a covenant—a pact to remain loyal to each other forever, even if future events or discoveries about one another cause them to lose favor in each other's eyes.

This, essentially, is the theme of Rosh Hashanah: a renewal of the covenant between G-d and the Jewish people. On Rosh Hashanah, when our love for G-d is strong (after our heartfelt *teshuvah* during the month of Elul), we commit ourselves to G-d unconditionally. We pray that G-d will enter this covenant with us, committing Himself to us unconditionally, even if later in the year our love may not be as obvious.

The covenant of Rosh Hashanah requires, however, that all members of the Jewish nation unite as one, just as the Jewish people did—men, women and children, from the elders to the converts—in Parshas Nitzavim. For in order to evoke G-d's unconditional commitment to us, we too must behave in a manner that transcends any reason or conditions. We do this by showing our sincere love and respect for *all* our fellow Jews, despite our understandable differences.

—*Likkutei Sichos, vol. 2, pp. 399–400*

29:13-14 | יג-יד : כט

וְלֹא אִתְּכֶם לְבַדְּכֶם אָנֹכִי כֹּרֵת אֶת הַבְּרִית הַזֹּאת וְאֶת הָאָלָה הַזֹּאת: כִּי אֶת אֲשֶׁר יֶשְׁנוֹ פֹּה עִמָּנוּ עֹמֵד הַיּוֹם לִפְנֵי ה' אֱלֹקֵינוּ וְאֵת אֲשֶׁר אֵינֶנּוּ פֹּה עִמָּנוּ הַיּוֹם

But not only with you am I making this covenant and this oath, but with those standing here with us today before Hashem our G-d, and with those who are not here with us, this day.

What Makes You Jewish Today?

The entire Jewish nation assembled to enter into a covenant with G-d. Moshe addressed them, explaining that this covenant was not only with the Jews of that generation who were all present, but also "with those standing here with us today before Hashem our G-d, and with those who are not here with us this day." Meaning, in the words of Rashi, "Even with future generations."

Various commentaries discuss how the covenant could be binding upon people who were not yet born (and even future converts to Judaism).[4] Some explain that the souls of the future generations were present when the covenant was made, even though their bodies were not. Others explain that since a child is the continuation of his parents,[5] the future generations were contained within those present at that covenant, and thereby automatically included.

Rashi, however, offers neither of these explanations, nor any other, implying that these rationalizations are unneces-

---

4. See Talmud, Shevuos 39a.
5. In the terminology of the Talmudists, "A child is the leg of his father."

sary. Ostensibly, Rashi is of the opinion that since G-d is not bound by the natural limits of time, He can enter a covenant with people of the future *directly*, just as He can with people of the present.

Support for this is found in the words of the verse: "...those standing with us here today... and with those who are not here with us." Having stated earlier (29:11) that everyone present was entering the covenant, why was it necessary to repeat that the covenant encompassed "those standing with us here today"? Evidently, the Torah wishes to equate G-d's covenant with the Jews of future generations ("who are not here with us") and His covenant with those present ("those standing with us here today"), emphasizing that they are identical.

Rashi therefore insists that the Jews of future generations enter this covenant not merely by virtue of their ancestors' presence, nor is the covenant merely with their souls (in contrast with those who were physically present at the time, whose bodies, too, entered in the covenant). Rather, every Jew for all eternity, body and soul, born Jew and convert alike, is a direct and equal partner in this covenant with G-d.

—*Likkutei Sichos, vol. 19, pp. 266-271*

30:1-2 | ל:א-ב

וְהָיָה כִי יָבֹאוּ עָלֶיךָ כָּל־הַדְּבָרִים הָאֵלֶּה...
וְשַׁבְתָּ עַד ה' אֱלֹקֶיךָ וְשָׁמַעְתָּ בְקֹלוֹ

It will be, when all these things come upon you... and you will return to Hashem your G-d, and you will listen to His voice.

Can Teshuvah Be an Obligation?

The Sefer Mitzvos Katan interprets this verse as a commandment to do *teshuvah*, meaning that a person who has sinned is obligated to repent, and has neglected to fulfill a mitzvah if he does not.[6] Others, however, read this verse as foretelling that the Jewish people will ultimately repent, but not necessarily as a commandment to do so. Indeed, according to some opinions, repentance is not an obligation of its own; it is only the means (along with the verbal confession) by which a person can atone for his sins if he so desires.[7]

This debate reflects two aspects of *teshuvah* as explained in the teachings of Chassidus. According to Chassidus, the soul comprises 613 spiritual "limbs" or faculties, each corresponding to a particular mitzvah,[8] and a deficiency in the fulfillment of a mitzvah causes a deficiency in the corresponding limb in one's soul.[9]

Teshuvah, however, has the ability to repair those "limbs" of the soul that have been damaged. This is because the profound

---

6. Mitzvah 53.
7. See Minchas Chinuch, mitzvah 364.
8. Tanya, chapter 4.
9. Likkutei Torah, Nitzavim 45c.

desire to reconnect with G-d draws from the very essence of the soul—the source from which the individual "limbs" of the soul extend. *Teshuvah* thus draws new life into all the "limbs," restoring them to their proper "health."

This explains the opinion that *teshuvah* is not one of the commandments. Feelings that stem from the depths of your heart, expressing the essence of your soul, must come from within; when you act out of duty, you are not expressing your most natural self. Therefore the Torah does not command you to repent, since only when *teshuvah* is motivated by your own free choice is it clear that it stems from the purest essence of the soul.

Nevertheless, the prevalent opinion is that *teshuvah* is in fact a mitzvah,[10] for the goal of *teshuvah* is not only feelings of regret and a burning desire to return to G-d, but the practical observance of His mitzvos that these feelings will engender in the future. As such, although *teshuvah* must stem from within and not be motivated by duty alone, it is still a mitzvah like all the others, in order to remind you of its objective—to invigorate your actual fulfillment of the mitzvos, your obligations toward G-d.

—*Likkutei Sichos, vol. 38, pp. 18-25*

---

10. See Tanya, Iggeres Hateshuvah, chapter 1.

30:6 | ל:ו

וּמָל ה' אֱלֹקֶיךָ אֶת לְבָבְךָ וְאֶת לְבַב זַרְעֶךָ

Hashem, your G-d, will circumcise your heart and the heart of your offspring...

To Cure the Heart

In Parshas Nitzavim, Moshe warns the Jewish people of the exile and desolation that will follow if they abandon their covenant with G-d. He foretells, however, that ultimately, "You will return to Hashem, your G-d... and He will bring back your exiles, and He will have mercy upon you." Finally, "Hashem, your G-d, will circumcise your heart and the heart of your offspring, so that you will love Hashem, your G-d, with all your heart and with all your soul, for the sake of your life."

The figurative circumcision of the heart is also mentioned in Parshas Eikev, where Moshe implores the Jewish people to take heed of G-d's greatness, justness and kindness, and to not be impervious to the love that He has shown them: "Circumcise therefore the foreskin of your heart, and do not be stiff-necked anymore."[11]

Noticeably, there Moshe speaks of circumcising "the foreskin of the heart," whereas here he refers to circumcising or unblocking the heart itself. In addition, the wording of the two verses indicates that removing the foreskin of the heart is in the hands of the people, whereas circumcising the heart is up to G-d.

---

11. Devarim 10:16.

The reason behind these differences is that the "foreskin of the heart" refers to a "cover" or blockage which causes the heart to be foolish and callous.[12] In Parshas Nitzavim, however, where Moshe speaks about the era *after* "you will return to G-d" (upon witnessing the destruction resulting from abandoning His covenant), obviously the "foreskin of the heart" that blocks it from being attuned to G-d will have already been removed—by the people themselves.

What will remain will be to circumcise the heart itself—meaning, to cure the heart of its natural tendency to be misled and tempted by *foreign* passions and desires, in order to ensure that the Jewish people will not breach the covenant again. (This reflects Moshe's earlier warning, "You have *seen* their detestable things... Lest there be among you a man, woman, family or tribe *whose heart strays* this day from Hashem...,"[13] implying that the issue being addressed here is not the heart's insensitivity, but its natural susceptibility to outside influences.) To sever ("circumcise") the natural association between the eyes' sights and the heart's desires, is in the hands of the Creator alone.

—*Likkutei Sichos, vol. 29, pp. 167-170*

---

12. See Rashi and Targum Onkelos ad loc.
13. Devarim 29:16–17.

30:6 | ל:ו

וּמָל ה' אֱלֹקֶיךָ אֶת לְבָבְךָ וְאֶת לְבַב זַרְעֶךָ לְאַהֲבָה אֶת ה' אֱלֹקֶיךָ בְּכָל לְבָבְךָ וּבְכָל נַפְשְׁךָ לְמַעַן חַיֶּיךָ

Hashem, your G-d, will circumcise your heart and the heart of your offspring, so that you will love Hashem, your G-d, with all your heart and with all your soul, for the sake of your life.

A Hint of Love

The mystics and Sages have long observed that by combining the first letters of each of the four words אֶת לְבָבְךָ וְאֶת לְבַב—"your heart and the hearts of" (from the phrase "Hashem, your G-d, will circumcise your heart and the heart of your offspring"), we form the word אלול—Elul, the name of the month during which this verse is traditionally read.[14]

The hint to the month of Elul in the context of "circumcising your heart" is interpreted by some as alluding to the prevalent theme of penitence that characterizes this month preceding the Days of Awe—Rosh Hashanah and Yom Kippur.

A simple reading of the verse, however, implies that the "circumcision of the heart" referred to here is not remorse and contrition. Rather, it is a Divine act enabling us to *love* G-d more genuinely and profoundly: "G-d will circumcise your heart... so that you will love Hashem, your G-d, with all your heart and with all your soul, for the sake of your life." When our hearts will be cured of their natural inclination toward foreign temptation and desire, we will be able to truly love

---

14. See Baal Haturim, Devarim 30:6; and others.

G‑d with *all* our being. As such, the hint in this verse to the month of Elul highlights another prevalent theme in this season: our loving relationship with G‑d.

This parallels the other acrostic associated with the word Elul, drawn from the words in Shir Hashirim[15] אֲנִי לְדוֹדִי וְדוֹדִי לִי—"I am my beloved's, and my beloved is mine."[16] In this verse, too, the emphasis is on our relationship with G‑d as "our beloved," and us as His.

Accordingly, the Alter Rebbe illustrates the spiritual potency of the month of Elul with the parable of a king who, prior to entering the capital, passes through the fields outside the city, where he graciously receives all who come to greet him, openly displaying his delight at encountering each of them.[17] Just as the king's radiant joy upon seeing his subjects undoubtedly inspires a reciprocal sense of love in all who come to greet him, G‑d's joyful acceptance of all who search for Him in the month of Elul arouses, in the heart of every Jew, profound feelings of love and attachment towards Him.

—*Likkutei Sichos, vol. 29, pp. 170–171*

---

15. Shir Hashirim 6:3.
16. See Avudraham, Seder Tefillas Rosh Hashanah; Pri Eitz Chaim, Shaar Rosh Hashanah, chapter 1; et al.
17. Likkutei Torah, Re'eh 32b.

וילך
Vayeilech

לא:ב | 31:2

בֶּן מֵאָה וְעֶשְׂרִים שָׁנָה אָנֹכִי הַיּוֹם לֹא אוּכַל עוֹד לָצֵאת וְלָבוֹא

Today I am one hundred and twenty years old; I can no longer go out or come in.

The Perfectly Timed Yahrzeit

On the last day of Moshe's life, he said, "Today I am 120 years old." The Talmud[1] interprets the word "today" to mean that it was his birthday. "This teaches," says the Talmud, "that G-d sits and completes the years of the righteous from day to day and month to month."

What is the significance of the righteous passing away on their birthdate?

The Tanya teaches that the soul of a *tzaddik*, a righteous person, can influence his disciples even more so after his passing than when he was alive. For in the *tzaddik*'s lifetime, when his soul was contained within a physical body, only a

---

1. Kiddushin 38a.

glimmer of his soul was able to radiate beyond his body, reaching his disciples only through his thoughts and words. After his passing, however, the *tzaddik* is no longer limited in this way. Moreover, the ascent of the *tzaddik*'s soul to its source causes sublime spiritual energy to radiate upon all whom he influenced to become servants of G-d, instilling thoughts of repentance and good deeds in their hearts.[2]

Thus, in a sense, the day of the *tzaddik*'s passing completes his birth. For on the day of his passing, his gift to the world is fully revealed and effective, whereas on the day he was born it was only in potential. G-d therefore "completes the years of the righteous from day to day and month to month," because a *tzaddik*'s *yahrtzeit* is synonymous with his birthday.

—*Likkutei Sichos, vol. 16, p. 350*

---

[2]. Tanya, Iggeres Hakodesh, epistle 27.

לא:יב | 31:12

הַקְהֵל אֶת הָעָם הָאֲנָשִׁים וְהַנָּשִׁים וְהַטַּף וְגֵרְךָ אֲשֶׁר בִּשְׁעָרֶיךָ לְמַעַן יִשְׁמְעוּ וּלְמַעַן יִלְמְדוּ וְיָרְאוּ אֶת ה' אֱלֹקֵיכֶם וְשָׁמְרוּ לַעֲשׂוֹת אֶת כָּל דִּבְרֵי הַתּוֹרָה הַזֹּאת

Assemble the people—the men, the women, the children, and your foreigner who is in your gates—in order that they will hear, and in order that they will learn and fear Hashem your G-d, and they will be careful to do all the words of this Torah.

Hakhel: Bracing for Change

Moshe's final message to Yehoshua included instructions regarding the mitzvah of Hakhel: every seven years, during the year following the Shemittah year, the entire Jewish nation should gather in the Beis Hamikdash, the Holy Temple, to hear the king read select portions of the Torah.

Why was this mitzvah not taught earlier, when Bnei Yisrael were instructed in the observance of Shemittah?

The mitzvah of Hakhel, more so than other mitzvos—including those that are likewise only obligatory in the Land of Israel—is particularly associated with the change that Bnei Yisrael were about to experience at the end of their desert journey.

The Rambam describes the observance of Hakhel:

> All must focus their attention and direct their hearing to listen with reverence, awe, and rejoicing while trembling, as on the day the Torah was given at Sinai... Scripture established it [Hakhel] to strengthen the true faith. One should view himself as though he was instructed now for the first

time regarding the Torah, as though he is hearing it now from the Almighty.[3]

Accordingly, Moshe taught Bnei Yisrael about Hakhel specifically at the end of their forty-year sojourn, as they prepared to enter the Land of Israel. The essence of the mitzvah of Hakhel is that when Bnei Yisrael are in circumstances drastically different from those in which they experienced the great G-dly revelation at Sinai, they should strengthen their commitment to the Torah by periodically recreating and reliving that Sinai experience. So, as Bnei Yisrael prepared to part from the desert in which they received the Torah, and from Moshe who had taught it to them, they were commanded to recreate the ambiance of the giving of the Torah through Hakhel, in order to strengthen their eternal adherence to the Torah's commands.

—*Likkutei Sichos, vol. 34, pp. 187–190*

---

[3]. Mishneh Torah, Hil. Chagigah 3:6.

לא:יב | 31:12

הַקְהֵל אֶת הָעָם הָאֲנָשִׁים וְהַנָּשִׁים וְהַטַּף וְגֵרְךָ אֲשֶׁר בִּשְׁעָרֶיךָ לְמַעַן יִשְׁמְעוּ וּלְמַעַן יִלְמְדוּ וְיָרְאוּ אֶת ה' אֱלֹהֵיכֶם וְשָׁמְרוּ לַעֲשׂוֹת אֶת כָּל דִּבְרֵי הַתּוֹרָה הַזֹּאת

Assemble the people—the men, the women, the children, and your foreigner who is in your gates—in order that they will hear, and in order that they will learn and fear Hashem your G-d, and they will be careful to do all the words of this Torah.

Welcome to the Faith. Hakhel!

In describing the observance of Hakhel, when the entire Jewish nation should gather in the Beis Hamikdash, the Holy Temple, to hear the king read select portions of the Torah, the Rambam makes particular mention that "even converts who do not understand" the Holy Tongue, in which the Torah is read, must attend the assembly.[4]

The source for the Rambam's unique emphasis on the attendance of converts who do not understand the reading of the Torah can be found in the words of the verse that enumerates the attendees: "The men, the women, the children, and your foreigner who is in your gates."

The Torah alternates between a number of expressions when referring to converts, including "The foreigner who dwells in your midst,"[5] "Your foreigner who is in your camp,"[6]

---

4. Mishneh Torah, Hil. Chagigah 3:5–6.
5. Shemos 12:49.
6. Devarim 29:10.

and "Your foreigner who is in your gates."[7] The simple difference between these expressions is that the terms "foreigner who dwells in your midst" and "foreigner who is in your camp" imply that the convert has long been part of the Jewish community, whereas the term "foreigner who is in your gates" can be interpreted as referring to a convert who is just barely "in the gate"—he has only recently joined the Jewish community.

Since the Torah mentions the convert's participation in the Hakhel assembly specifically using the expression "the foreigner that is in your gates," the Rambam understands that even the newest converts, for whom the original language of the Torah may still be foreign, are an integral part of the Hakhel assembly.

—*Sichos Kodesh 5735, vol. 1, pp. 50–51;*
Likkutei Sichos, vol. 36, p. 245

---

7. Shemos 20:10, Devarim 5:14, et al.

לא, יב-יט | 31:12-19

הַקְהֵל אֶת הָעָם... לְמַעַן יִשְׁמְעוּ וּלְמַעַן יִלְמְדוּ וְיָרְאוּ אֶת ה' אֱלֹקֵיכֶם וְשָׁמְרוּ לַעֲשׂוֹת אֶת כָּל דִּבְרֵי הַתּוֹרָה הַזֹּאת... וְעַתָּה כִּתְבוּ לָכֶם אֶת הַשִּׁירָה הַזֹּאת וְלַמְּדָהּ אֶת בְּנֵי יִשְׂרָאֵל שִׂימָהּ בְּפִיהֶם

Assemble the people... in order that they will hear, and in order that they will learn and fear Hashem, your G-d, and they will be careful to do all the words of this Torah... And now, write for yourselves this song, and teach it to the children of Israel; place it into their mouths...

Two Last Instructions

In his last days, Moshe conveyed to Bnei Yisrael two final positive commandments: the mitzvah of Hakhel and the mitzvah of writing a Sefer Torah.

These two mitzvos share a common objective: to allow future generations to experience some degree of what Bnei Yisrael experienced at the giving of the Torah. With Hakhel, we replicate the events at Sinai by gathering the entire Jewish nation in one place and listening to the king read select passages from the Torah, to "encourage them to perform mitzvos, and strengthen them in the true faith."[8] Everyone in attendance, says the Rambam, "should view himself as though he was instructed now for the first time regarding the Torah, as though he is hearing it now from the Almighty."[9] Similarly,

---

8. Mishneh Torah, Hil. Chagigah 3:1.
9. Ibid. 3:6.

when a person writes a Sefer Torah for himself, "Scripture regards it as if he had received it at Mount Sinai."[10]

Why do we need two such mitzvos, which fulfill the same purpose?

Prior to receiving the Torah, Bnei Yisrael declared, "We will obey, and we will listen,"[11] expressing their commitment to both aspects of the giving of the Torah that would take place at Mount Sinai: the giving of the Torah itself (to study and know it), and the giving of the commandments within it (to obey and observe them).

The mitzvos of Hakhel and of writing a Sefer Torah, whose shared purpose is to recreate the experience of receiving the Torah, each focus of one of these aspects. Hakhel focuses on invigorating our acceptance of the mitzvos, as the Torah articulates, "In order that they will... fear Hashem, your G-d, and they will observe to do all the words of this Torah." In contrast, the primary emphasis of writing a Sefer Torah is to strengthen our *study* of the Torah, as the Torah emphasizes, "And now, write for yourselves this song, *teach it* to Bnei Yisrael; place it in their mouths."

—*Likkutei Sichos, vol. 34, pp. 189–190*

---

10. Menachos 30a.
11. Shemos 24:7.

31:18 | לא:יח

וְאָנֹכִי הַסְתֵּר אַסְתִּיר פָּנַי בַּיּוֹם הַהוּא
But I, hide, I shall hide My face on that day.

When G-d Hides

In Parshas Vayelech, G-d foretells that the Jewish people will one day stray after foreign gods. As a result, His fury will rage against them and many troubles will befall them. "But I, hide, I shall hide My face on that day, because of all the evil they have committed," says G-d.

The Baal Shem Tov explains that the double expression "Hide, I shall hide" denotes a state of Divine concealment so great that not only does G-d seem absent, His concealment and seeming absence also go unnoticed! When G-d conceals His very concealment, and the darkness is mistaken for light, no one even searches for a way to remedy the situation, and that is truly the worst form of darkness.

There is, however, a silver lining even to this most dark and dire of conditions. In fact, in light of the Chassidic perspective that the curses stated in the Torah are actually hidden blessings,[12] the ominous (and double) threat "But I, hide, I shall hide My face on that day," must truly convey an extraordinary blessing.

That blessing is conveyed in the first word of this phrase, וְאָנֹכִי, "But I." The many names of G-d refer to the various manifestations of His infinite abilities; each name—even each letter—conveying a unique aspect of the Divine mys-

---

12. See Likkutei Torah, Bechukosai 48a.

tery.[13] Conversely, when G-d speaks of Himself in the Torah in the first person, not by any of His names but simply "I"—i.e., whoever I am—He refers to His unknowable essence, which cannot be described by any name nor hinted to by any letter.

This, then, is the truth behind the double-hiddenness of G-d, "But I, hide, I shall hide My face on that day": this extreme concealment of G-dliness is testimony to the presence of the inconceivable and inscrutable Divine "I," which not only is present *even* when unseen, indeed the hiddenness itself expresses its greatness and *inconceivableness*.

In the bleakest of situations, in which G-d's presence is doubly hidden and unseen, we must realize that the darkness is not what it seems to be. Rather, it is an opportunity to come in touch with and thereby reveal the truly unknowable "I" of G-d, which transcends even the greatest of G-d's "names" and manifestations.

—*Likkutei Sichos, vol. 6, p. 194; ibid., vol. 9, pp. 193-195*

---

13. See Zohar 3:257b.

לא:כח | 31:28

הַקְהִילוּ אֵלַי אֶת כָּל זִקְנֵי שִׁבְטֵיכֶם וְשֹׁטְרֵיכֶם
וַאֲדַבְּרָה בְאָזְנֵיהֶם אֵת הַדְּבָרִים הָאֵלֶּה

Assemble to me all the elders of your tribes and your officers, and I will speak these words into their ears.

Moshe's Retirement

On the last day of Moshe's life, he instructed the Levi'im to gather all of Bnei Yisrael so that he could address them. Rashi notes that Moshe did not summon the people with the sounding of trumpets, as he normally would,[14] affirming the words of Koheles, "There is no sovereignty on the day of death."[15] The trumpets were associated with Moshe's leadership, and because he did not reign over Bnei Yisrael on the day of his passing, he could not use them to summon the people.

But is it possible that Moshe's status was diminished on the last day of his life? A *tzaddik*, a righteous person, rises every single day, "from strength to strength."[16] Certainly, on the last day of Moshe's physical life he was at the height of his life's achievements, not the opposite!

Clearly then, the lack of rulership on the day of a *tzaddik*'s death is not a deficiency, but a sign of the truly exalted state he reaches on that day. For rulership requires an association between the ruler and the ones being ruled, albeit a relationship defined by authority of the ruler over the ruled. On the day of his death, however, the *tzaddik* becomes so transcendent that

---

14. See Bamidbar 10:2.
15. Koheles 8:8.
16. Tehillim 84:8; see Talmud, Berachos 64a.

he is removed even from the association inherent in "ruling over" the people and leading them.

Here we see the unique bond between Moshe and the Jewish people. Although "there is no sovereignty on the day of death," and it would seem that Moshe was completely detached from Bnei Yisrael on the day of his physical passing, he nevertheless insisted that the people assemble before him. For beyond the relationship of "sovereignty" (which Moshe transcended on the day of his passing), Moshe and Bnei Yisrael were still bound to one another intrinsically—"Moshe is Yisrael, and Yisrael is Moshe."[17]

—*Likkutei Sichos, vol. 24, pp. 220–221*

---

17. Rashi, Bamidbar 21:21.

האזינו
Ha'azinu

32:1 | לב:א

הַאֲזִינוּ הַשָּׁמַיִם וַאֲדַבֵּרָה וְתִשְׁמַע הָאָרֶץ אִמְרֵי פִי

Listen, O heavens, and I will speak; and let the earth hear the words of my mouth.

Close to the Heavens

The Sifri observes that when Moshe addressed the heavens he said הַאֲזִינוּ, which means "listen," whereas when he addressed the earth he said וְתִשְׁמַע, which means "hear." The Sifri explains that "listening" indicates a degree of closeness, while "hearing" can occur from afar: "Since Moshe was close to heaven, he said 'Listen, O heavens,' and since he was distant from earth, he said 'Let the earth hear the words of my mouth.'"

Parshas Ha'azinu is often read on the Shabbos between Rosh Hashanah and Yom Kippur, during the period known as the Ten Days of Teshuvah. Regarding these ten days, the Talmud cites the verse "Seek G-d when He is found, call Him when He is near,"[1] meaning that these ten days are the time when "G-d is found," and therefore the best time to "seek Him." As the Rambam explains, "Even though repentance and calling out [to G-d] are desirable at all times, in the ten days between Rosh Hashanah and Yom Kippur they are even more desirable, and are accepted immediately."[2]

The mystics teach that the content of every Parshah is associated with the time of year in which it is read.[3] Accordingly Sifri's description of Moshe's spiritual state can be understood as a prototype of the state of every Jew in the Ten Days of Teshuvah. In these ten days, when G-d is "found" and "near" to every Jew, each one of us is capable of feeling "close to the heavens"—sensing G-d's love and affection, and consequently being "distant from the earth"—detached and removed from earthly pursuits and concerns.

—*Likkutei Sichos, vol. 34, pp. 203-204*

---

1. Yeshayahu 55:6.
2. Mishneh Torah, Hil. Teshuvah 2:6.
3. Shnei Luchos Habris, Torah Shebichsav, Vayeishev.

לב:א | 32:1

הַאֲזִינוּ הַשָּׁמַיִם וַאֲדַבֵּרָה וְתִשְׁמַע הָאָרֶץ אִמְרֵי פִי

Listen, O heavens, and I will speak; and let the earth hear the words of my mouth.

When Distance is a Virtue

Chassidus interprets the heaven and earth in this verse as an allusion to two components of our Divine service: Torah study and mitzvah observance.[4] The heavens allude to the study of the Torah, which was given from the heavens—"From the heavens I have spoken with you,"[5] while earth alludes to the practical observance of the mitzvos, the fulfillment of which largely involves physical objects and "earthly" deeds.

We find, however, that when Moshe addressed the heavens, he said הַאֲזִינוּ הַשָּׁמַיִם, "Listen, O heavens," whereas when he addressed the earth, he said וְתִשְׁמַע הָאָרֶץ, "Let the earth hear." "Hearing," which can be from afar, denotes distance, in comparison to "listening." As the Sifri explains, "Since Moshe was close to heaven, he said, 'Listen, O heavens,' and since he was distant from earth, he said, 'Let the earth hear the words of my mouth.'"

How do we reconcile Moshe's "distance" from the earth (a distance portrayed here as a value to aspire to) with the Chassidic interpretation that "earth" refers to observance of the mitzvos? Evidently, "distance" in this context is not detachment; it describes a mode of Divine service that is positively characterized by a sense of "distance."

---

4. See Likkutei Torah, Ha'azinu 74b.
5. Shemos 20:19.

To serve G-d with a sense of "closeness" means to recognize and appreciate His greatness, and to love and feel attached to Him. In contrast, to serve G-d with a sense of "distance" means that even if we do not feel intellectually or emotionally attached, we dutifully abide by His will with a spirit of *kabblas ol*—accepting the yoke of heaven.

In light of this distinction, we can understand the difference between Torah study and mitzvah observance, and the virtue of "distance" with regard to the mitzvos.

To study Torah is to endeavor to absorb G-d's wisdom in our mind, to unify our intellect with His— it is an experience of closeness and intimacy like no other. The observance of mitzvos, conversely, is primarily an exercise in obedience. Even the meanings behind the mitzvos, which help us to somewhat understand and appreciate their value, are only secondary to actually fulfilling them—i.e., dutifully carrying out G-d's commands. We are therefore encouraged to be "distant from the earth," to devote ourselves to fulfilling G-d's mitzvos with *kabblas ol*, regardless of how close we feel to Him.

—*Likkutei Sichos, vol. 34, pp. 204–205*

לב:י | 32:10

יְמְצָאֵהוּ בְּאֶרֶץ מִדְבָּר

He found them in a desert land.

Finding Faith

Rashi explains this verse as praise of the Jewish people: "G-d found them faithful to Him in a desert land, for they accepted His Torah, His sovereignty and His yoke upon themselves."

Why does the Torah refer to the Jewish people's faith as something that G-d "found"?

A "find" is an object of value that comes to a person unexpectedly. In the words of the Talmud,[6] a find happens without planning—*b'hesach hadaas*, "in absence of cognizance." As such, the idea of G-d "finding" Bnei Yisrael alludes to His bond with the Jewish people that transcends any "cognizance," order, structure or limit.

G-d's "unplanned" and unrestricted attachment to the Jewish people mirrors our faithfulness to Him, which can likewise be described as a "find." Our faith, by definition, is a commitment to G-d that transcends reason: we follow G-d loyally, whether we understand His ways or not. Our faith is therefore comparable to a "find" that is not the product of rational thinking alone.

Rashi alludes to this idea when he says that the Jews "accepted G-d's Torah, His sovereignty and His yoke upon themselves." These words emphasize that in addition to accepting G-d's Torah, which they could learn and comprehend, the

---

6. Sanhedrin 97a.

Jewish people also accepted G-d's kingship and yoke, submitting themselves to Him unconditionally, without any (rational) limits whatsoever.

Therefore, just as our suprarational faith is comparable to a "find," so is G-d's commitment to us like a "find"—it utterly transcends any system or reason.

—*Likkutei Sichos, vol. 34, p. 210*

לב:יא | 32:11

כְּנֶ֙שֶׁר֙ יָעִ֣יר קִנּ֔וֹ עַל־גּוֹזָלָ֖יו יְרַחֵ֑ף יִפְרֹ֤שׂ כְּנָפָיו֙ יִקָּחֵ֔הוּ יִשָּׂאֵ֖הוּ עַל־אֶבְרָתֽוֹ׃

Like an eagle awakening its nest, hovering over its fledglings; it spreads its wings when taking them, and carries them on its wings.

Angels At Risk

In the song of Ha'azinu, Moshe likens G-d's care of Bnei Yisrael to an eagle's care of its young. Rashi explains that when moving its young from place to place, the eagle does not carry them with its feet as other birds do. The eagle is not threatened by any other bird; it fears only the hunter's arrow, so it carries its young on its wings, saying, "Better that the arrow pierce me than my children." Similarly, explains Rashi, "When the Egyptians pursued and reached Bnei Yisrael at the sea, they shot arrows and catapulted rocks at them. Immediately, 'the angel of Elokim moved... and came between the camp of Egypt and the camp of Israel.'"[7]

But can an angel intercepting the Egyptian arrows and rocks truly be compared to an eagle? Angels are, after all, spiritual beings, and not vulnerable to physical arrows. Whereas the eagle exposes itself to actual harm in order to protect its young!

The angel that protected Bnei Yisrael at the Sea, however, did in fact make a sacrifice comparable to that of an eagle for its young. The Torah emphasizes that the angel that

---

7. Shemos 14:19–20.

positioned itself "between the camp of Egypt and the camp of Israel" was "the angel of Elokim."[8] Rashi notes there that the Torah generally refers to angels as "an angel of Hashem" (spelled Yud-Hei-Vav-Hei), whereas this angel is called "the angel of Elokim." Rashi explains: "[The Divine name] Elokim denotes G-d's attribute of judgment. This teaches that at that moment, Bnei Yisrael were being judged whether to be saved or to perish with the Egyptians."

Accordingly, we can understand the full extent of the angel's sacrifice.

An angel may not deviate from the Divine mission it has been designated. Now, the mission of an angel of Elokim—G-d's attribute of judgment—is to carry out strict justice, whereas an angel of Hashem—G-d's attribute of mercy—intercedes on behalf of the condemned and goes on missions of mercy. Therein lies the sacrifice of the angel of Elokim that "came between the camp of Egypt and the camp of Israel," protecting Bnei Yisrael while G-d was deciding whether or not to save them. Like the eagle that puts its own life at risk in order to protect its young, the angel of Elokim defied its very identity as an agent of "justice," in order to mercifully save Bnei Yisrael from harm!

—*Sichos Kodesh 5737, vol. 1, pp. 58–59*

---

8. Shemos 14:19.

לב:מד | 32:44

וַיָּבֹא מֹשֶׁה וַיְדַבֵּר אֶת כָּל דִּבְרֵי הַשִּׁירָה הַזֹּאת בְּאָזְנֵי הָעָם הוּא וְהוֹשֵׁעַ בִּן נוּן.

Moshe came and spoke all the words of this song in the ears of the people, he, and Hoshea son of Nun.

Humble As Ever

The Torah recounts the first time that Moshe and Yehoshua jointly addressed Bnei Yisrael: "Moshe came and spoke all the words of this song… he and Hoshea son of Nun."

Drawing from three distinct sources, Rashi comments on this episode:

> It was a Shabbos of joint leadership; authority was taken from one and given to the other.[9] Moshe appointed a spokesperson for Yehoshua (to disseminate his lectures to the public), so that he could teach in Moshe's lifetime, so that the Jewish people would not say, "During your teacher's lifetime you would not raise your head!"[10] And why does Scripture here call him Hoshea [though his name had long since been changed to Yehoshua[11]]? To teach us that he did not become haughty. Though he was given high status, he humbled himself as he had formerly.[12]

Though seemingly independent points, Rashi's second and third comment each answer a question that the previous comment creates.

---

9. Sotah 13b.
10. Sifri, Devarim 31:1.
11. See Bamidbar 13:16.
12. Sifri, Devarim 32:44.

First, Rashi notes that Moshe and Yehoshua's *joint* address was, in effect, a compromise on Moshe's exclusive leadership—"authority was taken from one and given to the other."

Why was this necessary here, unlike any other transfer of leadership in the Torah and the Prophets, where the successor began to lead only after his predecessor's passing?

Rashi answers this question with a quote from the Sifri.

During his predecessor's lifetime, Yehoshua was the quintessential follower. He was known as Moshe's "attendant,"[13] not as a leader. As such, the people might believe he was too meek to lead, saying (in Rashi's words), "During your teacher's lifetime you would not *raise your head*!" Hence the necessity of establishing Yehoshua's leadership—to raise his head, as it were—while Moshe was still alive.

This, however, leads to another question: if the objective here was to dispel the notion that Yehoshua was timid, why does the Torah revert to calling him Hoshea, a name that recalled his *early years* as Moshe's attendant, before it was changed to Yehoshua?

This is to illustrate Yehoshua's extraordinary humility, says Rashi, drawing from elsewhere in Sifri. The Torah refers to Yehoshua as Hoshea here to underscore that despite Moshe's *specifically elevating him* and imbuing him with the preeminence necessary to lead, Yehoshua actively maintained his trademark humility—"He humbled himself, as he had formerly."

—*Likkutei Sichos, vol. 29, pp. 198-201*

---

[13]. Shemos 33:11.

32:48-49 | לב:מח-מט

וַיְדַבֵּר ה' אֶל מֹשֶׁה בְּעֶצֶם הַיּוֹם הַזֶּה לֵאמֹר:
עֲלֵה אֶל הַר הָעֲבָרִים הַזֶּה הַר נְבוֹ

G-d spoke to Moshe on that very day, saying: Ascend this Mount Avarim [to] Mount Nevo...

Some Things Can't Wait

Rashi notes that the Torah employs the phrase בְּעֶצֶם הַיּוֹם הַזֶּה (literally, "at the strength of this day") in three places: when Noach entered the ark; when the Jews left Egypt; and when Moshe ascended Mount Nevo, where he would pass away. Rashi explains that in all three instances there were people who intended to stop these events from materializing, and G-d said, "It will take place at midday. Let anyone who has the power to prevent it from happening come and do so." Hence the Torah's use of the expression בְּעֶצֶם הַיּוֹם הַזֶּה, meaning "at the peak of daylight," i.e., midday.

But Rashi omits a fourth time the Torah uses this expression—regarding Avraham's circumcision. There, too, the Torah states[14] that it took place בְּעֶצֶם הַיּוֹם הַזֶּה, and for a similar reason. As Rashi explains there, this phrase emphasizes that Avraham circumcised himself in the daytime rather than at night, because "he was afraid neither of the heathens nor of the scorners. And so that his enemies and his contemporaries would not say, 'Had we seen him, we would not have allowed him to circumcise and fulfill G-d's command.'"

Rashi nevertheless omits this reference, because unlike the

---

14. Bereishis 17:23.

other instances, in which the expression בְּעֶצֶם הַיּוֹם הַזֶּה teaches us that an event that could have taken place earlier or later was *timed* for midday, in Avraham's case this could not be so. Granted, the phrase בְּעֶצֶם הַיּוֹם הַזֶּה highlights that Avraham's circumcision took place in broad daylight, despite the possibility that others might have attempted to stop him. But Avraham circumcised himself at G‑d's command, and thus certainly did so at the absolute *earliest* opportunity. If it were possible to perform the circumcision earlier, Avraham would not have waited until midday for any reason whatsoever, for when fulfilling a mitzvah, the most auspicious moment is the soonest one.

—*Sichos Kodesh 5741, vol. 1, pp. 36–39*

וזאת הברכה
Vezos Habracha

לג:ב | 33:2

ה' מִסִּינַי בָּא וְזָרַח מִשֵּׂעִיר לָמוֹ הוֹפִיעַ מֵהַר פָּארָן וְאָתָה מֵרִבְבֹת קֹדֶשׁ מִימִינוֹ אֵשׁ דָּת לָמוֹ

G-d came from Sinai, He shone forth to them from Seir, He appeared from Mount Paran, He came with some of the holy myriads; from His right hand was a fiery Law for them.

The Choicest Choice

The Talmud remarks:

> What did G-d seek in Seir, and what did He seek in Mount Paran? Said Rabbi Yochanan: This teaches us that G-d offered the Torah to every nation and every tongue, but none

accepted it, until He came to the Jewish people, who accepted it.[1]

Why did G-d offer the Torah to the gentile nations, *knowing* that they would not accept it? The Midrash[2] explains that this was to refute any later claims by the nations that they would have accepted and observed the Torah if only they had been given a chance.

Alternatively, by offering the Torah to others, G-d revealed the extent to which He chooses the Jewish people as His nation—a central theme in the giving of the Torah.[3]

To select an item for its merits is not free choice; it is a logical imperative. True "free" choice is to select between options that seem entirely equal, and to choose one of them solely because that is what you opt for, not because of any virtue or draw that particular option holds. It follows, then, that the Jewish people's distinction as G-d's "chosen nation"[4] means that G-d's attachment to the Jew stems from a place where the individual qualities of the chosen and the unchosen are insignificant, where those who accept the Torah are as indistinctive as those who refuse it, yet G-d chooses them nonetheless.

This idea is expressed in the words of the prophet Malachi, "'Was not Eisav a brother to Yaakov?' says G-d. 'Yet I loved Yaakov, and I hated Eisav.'"[5] Even where Eisav and Yaakov are brothers—equally good options—G-d still chooses Yaakov, the Jewish people.

---

1. Avodah Zarah 2b.
2. Mechilta, Yisro 5.
3. See Shulchan Aruch Admor Hazaken, Orach Chaim 60:4.
4. See Devarim 14:2, et al.
5. Malachi 1:2-3.

Accordingly, we can understand why G-d offered the Torah to everyone equally before giving it to the Jewish people (in fact, *compelling* them to accept it!)[6] By leveling the playing field, as it were, between those who He knew would accept the Torah and those who He knew would reject it, G-d revealed that even in His very essence, before which all qualities and nations are equally insignificant, He desires and chooses the Jewish people as the lucky recipients of His Torah.

—*Likkutei Sichos, vol. 4, pp. 1308–1309*

---

6. See Talmud, Shabbos 88a.

33:4 | לג:ד

תּוֹרָה צִוָּה לָנוּ מֹשֶׁה מוֹרָשָׁה קְהִלַּת יַעֲקֹב

*The Torah was commanded to us by Moshe;
it is the inheritance of the congregation of Yaakov.*

The Inheritance

Inheritance is spontaneous; to inherit requires no act or effort on the part of the heir. It is also indiscriminate—the age, maturity or mental capacity of the legal heir is of no significance; even if the heir is a newborn baby, he immediately and fully replaces his ancestors as owner of the inherited property.[7]

Our Sages taught that "from the moment your son knows how to speak, teach him [the verse] *Torah tziva lanu Moshe...*"[8] By beginning a Jewish child's education with this verse, stating that "the Torah was commanded to us by Moshe; it is the *inheritance* of the congregation of Yaakov," we are telling them that like every Jewish man, woman and child, without distinction, they are natural and complete heirs to the entire Torah.

The first segment of this verse also conveys that no matter how much of the Torah one has learned or will learn and understand in the future, it is all but a part of the Torah that "was commanded to us by Moshe." For "the Torah"—all of it, including the innovations and extrapolations made by Sages in future generations, and even the secrets that Moshiach will teach—is included in the very Torah that Moshe taught.[9]

---

7. Mishna, Niddah 5:3.
8. Rashi on Devarim 11:19; cf. Talmud, Sukkah 42a.
9. See Talmud, Megillah 19b; Talmud Yerushalmi, Peah 2:4, et al.

Essentially, this hints that no matter how well we know and understand the Torah, it remains infinitely deeper and more profound.

We thereby begin the child's lifelong study of the Torah with the understanding that at its core the Torah transcends *all* grasp and comprehension, his and the most advanced scholar's alike. Why is that? Because through our reading and study of the Torah we connect with G-d Himself, who has vested Himself into the Torah;[10] thus the essence of the Torah far surpasses what the human mind can read and discover in its words. At the same time, the conclusion of the verse *Torah tzivah* reminds us that, as rightful heirs, this connection with G-d forged through Torah study is the inheritance of every Jew, whether a young child just learning to repeat the Torah's words or a scholar exploring its most profound ideas.

—*Likkutei Sichos, vol. 4, pp. 1165–1167*

---

10. See Shemos Rabbah 33:1.

33:18 | לג:יח

וְלִזְבוּלֻן אָמַר שְׂמַח זְבוּלֻן בְּצֵאתֶךָ וְיִשָּׂשכָר בְּאֹהָלֶיךָ

And to Zevulun he said: "Rejoice, Zevulun, in your departure, and Yissachar, in your tents."

The Joy of Achievement

Moshe's blessing to Zevulun and Yissachar distinguishes itself by its emphasis on their roles being a source of joy: "Rejoice, Zevulun, in your departure, and Yissachar, in your tents."

This can be explained by the Talmudic maxim, "A man prefers one *kav* [a measurement] of his own to nine *kav* of his neighbor's."[11] Meaning that we prefer and enjoy things we have earned through our own toil and effort, even if small, more than we enjoy something which is handed to us without any effort on our part, even if it is plentiful or grand.

In his blessings to the other tribes, Moshe focused primarily on the gifts, spiritual or physical, that G-d would bestow upon each tribe. Conversely, Moshe blessed Zevulun and Yissachar with success in their *endeavors*. As Rashi explains, "Zevulun… prosper when you go out to trade, and Yissachar, prosper when you sit in your tents to study the Torah."

Since their blessing emphasized not only the gifts G-d would grant them, but also their effort and participation in seeing those blessings bear fruit, Zevulun and Yissachar had even greater reason to rejoice than the other tribes.

—*Toras Menachem 5742, vol. 1, pp. 163–165*

---

11. Bava Metzia 38b.

לג:כז-כט | 33:27-29

וַיְגָרֶשׁ מִפָּנֶיךָ אוֹיֵב וַיֹּאמֶר הַשְׁמֵד...
וְיִכָּחֲשׁוּ אֹיְבֶיךָ לָךְ וְאַתָּה עַל בָּמוֹתֵימוֹ תִדְרֹךְ

He drove out the enemy from before you, and said, 'Destroy!' ... Your enemies will deny [their identities] to you, but you will tread upon their heights.

Keep Your Enemies at a Distance

In the blessings Moshe gives to the Jewish people, we find two distinct attitudes toward our enemies. Initially Moshe says that G-d drives away our enemies entirely, and likewise instructs us to destroy them—"He drove out the enemy from before you, and said, 'Destroy!'"[12] Later, however, the verse implies that enemies will exist but will hide in fear, ultimately serving as platforms by which the Jewish people will ascend to great heights—"Your enemies will deny [their identities] to you, but you will tread upon their heights."[13] So, which is it? Are enemies to be expelled and eradicated, or are they to be subdued so they can assist the Jewish people?

It depends from where.

From some environments, the enemy must be expelled entirely; as a result, the enemy elsewhere will be subdued and utilized positively.

The verse that speaks of being assisted "by your enemies" refers to the "enemies" found in the world outside us—i.e., challenges to G-dliness and holiness in the broader society. We cannot deny that such elements exist, nor should we fool

---

12. Devarim 33:27.
13. Ibid. 33:29.

ourselves into believing that we can avoid interaction with them or that we are incapable of influencing them. It is every Jew's duty to influence the "enemy"—to bring justice and morality into the world, and to remove the concealment of G-dliness that the material world naturally presents.

In order to succeed at this, however, we must first abide by the verse "He drove out the enemy from before you, and said, 'Destroy!'" This verse refers to the "enemies" found at home. A Jewish home is no place for influences that are not inherently holy. Therefore G-d tells us to "drive out" and "destroy" any enemies, to remove any trace of unholy influences from the Jewish home, and allow it to be a perfectly holy temple for G-d.

Only then can we succeed in fulfilling our duty to positively influence what takes place outside our homes as well.

—Toras Menachem 5742, vol. 1, pp. 179-180

34:12 | לד:יב

וּלְכֹל הַיָּד הַחֲזָקָה וּלְכֹל הַמּוֹרָא הַגָּדוֹל אֲשֶׁר עָשָׂה מֹשֶׁה לְעֵינֵי כָּל יִשְׂרָאֵל׃

And all the mighty hand, and all the great awe which Moshe performed before the eyes of all Israel.

The Greatest Praise of All

The final verses of the Torah describe Moshe's unparalleled level of prophecy and his unmatched accomplishments. Rashi adds that the words "…which Moshe performed before the eyes of all of Israel" refer to yet another one of Moshe's achievements, namely, "His heart emboldened him to smash the Luchos before their eyes, as it is written, 'And I shattered them before your eyes.'"[14]

Now, it was certainly daring of Moshe to break the Luchos that G-d Himself formed and inscribed. But according to Rashi's explanation, the greatness referred to here is not only that he broke the Luchos, but that he did so boldly, "before the eyes of all Israel." What was the great "boldness of heart" inherent in breaking the Luchos where Bnei Yisrael could see? And why does the Torah regard this as Moshe's crowning achievement?

Why, in fact, did Moshe break the Luchos so publicly? Moshe hoped that smashing them in the presence of the entire nation would move the people to truly regret having made and worshipped the Golden Calf. He hoped that by demonstrating that their actions made necessary the destruction of the holy

---

14. Devarim 9:17.

Luchos, Bnei Yisrael would realize the severity of what they had done, and would immediately repent.

This conviction, says Rashi, demonstrated "boldness of heart," for such faith in Bnei Yisrael was revolutionary. Despite seeing their low spiritual state, evidenced by their grave sin only weeks after G-d's revelation at Sinai, Moshe still believed in the Jewish people's inherent devotion to G-d! He trusted that when they realized that transgressing the Torah severs a Jew's relationship with G-d, they would immediately repent and abandon their sinful ways.

This faith in the Jewish people, explains Rashi, was Moshe's greatest virtue, more so than his many other merits and accomplishments.

—*Toras Menachem, vol. 45, pp. 92-95*

לד:יב | 34:12

וּלְכֹל הַמּוֹרָא הַגָּדוֹל אֲשֶׁר עָשָׂה מֹשֶׁה לְעֵינֵי כָּל יִשְׂרָאֵל

...and all the great awe which Moshe performed before the eyes of all Israel.

The Peak

Based on the Sifri, Rashi interprets the final words of the Torah, "Before the eyes of all Israel," as a reference to one of the darkest moments in the Jewish people's history: when Moshe reacted to the sin of the Golden Calf by smashing the Luchos "before their eyes" (as described in Devarim 9:17).

On its surface, the episode of Moshe breaking the Luchos hardly seems an appropriate conclusion for the Torah. Why end with an episode so uncomplimentary to the Jewish people, so uncomfortable for Moshe, and so irreverent of the Torah (embodied in the Luchos)? In addition, this mention of the breaking of the Luchos seems out of context in these final verses of the Torah, which are a tribute to Moshe's unparalleled greatness!

The opposite, however, is true.

What was Moshe's thought process when he broke the Luchos? The Midrash explains:

> This can be compared to a king who went abroad, and left his bride with the maidservants. Because of the immoral behavior of the maidservants, she acquired a bad reputation. Her escort arose and tore up her marriage contract. He said, "If the king decides to kill her, I will say to him, 'She is not yet your wife.'" ...Likewise, the king represents G-d. The maidservants represent the *eirev rav* [the "mixed multitude" who

joined the Jewish people when they left Egypt, and who were responsible for the making of the Golden Calf], the escort is Moshe, and G-d's bride is the Jewish people.[15]

If there ever was anyone who appreciated and cherished the Luchos and the Torah, it was Moshe, who merited receiving the tablets from G-d Himself. Yet, when Moshe realized that the existence of the Luchos—the "marriage contract"—posed a threat to the Jewish nation, he immediately destroyed the Luchos to save the people. The breaking of the Luchos thus demonstrates Moshe's true legacy and his greatest acclaim—his extraordinary devotion to the Jewish people.

Moreover, Moshe's breaking of the Luchos demonstrated how cherished the Jewish people are—saving even a sinful Jew takes precedence over protecting the holy Luchos!

How fitting it is, then, to complete the Torah on this note, highlighting the value of the Jewish people for whom the Torah was written, and whose importance exceeds even that of the Torah itself.

—*Likkutei Sichos, vol. 34, pp. 217–223*

---

15. See Rashi, Shemos 34:1.

In loving memory of

הוו"ח

ר' **ישכר דוב ומרים**
וייס
ע"ה

R' Yissochor Dov (Berel)
and **Miriam** ע"ה
Weiss

※

הוו"ח

ר' **שלום וצפורה**
לפידות
ע"ה

R' Sholom
and **Tziporah** ע"ה
Lapidus

Their love and care for every Jew was exemplary,
and they served God with all their heart.

※

May the study of the Rebbe's sichos from this "Lightpoints"
Sefer be a merit for them, and may they intercede with
our Father in Heaven to send Moshiach now!

Sponsored by:
Rabbi Moishe and **Ruty Weiss**
Sherman Oaks, CA

לזכרון עולם בהיכל ה'

הנגיד החסידי הנודע לשם ולתהילה,
שמו מפארים בכל החוגים, איש החסד והצדקה אשר פיזר נתן לאביונים,
מגדולי תמכין דאורייתא, בר אוריין ומוקיר רבנן,
קבע עיתים לתורה בכל עת ובכל זמן, טוב לשמים וטוב לבריות

הרה"ח הנעלה
ר' יששכר דוב
ב"ר יונה ע"ה
נפטר ז"ך אייר, ה'תשע"א

האשה החשובה הצנועה והחסודה
שעמדה לימין בעלה במעשה הצדקה

מרת מרים
בת ר' אלטער מרדכי ע"ה
נפטרה ר"ח שבט, ה'תשע"א

וייס

הרה"ח הוו"ח אי"א בעל
מידות טובות רודף צדקה וחסד
ר' שלום
ב"ר יואל ע"ה
נפטר יו"ד שבט, ה'תשל"א

אשת חבר האשה
החשובה הצנועה והחסודה
מרת צפורה
בת ר' אברהם ע"ה
נפטרה ליל שמיני עצרת, ה'תש"ע

לפידות
תנצב"ה

נדפס על ידי חתנם ובתם
הרה"ת ר' **משה אהרן צבי**
וזוגתו מרת **העניא רבקה רות** שיחיו
וייס
שערמאן אוקס, קאליפורניא